Salty Wives, Spirited Mothers, and Savvy Widows

Salty Wives, Spirited Mothers, and Savvy Widows

CAPABLE WOMEN
OF PURPOSE AND PERSISTENCE
IN LUKE'S GOSPEL

F. Scott Spencer

WILLIAM B. EERDMANS PUBLISHING COMPANY
GRAND RAPIDS, MICHIGAN / CAMBRIDGE, U.K.

Published 2012 by
Wm. B. Eerdmans Publishing Co.
2140 Oak Industrial Drive N.E., Grand Rapids, Michigan 49505 /
P.O. Box 163, Cambridge CB3 9PU U.K.
www.eerdmans.com

Printed in the United States of America

18 17 16 15 14 13 12   7 6 5 4 3 2 1

Library of Congress Cataloging-in-Publication Data

Spencer, F. Scott (Franklin Scott)
    Salty wives, spirited mothers, and savvy widows: capable women of
    purpose and persistence in Luke's gospel / F. Scott Spencer.
        p.   cm.
    Includes bibliographical references and index.
    ISBN 978-0-8028-6762-9 (pbk.: alk. paper)
    1. Bible. N.T. Luke — Criticism, interpretation, etc.
    2. Women in the Bible.   I. Title.

BS2595.52.S64   2012
226.4′0922082 — dc23

                                           2012020151

"Lot's Wife" from *Poems of Akhmatova,* by Anna Akhmatova and translated by Stanley Kunitz and
Max Hayward. Originally published by Little, Brown & Co. © 1973 by Stanley Kunitz and Max
Hayward. Used courtesy of the author's estate. All rights reserved.

"Lot's Wife" by Gene Fendt. *Theology Today* 50 (1993): 116.

To the consummately capable cadre of women FBI agents from whom I've learned so much

Contents

PREFACE   viii

1. Toward Bluer Skies: Reducing the Threat Level
   and Resurrecting Feminist Studies of Women in Luke   1

2. Can We Go On Together with Suspicious Minds?
   Doubt and Trust as Both Sides of the Hermeneutical "Coin"
   (Luke 15:8-10)   24

3. A Woman's Right to Choose? Mother Mary as
   Spirited Agent and Actor (Luke 1–2)   55

4. The Quest for the Historical Joanna: Follower of Jesus,
   Friend of Mary Magdalene, and Wife of Herod's Official
   (Luke 8:1-3; 24:10)   101

5. A Testy Hostess and Her Lazy Sister? Martha, Mary,
   and the Household Rivals Type-Scene (Luke 10:38-42)   145

6. A Hungry Widow, Spicy Queen, and Salty Wife:
   "Foreign" Biblical Models of Warning and Judgment
   (Luke 4:25-26; 11:31; 17:32)   190

7. The Savvy Widow's Might: Fighting for Justice in an
   Unjust World (Luke 18:1-8)   264

8. A Capable Woman, Who Can Find?
   We Have Found Some in Luke!   315

INDEX   342

Preface

I can't find the reference now, but I recall reading years ago how the graduate students at Harvard working with Elisabeth Schüssler Fiorenza, the most influential feminist NT scholar of our time, dubbed themselves, tongue in cheek, FBI agents — that is, diligent practitioners of Feminist Biblical Interpretation. I instantly loved and coveted the label, partly because I loved *The F.B.I.* TV show growing up (a Quinn Martin production starring Efrem Zimbalist Jr., we were solemnly told at the beginning of each episode; the show had nothing to do with budding "second wave" feminism of the 1960s and 1970s, but I guess it counts for something that daughter Stephanie Zimbalist went on to star in her own show in the mid-1980s as an unmarried private eye who owned her own detective agency) — but mostly because a good bit of my postdoctoral academic career has been engaged with feminist biblical scholarship. I tell my students that I'm a card-carrying feminist (some actually think I have a laminated card in my wallet), but truth be told, I really want a shiny FBI badge to flash and maybe a special pen to write with (no guns, thank you, which are not part of the program anyway, despite the gross caricature of feminist critics as threats to civilization). I've applied for a badge but not received one yet. Maybe it's because I never went to Harvard or, more likely, because a background check would turn up Texas fundamentalist roots sure to red-flag my file.

In all seriousness, I have been immeasurably challenged and enriched by the rising tide of feminist biblical scholarship over the past three decades (flowing way beyond the banks of the Charles River). I continue to regard feminist criticism in its manifold expressions as an "essential" (to use a rather unfeminist term) and necessary, rather than optional and ancillary, component of informed critical biblical interpretation — for men as well as women. In fact, I might argue, feminist criticism is *especially* crucial for male interpreters whose blind spots are apt to be larger, less acknowledged, and thus more in need of therapeutic feminist-critical illumination. I'm aware of the problems here, not least the rich core of women's experiences that feminist critics draw upon, which I have no direct access to and often skew and misunderstand, as my wife of almost forty years and two young adult daughters regularly remind me (in love, of course). But I don't have any more personal, immediate access to the experiences of a male Galilean Jew who lived two thousand years ago — *except* through sympathetic reading, study, dialogue, and debate with others who are trying to get to know him better. So, too, with feminist thought, especially that which wrestles with the significance of the "misunderstood Jew"[1] from first-century Galilee for today, I read, think, discuss, keep up as best I can, *and* dare to try my own hand at feminist biblical interpretation — *not* in any sense to co-opt the approach or show the girls how it's done, but out of deep respect for the contributions of pioneering FBI agents with whom I interact and sometimes disagree, as they do among themselves. My halting attempts at imitation are indeed offered as a sincere form of admiration and appreciation (flattery). As best I can tell from the literature, we are now rocking in the swells of a "third wave" feminist movement flowing into some indeterminate form of postfeminism.[2] Be that as it may, I dive in as an amateur surfer, enjoy the ride, and try not to drown in the process.

I come to this present project on women in Luke with no rigid feminist-critical methodology, which generally fits the more eclectic strategies employed by feminist biblical scholars. Feminist criticism(s) coheres more around a political commitment to women's liberation and equality than a set of hermeneutical techniques. In a recent article on feminist criticism, I do sketch a series of investigative questions around four areas of interest — place and occupation, voice and rhetoric, power and experience, and suspicion and trust[3] — which I keep in view throughout the present study. The first two chapters unpack my theoretical framework more fully. Without going into detail here, I will alert readers to my aim to tilt feminist

1. Amy-Jill Levine, *The Misunderstood Jew: The Church and the Scandal of the Jewish Jesus* (New York: HarperOne, 2006).

2. See Jennifer Baumgardner and Amy Richards, *Manifesta: Young Women, Feminism, and the Future* (2nd ed.; New York: Farrar, Straus and Giroux, 2010).

3. F. Scott Spencer, "Feminist Criticism," in *Hearing the New Testament: Strategies for Interpretation* (ed. Joel B. Green; Grand Rapids: Eerdmans, 2010), 289-325.

scholarship toward a slightly more positive — though still critical — evaluation of the *creative agency and capable activity* of women in Luke's Gospel. I seek to strike a more celebratory than lamentable chord — beyond my own previous work exposing Luke's silencing and subordinating strains — in hopes of encouraging more direct liberating readings of Luke today.

All these chapters appear in print here for the first time. However, I have aired portions of two chapters in academic conferences: I presented a version of chapter 2 ("Can We Go On Together with Suspicious Minds?") as the presidential address for the southeast regional meeting of the Society of Biblical Literature in Greensboro, North Carolina (2009); and I delivered part of chapter 3 ("A Woman's Right to Choose?") for the Feminist Hermeneutics section of the national Society of Biblical Literature meeting in Atlanta (2010). I'm grateful to both organizations for accepting my papers and offering helpful feedback.

The cadre of brilliant feminist biblical scholars to whom I'm indebted (and to whom I dedicate this book) are too numerous to mention. Plus, more than most critical movements, feminism tends toward valuing a diverse community of thinkers, activists, and scholars, from popular grass roots to academic ivy walls. I'm grateful to be a small part of this vibrant community. I also continue to be grateful for the opportunity to work in a context of supportive freedom at the Baptist Theological Seminary at Richmond. Thanks to all my wonderful colleagues — faculty, staff, and students — as we continue to work together to promote the consummate capabilities and equal opportunities of our many women students.

Finally, I'd like to express a word of warm appreciation to Senior Editor Allen Myers at Eerdmans Publishing, who graciously invited me to lunch after my first paper mentioned above. That meeting began discussions of this book and much encouragement to see it through to publication. Allen's gracious spirit and seasoned experience in publishing biblical scholarship have buoyed me every step of the way.

1. Toward Bluer Skies: Reducing the Threat Level and Resurrecting Feminist Studies of Women in Luke

In our post–9/11 world (I draft this a few days after the ten-year anniversary), we have become all too familiar with warnings of terrorist threat levels, accompanied by various scanning and stripping probes in airports and other public venues. Although the labels have recently changed to the simpler dual options of either "imminent" or "elevated" risks of danger (we mustn't overwhelm an already stressed-out, panic-stricken society, though allowing nothing less than an "elevated" threat is not exactly comforting), the original five-stage, color-coded advisory system (see p. 2) seems more vividly suited for the complex "war on terror." Forget the colored beads of the Jesus Seminar assessing the authenticity of Jesus' words. This is really critical, life-and-death business, right now! Oh, for some "bluer" skies under which we remain cautiously "guarded" about our security (mustn't ever completely let down our guard) but generally optimistic about the future and snug and cozy in our beds at night. It's probably too much to hope for nothing but "green" pastures in our perilous world, but we'll settle for clear skies.

In the world of NT scholarship concerning Luke's treatment of women — which again scarcely equates to the crisis of global terrorism, though women can be deeply affected, even oppressed and damaged, by misguided biblical interpretation — the threat level has been rising since the 1990s through the investigations of highly trained, trenchant FBI agents, that is, those engaged in frontline Feminist Biblical Interpretation.[1] Whereas Luke

---

1. As noted in the preface, the FBI acronym was coined, as far as I know, tongue in cheek, by Harvard graduate students of Elisabeth Schüssler Fiorenza in feminist biblical criticism.

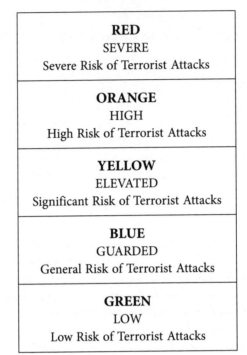

RED
SEVERE
Severe Risk of Terrorist Attacks

ORANGE
HIGH
High Risk of Terrorist Attacks

YELLOW
ELEVATED
Significant Risk of Terrorist Attacks

BLUE
GUARDED
General Risk of Terrorist Attacks

GREEN
LOW
Low Risk of Terrorist Attacks

was long regarded as the NT writer most supportive of women's interests, largely because of the sheer number of women characters in the Third Gospel and Acts and a major literary pattern of pairing male and female figures, closer analysis of what Lukan women actually say (not much) and do (primarily serve men) began to raise some disturbing red flags. But isn't that just a product of feminists' extremist tendencies to "see red" in everything, in the present case to push Luke's terrorist threat level against women to "red" and all but call for Luke's canonical defrocking? Who are the real fanatical terrorists here: Luke or feminist scholars? We might concede the evidence of some truly horrifying "texts of terror" in the OT, such as those chillingly exposed by Phyllis Trible in her classic feminist work,[2] but not in Luke, surely. Luke has nothing approaching the slave-girl mistreatment (Hagar), rape-assault (Tamar), daughter killing (Jephthah), or dismemberment (Levite's concubine) Trible uncovers in OT narratives. Luke's Jesus heals several women and shows special care for widows, for goodness' sake.

2. Phyllis Trible, *Texts of Terror: Literary-Feminist Readings of Biblical Narratives* (Philadelphia: Fortress, 1984).

Without a doubt Luke's terrorism toward women, if in fact present in his two volumes, is of the more subtle variety, with the exception of the shocking drop-dead story of Sapphira (and husband Ananias) that Luke candidly admits is cause for "great fear" (Acts 5:5, 11). But subtle terrorism is no less insidious and may be even more threatening for its camouflage. That's precisely why we need skilled feminist critics to see through the subterfuge and expose the danger. But do these critics themselves (like all critics) not run the risk of being blinded by their own biases and seeing spooks that are not really there? In other words, is Luke really as bad as all that for women?

As it happens, as I have tried to engage sympathetically with feminist biblical scholarship over the past two decades, I have contributed to raising the threat level of Luke's writings against women, particularly in exposing Luke's lamentable reluctance to give women adequate *voice* after the promising start in Luke 1–2 (and the hopeful promise in Acts 2:17-18).[3] I'm sad to say that overall Luke and Acts do not — without critical deconstruction and reconstruction — significantly advance the cause of women preachers and pastors, which remains a major issue in my ecclesiastical context. As with all parts of the Bible and all its interpreters (none of us comes to the Bible without thick layers of interpretive encrustation), we must approach Luke and Lukan scholars — and ourselves! — with due diligent caution and critical acumen. But we need not be Bible-phobic or put an XXX Poison label on Luke, and we must not be so rigidly reductionist as to deny the Bible's enormous life-giving and right-making potential for millions across history to the present day — including millions of *women,* many on the lower end of society, who find their consciousnesses, whether pro-, anti-, or nonfeminist, comforted and strengthened by biblical faith — including that based upon Luke's writings, which have particularly nurtured modern sociopolitical liberation causes.[4]

---

3. See chapter 6, "Out of Mind, Out of Voice: Slave-Girls and Prophetic Daughters in Luke-Acts," in F. Scott Spencer, *Dancing Girls, "Loose" Ladies, and Women of "the Cloth": The Women in Jesus' Life* (New York: Continuum, 2004), 144-65; an earlier version appeared in *Biblical Interpretation* 7 (1999): 133-55.

4. See, e.g., Justo L. González, *Luke* (Louisville: Westminster John Knox, 2010); Sharon H. Ringe, *Jesus, Liberation, and the Biblical Jubilee: Images for Ethics and Christology* (Philadelphia: Fortress, 1985); Loretta Dornisch, *A Woman Reads the Gospel of Luke* (Collegeville, Minn.: Liturgical Press, 1996); Richard J. Cassidy and Philip J. Scharper, eds., *Political Issues in Luke-Acts* (Maryknoll, N.Y.: Orbis, 1983); Cassidy, *Jesus, Politics, and Society: A Study of Luke's Gospel* (Maryknoll, N.Y.: Orbis, 1978); Cassidy, *Society and Politics in the Acts of the Apostles* (Maryknoll, N.Y.: Orbis, 1987).

So, regarding the portrayal of women in Luke's Gospel, I endeavor in this project to pull the pendulum back a tad from the feminist-critical pole toward the center, or to lower the threat level toward "bluer" hues — still *GUARDED*, still applying sharp feminist-critical analyses, but pressing through to more salutary results, to a somewhat sweeter concentration in Luke's bittersweet, "mixed message" regarding women's agency and action. Short of remixing Luke's sound track, I see, or rather hear, no way to amplify women's virtual silence (after the birth narratives) in this Gospel. And short of anachronistic revisionism, I see no rhyme or reason to profiling Jesus or Luke as first-century feminists, of which there were none any more than there were astronauts, nuclear scientists, or rap artists. But I do see room to expand our positive engagement with "capable women of purpose and persistence" within their Lukan literary and social worlds.

To use a major Lukan (and NT) theological image, I try to *resurrect* Luke's presentation of women toward more life-enhancing ends. Though not cases I focus on in this book, the two incidents where Luke's Jesus raises someone from the dead both involve restoring women's capacities for full lives: resuscitating a widow's deceased only son (and likely major source of her support) on his funeral mat (Luke 7:11-17), and the only daughter of her parents, a twelve-year-old girl on the brink of womanhood (8:40-42, 49-56). Moreover, the *women disciples* of Jesus remain most faithful to him to the end of his life (23:49, 55) and become the first witnesses to his resurrection. Of course, Luke also notes that the male apostles dismissed the women's testimony as an "idle tale" until they could corroborate it for themselves (24:1-12). But corroborate it they did, which confirms the women's priority and probity all along as "apostolic" witnesses. While the "idle tale" reference unfortunately lingers as a slight to women's proclamation, the final chapter of Luke's Gospel deconstructs it as men's idle opinion about women's idle speech: thus, two "idle's" make a "capable."

Without engaging a full history of contemporary scholarship on women in Luke, I situate my own work within a sample of salient studies from three major feminist critics, with particular attention to their perspectives on the resurrection narrative in Luke 24. I then close this introductory chapter with a brief preview of the cases treated in this book and the methodology employed.

Sampling the FBI Files

The closing decade of the twentieth century featured the landmark publication of two one-volume feminist commentaries on the entire NT, with substantial articles on the respective books written by leading feminist scholars. *Women's Bible Commentary,* edited by Carol Newsom and Sharon Ringe (1992 [rev. 1998]), so named in honor of Elizabeth Cady Stanton's monumental *The Women's Bible* a century before, offers a provocative chapter on Luke by Jane Schaberg.[5] The second volume of *Searching the Scriptures: A Feminist Commentary* (1993), edited by Elisabeth Schüssler Fiorenza, the most prominent "dean" of feminist NT criticism, presents the stimulating analysis of Luke's Gospel by Turid Karlsen Seim.[6] Both Schaberg and Seim also have separate monographs supporting their articles.[7] Equally substantive and incisive during the same period, though not a part of the two one-volume commentaries, is the work of Barbara Reid, exhibited in *Choosing the Better Part? Women in the Gospel of Luke* (1996) and numerous articles.[8] She is also the general editor of a massive new series in the making of full-scale feminist commentaries on every book of the Bible.[9]

Jane Schaberg and Luke's "Oppressive Dynamics"

Schaberg opens her contribution to *Women's Bible Commentary* under the heading of "Warning" with this "red" threat level advisory: "The Gospel of Luke is an extremely dangerous text, perhaps the most dangerous in the Bible."[10] While granting that Luke (when read critically) "also contains challenge and promise" and some "liberating elements" for women, partic-

5. Jane Schaberg, "Luke," in *Women's Bible Commentary* (ed. Carol A. Newsom and Sharon H. Ringe; 2nd ed.; Louisville: Westminster John Knox, 1998), 363-80.

6. Turid Karlsen Seim, "The Gospel of Luke," in *Searching the Scriptures,* vol. 2: *A Feminist Commentary* (New York: Crossroad, 1994), 728-62.

7. Schaberg, *The Illegitimacy of Jesus* (New York: Crossroad, 1990); Schaberg, *The Resurrection of Mary Magdalene: Legends, Apocrypha, and the Christian Testament* (New York: Continuum, 2004); Seim, *The Double Message: Patterns of Gender in Luke and Acts* (Nashville: Abingdon, 1994).

8. Barbara E. Reid, *Choosing the Better Part? Women in the Gospel of Luke* (Collegeville, Minn.: Liturgical Press, 1996).

9. To be published by Liturgical Press.

10. Schaberg, "Luke," 363.

ularly acknowledging Mary's Magnificat as "the great New Testament song of liberation,"[11] Schaberg admittedly devotes most attention to exposing the "oppressive dynamics" driving this Gospel, which she regards as a "formidable opponent" of women's rights.[12] The overall tone of her article is ominous and inimical, less concerned with negotiating Luke's mixed message than with negating its malevolent manifesto keeping women in their subordinate, silent places.

Some of the evidence Schaberg adduces resonates with others' findings, such as the paucity of women's speech in Luke (and Acts) compared to men's and the tendency to confine women to supportive, serving roles in the Jesus movement rather than develop their leadership and decision-making capabilities. Other points press Luke's antifeminist agenda further than the text seems to allow. For example, Schaberg too often grounds her arguments about women's silencing in Luke not only in explicit narrative portrayals, but also in presumed silences or absences in Luke's presentation compared to other Gospels (e.g., Luke's omission of Mark's Syrophoenician woman episode for supposed polemical reasons).[13] As narrative criticism has demonstrated, redactional arguments from silence are methodologically weak in Gospel study: what we have to interpret is a finished narrative product, not a clear record of its literary history; probing an ancient author's psychological motivation for *not* including this or that material remains a precarious enterprise.[14] Also, when Schaberg decries women's restricted roles related to speaking and leading (a concern I share), I think she devalues, on the other side, the valued listening and serving ("hearing the word of God and doing it" [cf. 8:21]) dimensions of discipleship exemplified by women — and Jesus! — and incumbent on all followers of Jesus, male and female. Instead of pressing women into passive silence and submission, the aural component always assumes in Luke

11. Schaberg, "Luke," 363, 373, 380. The full Magnificat reference runs: "The Magnificat is the great New Testament song of liberation — personal and social, moral and economic — a revolutionary document of intense conflict and victory. It praises God's liberating actions on behalf of the speaker, which are paradigmatic of all of God's actions on behalf of marginal and exploited people" (373).

12. Schaberg, "Luke," 380.

13. I engage with feminist concerns about Luke's omission of Mark's Syrophoenician woman story in an excursus in chapter 6.

14. Cf. F. Scott Spencer, "Acts and Modern Literary Approaches," in *The Book of Acts in Its First Century Setting* (vol. 1, *Ancient Literary Setting*, ed. Bruce W. Winter and Andrew D. Clarke; Grand Rapids: Eerdmans, 1993), 381-414.

capacities for active thought and practice: to hear necessitates reflection and response, deliberation and deed. Schaberg misses these connections in her reductive assessment: "Luke thinks of a woman's proper attitude as that of a listener, pondering what is not understood, learning in silence."[15] As I will argue at some length in chapter 3, the repeated "pondering" of Mary of Nazareth, far from shutting her up or shunting her off to a quiet corner, accentuates her intelligent engagement with God's revelatory word and precipitates her active — and creative — partnership in God's redemptive work.

Perhaps Schaberg's most extreme point concerns Luke's implicit endorsement of domestic abuse: "Several passages from Luke's Gospel if seen through the eyes of a battered woman can be read to condone violence."[16] Of course, any such reading should be staunchly deplored and resisted. But just because a text *can* be read a certain way (texts can be read and twisted in all sorts of ways, for good or ill) doesn't mean that is the most cogent interpretation from either authorial or textual angles. Schaberg cites four main examples of potentially violent, misogynistic texts: (1) Luke 16:18 — which "omits Mark's prohibition against divorce, but retains the prohibition of remarriage after divorce, with no exceptions," thus proving deleterious to divorced women's chances for security and sexual fulfillment; (2) Luke 6:27-29, 9:23, and 24:26 — which string together victim-glorifying notions of loving enemies, turning the other cheek, bearing "daily" crosses, and the "necessity" of suffering, all of which reinforce women's common daily oppressive experiences; (3) Luke 4:18-20 — which sets forth, via Isaiah, Jesus' programmatic liberating vocation, but is not enacted in the balance of Luke's narrative on behalf of freeing *women* from physical, psychological, or spiritual bondage (Schaberg does admit, however, occasional scenes like Jesus' deliverance of the bent-over woman bound by Satan [13:10-17], "which some women have read as allegories of their oppression and release"); and (4) Luke 10:29-37 and 15:11-32 — which present special Lukan parables of the Good Samaritan and prodigal son in which "the male experience is presented . . . as universal human experience" (male victim in the ditch; father's dealings with younger and elder sons, with no mother in sight), exposing the "urgent need for women's own parables, women's own narratives."[17] In this last case, Schaberg curiously makes no

15. Schaberg, "Luke," 369.
16. Schaberg, "Luke," 370.
17. Schaberg, "Luke," 370.

mention of the parables of the baker woman (13:20-21), sweeper woman (15:8-10), or widow and unjust judge (18:1-8), the latter two of which will receive major attention in this book. Apart from suggesting lacunae where none exist, Schaberg again makes too much of certain real absences and omissions. But most problematic is that none of the texts Schaberg indicts in this section *requires* or even *implies* a particular abusive stance against women (except obliquely, perhaps, Jesus' brief statement about divorce in 16:18). Jesus addresses his radical "love your enemies" and "turn the other cheek" message to "his disciples" (6:20), all of whom are male at this stage of the story (5:1-10, 27-28; 6:12-16); he in no way targets women here or in his cross-bearing requirement for discipleship later. And while we may wish for more Lukan scenes depicting women's liberation, there is no reason to think that Isaiah's redemptive agenda for the poor, the captives, and the oppressed adopted by Jesus is gender-restricted. It is indeed tragic and reprehensible when these texts are twisted to do violence toward women — but especially so since such misinterpretations also do violence to Luke's Gospel.

Finally, regarding the closing crucifixion and resurrection narratives in Luke, Schaberg laments the "near disappearance of women" in comparison with the other Gospels. She particularly highlights that Jesus' female followers in Luke receive neither a special appearance of the risen Jesus nor a direct commission to bear witness to his resurrection to the male apostles; rather, they simply take it upon themselves to report the news the apostles first regard as an "idle" bit of hysterical nonsense. Moreover, though Luke does uniquely have the heavenly messengers ("two men [!]") at the empty tomb exhort the women to "remember how [Jesus] told you [about his resurrection], while he was still in Galilee" (24:6-7), the actual Galilean passion/resurrection prediction earlier in the Gospel (9:22) seems directed to the inner circle of twelve male disciples (cf. 9:10-50) with no mention of women in the background.[18] I agree that the narrative gap is a yawning one between Jesus' original prediction and the messengers' call for the women to remember it, and that the women's discipleship is somewhat blurred in the process. While I have cautioned against making too much of arguments from absence, I think that women's virtual fading

---

18. Schaberg, "Luke," 378-80. Jesus makes a second passion prediction in 9:44 (to the same audience as 9:22), but with no mention of his resurrection. A third prediction comes later in 18:31-34, in this case outside Galilee and directed privately to "the twelve" male apostles (18:31).

from clear view as Jesus' companions in the long section from 8:1-3 to 23:49–24:10, *where Luke leads us to expect women's involvement,* remains problematic and smacks of some subordinate concept of women's discipleship.[19] Still, I see no reason to discount the women's true testimony to the resurrection in Luke because it wasn't explicitly predicted or commissioned. To the contrary, their apprehension of Jesus' words ("then they remembered" [24:8]) not directed primarily to them and their decision to announce Jesus' resurrection to the apostles without being told to do so commend their initiative, courage, and independence. They know what they know, regardless of men's doubts, and are not afraid to say it and act upon it.

Turid Karlsen Seim and Luke's "Double Message"

Methodologically, Seim starts with a more positive, "constructive" disposition toward Luke's text. "My reading of Luke tries to understand the Lukan construction and does not aim at the reconstruction of another story or subtext using the Lukan text as a pretext. For the most part it ignores the history behind the Lukan screen and concentrates on the given text. This approach may, of course, be seen as lacking a certain feminist suspicion, but the rationale behind it is the wish and the need to see the full construction before deconstruction and reconstruction can take place."[20] This self-assessment somewhat understates Seim's work, which in fact demonstrates judicious employment of both historical analysis, including redaction criticism, and a feminist hermeneutic of suspicion. But in all this, Seim maintains prime focus on the final Lukan narratives in all their rich complexity, "ambiguity," and "polyphony," resisting a consistent, monolithic presentation of women.[21] (Here I find a strong affinity with my own approach.) Not surprisingly, then, Seim's conclusions about Luke's treatment of women moderate those that maximize either the support factor or the threat level. "It is a preposterous simplification to ask whether Luke's writ-

19. In the long central travel section of Luke, the only women disciples who appear are Martha and Mary in the brief episode in 10:38-42. But Jesus just pops in for a short visit in their home: they do not accompany him on the journey.
20. Seim, "The Gospel of Luke," 729.
21. While the large number of women characters in Luke's narrative does not guarantee women's altogether positive portrayal, it does tilt toward a multiplicity and complexity of perspectives.

ings are friendly or hostile to women. Luke's version of the life of Jesus and of the first believers cannot be reduced either to a feminist treasure chamber or to a chamber of horrors for women's theology. It contains elements that bring joy to 'dignity studies' and other elements that give support to 'misery studies.'"[22]

On the "misery" side, Seim echoes the concern Schaberg and others have with women's lack of speaking and leading roles in Luke's story, an absence that becomes more conspicuous as the plot progresses, especially into its second volume (Acts). On the "dignity" side, Seim stresses Luke's advocacy of "ascetic liberation" for unmarried women and "liberating acts" of healing for infirm women, both experiences fraught with eschatological significance.[23] The preponderant state for women characters in Luke's narrative is single, unattached to any male kin; for example, Luke features more widows than any NT writer. Far from being a lamentable, limiting condition, celibacy and singlehood afforded women in the Jesus movement and early church "the possibility of a power and an authority from which they were otherwise excluded and an opportunity to move outside the limiting constraints of their conventional roles as daughter, wife, and mother. By withdrawing their sexuality from control by others, they achieved a sort of control over their lives and their possessions." More specifically, ascetic women could become

Free from the patriarchal dominance by either father or husband,
Free from risky pregnancies,
Free from painful and often life-threatening childbirth,
Free from the demands of constant caring, and even
Free from great economic worries.[24]

Of course, this is an idyllic portrait of freedom not always matched by reality. Widows might just as easily find themselves neglected and destitute, like the widow at Zarephath, widows who had their homes "devoured" by unscrupulous lawyers, the widow who gave her last two pennies to the temple treasury, and Hellenist widows edged out of the early church's soup line (see Luke 4:25-26; 20:47–21:4; Acts 6:1-7). But other wid-

---

22. Seim, *The Double Message*, 249.

23. Seim, "The Gospel of Luke," 735-39, 755-61; *The Double Message*, 39-57, 185-248.

24. Citing Seim, "The Gospel of Luke," 760, I add capitalization and italics in a poetic-style layout for emphasis.

ows get along just fine (like Anna in Luke 2:36-38), and in any case, single ascetic women fit Jesus' model of the spiritual household of God (8:19-21; 11:27-28), led by the single, celibate Jesus himself, and the eschatological kingdom of God where the resurrected ones "neither marry nor are given in marriage" (20:34-36).

The many women in Luke's Gospel delivered of various bodily ailments and disabilities by Jesus' touch with the "finger of God" also partake of God's eschatological power (11:20). A banner example (which Seim appreciates much more than Schaberg) involves Jesus' Sabbath restoration of the bent-over woman "whom Satan bound for eighteen long years" (13:16). Significantly accompanying Jesus' healing is his matter-of-fact identification of this woman as "a daughter of Abraham" (3:16). As Seim emphasizes, "the formulation in Luke 13:16 is an observation of fact, not an emphatic bestowal of a designation. The woman *is* Abraham's daughter; she does not become one."[25] In other words, she is not some special case, the proverbial exception that proves the rule, in which a woman, like the martyred mother of Eleazar, miraculously surmounts her "weaker sex" to assume the "mind of Abraham," to exhibit rare faith and fortitude "as the daughter of God-fearing Abraham" (see 4 Macc 14:20–15:28). In the Lukan incident, the woman has nothing to prove, no deficient identity to overcome in Jesus' eyes: "The healing on the day of rest, which was an essential sign of the covenant, realizes [the woman's] status as daughter. As a daughter of Abraham, she shares in the blessing that is promised to Abraham's progeny, and this is having a liberating effect on her life."[26]

Sliding into a more "mixed" perspective, however, Seim admits that the dignifying and liberating portraits of ascetic and healed women in Luke exact a toll, at least potentially. Sexual asceticism can easily become asexual, unisexed, or de-gendered, denying any distinctive value to femaleness, or worse, transmuting female identity wholly into dominant male essence (the one normative sex), as occurred in certain Gnostic traditions.[27] Luke gets close to this by identifying all the unmarried and unmarrying

---

25. Seim, "The Gospel of Luke," 736 (emphasis in original).

26. Seim, "The Gospel of Luke," 737.

27. See the (in)famous final logion in the *Gospel of Thomas*: "Simon Peter said to them, 'Mary should leave us, for females are not worthy of life.' Jesus said, 'Look, I shall guide her to make her male, so that she too may become a living spirit resembling you males. For every female who makes herself male will enter heaven's kingdom'" (114; citation from Marvin Meyer, *The Gospels of Mary: The Secret Tradition of Mary Magdalene, the Companion of Jesus* [New York: HarperCollins, 2004], 35).

offspring of God in the age to come as angel-like "*sons (huioi)* of God" and "*sons (huioi)* of the resurrection" (Luke 20:36). But this may simply reflect typical male generic language, reinforced by Jesus as Everyman, the ideal "*son* of Adam, *son* of God" (cf. 3:38). In any event, Seim concludes that "there is no clear trace in Luke of the idea that the ascetic life for women is a way of becoming male."[28] A more serious difficulty of the ascetic ideal from a feminist perspective, as I see it, is the devaluation of marriage and motherhood, sexuality and family engagement, for women *who still choose these options on their own terms.* Of course, opportunities for women's "right to choose" were severely restricted in Luke's world. But even in the frame of Mary's arranged marriage to Joseph, which Luke downplays, and her unique experience of virginal conception and prophetic expression, which plays into Seim's emphasis on independent, ascetic women disciples,[29] I see considerable development within Luke 1–2 of Mary's personal embrace and critical exercise of her natural childbearing and child-rearing opportunities, which I discuss at length in chapter 3. Moreover, I explore in chapter 4 the interplay of Joanna's roles as disciple *and* wife.

As for those healed by Jesus, Seim sees the impact of afflicted women's deliverance blunted somewhat by their stigmatic *impurity,* as well as their illness, which Jesus must overcome,[30] and their phlegmatic *passivity* in contributing to their own restoration. However, beyond Mary's ritual purification after giving birth — which Luke treats as a thoroughly positive move "according to the law of Moses" with no prior shame attached (2:22) — Luke never raises purity issues with any woman (this is a telling silence!). Moreover, recent studies have rightly exposed the purity obsession of NT scholars as misrepresenting the (largely restorative) function of the purity system in ancient Judaism as unduly oppressive toward women (purity regulations were also incumbent on priests and ordinary men).[31] In

28. Seim, "The Gospel of Luke," 760.

29. See Seim, "The Virgin Mother: Mary and Ascetic Discipleship in Luke," in *A Feminist Companion to Luke* (ed. Amy-Jill Levine and Marianne Blickenstaff; London: Sheffield Academic, 2002), 89-105.

30. Seim, "The Gospel of Luke," 737-38: "Thus, it is noteworthy that both of the women who are called (Abraham's) daughters [hemorrhaging (8:48) and bent-over (13:16) women] are sick, socially stigmatized, and impure. Impure persons were normally regarded as a threat to the collective purity of the people. This was why the question of purity was a matter of social and religious importance" (cf. 736).

31. Note especially the important studies of various Jewish scholars, e.g.: Paula Fredrickson, *Jesus of Nazareth, King of the Jews: A Jewish Life and the Emergence of Christianity* (New York: Knopf, 1999), 105-10, 197-214; Fredrickson, "Did Jesus Oppose the Purity

terms of women's roles as "passive partners" in their healing, it is true that Jesus sometimes takes the initiative without the needy women even asking for his help (4:38-39; 7:10-17). But regarding the hemorrhaging woman — the key case where a woman does seek out Jesus' curative power and obtains it without his permission! (8:43-48) — Seim curiously downplays her action in contrast to the male ruler Jairus's approach (on behalf of his sick daughter) in the related story: "The distinguished Jairus appeals very humbly but still directly to Jesus and begs him to come to his home. The woman with the hemorrhage does indeed reach out to get help for herself, but she comes under the cover of the crowd of the people, hidden and approaching Jesus from behind, fearful and afraid."[32] Whereas Seim intimates that Luke hereby contrasts and subordinates the bleeding woman to the synagogue ruler, I see a remarkable affirmation of the woman's initiative, persistence, and courage in the face of social obstacles and her own debilitated physical and economic condition — an affirmation echoing Jesus' final words to her: "Daughter, your faith has made you well; go in peace" (8:48). It's a terrible shame that the woman had to go through all this after her protracted twelve-year struggle — but she was still determined to get what she needed from Jesus. Though I do not focus on this woman's case in the present book,[33] I see her as a model of the "capable women of purpose and persistence" I do treat.

Finally, Seim also paints a mixed picture of Mary Magdalene, Joanna, and the other Galilean women who follow and "serve" *(diakoneō)* in Luke 8:1-3 and become the first witnesses to Jesus' resurrection in 24:8-11. While recognizing the high value Luke and Jesus accord to "service" *(diakonia)* for both men and women, Seim still detects tendencies for women's traditional, domestic service to function in an auxiliary mode undergirding men's higher callings of leadership and proclamation. In the case of Joanna and company in 8:1-3, "the women are no longer seen as disciples but are

---

Laws?" *Bible Review* 11 (1995): 20-25, 42-47; Amy-Jill Levine, *The Misunderstood Jew: The Church and the Scandal of the Jewish Jesus* (New York: HarperOne, 2006), 121-25, 145-66, 173-77; Levine, "Discharging Responsibility: Matthean Jesus, Biblical Law, and Hemorrhaging Woman," in *Treasures New and Old: Contributions to Matthean Studies* (ed. David R. Bauer and Mark Allan Powell; Atlanta: Scholars, 1996), 379-97; Shaye J. D. Cohen, "Menstruants and the Sacred in Judaism and Christianity," in *Women's History and Ancient History* (ed. Sarah B. Pomeroy; Chapel Hill: University of North Carolina Press, 1991), 273-99.

32. Seim, "The Gospel of Luke," 738.

33. See my discussion of this incident (though focused on Mark's account) in *Dancing Girls,* 57-61.

directed to a special function of care that is determined in material terms."[34] I will argue in chapter 4 for a stronger, more inclusive (though not fully egalitarian) view of women's discipleship in Luke and will reinforce my earlier work on Luke's deliberate toppling of traditional hierarchies between service/ministry at table (*diakonein trapezais*) and service/ ministry of the word (*diakonia tou logou*) (Acts 6:2-3). I put greater emphasis than Seim on Jesus' Last Supper call for his apostles to emulate his diaconal vocation — "I am among you as one who serves (*diakanōn*)" (Luke 22:27). Seim interprets Jesus' simile ("the leader is *like* [*hōs*] one who serves"; "I am among you *as* [*hōs*] one who serves" [22:26-27]) as a conscious maintenance of leader/servant boundaries (becoming more servant-like is good, but don't overdo it),[35] whereas I see the force of the simile in its context (the apostles are crassly jockeying for rank while Jesus table-waits on them) as dismantling the boundaries. Jesus fundamentally makes a strong identity statement of who he *is* ("I am [*egō eimi*])" in servant-terms normally reserved for women, not merely an allusion to his occasional servant-like, womanish conduct.

Coming to the empty tomb scene, Seim regards the discipleship status of the Galilean women as more elevated. Though they come to the tomb to perform typical material-servant operations of anointing Jesus' body, his absence nullifies such duty. Instead the women are reminded what Jesus said *to them* previously about his resurrection and become the first to proclaim his resurrection to the apostles without being commissioned to do so. While Schaberg and others demean the lack of commissioning in Luke as less respectful of their capacity for witness, Seim takes an opposite tack. Mark's Gospel, in which they are told by an angelic "young man" to report to the male disciples (Mark 16:5-7), treats them like "errand girls," whereas Luke features "their own spontaneous initiative as a continuation of what they themselves have heard and remembered."[36] Moreover, though the apostles don't believe the women until Peter dashes to the tomb and becomes "amazed at what had happened" — just as the women announced — Peter "comes across as a pale variant" of the women witnesses.[37] Overall, the empty tomb incident exemplifies Luke's "double message: the women from Galilee were indeed capable and qualified, but the men sus-

---

34. Seim, "The Gospel of Luke," 740.
35. Seim, "The Gospel of Luke," 744-45.
36. Seim, "The Gospel of Luke," 748-50.
37. Seim, "The Gospel of Luke," 751.

pected and rejected them. The male consolidation of power occurs against a story in which the men have shown weakness and failure rather than strength."[38] This factor of women's "capability" is a major component of my project.

Barbara Reid and Luke's "Better Part"

Reid's important monograph on the Third Gospel continues the feminist exposé of Luke's limitation of women's roles in Jesus' ministry and community. In the face of women's dynamic activity and leadership in the early Christian movement, Luke, in Reid's view, "like the author of the Pastoral letters . . . is intent on restricting them to silent, passive, supporting roles." Further, Luke "convey[s] the message that women and men have different ways of being disciples" — which reinforce a male-dominated hierarchy and resist gender equality.[39] The famous snapshot of Jesus' visit to the home of sisters Mary and Martha is paradigmatic, as Jesus affirms Mary's quiescent sitting at his feet as the "better choice" over against Martha's angry protest and agitated ministry (Luke 10:38-42). Mary epitomizes women's "silent, passive, supporting" part in contradistinction to men's vocal, active, leading roles.

However, while adopting this critical perspective on women's circumscribed place in Luke, Reid by no means leaves it there. Much more purposefully and pervasively than Schaberg or Seim, Reid utilizes a range of biblical-critical tools (historical, literary, sociological, and especially feminist) to explore how Luke's narrative can be reclaimed and reconstituted against its patriarchal grain toward liberating ends for women in contemporary communities of faith. How can preachers and teachers communicate the gospel (good news) of Luke for women today? This question pulses at the heart of Reid's study: "If one engages in the difficult task of reinterpreting the text from a feminist perspective, reading against Luke's intent, then the stories can be recontextualized to proclaim a message of good news for women and men called equally to share in the same discipleship and mission of Jesus."[40] The question mark in Reid's title is critical:

38. Seim, "The Gospel of Luke," 761.
39. Reid, *Choosing the Better Part?* 53. Cf. 3-4: "If we are looking to Luke's narrative to show that women and men shared equally in Jesus' mission in the first century, we will be disappointed."
40. Reid, *Choosing the Better Part?* 205.

"Choosing the Better Part?" moves from an exegetical conclusion of the Mary/Martha story to an ethical challenge to contemporary interpreters of Luke to make their own *better choices* generative of women's full and equal flourishing. Notice from the first page of Reid's book: "It is my hope that this book will help both women and men, particularly those who preach and teach the Scriptures, to do so in a way that will promote a Church of equal disciples, where gender differences would no longer determine ministerial roles. This would be today's way of 'choosing the better part.'"[41] And the closing word on the last page: "The better part awaits our choice."[42]

Reid offers fruitful possibilities of better interpretive choices at the end of every chapter spotlighting key members of the large cast of women characters in Luke's Gospel. Following the summary in her concluding chapter, we may briefly survey Reid's perspective, and make some comparisons with our own project, under five categories.

1. Prophetic Women in Luke 1–2   Reid appreciates the extraordinary cases of the Spirit-inspired "strong, vocal, prophetic" women in Luke's opening birth narratives — namely, Mary, Elizabeth, and Anna — as "promising" models for liberation. However, she also raises a critical red flag, not only noting these women's contrasts with the more staid and silent sisters that follow in the Gospel, but also regarding their stylized biblical characterizations as Luke's consignment of these dynamic women to the old "era of Judaism," deliberately pushing them back and marking them off from the more modest, "respectable" female disciples of Jesus and the "New Age" he inaugurates.[43] While I, too, stress the patterning of Mary, Elizabeth, and Anna after OT models (especially Miriam, Sarah, and Hannah) and the lamentable drop-off in prophetic women after Luke 2, I do not see Luke following a rigid periodic scheme separating "old" covenant and "new" kingdom eras.[44] Quite the contrary, I see Luke's whole

41. Reid, *Choosing the Better Part?* 1.
42. Reid, *Choosing the Better Part?* 207.
43. Reid, *Choosing the Better Part?* 52, 206.
44. Reid (*Choosing the Better Part?*) candidly states that these women "are not disciples" (52) and "Luke does not consider them the ideal for Christian women" (206). Reid's perspective is reminiscent of Hans Conzelmann's (*The Theology of St. Luke* [trans. Geoffrey Buswell; New York: Harper, 1961]) influential "periodizing" assessment of Luke-Acts as promoting the ministry of Jesus and the primitive church as the "Middle of Time," segmented off from the bygone age of the OT and the future delayed parousia of Christ. However, recent Lukan

narrative-theological project as intricately developing continuities and connections with, as well as disjunctions and distinctions from, the Jewish scriptures. I explore these complex intertextual links in some detail, not only in relation to Mary of Nazareth's portrait (chapter 3), but also concerning the "rivalry" between vocal-active Martha and silent-passive Mary (chapter 5).[45] And in both cases, I push for a richer, more promising understanding of women's discipleship in Luke — not yet reaching full equality with men, to be sure, but neither relegated to a bygone era nor restricted to a static role.

2. Women Healed by Jesus   While aware that the anonymous afflicted women Jesus restores remain largely silent and subordinate, Reid detects and accentuates traces of liberating possibilities in their stories: "beyond being nameless objects of compassion, each has further potential for discipleship." For example, Simon's mother-in-law rises to resume her hosting duties after being healed of her fever and "respond[s] to Jesus with service that matches his own mission"; the widow at Nain may be imagined as offering "a voiceless protest against death that ends with restoration of life"; and in cases we've already treated above: the hemorrhaging woman demonstrates a "gutsy faith" contributing, against considerable odds, to her own healing, and the long-suffering, bent-over woman who praises God for her deliverance (13:13) inspires "all who are bent under the weight of oppression to stand erect so that the whole people may glorify God."[46]

3. Women Featured in Jesus' Parables   Reid stands out for the remarkably careful attention she gives to the three brief parables in Luke showcasing women protagonists (13:20-21; 15:8-10; 18:2-5). However brief these snippets, she refuses to give them short shrift.[47] Moreover, while these women all do typical women's work (baking, sweeping, pleading for help), Reid sees them modeling significant acts of ministry (spreading the "yeast" of

---

scholarship has tended to view Luke's narrative-theological program in more fluid (less rigid) temporal terms, especially related to continuities with the OT.

45. Further, I devote the entirety of chapter 7 to exploring Luke's treatment (positive, negative, and ambiguous) of three "foreign" OT women (see more below).

46. Reid, *Choosing the Better Part?* 206.

47. Reid, *Choosing the Better Part?* 169-94 (chapters 13–15). See also by Reid: "Beyond Petty Pursuits and Wearisome Widows: Three Lukan Parables," *Interpretation* 56 (2002): 284-94; *Parables for Preachers: The Gospel of Luke (Year C)* (Collegeville, Minn.: Liturgical Press, 2000).

God's kingdom; seeking lost "sinners") and, in the case of the exploited widow, upending "the stereotype of poor helpless widows, exemplifying instead the strength of weakness and the power of persistent pursuit of justice." Most dramatically, Reid envisions all three parable women as "feminine images of *God*."[48] The downside, however, especially concerning the widow's judicial tale, is that Luke's surrounding context, in Reid's view, severely blunts the parable's original liberating thrust. Here I take an opposite position: in chapter 7 I will argue in detail for a more positive, reinforcing relationship between parable and context in Luke 18:1-8.

4. Women Who Model Jesus' Self-Sacrifice   Jesus' call to self-giving and cross-bearing sacrifice in all the Gospels (not just Luke) has posed a particular burden, from a feminist-critical perspective, for women who already expend themselves serving others. Doesn't the charge to "take up the cross daily" (only Luke adds the "daily" component [Luke 9:23]) only drive more nails into women's subordinate, servile coffins, keeping them buried at the bottom of the social ladder? Of course, Reid is fully alert to these adverse tendencies. But she also presses toward the "better choice" of viewing three Lukan women in particular not as generic women's cases, but as models for Jesus himself, "who pours out his life on behalf of others" and calls all his disciples, men as surely as women, to follow his example: the profuse anointing/kissing/weeping woman demonstrates in attending to Jesus his own vocation of "self-emptying love" (7:36-50); the woman searching for her missing coin exemplifies Jesus' diligent, indefatigable seeking for socially and morally lost persons (15:8-10); and the widow who throws her last pennies into the temple treasury chute effectively surrenders her whole life (*bios* [21:1-4]), as Jesus will soon do. Above all, these women help concretize Jesus' mission as a "fully embodied" project of loving actions for all needy "neighbors" in the community of God's people.[49]

5. Galilean Women Followers of Jesus   Concerning Luke's treatment of Mary Magdalene, Joanna, and company — restricting their contribution to the Jesus movement to material service in 8:1-3 and reducing their inaugural witness to Jesus' resurrection to nonsense ("idle tale") and silence in

---

48. Reid, *Choosing the Better Part?* 207 (emphasis added).

49. Reid, *Choosing the Better Part?* 207; also see Reid's sensitive, insightful volume, *Taking Up the Cross: New Testament Interpretations through Latina and Feminist Eyes* (Minneapolis: Fortress, 2007).

23:49–24:12 — Reid speaks of a "mixed message," à la Seim, but seems more inclined to Schaberg's feminist critique. In particular, Reid follows Schaberg in exposing the larger company of "acquaintances" with the Galilean women at the cross (mitigating Mark's clear statement of the male disciples' desertion with an implication of their continuing presence [Luke 23:49; cf. Mark 14:50; 15:40-41]), the women's lack of direct resurrection appearance by Christ and commission to testify, and the blanket dismissal of their word by the apostles. Also, far from seeing Peter as a "pale variant" (Seim) of the women witnesses, Reid stresses that Luke maintains "the primacy of Peter's witness" on the basis of the (belated and brief) report that "the Lord . . . has appeared to Simon!" (Luke 24:34).[50] From this critical standpoint, however, Reid again seeks for liberating potential. She finds it in this case more in turning Luke's text against itself than in sifting out some gold nuggets within, but in the process she develops a powerfully creative and challenging hermeneutic of proclamation rooted in "ritualized grief": "Today our proclamation of Luke's version of the empty tomb story can serve to ritualize the grief that Christian women have experienced for twenty centuries when their faithful and true witness is diminished as 'nonsense.' It can remind us of the deprivation imposed on the whole Christian community when its female members are silenced. It can move believers to choose the better part by taking actions to ensure that the faithful preaching of women be heard and accepted in our day."[51]

It should be evident by now that overall my approach in this book aligns more closely with Seim's and Reid's more nuanced negotiations of Luke's "mixed" treatment of women than with Schaberg's more sustained "red alert" position. But even within the mixture, I seek to sweeten the pot somewhat with sunnier depictions of capable, intelligent, determined women in Luke without, I trust, becoming sappy and a Little Mister Sunshine. Throughout this work, I remain enormously indebted to the three scholars just discussed and to a host of other feminist biblical critics.

Sketching the Cases in This Book

Having offered some orientation to my work above, I now sharpen that with brief previews of the cases I will treat. In methodology, my approach

---

50. Reid, *Choosing the Better Part?* 198-204; 206-7 (the "primacy of Peter" reference is on p. 201 and "mixed message" is on p. 206).

51. Reid, *Choosing the Better Part?* 204.

varies somewhat in each chapter depending on the issues, texts, and characters under investigation, but it generally reflects an eclectic use of grammatical, historical, sociological, literary, canonical, theological, postmodern, and feminist tools. I thus follow in the train of the multifocused feminist Lukan scholars discussed above, while pursuing three lines of inquiry more assiduously: (1) on the *literary* side, I give more attention to narrative-critical than redaction-critical analysis of Luke's composition; (2) on the *canonical* side, I frequently engage in detailed intertextual comparisons and contrasts with OT (including the Apocrypha) passages, patterns, and models; and (3) on the *feminist* side, in addition to interacting closely with feminist biblical scholarship, I utilize insights from feminist theologians, like Serene Jones, and feminist political philosophers, such as Martha Nussbaum, Susan Moller Okin, and Iris Marion Young. Nussbaum's "Capabilities Approach" to equal justice, freedom, and human development especially influences the study of Mary of Nazareth's "right to choose" (chapter 3) and Martha's and Mary's "good/better choices" (chapter 5) and serves as the matrix for the concluding chapter summarizing and assessing the capabilities of all the Lukan women featured in this book.[52]

The Case of the Suspicious Feminist (Chapter 2)

This is the most developed methodological chapter in the book, focusing on a major — and much maligned and misunderstood — component of feminist criticism, namely: the hermeneutics of suspicion. Here I seek to steer a middle course between the extreme poles of skepticism, on the left, and fideism, on the right — allowing for genuinely positive, constructive portraits of faithful, capable women in Luke without airbrushing away the subordinating and suppressing elements or, to shift the image, without sweeping the dusty residue of kyriarchal (lord-ruled) domination of women under the rug. Doubt and faith must dwell together as both sides of the hermeneutical "coin." Following an extended theoretical introduction to the problem, I apply a moderate hermeneutic of suspicion, combined

---

52. The most recent and convenient summary may be found in Martha C. Nussbaum, *Creating Capabilities: The Human Development Approach* (Cambridge: Harvard University Press, Belknap Press, 2011). A fuller bibliography of Nussbaum's numerous writings will appear in later chapters.

with a hermeneutics of remembrance, imagination, and transformation, to Jesus' story of the woman who diligently sweeps her house to find a valued lost coin, as God in Christ searches and finds "lost sinners" (15:8-10).

The Case of the Pregnant Teenager (Chapter 3)

Here I track the young virgin Mary's cognitive, affective, and active responses to Gabriel's annunciation of Jesus' conception in her womb and her consequent pregnancy, delivery, and maternal care. While God's choice of her to bear and nurture Israel's Messiah is primary and programmed — so decreed by the Most High Lord God (1:32) — Mary is not portrayed as simply a passive, pliant, and compliant vessel for God's use. Across Luke 1–2 she questions, challenges, ponders, expounds upon, acts, and reacts to her maternal vocation, proving herself to be a capable, creative partner with God and God's work of salvation through Jesus. Mary's characterization as "Spirited agent and actor" comports to a significant degree with seven items on Nussbaum's "capabilities list," which I introduce in this chapter.

The Case of the Independent Wife (Chapter 4)

Though briefly identified in only two verses (8:3; 24:10), Joanna offers a tantalizing snapshot of a named female follower of Jesus (from Galilee to empty tomb), friend of Mary Magdalene, and wife of a Herodian official (Chuza). Particularly rare for Luke is the glimpse Joanna affords into a *married* woman disciple — with a Herodian husband no less! — who appears to accompany and support the Jesus movement independently of her spouse. But many questions remain open in Luke's meager account, which various scholars have addressed in remarkably imaginative — and speculative — ways. After analyzing all the information Luke does provide about Joanna, I describe and critique several reconstructions of her role in Jesus' ministry and early Christianity. This is by far the most historically oriented chapter in the book (it's titled "The Quest for the Historical Joanna"), though I endeavor throughout not to lose sight of the primary Lukan context. Although some have tried to identify Luke's Joanna with Paul's Junia in Romans 16:7, the connection remains far from certain. As I see it, while I'm happy to grant that Joanna was a "real" historical figure, she appears only in Luke's narrative as part of its overall presentation of women disciples.

The Case of the Angry Hostess (Chapter 5)

Here I take up what is probably the most overworked, overanalyzed case in Lukan feminist studies, certainly in proportion to its size: the Martha and Mary incident in 10:38-42. As noted above, this snippet has become a *locus classicus* for Luke's proclivity to muzzle vocal, vibrant women like Martha in favor of silent, submissive sisters like Mary. While not denying the suspicious, limiting tendencies in this story, I will follow the more positive lead of some scholars who seek to rehabilitate the "testy hostess" Martha and to accentuate the complementary, more than competitive, nature of the sisters' roles *within* Luke's account. My approach supplements previous studies of Luke's Martha/Mary story with extensive comparative analysis of several OT household rivals type-scenes,[53] examination of the story's reception history into medieval and Reformation periods, and appropriation of concepts of "capability" and "motility" from feminist philosophers Martha Nussbaum and Iris Young, respectively.

The Case of the Threatening Foreigners (Chapter 6)

By contrast with the oft-treated Martha/Mary episode, to my knowledge no one has investigated the trio of anonymous OT Gentile ("foreign") women alluded to in Luke: the widow at Zarephath (4:25-26), the queen of the South (11:31), and the wife of Lot (17:32). Moreover, whereas the four OT Gentile (or Gentile-related) women in Matthew's genealogy of Jesus (Tamar, Rahab, Ruth, and the wife of Uriah) have garnered considerable scholarly attention in recent years, Luke's scattered references to three "foreign" OT women have scarcely received honorable mention — despite Jesus' admonition to "*remember* [Lot's wife]." In remembering the three "strange" women from Israel's past, I pay close attention to their original biblical stories and subsequent interpretations in Hellenistic-Jewish literature, as well as to their function in Luke's narrative. I especially address the issue of alien women's stereotypical threat to Israelite piety and security (an FBI concern, if there ever was one), finding it to be much more ambiguous and complex than commonly assumed. There is as much to learn as to fear from these borderline cases.

---

53. A fruitful approach whose idea I owe to Amy-Jill Levine (in conversation).

The Case of the Feisty Widow (Chapter 7)

While I have used the image of forensic-legal "cases" to introduce the women investigated in this book, this chapter features an actual courtroom scene from one of the most vivid parables spun by the Lukan Jesus, in which a widow pleads for justice against an unjust opponent before an unjust judge (18:2-5). Remarkably, however, despite conventional portrayals of widows as vulnerable victims — including some in Luke's writings (e.g., Luke 20:47; Acts 6:1) — the widow in the parable not only wins her case against incredible odds, but also wins it in a remarkable display of strategic savvy and strength by an underdog fighter (boxer) for justice. Nevertheless, as feminist interpreters celebrate the widow's achievement in the parable, many also lament the confining (boxing) ring that Luke has roped around this feisty woman (Luke 18:1, 6-7). I, however, find plenty of space within Luke's arena in 18:1-8 for affirming the indomitable widow as a model of prayerful and faithful pursuit of justice. Indeed, in my judgment, she stands out as the quintessential "capable woman of purpose and persistence" the coming Son of Man hopes to find vigorously advancing God's just reign on earth (18:8).

2. Can We Go On Together with Suspicious Minds? Doubt and Trust as Both Sides of the Hermeneutical "Coin" (Luke 15:8-10)

Elvis didn't think so. "We *can't* go on together with suspicious minds," he crooned. "And we *can't* build our dreams on suspicious minds." Loving relationships and communities do not thrive in the throes of mistrust, angst, and accusation; indeed, they eventually die, along with their hopes and dreams, under suspicion's corrosive tyranny.

So it can be in relating to the Bible in interpretive communities of faith, which engage the "Good Book" less as an inanimate object of gaze than as an intimate subject of love — reaching out to its readers, addressing issues that matter to them, and compelling active responses of love, devotion, and obedience. To sharpen the point theologically, the Bible bears consistent witness to the creative, redemptive character of *God,* who personally engages and challenges people as loving — and demanding — subject.[1] And thoroughgoing suspicion of God's intentions toward us and purposes for

---

1. See Jacqueline E. Lapsley, *Whispering the Word: Hearing Women's Stories in the Old Testament* (Louisville: Westminster John Knox, 2005), 19: "[A] hermeneutic of informed trust (informed by history, tradition, and experience) frees us to encounter God in Scripture — frees us to expect that God is telling us something significant, even revelatory, about ourselves, about who God is, and about our life together" (cf. 1-19); Joel B. Green, "Scripture and Theology: Uniting the Two So Long Divided," in *Between Two Horizons: Spanning New Testament Studies and Systematic Theology* (ed. Joel Green and Max Turner; Grand Rapids: Eerdmans, 2000), 31: "[T]he interpretive model to which we object treats the biblical text solely or primarily as a source of data, of knowledge. . . . How do these texts impinge on their readers? What processes do they set in motion? In this accounting the text cannot be regarded as mere object; it, too, is subject in the communicative discourse." Stephen E. Fowl and L. Gregory Jones, *Reading in Communion: Scripture and Ethics in Christian Life* (Grand Rapids: Eerdmans, 1991), 42: "[W]e must be willing to be interrogated *by* Scripture in addition to interrogating Scripture" (emphasis in original).

us, as mediated in the Bible, scarcely provides a propitious foundation on which to build a healthy relationship with God and God's word.

The serpent's opening gambit casts *false* suspicion on God: "Did God [really] say, 'You shall not eat from *any* tree in the garden'?" (Gen 3:1). (What a cheeky deity to plant all these luscious trees around you and not let you sample *any* of their delights!) Of course, God commanded no such thing, as the woman promptly clarifies; but then she springs her own suspicious trap, suggesting *wrongly* that God had prohibited *touching* as well as tasting the fruit of a single, exceptional tree (3:2-3). Where does this truncated, hyper-fastidious view of God come from — this God who had done nothing but provide human beings with life, companionship, employment, housing, and an abundance of food, minus *one lone* forbidden tree ("You may *freely eat* of every tree of the garden [but one!]" [2:16-17])? Suspicion begets disobedience, which in turn begets further suspicion: surely, the first couple supposes, God wants nothing to do with them now — hence, their fig-leaf cover-up and bush-league hideout (3:7-8). And who knows what kind of horrible "death sentence" awaits them on this ominous "day" of transgression (2:17)?

Although God is scarcely pleased with the first couple and has good cause to doubt their faithfulness, God in fact *seeks them out*, confronts them with the consequences of their wrongdoing — including eventual, but not imminent, death — *and* clothes them with more durable, protective garments (3:8-21). The divine-human relationship is unquestionably scarred, but not severed. For God's part, grace and love prevail; but on the human side, suspicion still lurks. Cain's boiling anger toward his brother is fueled in large measure by suspicion of God's preferential intentions in accepting Abel's offering and rejecting Cain's. Why, exactly, does the Lord not "regard" Cain's produce? The text does not say, leaving a gap for suspicion to erupt and fester.[2] And the result is disastrous: Cain's suspicion-sparked anger explodes into Abel's murder and Cain's exile (4:1-16).

So from the beginning, the Bible testifies to suspicion's corrosive effect on healthy relationships among God, God's people, and God's world. But for all its initial suspicion of human suspicion toward God, the Bible soon makes a measure of space for this inquisitive, even inquisitorial, side of human nature. The unfathomable depth and complexity of God and God's

---

2. Terence E. Fretheim confirms the inscrutability of God's rejecting Cain's offering as "an election for reasons known only to God" (*God and the World in the Old Testament: A Relational Theology of Creation* [Nashville: Abingdon, 2005], 78).

word unfolding through time to fallible, finite human beings (created in God's image, but still limited in capacity to comprehend God fully) inevitably call forth human questions, concerns, and suspicions. Starting from a position of faith does not guarantee twenty-twenty spiritual vision; we often see "in a mirror, dimly" (1 Cor 13:12),[3] "people [that] look like trees, walking" (Mark 8:24), requiring progress "through faith for faith" (Paul [Rom 1:17]) or "faith seeking understanding" (Anselm, *Proslogion*).

And this faith journey may well wind through critical paths of lament, laced with doubt and suspicion. Faithful Abraham suspects God of indiscriminate judgment against Sodom and Gomorrah and tells God so, more or less (Gen 18:22-33); likewise, Moses questions God's intentions to wipe out the whole lot of golden-calf-making Israelites at Sinai (Exod 32:11-14); Job accuses God of unnecessary roughness and pleads for an "umpire" to make God play fair (Job 9:32-33); the psalmist, echoed by Jesus on the cross, wonders in anguish why God has forsaken him in his hour of need (Ps 22:1; Matt 27:46/Mark 15:34); and Habakkuk laments God's deaf ear to the cries of God's suffering people in a violent world (Hab 1:2-17). In each case suspicion is born of faith: because we believe you are a just, compassionate, gracious, present God, as disclosed through your word, we suspect something is out of kilter when you seem to act differently. And as faithful human beings express suspicion of God's acts and aims, God engages them in productive dialogue toward a fuller understanding of God's will and ways. Suspicion serves faith by calling God out, as it were, to be true to God's nature, as we have come to know it, and calling forth richer and deeper modes of knowing and loving this God with whom we have to do.

But while the lament tradition provides a candid and creative nexus for doubt and faith in biblical-theological interpretation, does it sufficiently justify the prevailing practice of a hermeneutic of suspicion in contemporary biblical scholarship? Does unbridled suspicion not still run the risk of divorcing itself from or directing itself against faith, of crossing the line into scoffing and scorning God, as Proverbs warns?[4] Such concerns have sparked renewed suspicions, in certain theological quarters, about the ultimate value of suspicion as a principal hermeneutical strategy and its compatibility with faithful response to God's revelation.[5]

---

3. Fowl and Jones, *Reading in Communion*, 110.

4. E.g., Prov 1:20-25; 3:34; 9:7-12; 21:24; 29:8; cf. Dick Keyes, *Seeing through Cynicism: A Reconsideration of the Power of Cynicism* (Downers Grove, Ill.: IVP, 2006), 84.

5. Merold Westphal, *Suspicion and Faith: The Religious Uses of Modern Atheism* (Grand Rapids: Eerdmans, 1993), 284: "Suspicion is dangerous, but that does not mean that we

Suspecting and Suspending Suspicion

As David Jasper sketches in broad terms, biblical hermeneutics since the Enlightenment has consistently coursed through dual currents of faith and suspicion — not, however, always flowing in the same direction or in healthy tension with each other.[6] Indeed, the suspicion of early scientific rationalists gravely undermined the historical veracity of biblical miracles and other supposed supernatural phenomena, prompting spirited apologetic rejoinders from Bible "believers." Later ideological critics, led by the so-called triumvirate "masters of suspicion" — Nietzsche, Marx, and Freud — unmasked oppressive and repressive tendencies of religion and other sociopolitical establishments serving elite interests; in the process, they left little room for faithful engagement with or salutary submission to the Bible as God's authoritative word.[7]

Newer methods of biblical analysis have adopted a "hermeneutics of suspicion" platform with fresh vigor. Feminist criticism, in particular, typically approaches the Bible with all due caution as a text written by (dominant) men for men — that is, from a thoroughly androcentric (male-centered), patriarchal (father-ruled), and kyriarchal (master-dominated) perspective. Let women and other "others" beware! Post-Holocaust investigation of the NT trains a wary eagle eye on harsh statements about "the Jews" and Jewish unbelief and hypocritical practice, suspecting Christian polemical propaganda and supersessionist ideology. Recent ecological hermeneutics suspects and resists the Bible's largely anthropocentric (human-oriented) perspective of the world, which tends to neglect, distort, and exploit the wider interests of creation and "Earth" as living subject.[8] Apart from the problematic language of the biblical text itself,[9] suspicion has also

---

should suspend our suspicions. It means, rather, that we should suspect our suspicions, knowing of their danger." Cf. Keyes, *Seeing through Cynicism*, 75-79, 89-97.

6. David Jasper, *A Short Introduction to Hermeneutics* (Louisville: Westminster John Knox, 2004), 7-24, 69-87.

7. Westphal, *Suspicion and Faith*; Keyes, *Seeing through Cynicism*, 50-56.

8. Norman C. Habel and Peter Trudinger, eds., *Exploring Ecological Hermeneutics* (Atlanta: Scholars, 2008); David G. Horrell et al., eds., *Ecological Hermeneutics: Biblical, Historical, and Theological Perspectives* (London: T. & T. Clark, 2010).

9. Leading feminist NT scholar Elisabeth Schüssler Fiorenza gives special attention to the biblical text as a "site of struggle over language and theory" in *Sharing Her Word: Feminist Biblical Interpretation in Context* (Boston: Beacon Press, 1998), 88-104; e.g., "In my view, a hermeneutics of suspicion does not have the task of unearthing or uncovering historical or theological truth but of disentangling the ideological workings of andro-kyriocentric language" (90).

been fueled by two millennia of accumulated interpretive record, including (mis)use of the text to support so-called holy wars and ethnic "cleansings," subordination and even battering of women, pogroms against Jews, enslavement of African laborers, and exploitation of the environment. For some concerned critics, the Bible's deleterious rhetoric and history of interpretation are enough to merit it a stark label, Warning: Dangerous to Your Health. Read at Your Own Risk. Even the prominent Lutheran bishop and biblical theologian Krister Stendahl classified the Bible as a major "public health" hazard in its — and its interpreters' — often-toxic treatment of women and Jews and spoke of "increasingly . . . moving my teaching situation to what you might call the Public Health Department of biblical studies."[10]

But come on now. Warning labels and public health alerts? Putting the Bible on a par with cigarettes and smallpox? Isn't that pushing suspicion too far — from healthy, faithful lament to harmful, foolish paranoia? Conceding, even confessing as sin (on biblical grounds), the sad history of (ab)using the Bible for violent, oppressive purposes does not abrogate the witness of millions through the ages to the Bible's life-giving, liberating power. So enough already with this dour drumbeat of hermeneutical suspicion! Is it not high time to return dispositions of faith, trust, and submission to the hermeneutical throne,[11] with suspicion, if present at all, firmly relegated to footstool (and footnote) status? An increasing scholarly chorus has been calling for greater integration between biblical and theological disciplines around the "rule of faith," which not merely suspends disbelief (suspicion) in God's revealed word, but actively affirms orthodox faith and practice.[12] A cynical hermeneu-

10. Krister Stendahl, "Ancient Scripture in the Modern World," in *Scripture in the Jewish and Christian Traditions: Authority, Interpretation, Relevance* (ed. Frederick E. Greenspahn; Nashville: Abingdon, 1982), 205; on the "warning" or "caution" label, see Schüssler Fiorenza, "The Will to Choose or to Reject: Continuing Our Critical Work," in *Feminist Interpretation of the Bible* (ed. Letty M. Russell; Philadelphia: Westminster, 1985), 130 (cf. discussion below).

11. See Joel Green, *Seized by Truth: Reading the Bible as Scripture* (Nashville: Abingdon, 2007), 11: "[M]ore basic than learning the biblical languages, and more essential than good technique in interpretation are such dispositions and postures and gestures as acceptance, devotion, attention and trust" (cf. 24, where Green elaborates on these dispositions as "yielding" and "obedience" to Scripture's claims).

12. See the helpful essay collections in Green and Turner, eds., *Between Two Horizons*; Ellen F. Davis and Richard B. Hays, eds., *The Art of Reading Scripture* (Grand Rapids: Eerdmans, 2003); Stephen Fowl, ed., *The Theological Interpretation of Scripture: Classic and Con-*

tics of suspicion must give way to a more civil and congenial hermeneutics of trust and consent.

For example, in his collection of detailed literary and historical studies of key women in the Gospels, Richard Bauckham takes a cautious (suspicious) stance toward feminist biblical criticism.[13] Although applauding its "considerable achievements" in uncovering significant women characters in the Bible, largely neglected in the history of interpretation, and in "discovering," in certain cases, hopeful "possibilities of the text as possibilities for new living today,"[14] Bauckham expresses grave concerns over feminist criticism's typical employment of the hermeneutics of suspicion. The "proper use" of this hermeneutic, he argues, should be limited to exposing both the rather banal fact that men and women occupied different social positions in biblical society, with men mostly on top, and also the more provocative reality that texts, not least biblical texts, "are not ideologically neutral" but rather serve a variety of social and political interests.[15] However, Bauckham worries that feminist criticism too readily succumbs to a "blinkered use" of suspicion as "the only exegetical tool" in the service of a "one-issue" obsession.

> [T]he issue of patriarchal oppression of women is the only interest the exegete brings to the text and therefore the feminist hermeneutic of suspicion is the only exegetical tool that is employed. It is hard to attend fairly and openly to a text unless one is genuinely interested in all that the text is about, and unless one takes the trouble to approach it with

---

temporary Readings (Malden, Mass.: Blackwell, 1997); A. K. M. Adam et al., *Reading Scripture with the Church: Toward a Hermeneutic for Theological Interpretation* (Grand Rapids: Baker Academic, 2006). Cf. also Kevin J. Vanhoozer, gen. ed., *Dictionary for Theological Interpretation of the Bible* (Grand Rapids: Baker Academic, 2005); Daniel J. Trier, *Introducing Theological Interpretation of Scripture: Recovering a Christian Practice* (Grand Rapids: Baker Academic, 2008); and two monographs by Stephen Fowl: *Engaging Scripture: A Model for Theological Interpretation* (Malden, Mass.: Blackwell, 1998) and *Theological Interpretation of Scripture* (Eugene, Oreg.: Cascade, 2009).

13. Richard Bauckham, *Gospel Women: Studies of the Named Women in the Gospels* (Grand Rapids: Eerdmans, 2002). Cf. my fuller summary and assessment of Bauckham's approach in F. Scott Spencer, *Dancing Girls, "Loose" Ladies, and Women of "the Cloth": Women in Jesus' Life* (London: Continuum, 2004), 8-11.

14. Bauckham, *Gospel Women*, xiii-xiv. On the criterion of feminist-liberating "possibility" in biblical interpretation, Bauckham draws on Schüssler Fiorenza, *Jesus and the Politics of Interpretation* (New York: Continuum, 2000), 51-53.

15. Bauckham, *Gospel Women*, xv.

the rich resources of interpretation available in the form of historical and literary methods that are designed to open up the text for its own sake and not just for ideological illustration.[16]

Bauckham further laments a hermeneutic of suspicion's tone deafness to "genuinely gynocentric" counterstrains in otherwise male-dominated biblical literature. He draws a sharp methodological line in the sand: "Unlike many feminist biblical critics I do not regard the canon of Scripture as a hopelessly patriarchal construction."[17] The book of Ruth in the Hebrew Bible and the Mary-Elizabeth exchange in Luke 1 represent banner examples, in Bauckham's judgment, offering "authentically women's perspectives" on biblical events (even if written by a man) and allowing feminist critics positively to read "with the grain" of the text, if they just would.[18] He pushes his case further with Luke's Gospel by saying that, although Elizabeth drops out of the story entirely after the first chapter and Mary (Jesus' mother) after the second,[19] Mary Magdalene, Joanna, and "many other" Galilean women join the company of Jesus' closest followers in Luke 8:2-3, thus inviting readers, male and female, to consider the balance of Luke's narrative from women's points of view, even though these particular women say nothing and remain hidden until the closing scenes in 23:55–24:10 (cf. 24:22).[20]

Richard Hays mounts a more vigorous assault, trumpeting a "hermeneutic of trust *(pistis)*" as a "dramatic and life-giving alternative to the corrosive hermeneutic of suspicion that has come to dominate the modern academy."[21] Here suspicion equates with *apistia* — unbelief, unfaithfulness. Although Hays acknowledges that many "suspicious interpreters . . . believe [the Bible] can contain both liberating and oppressing messages," he focuses on their overriding tendency to "portray the apostolic witnesses

16. Bauckham, *Gospel Women*, xv-xvi.

17. Bauckham, *Gospel Women*, xix.

18. Bauckham, *Gospel Women*, xix-xxi, 14; and the chapters "The Book of Ruth as a Key to Gynocentric Reading of Scripture," 1-16, and "Elizabeth and Mary in Luke 1: Read a Gynocentric Text Intertextually," 47-76.

19. Mary reappears briefly by name as part of the earliest Christian community in Acts 1:14, but is never mentioned again in Luke's writings.

20. Bauckham, *Gospel Women*, 199-202; cf. Robert J. Karris, "Women and Discipleship in Luke," *Catholic Biblical Quarterly* 56 (1994): 1-20.

21. Richard Hays, *The Conversion of the Imagination: Paul as Interpreter of Israel's Scripture* (Grand Rapids: Eerdmans, 2005), xv. The focal essay is entitled "A Hermeneutic of Trust" (190-201). For a recent, largely sympathetic, assessment of Hays's study, see Martin E. Marty, *Building Cultures of Trust* (Grand Rapids: Eerdmans, 2010), 61-63.

less as revelatory witnesses to God's mercy than as oppressive promulgators of abusive images of God." He particularly seizes on Schüssler Fiorenza's contention, alluded to above, that "a feminist critical hermeneutics of suspicion places a warning label on all biblical texts: *Caution! Could be dangerous to your health and survival*."[22] Having thus tarred the Bible with a dubious and dangerous brush, Schüssler Fiorenza and her suspicious cohorts supposedly supplant biblical authority with the rule of *experience*, which they elevate, in Hays's opinion, with "remarkably credulous" arrogance as "unambiguously revelatory." Hence, "they endlessly critique the biblical texts but rarely get around to hearing Scripture's critique of us, or hearing its message of grace."[23]

Hays turns the tables on feminist and other ideological critics in calling for *suspicion of human experience and academic institutions* inevitably "corrupted and shaped by the present evil age" (cf. Gal 1:4) and polluted by "filth in our own souls" (T. S. Eliot). As sinful beings, we must humbly and trustingly allow God's word to rub hard against the grain of our fickle and misguided experience.[24] We should take our foundational hermeneutical cues from (1) *Abraham*, who, according to Paul, distrusted (suspected) his own geriatric impotence and Sarah's barrenness in favor of believing God's remarkable word of promise (Rom 4:18-21, using *apistia* and *pistis/ pisteuō*); and (2) *Mary*, who overcame her suspicion of virginal conception ("How can this be?") with faithful submission to God's purpose ("Let it be with me according to your word") (Luke 1:34, 38).[25] Thus, Hays principally advocates suspicion as an obstacle to surmount or a practice to suspend — replaced by a *hermeneutic of consent/trust*.

Sustaining and Struggling with Suspicion

While turning the critical spotlight on a hermeneutic of suspicion exposes valid concerns — by definition, this hermeneutic should train its suspicious eye inward as well as outward — questions concerning balance and

22. Hays, *Conversion*, 190-91, referencing Schüssler Fiorenza, "The Will to Choose or Reject," in *Feminist Interpretation* (ed. Russell), 130.

23. Hays, *Conversion*, 191.

24. Hays, *Conversion*, 197-200, drawing the Eliot "filth" allusion from Frank Lentricchia, "Last Will and Testament of an Ex-Literary Critic," *Lingua Franca* (September/October 1996): 60 ("'Tell us truly, is there no filth in your soul?'").

25. Hays, *Conversion*, 192-97.

proportion persist. How far must the pendulum swing away from an engaged suspicious approach to biblical interpretation to be regarded as "faithful"? The lament tradition notwithstanding, does suspicion operate more as faith's foe than as its friend? Are Bauckham's and Hays's negative assessments of suspicious practices of feminist biblical criticism, in particular, squarely on target? Do they fairly reflect typical use of a hermeneutic of suspicion by feminist scholars?

My take on the broad sweep of contemporary feminist biblical criticism is that it generally plays the "suspicion" card in a more limited, sophisticated, and optimistic fashion than is often assumed. Moreover, I suggest that suspicion and trust, doubt and faith, can and should *mutually* inform biblical-theological interpretation, feminist and otherwise, spurred by the lament tradition but also extending beyond it across the biblical canon. Consider the following four issues.

Methodological Complexity

First, tarring feminist biblical interpreters as "blinkered," "one-issue" critics armed only with a suspicious sledgehammer in their exegetical toolbox, which they ruthlessly wield to bash the "abusive" biblical God, is itself a myopic, reductive caricature, woefully out of touch with the rich complexity and diversity — and even piety — of much feminist engagement with the Bible as it has developed over the past four decades. Shifting the image from toolshed to music hall, Amy-Jill Levine observes,

> Today there are countless readings that could be labeled feminist, even as there are countless ways that the term has been and can be defined. The feminist choir no longer sounds the single note of white, Western, middle-class, Christian concerns; "feminist biblical studies" is now a symphony. It acknowledges the different concerns social location and experience bring to interpretation and recognizes the tentativeness and partiality of each conclusion: no instrument alone is complete; no two musicians play the music exactly alike.[26]

Moreover, along with employing a variety of tools and instruments, feminist biblical scholars come to their work with a range of theological

---

26. Amy-Jill Levine, introduction to *A Feminist Companion to Matthew* (ed. Amy-Jill Levine and Marianne Blickenstaff; Sheffield: Sheffield Academic, 2001), 14.

commitments, but rarely with no commitment at all. Simply conceding that most feminist interpreters recognize helpful as well as harmful elements within the Bible understates the situation. Most in fact are passionate women (and supportive men) of faith *(pistis)* — not unfaith *(apistia)* — involved in synagogues, churches, hospitals, prisons, and other faith communities struggling to discover and experience the Bible's God-gracing, life-giving power. If the Bible is so hopelessly deleterious to women, why bother? If it is so incorrigibly riddled with patriarchy, why "love it," as Phyllis Trible confessed, to devote so many years of professional training and so much critical energy to studying it?[27]

Although Schüssler Fiorenza's students have playfully dubbed themselves and their mentor as FBI agents (**F**eminist **B**iblical **I**nterpreters), in truth their sole mission has not been to spy and smoke out dangerous threats to women and other oppressed persons lurking in the biblical text. Identifying seven interweaving "hermeneutical moves and turns" in the "circle dance" of feminist biblical interpretation, Schüssler Fiorenza lists "suspicion" third (after "experience" and "domination and social location"), followed by four *constructive steps:* "critical evaluation," "creative imagination," "remembering and reconstruction," and ultimately "transformative action for change."[28] Further, she strongly argues that biblical interpreters "need to develop and engage not only a deconstructive but (re)constructive methodology. The feminist coin, if it should retain its currency, must have two sides: deconstruction and reconstruction!"[29] And she decries the cynicism of some (a minority, I would say) feminist critics who assert that any attempt to reclaim androcentric biblical texts for women's emancipatory interests is a disingenuous and hopeless act of "wishful thinking."[30] On the contrary, Schüssler Fiorenza's appreciation for the theologically imaginative, literarily open, and historically contingent nature of the Bible spurs her to creative, salutary (re)interpretations for women today.

27. Trible, "If the Bible's So Patriarchal, How Come I Love It?" *Bible Review* 8 (1992): 44-47, 55.

28. Schüssler Fiorenza, *Wisdom Ways: Introducing Feminist Biblical Interpretation* (Maryknoll, N.Y.: Orbis, 2001), 165-91; "Invitation to 'Dance' in the Open House of Wisdom: Feminist Study of the Bible," in *Engaging the Bible: Critical Readings from Contemporary Women* (ed. Choi Hee An and Katheryn Pfisterer Darr; Minneapolis: Fortress, 2006), 97-104; *Sharing Her Word,* 76-77; *The Power of the Word: Scripture and the Rhetoric of Empire* (Minneapolis: Fortress, 2007), 163-64.

29. Schüssler Fiorenza, *Sharing Her Word,* 80.

30. Schüssler Fiorenza, *Sharing Her Word,* 97-101.

Biblical-Theological Tension

Second, careful attention must be paid to the thick textures, creative tensions, suggestive gaps, and dynamic ebbs and flows of biblical narrative, which permit, if not invite, a wide array of reader responses across the doubt-faith, suspicion-trust spectrum. John Goldingay issues a strong and persuasive appeal to biblical-theological interpreters to take seriously the predominantly narrative nature of the Bible and, in turn, the nature of narrative as richly "open-ended, allusive, and capable of embracing questions and ambiguity," in distinction from "traditional systematic theology," which "by its nature . . . is [more] concerned with the unequivocal; it presupposes a quest for unity."[31] In particular, meaningful narrative plots mount and maintain various levels of suspense (suspicion), which lead to a range of partial and frustrating, as well as more complete and satisfying, resolutions. Complex narratives have no problem with leaving their readers dangling in deliberative thought. Applied to the canonical NT Gospel plot(s) — unfolding in four (or five, if Acts is treated separately) distinctive narratives — various "dialectical tensions" can be appreciated, not least one with provocative implications for gendered status among Jesus' followers. "[T]he Gospel story portrays Jesus choosing twelve men as members of his inner circle, which might confirm men's special status in the leadership of the people of God. It then portrays him watching them misunderstand, betray, and abandon him, so that the people who accompany his martyrdom and first learn of his transformation are women — which might subvert men's special status in the leadership of the people of God."[32]

It's at this point of keenly attending to narrative-theological plots and tensions that Hays falls short in his antifeminist readings of Abraham's and Mary's "faithful" surmounting of doubt to believe God's word. On the one hand, these cases don't really address the feminist-critical hermeneutic of suspicion. The suspicion Abraham and Mary overcome focuses not on withering, unjust life experiences they interrogate God about, as with biblical laments, but rather on incredible promises of God's life-giving power. Their problem is not theodicy, but theophany. Abraham resists false hopes of Sarah's childbearing in old age, while Mary queries the prospect of her own childbearing without a man's seed. They suspect God's overreaching

31. John Goldingay, "Biblical Narrative and Systematic Theology," in *Between Two Horizons* (ed. Green and Turner), 131-32.

32. Goldingay, "Biblical Narrative," 125.

blessing, not God's overbearing oppressing; and such blessing — focused on enlivening and empowering both elderly and young women — nicely fits feminism's liberating agenda.

On the other hand, however, the overall narratives surrounding Abraham and Mary open up a range of character and reader responses, both problematic and promising. Paul's subsuming the career of Abraham under the banner "He believed the LORD; and the LORD reckoned it to him as righteousness" (Gen 15:6) represents a highly selective generalization. Abraham also schemed to adjust the Lord's will (16:1-4; 17:18), laughed at the Lord's promise (17:17), questioned the Lord's judgment (18:23-33), and jeopardized the Lord's plan — and Sarah's life, twice! — by lying about his relationship with her and selling her into a foreign king's harem to save his own neck (12:10-20; 20:1-18). And the outrageous "binding" of the covenant son Isaac *without Sarah's knowledge* (22:1-14), while capable of being read as the acme of Abraham's faithful obedience to God, does not yield such an interpretation without engaging some hard-hitting, "suspicious" questions, such as: Why does this patriarch who queried the fairness of God's judgment against Sodom in order to spare nephew Lot's life not utter a peep of doubt about God demanding the sacrifice of son Isaac at Moriah?[33]

As for Mary's role in Luke, some feminist scholars echo Bauckham's gynocentric reading of Luke's birth narrative as a "critical counterbalance" or welcome "interruption of the dominant androcentricity of Scripture"[34] — including the rest of Luke. In Brigitte Kahl's terms, Luke 1 stitches a "feminist-egalitarian" pattern, "something like a 'feminist code' woven into the texture of the biblical 'textile.'"[35] Likewise, including Mary Magdalene, Joanna, Susannah, and other women among Jesus' disciples in Luke 8 and 23–24 militates against a hyper-suspicious reading of Luke's male-dominated story. But such gains are easily lost. The total *dropping* of Mary and Elizabeth from Luke's script after such a propitious beginning

33. See R. W. L. Moberly, *The Bible, Theology, and Faith: A Study of Abraham and Jesus* (Cambridge: Cambridge University Press, 2000), 162-83, for a superb, nuanced study of Abraham's offering of Isaac in Gen 22. Moberly vigorously argues for a positive theological understanding of Abraham's faith against a hyper-suspicious viewpoint. But he does not entirely dismiss a hermeneutic of suspicion (see more below) and seriously engages with feminist-critical analysis, particularly that of Phyllis Trible.

34. Bauckham, *Gospel Women,* xix-xx, 13.

35. Brigitte Kahl, "Toward a Materialist-Feminist Reading," in *A Feminist Introduction* (vol. 1 of *Searching the Scriptures,* ed. Elisabeth Schüssler Fiorenza; New York: Crossroad, 1993), 237-38.

and yawning *gap* between mentions of Mary Magdalene and cohorts "repatriarchalize"[36] Luke's narrative and recharge suspicious minds. To assume women's continuing presence without regularly checking roll and recording their contributions is better than ignoring them altogether, but it also assumes a largely passive and subordinate role and raises red flags about the depth of Luke's commitment to inclusive discipleship and equal opportunity. In any case, negotiating tensions between liberating and limiting elements of Luke's "mixed messages" regarding women seems to demand a dialectical hermeneutic of faith and suspicion.

Personal Experience

Third, a hermeneutic of suspicion's alleged valorization of personal experience and arrogant devaluation of the corruptive power of human sinfulness beg for clarification and nuance. Without a doubt, feminist biblical criticism in its various forms places a high premium on experience, especially women's experience. Convinced that interpreters inevitably bring their experience to the interpretive table, a feminist critic lays her cards faceup on the table, calls for others to do the same, and unabashedly argues that it's high time *her* experience plays a bigger role in the conversation. But that does not mean that feminist biblical interpreters glorify their experience as "unambiguously revelatory."[37] Quite the contrary, feminists have paid increasing attention to the kaleidoscope of women's global experiences that necessarily *relativizes, qualifies, and criticizes* any singular expression. If modern feminist biblical criticism sprang up in the 1970s-1980s among predominantly white, middle-class, educated, Euro-American Christian women, it has long since repented of its patronizing monoculturalism to embrace a multitude of perspectives from women of various colors, classes, confessions, and cultures. Only in the face of *alternative* experiences can deep self-critique effectively take place. Indeed, such self-critique is perhaps the greatest motivation for *men* to suspect their own blind spots and engage feminist criticism seriously.[38]

As for their sense of sin, suspicious feminist interpreters are scarcely

36. Kahl, "Materialist-Feminist Reading," 236-37.

37. Hays, *Conversion*, 191.

38. See F. Scott Spencer, "Feminist Criticism," in *Hearing the New Testament: Strategies for Interpretation* (ed. Joel B. Green; 2nd ed.; Grand Rapids: Eerdmans, 2010), 300-304, 315-18.

squeamish about prophetic denunciations or stiff-necked about personal confessions. To be sure, more emphasis falls on public-institutional than private-individual sin; as Schüssler Fiorenza states, "liberation feminism understands all [women] as the people of [God] created in Her image and hence it indicts the death-dealing powers of exclusion and oppression as structural sin and life-destroying evil."[39] But such an announcement has a strong biblical-prophetic ring and provides a critical counterweight to the still dominant "introspective conscience of the West."[40] As for personal confession of wrongdoing and wrong reading, whether invoking traditional "sin" language or not, feminist critics — *because,* rather than in spite of, their suspicious outlook — remain among the most frank and forthcoming biblical interpreters about their own autobiographical journeys, *including* changes of mind (repentance) and admissions of mistakes (confession). As a key case in point, more than a few early feminist Christian scholars have humbly disavowed tendencies, both subtle and overt, deliberate and unintended, to smear ancient Judaism as hopelessly misogynistic or patriarchal, usually to make an inclusive, even "feminist" Jesus look good in contrast.[41]

Among those advocating a more explicit confessional approach to biblical interpretation and cautioning against a thoroughly deconstructive hermeneutic of suspicion, some scholars retain more than grudging or backhanded respect for suspicion's necessary function alongside faith, refusing to dump out the healthy suspicious baby with the hyper-cynical bathwater. Walter Moberly, for example, who resists a particularly virulent

39. Schüssler Fiorenza, *Power of the Word,* 48. Where I have bracketed "women" and "God," she uses the neologisms "wo/men" and "G*d" that she regards as more inclusive. Most feminist biblical scholars, however, still retain traditional spellings.

40. See Krister Stendahl, "The Apostle Paul and Introspective Conscience of the West," in his *Paul among Jews and Gentiles, and Other Essays* (Philadelphia: Fortress, 1976), 78-96.

41. See the pioneering challenges issued by Judith Plaskow in the following essays: "Christian Feminism and Anti-Judaism," *Cross Currents* 28 (1978): 306-9; "Feminist Anti-Judaism and the Christian God," *Journal of Feminist Studies in Religion* 7 (1991): 99-108; and "Anti-Judaism in Feminist Christian Interpretation," in *A Feminist Introduction* (vol. 1 of *Searching the Scriptures,* ed. Schüssler Fiorenza), 117-29. More recently, see Amy-Jill Levine, "Anti-Judaism and Postcolonial Biblical Interpretation," *Journal of Feminist Studies in Religion* 20 (2004): 91-106; Levine, *The Misunderstood Jew: The Church and Scandal of the Jewish Jesus* (New York: HarperCollins, 2007), 132-43, 173-78; Luise Schottroff, *Lydia's Impatient Sisters: A Feminist Social History of Early Christianity* (trans. Barbara Rumscheidt and Martin Rumscheidt; Louisville: Westminster John Knox, 1995), 11-16; Luise Schottroff, Silvia Schroer, and Marie-Theres Wacker, *Feminist Interpretation: The Bible in Women's Perspective* (trans. Martin Rumscheidt and Barbara Rumscheidt; Minneapolis: Fortress, 1998), 55-62; Schüssler Fiorenza, *Jesus,* 115-44.

feminist-deconstructive strain that debunks the OT God as abusive and capricious, still contends that "a Christian theologian should not be quick to dismiss a hermeneutic of suspicion." Indeed, "suspicion touches on something that is basic within a Christian account of life, the recognition that there is nothing which cannot be abused and that humans have an enormous capacity for self-deception in the ways they try to rationalize and justify their greed, desires, and idolatries. The religious life is not exempt from this; rather it may be a prime exemplar of it."[42]

Similarly, Ellen Davis, who clings to "a more excellent way than outright repudiation or public silencing of texts that repel us and seem to present a threat to the marginalized and powerless," understands that the Bible does not always make that way easy.[43] She appreciates that as much as "the North American church is under suspicion for not taking the Bible seriously, it is equally true that the Bible is under suspicion in the North American church for not being a trustworthy guide for faith and life, for claiming too many victims through the centuries."[44] Ironically, however, suspicion of our own stale, parroted views of the Bible can open fresh interpretive paths. If we read the Bible in sin- and faith-confessing communities, "it is well," Davis exhorts, "to begin by suspecting our own interpretations. Most of them have probably not been reconsidered in a long time — years in our own lives, generations in the church."[45]

Hermeneutical Struggle

Fourth, though not calibrating precise amounts of suspicion and faith in the hermeneutical stew, feminist and other liberationist approaches to biblical interpretation typically combine healthy portions of both ingredients under the main element of *struggle*. Whatever the mix — so many parts faith to so many parts suspicion — the key is to stir, whip, beat, and knead vigorously and indefatigably until freedom and justice, grace and peace emerge. Suspicion and doubt alert us that this is no easy-bake, microwaveable fare; the biblical text can be hard to handle. But faith and trust keep us

---

42. Moberly, *Bible, Theology, and Faith,* 162.

43. Ellen F. Davis, "Critical Traditioning: Seeking an Inner Biblical Hermeneutic," in *Art of Reading Scripture* (ed. Davis and Hays), 166.

44. Davis, "Critical Traditioning," 165.

45. Davis, "Teaching the Bible Confessionally in the Church," in *Art of Reading Scripture* (ed. Davis and Hays), 16.

in the kitchen however long it takes until God's word is ready — or better put, until we're ready to hear God's word.[46]

Shifting from kitchen to gymnasium, many feminist critics take seriously the work of *wrestling* with the biblical text in all its power to break and bruise, challenge and chasten — but still with the hope of somehow emerging blessed from the contest. Trible's preface to her monumental treatment of biblical "texts of terror" invokes Jacob's nocturnal wrestling match at the Jabbok with the divine-demonic "man" as paradigmatic of the fervent feminist struggle to wrest something redemptive out of terrible stories: "The fight itself is solitary and intense. We struggle mightily, only to be wounded. But yet we hold on, seeking a blessing: the healing of wounds and the restoration of health. If the blessing comes — and we dare not claim assurance — it does not come on our own terms. Indeed, as we leave the land of terror, we limp."[47] Suspicion and faith meet most poignantly at Jacob's desperate plea — "I will not let you go, unless you bless me" (Gen 32:26) — suspended between his old "cheater," heel-grabbing Jacob-self and his new "God-wrestled," hip-wrenched Israel-identity.

Again, Ellen Davis chimes in from a more traditional-confessional perspective, but with a critical twist. She pulls no punches. "This is, or should be," she says, "the scandal of every introductory Bible course, in seminary and in parish: the Scriptures are chock-full of embarrassing, offensive, and internally contradictory texts, texts we do not wish to live with, let alone live *by*."[48] But with equal conviction, she also contends that this "scandal" is no surprise to the Bible itself, which routinely engages in "critical traditioning," as Davis dubs it, across the canon — critiquing, correcting, and clarifying *its own* previous murky, misguided viewpoints in the spirit of repentance *(metanoia)*.[49] Banner examples include Rahab's "radical relativizing" of the ethnic cleansing tradition in Joshua and the

---

46. My imagery is inspired here by Jesus' parable of the baker woman in Matt 13:33// Luke 13:20-21, which has received increasing attention from feminist scholars. See, e.g., Barbara E. Reid, "Beyond Petty Pursuits and Wearisome Widows: Three Lukan Parables," *Interpretation* 56 (2002): 284-87; Holly Hearon and Antoinette Clark Wire, "Women's Work in the Realm of God (Mt. 13.33; Lk. 13.20, 21; *Gos. Thom.* 96; Mt. 6.28-30; Lk. 12.27-28; *Gos. Thom.* 36)," in *The Lost Coin: Parables of Women, Work, and Wisdom* (ed. Mary Ann Beavis; London: Sheffield Academic, 2002), 136-57.

47. Phyllis Trible, *Texts of Terror: Literary-Feminist Readings of Biblical Narratives* (Philadelphia: Fortress, 1984), 4-5.

48. Davis, "Critical Traditioning," 177.

49. Davis, "Critical Traditioning," 168-69; Davis, "Teaching the Bible Confessionally," 16-18.

Canaanite woman's strategic reorientation of Jesus' own ethnocentric, charity-begins-at-home position in Matthew.[50] Significantly, however, the Bible accomplishes this critical (re)traditioning through a dialogic rather than despotic approach. That is, it openly retains rather than removes the problematic tradition as a partial witness to God's purpose and gives us a front-row seat to the wrestling match for a faithful understanding of suspicious texts. Beyond that, it provides a vital hermeneutical touchstone: although the Bible by no means poses all the suspicious, critical questions we might raise today, it does allow, if not encourage, us to engage in further inner-biblical, critical traditioning, to join the struggle for edifying, redemptive interpretation and to not let the text go, without a knockdown fight, "as a potential source of valid theological insight."[51]

Test Case: Flipping the Coin (Luke 15:8-10)

With this warrant to exercise both doubt and faith in the struggle for redemptive biblical interpretation, we turn to a short sample text, chosen for its suggestive resonance with Schüssler Fiorenza's call for the "feminist coin" to retain its double-sided "currency" of both "deconstruction and reconstruction."[52] Consider Jesus' parable of a woman's search for her lost coin in Luke 15:8-10, in light of the four points just discussed.

Methodological Complexity

First, it is true that some feminist critics take a one-sided negative stance, finding no redeeming value at all for women in this "coin." Susan Durber,

---

50. Davis, "Critical Traditioning," 170-77. Davis does not explore the tight connection between the OT Rahab and NT Canaanite woman stories (both involve exceptional Canaanite women subverting ethnocentric boundaries), which would strengthen her case. Though it employs a different, postcolonial perspective, see the extended analysis of the Canaanite woman incident in Matt 15:21-28 through "Rahab's reading prism" in Musa W. Dube, *Postcolonial Feminist Interpretation of the Bible* (St. Louis: Chalice, 2000), 127-95.

51. Davis, "Critical Traditioning," 164.

52. Schüssler Fiorenza, *Sharing Her Word*, 80. The parable of the woman's search for her lost coin has inspired much feminist-biblical and feminist-theological reflection. See, e.g., Phyllis Trible, *God and the Rhetoric of Sexuality* (Philadelphia: Fortress, 1978), 200-202; Ann Loades, *Searching for Lost Coins: Explorations in Christianity and Feminism* (Allison Park, Pa.: Pickwick, 1988); Beavis, *The Lost Coin*.

for example, contends that, as a tale spun by a man for men, this parable assumes an exclusive circle of male readers that women can only penetrate by becoming "immasculated" — one of the boys — conceding "the male point of view as . . . normative." Whereas the preceding parable of the lost sheep directly identifies Jesus' audience with the story's male shepherd protagonist ("Which one *of you* [*ex hymōn*], having a hundred sheep and losing one" [Luke 15:4]), the lost coin story casts the woman as a wholly "other" object of male gaze ("Or a *certain woman* [*tis gynē*], having ten coins and losing one" [cf. 15:8]).[53] Female readers have no place or stake in this text; they remain "lost" in Lukan space.

But while granting the text's male viewpoint, some Christian feminist interpreters refuse to be corseted in such a perspective or disenfranchised from the Gospel story that remains their story, too, whatever its linguistic limitations. Some even accept that the parable reflects an authentic gynocentric view of a housekeeper's financial and janitorial duties. In a fascinating study informed by a five-month sojourn in Yemen and interviews with Arab-Christian women in the United States, feminist biblical scholar Carol Schersten LaHurd reports that these women find Jesus' parable quite consistent with their experience and by no means demeaning or delimiting to women in its domestic orientation.[54] From her biblical and sociological research, she concludes that the parable's searching housekeeper operates freely "by choice," not by coercion from an oppressive patriarchy that confines her to private space.[55] Indeed, it is precisely within

---

53. Susan Durber, "The Female Reader of the Parables of the Lost," *Journal for the Study of the New Testament* 45 (1992): 69-78; cf. the discussion of Durber's study in Stephen D. Moore, *Poststructuralism and the New Testament: Derrida and Foucault at the Foot of the Cross* (Minneapolis: Fortress, 1994), 50-52.

54. Carol Schersten LaHurd, "Re-Viewing Luke 15 with Arab Christian Women," in *A Feminist Companion to Luke* (ed. Amy-Jill Levine and Marianne Blickenstaff; London: Sheffield Academic, 2002), 246-57. Though "inspired" by the many influential studies of Jesus' parables by Kenneth E. Bailey, based on his extensive experiences in Beirut and around the eastern Mediterranean world, LaHurd notes that Bailey limited his interviews to male Arab-Christian subjects. In contrast, "my feminist commitment to hearing women's voices encouraged me to test [Bailey's] exegesis by interviewing Christian women who had come to the United States from Egypt and Lebanon" (247).

55. LaHurd, "Re-Viewing Luke 15," 254. Of course, as political philosophers and international activists in the "Human Development" movement, Martha Nussbaum and Amartya Sen stress that women's domestic and economic "choices" are often so determined by entrenched, internalized social traditions and conditions as to constitute no free choice at all; in other words, women so choose because they can't conceive of any other options or are

the home that some Middle Eastern women, then and now, exert leadership in society by responsibly managing family finances, superintending the environment, and raising children.[56] Though perhaps not able to hoist a wayward seventy-pound sheep on her shoulders and haul it home, the woman in Jesus' story is no weak figure engaged in some trivial pursuit: "In a culture where men and women value household, this woman has the power to restore wholeness and order and to celebrate that restoration."[57]

Biblical-Theological Tension

Second, Luke's narrative context raises issues on both the suspicion and faith sides of the interpretive "coin." Most immediately, Luke 15 clusters three parables featuring single lost-and-found items in a descending economy of scale: one sheep among a hundred; one coin among ten; one son among two. As the totals go down, the value of the lost one goes up, building to the climactic final parable, by far the longest of the trio. The shepherd/sheep and homemaker/coin cameos serve as preludes to the father/son main event. And whatever might be gained from a feminist perspective in the sweeper woman's story is lost in the final parable, where women are either glaringly absent (no mother, sisters, or female servants in the picture; even the fatted calf is a young bull!) or stereotypically corrupt (whores who milk the prodigal youth's fortune [15:30] — the antithesis of the money-saving homemaker). Even in comparison with the shepherd

---

paralyzed by fear of bucking the system. Women's choices to embrace traditional societal roles may be affirmed, provided they have the agency and capability to choose otherwise. For Nussbaum, see *Women and Human Development: The Capabilities Approach* (Cambridge: Cambridge University Press, 2000), 34-166; *Sex and Social Justice* (Oxford: Oxford University Press, 1999), 3-80; "Human Capabilities, Female Human Beings," in *Women, Culture, and Development: A Study of Human Capabilities* (ed. Martha Nussbaum and Jonathan Glover; Oxford: Oxford University Press, 1995), 91-104; for Sen, see *Development as Freedom* (New York: Anchor, 1999), 189-203, 282-89; *The Idea of Justice* (Cambridge: Harvard University Press, 2009), 155-73, 225-52; "Gender Inequality and Theories of Justice," in *Women, Culture, and Development* (ed. Nussbaum and Glover), 259-73.

56. The house/household *(oikos)* is the principal locus of mission and fellowship for the Jesus movement and early church in Luke and Acts.

57. LaHurd, "Re-Viewing Luke 15," 257; cf. 251. Note also Reid, "Beyond Petty Pursuits," 288: "[S]ome scholars depict the woman's search for a lost coin . . . as trivial. She is seen as scrounging for a lost bit of 'pin money,' a find that is only important to her women friends. Such interpretations have no basis in the text and reveal sexist biases."

parable, the woman still winds up with the short end of the (broom) stick. Luke's well-known technique of pairing male and female stories does not guarantee equal treatment; pairing is not parity.[58] For sheer dramatic effect, the shepherd's crook, broad shoulders, and daring wilderness trek overshadow the woman's broom, hunched shoulders, and menial floor sweep, not to mention the fact that the shepherd's tale, though brief, is still about a third longer than the housekeeper's snippet.

Expanding the context, most parables in Luke's central section feature men and men's business, and the quick snapshot of a fictional woman in her home adds nothing to the presence of actual women among Jesus' disciples. Furthermore, the woman's action of housecleaning, though treated positively in Luke 15, recalls a sinister case a few chapters earlier where Jesus images an orderly, neatly swept residence as the optimal environment for an expelled demon's return and reoccupation with seven nastier cohorts (11:24-26).

Thus, various suspicious narrative factors have helped "sweep [this parable] under the rug" in the history of interpretation.[59] But for those refusing to lose this woman and her coin without a fuss, other, more promising narrative perspectives emerge. For example, slotting her story *between* that of the shepherd and that of the father may mark it as the *hub* or *hinge* of the triad rather than the squeezed-out item.[60] Its focus on economic and domestic management leads more naturally than the shepherd's tale into the final parable. The shepherd handles no money and dubiously "*leaves* the ninety-nine *in* the wilderness" while he tracks after the one lost animal (presumably also in the wilderness) and then returns *home* after retrieving it (15:3-6). What about the ninety-nine? Chances are they've all wandered away and gotten themselves lost in the meantime. By contrast, the woman and the father both stay home safeguarding their remaining assets, even as they look for the lost one, the woman's hands busy at work, the father's eyes peeled toward the horizon (15:8, 20).

---

58. On the male-female pairing pattern in Luke's narratives, see F. Scott Spencer, *The Gospel of Luke and Acts of the Apostles* (Nashville: Abingdon, 2008), 41-44.

59. Linda Maloney, "'Swept under the Rug': Feminist Homiletical Reflections on the Parable of the Lost Coin (Lk. 15:8-9)," in *The Lost Coin* (ed. Beavis), 34-38.

60. For a similar sandwiching of a woman's episode between two related men's stories, see Tabitha/Dorcas's story of "good works" and resuscitation in Acts 9:36-43 between the accounts of Aeneas's healing (9:32-35) and Cornelius's God-fearing service (10:1-23). Cf. F. Scott Spencer, *Journeying through Acts: A Literary-Cultural Reading* (Peabody, Mass.: Hendrickson, 2004), 112-23.

While most other Lukan parables feature men, many of these appear in a negative light (especially rich men). And the woman searching for her lost coin is not entirely alone, celebrating her find with "women friends and neighbors" (*tas philas kai getonas* [feminine forms; 15:9]) and sharing the larger parable stage with two other positive female role models: a baker woman representing God's subtle yet sure advance of God's rule (13:20-21) and a feisty widow imaging the believer's unrelenting quest for God's justice on earth (18:1-8).[61] Moreover, just as the sweeper woman reflects *God's* joyous reclamation of everything in God's household,[62] she also models Jesus' gracious mission of "seeking *(zēteō)* and saving the lost" (19:10). Indeed, Jesus' search-and-rescue mission with the verb *zēteō* finds its *only direct counterpart* in the woman's retrieval of the missing coin: the shepherd "goes after" *(poreuomai)* the lost sheep (15:3), and the father "sees" *(horaō)* and "runs after" *(trechō)* the returning son (15:20); only the woman explicitly "seeks" *(zēteō)* and finds the misplaced coin (15:8).

Finally, although the parable's housecleaning woman is not a "real" woman devoted to or encountered by Jesus, her economic and domestic concerns fit "real" women accepted or admired by Jesus, namely: Mary Magdalene, Joanna, and company who bankroll Jesus' mission (8:2-3); Martha and Mary who host Jesus (10:38-42); and the poor widow whom Jesus commends over hypocritical male scribes for contributing her last coins to God's house (20:45–21:4) — all of whom we will examine in some detail in this book. To be sure, these do not constitute a great bounty of dynamic female disciples (none says a word, except Martha, and she more suspects than supports Jesus' true "word" on this occasion). But they do provide some hard "currency" to invest, and in tight times, we need to value all the coins we have.

Personal Experience

Third, the swirl of hermeneutical issues surrounding sin, experience, suspicion, and faith takes a provocative turn in a Dutch study of responses to

61. See Reid, "Beyond Petty Pursuits and Wearisome Widows."

62. See the parenthetical aside of Durber, "Female Reader," 72: "(The suggestion of recent [feminist] times that the woman may, after all, be an appropriate image for God does not undo the construction by these texts of the reader as male, although it might begin to subvert that construction.)" I think that greatly understates the issue: the searching woman, in my view, at the heart of these "lost and found" parables, offers a clear, central image of the searching God.

our parable from survivors of incest abuse, reported by Mary Ann Beavis.[63] Although the housecleaner's story seems to have nothing to do with sin or sinners — no dissolute pig-slopper or prostitutes here — it is still told, like all three "lost" parables, to vindicate Jesus' table fellowship with sinners (15:1-2), concluding with the punch line: "Just so, I tell you, there is joy in the presence of the angels of God over one sinner who repents" (15:10).

So how in the world could doubt and suspicion possibly dampen such a celestial celebration? Well, if this "sinner" honoree at heaven's party happens to be a former sexual offender, his victims might not be so ready to whoop it up with the angelic band. If God wants to forgive and embrace this guy, that's God's business, but forgive us who've long suffered his violent abuse for not being so charitable. And for goodness' sake, how can you throw a big happy-hour bash for this lowlife? Why should we want any part of that? So ran the responses from Beavis's report of incest survivors. Is their hermeneutical suspicion driven down a one-way street by their experience of male abuse? Of course it is — but hardly in some whiny, picayune fashion. These women in no way resemble the privileged elder brother with his sniveling, juvenile bleat, "You never threw a party for me and my friends!" (cf. 15:29). And even less do they compare with the sinner himself, as if they were somehow complicit in his crime (like the prostitutes who dallied with the prodigal) or have now become just as guilty because they *can't forgive him.*

Sadly, a long interpretive tradition of sexually shaming and blaming innocent biblical women — like Eve, Bathsheba, Mary Magdalene, and the Samaritan woman — justifies feminist suspicion about the Bible's treatment of female victims.[64] Does such suspicion run the risk of closing off abused women to God's grace, which they so desperately need?[65] It certainly hardens them against *cheap grace* and *partial grace,* but not authen-

---

63. Mary Ann Beavis, "Joy in Heaven, Sorrow on Earth: Luke 15.10," in *The Lost Coin* (ed. Beavis), 39-45.

64. Beavis, "Joy in Heaven," 40-43. Beavis also acknowledges that these texts do not have to be read in oppressive ways. Indeed, feminist interpreters have reclaimed all these women's stories toward various positive, liberating ends — often by more careful readings of what the texts actually say and don't say.

65. See the sobering critical study of an array of biblical texts that have proven either harmful or helpful to religiously inclined abused women in Susan Brooks Thistlethwaite, "Every Two Minutes: Battered Women and Feminist Interpretation," in *Feminist Interpretation of the Bible* (ed. Russell), 96-107.

tic grace *genuinely directed toward them*. And to this end, Beavis proposes a faithful rewording of the text: "Likewise, I tell you, the angels of Godde rejoice more over one innocent person who is vindicated than over the repentance of the sinners who have abused them!"[66]

But must we resort to changing the text in order to find grace? Can we hold on a little longer, search a tad harder, until it blesses us?

Hermeneutical Struggle

And so, fourth, we *struggle* for faith amid suspicion. Among the three seekers/finders featured in the Luke 15 parables, the woman stands out as the one who actively struggles most, who expends the most energy and effort. The shepherd travels farther, and the father celebrates bigger; but the woman flat works harder *at the search*. Three action verbs and one adverb propel her quest: she *"lights"* (*haptei*) a lamp, *"sweeps"* (*saroi*) the house under furniture and in the cracks and crevices of the mud-packed floor, and *"searches carefully"* (*zētei epimelōs*) for her precious lost coin (15:8). Though the parable does not explicitly identify the woman's socioeconomic status, her desperate diligence in retrieving one drachma (out of ten) — equivalent to a denarius, the customary single-day subsistence wage for a field laborer (cf. Matt 20:1-16) — suggests, according to Luise Schottroff, a poor working woman embroiled in a "daily struggle for money and bread" (cf. Luke 11:3, 5-8), "the very struggle for survival of women," made all the more onerous by an unjust economic scale where women typically earned half of men's wages for the same labor.[67] This woman simply could not afford to lose one part of a ten-day, barebones budget she had worked so hard to acquire; not finding this one coin in tight times might mean an entire day that she doesn't eat. This scenario of a struggling, hardworking woman seems more suited to Jesus' story than Jeremias's famous — and frivolous — speculation that the woman is searching for a missing coin-gem from her dowry head-

66. Beavis, "Joy in Heaven," 45. "Godde" reflects archaic English spelling for "God" used by a New Zealand group of Sisters of the Mission and adapted by Edwina Gateley to represent the deity essentially as beyond gender and metaphorically as both god and goddess, with joint male/female identity (similar to Schüssler Fiorenza's use of G*d). See Mary Ann Beavis, "Introduction: Seeking the 'Lost Coin' of Parables about Women," in *The Lost Coin* (ed. Beavis), 31-32.

67. Schottroff, *Lydia's Impatient Sisters*, 91, 100; cf. 91-100.

dress.[68] Nourishment, rather than adornment, more likely preoccupies this woman.

In any case, the sweeper woman in Jesus' parable will not be denied, and neither will interpreters who look to her as a hermeneutical model. Linda Maloney marks a 1985 conference of feminist-liberation theologians in Buenos Aires as a critical moment when this little parable "first came into its own."[69] Out of their experience of intense social and political struggle *(lucha)*, these theologians rallied around the sweeper woman's story as a manifesto for their interpretive practice. They discovered that biblical-theological "work," as Maloney puts it, "is contextual and concrete; it sees the ordinary and the everyday as the place God is revealed; it takes place 'in the house' — long a symbol of believing community. It is hard work; it is a *struggle* to find what has been lost in the darkness that has covered it for so many centuries. But it is also characterized by joy and celebration, and by hope: the hope that 'God is with us' (Mt. 1.23). Like the woman in the parable, God has her skirts tucked up and is busy sweeping and searching, too."[70]

Moreover, Maloney deftly adds an aural dimension to this interpretive challenge of "searching the Scriptures," inspired by imagining the sweeper woman's likely craning her neck and tuning her ears to the slightest tinkle of the missing silver coin: "The theological task of wo/men, like the work of the woman in the parable, is to sweep, and listen, and sweep again, and listen again — until there is a tiny sound that provides the impetus to go on searching for 'something' until at last it is found; 'something' that may seem so miniscule, so insignificant, that it has gone unnoticed and uncelebrated for centuries."[71]

Similarly, OT scholar Jacqueline Lapsley — intentionally reading Scripture from a dual position of confessional faith in God's revelatory word *and* a feminist-critical hermeneutic of suspicion — fully recognizes the difficulty of hearing God's liberating word for women in male-centered narratives. But rather than turning the channel, she summons in-

---

68. Joachim Jeremias, *The Parables of Jesus* (trans. S. H. Hooke; rev. ed.; New York: Scribner, 1963), 134-35; even with this theory, Jeremias regards the woman as impoverished: "If the woman's 10 drachmas were on her head-dress, she was indeed a very poor creature, considering that today many a [Palestinian Arab] woman prides herself on a head-dress of hundreds of gold and silver coins" (134-35). Cf. Schottroff, *Lydia's Impatient Sisters*, 96.

69. Maloney, "'Swept under the Rug,'" 35.

70. Maloney, "'Swept under the Rug,'" 35 (emphasis added).

71. Maloney, "'Swept under the Rug,'" 37.

terpreters to tune their theological antennae more finely to pick up God's "sometimes soft voice," delicate "whisper," and "surplus of meaning" mediating grace to all God's people.[72] Suspicion combined with struggle can hone our minds and make us more careful, discriminating listeners for God's "still small voice" (cf. 1 Kings 19:12). I think Elijah might concur, even if Elvis doesn't.[73]

In addition to modeling a rigorous quest to hear the subtle tones of God's redemptive word, the sweeper woman exemplifies another dimension of struggle in seek-and-find missions — whether for missing coins or hidden meanings in biblical texts — in her unique awareness of personal responsibility for what was lost. She alone among the three parable seekers in Luke 15 confesses, "I have found the coin that *I had lost (apōlesa)*" (Luke 15:9). The shepherd and the father own no responsibility for their losses.[74] But why should they? They're not the wayward wanderers in these stories, but rather the God figures who mercifully restore and receive the lost "sinners." With the housekeeper, then, who admits losing her coin, are we back to the problem — not just with readers, but with *the text* also — of too readily implicating women with sin and sinners, of blaming them unjustly, of diminishing their achievements to keep them in their humble places?

Not necessarily. For one thing, unlike the live sheep and son, the inanimate coin has no self-capacity to go astray and become lost. By the laws of physics, someone or some external force (like wind or gravity) controls its movement. So it's quite natural, especially since no break-in by a robber or purse rummaging by an insider seems in view here, for the woman to acknowledge that *she* misplaced the coin. The same situation would apply with a man and his missing money. But in fact, Jesus selects a woman, not a man, for this scenario. We might wonder about Jesus' choice: Why not have a businessman mislay his money bag and launch a search to find it? Or

72. Jacqueline E. Lapsley, *Whispering the Word: Hearing Women's Stories in the Old Testament* (Louisville: Westminster John Knox, 2005), 1-19.

73. While this aural emphasis on hearing *(akouō)* God's word runs throughout the Bible, it is in fact especially prominent in Luke's Gospel: see, e.g., Luke 2:18-20, 46-47; 6:46-49; 8:1-21; 9:28-36, 43-45; 10:16, 24, 38-42; 14:35; 16:29-31.

74. The shepherd says — "I have found my sheep that was lost" — claiming responsibility for the animal's retrieval, but not its loss. The father announces — "This son of mine . . . was lost and is found" (15:24, 32) — distancing himself, through passive voice, from his son's return as well as departure. Schottroff (*Lydia's Impatient Sisters*, 98) notes that the issue of the woman's blameworthiness for her missing coin was taken up a century ago in Adolph Jülicher's pioneering parable study (*Die Gleichnisreden Jesu* [1910]). Julicher, in fact, argued *against* scholars in his day who stigmatized the woman's carelessness.

better yet: Why not have a *shepherdess* lose track of an animal or a *mother* become separated from her child, where responsibility for the loss might at least be shared with the missing party? Then again, the story of a son, say, leaving his mother might raise as many questions about her character as his (what kind of horrible woman must she have been to drive him away?).[75] Ultimately, of course, all this speculation is moot: we must deal with the parables' characters and plots that the Lukan Jesus has given us, and that includes, along with the sweeper woman's more meticulous search process, her more conscious sense of involvement in the loss. "*I found* [through much diligence] what *I lost* [through some degree of negligence]."

However, rather than giving full suspicious vent to depicting a woman as negligent and culpable for loss in a manner unbefitting more competent and capable men — and certainly God — a more constructive feminist hermeneutic that struggles to balance doubt with faith might daringly probe a richer, more complex portrait of divine-human relations. For nestled in between two parables that obviously represent traditional biblical God-figures of Shepherd and Father is this companion vignette that, by close literary-thematic association, also features a God character, albeit in the less conventional configuration of a Sweeper Woman.[76] Accordingly, apart from encountering different images of occupation (sweeper) and gender (woman), we also confront an unsettling, yet potentially refreshing, prospect of God's vulnerability and responsibility: "I have found what *I have lost.*"[77]

Does God not keenly feel the personal diminution of what *God* loses when one of her children drifts away from her presence into perilous territory? In the process of seeking out and looking for this lost one's return, can God not be struck by and spurred on by some sense of gnawing re-

---

75. We might note, as an aside, that Luke does include a story of a frantic mother's search for her missing son, namely, Mary's hunt for the "lost" twelve-year-old Jesus (Luke 2:40-52)! In this case, the "fault" is all Jesus', but that does little to ease Mary's (together with Joseph's) sense of parental anxiety and responsibility. Upon finding Jesus in the temple, Mary bemoans: "Child, why have you treated us like this? Look, your father and I have been searching for you in great anxiety" (2:48). Cf. my discussion of this incident in the next chapter.

76. Cf. Schottroff, *Lydia's Impatient Sisters*, 100: "Luke 15:8-10 is a parable of God's searching for lost human beings. . . . The very struggle for survival of women . . . is a parable for the struggle of God, the One searching for lost human beings who repent."

77. Cf. LaHurd, "Re-Viewing Luke 15," 252: "In pre-banking culture this woman in Lk. 15 is entrusted with responsibility of guarding the family income and so accepts responsibility for recovery of the coin 'that I had lost.'"

sponsibility, if only partial, for the lost one's leaving the fold, spurning the family? What more might God have done or how might God have acted differently to keep the lost one safer in hand? In the famous "love song concerning his vineyard" people (Israel and Judah) mediated through Isaiah, God recalls all he had put into making his vineyard productive, only to lament in minor key the failure of this project:

> What more was there to do for my vineyard
>> that I have not done in it?
> When I expected it to yield grapes,
>> why did it yield wild grapes? (Isa 5:4; cf. vv. 1-4)

God's vineyard-people had lost their way and failed to realize God's purpose. While the song then abruptly strikes a bold counterchord, in which the angry vineyard owner threatens to uproot his fruitless plants (5:5-7),[78] the strain of his personal regret and frustration still haunts this emotionally complex song: "What more was there to do . . . that I have not done?" Why did my people not respond as "I expected" (5:4)?

This tragic song runs on the same track as Jesus' passionate lament over rebellious Jerusalem in the heart of Luke's central section, not long before his trio of "lost" parables: "How often have I desired/willed *(ēthelēsa)* to gather your children together as a hen gathers her brood under her wings, and you were not desiring/willing *(ēthelēsate)!*" (Luke 13:34). Here Jesus' striking maternal-natural self-image should not be missed, combined with deep "desire" for protecting the children and keeping them close.[79] Of course, vibrant chicks soon develop a mind of their own and a will to wander from the shade of their mothers' wings, which does not, however, dampen the hen's desire to regather her wayward brood in times of trouble. Such an image poignantly captures the heart of Jesus' mission: to restore God's "lost," scattered people to the redemptive care of God's wing, akin to restoring "sheep" to God's fold and "sons" to God's family. But tragically, God's Jerusalem-centered "chicks" seem "unwilling" to be

---

78. Balancing this ominous threat of Israel's uprooting and dislocation in the book of Isaiah is a hopeful countertheme of replanting and restoration; see, e.g., Isa 4:2-6; 11:1-16; 14:1-2; 27:1-13; 35:1-10; 40:1-31; 61:1-4.

79. This passionate identification of the male Jesus with a maternal, child-nurturing image resonates with Susan Moller Okin's case for equal involvement of men and women in child care, persuasively argued throughout her brilliant book *Justice, Gender, and the Family* (New York: Basic Books, 1989).

restored and thereby, in their "lost" state, court terrible impending disaster.[80] At the end of the day, their ominous fate will be the fault of their obstinacy. But that judgment in no way detaches Mother-Hen Jesus from *her* chicks or diminishes *her* aching loss and persistent longing for their restoration. *"How often I wanted (ēthelēsa) you but you didn't want (ouk ēthelēsate) me!"* A clash of wills, and Jesus, for the moment at least, loses the contest. His/her will isn't strong enough to keep his/her people safe. However much we underscore Israel's stiff-necked rebellion against God and God's Messiah, we must not undercut the tragedy of God's and Jesus' excruciating sense of personal loss.

In correlating Jesus' mother hen and sweeper woman images, the emphasis on the contending wills of mother bird and her brood in the context of separation and restoration more deeply personalizes the sweeper woman's quest for her lost (inanimate) coin; conversely, the housecleaner's final stress on finding what *she* had lost intensifies the hen's responsibility for protecting her little ones. And together, both feminine scenarios expand and enrich our understandings of God's and Christ's purposes, actions, and emotions.

When we toss the hermeneutical coin in the air and watch it flip end over end between suspicion and confession, doubt and faith, we cannot predict on which side it will land. But we can know that the more we toss it, the better chance we have of getting fairer and more balanced outcomes, as we appreciate the interpretive power of both sides. We cannot look for long, even in faith, at the full face of God (heads) and hope to live; in our finite states, we must also consider — quizzically, probingly, suspiciously — the shadows of God's backside (tails) that present themselves in the biblical witness. A feminist hermeneutic of faithful suspicion is well suited to helping us stumble through the shadows.

A Final Bit of Housecleaning

While I have found positive metaphorical and theological potential — amid genuine grounds for caution and suspicion — in our hermeneutical

80. On Jesus' struggle with the "tragic" dimension of Israel's rejection of God's Messiah, see further Luke 19:41-44; 21:20-24; 23:27-31; discussed in Robert C. Tannehill, "Israel in Luke-Acts: A Tragic Story," *Journal of Biblical Literature* 104 (1985): 69-85; reprinted in Tannehill, *The Shape of Luke's Story: Essays on Luke-Acts* (Eugene, Oreg.: Cascade, 2005), 105-24.

search of Jesus' parable of the woman's search for her lost coin, I do not want to leave this study without returning to ground level — literally, physically — the dirt floor (likely) the woman scours for her missing drachma. To raid this brief tale simply for hermeneutical insight devalues and exploits the woman's labor. In any case, an incarnational theology, like Jesus' and Luke's, demands an incarnational hermeneutics — fully embodied, deeply earthed. And lest we set the woman to flight on her broomstick, we must keep her, her broom, and her coin quest down in the everyday domestic world of *housework,* specifically *housecleaning.*

However, to put it mildly, women's typical housecleaning duties throughout history have not been a source of feminist celebration. No one puts it stronger than Simone de Beauvoir:

> Legions of women have in common only endlessly recurrent fatigue in a battle that never leads to victory. Even in the most privileged cases, this victory is never final. Few tasks are more similar to the torment of Sisyphus than those of the housewife; day after day, one must wash dishes, dust furniture, mend clothes that will be dirty, dusty, and torn again. The housewife wears herself out running on the spot . . . ; she never gains the sense that she is conquering a positive Good but *struggles* indefinitely against Evil. It is a *struggle* that begins again every day.[81]

> Washing, ironing, sweeping, routing out tufts of dust in the dark places behind the wardrobe, this is holding away death but also refusing life: for in one movement time is created and destroyed; the housewife only grasps the negative aspect of it. . . . All doctrines of transcendence and freedom subordinate the defeat of evil to progress toward good. But the wife is not called to build a better world; the house, the bedroom, the dirty laundry, the wooden floors, are fixed things: she can do no more than rout out indefinitely the foul causes that creep in; she attacks the dust, stains, mud, and filth; she fights sin, she fights with Satan. But it is a sad destiny to have to repel an enemy without respite instead of being turned toward positive aims; the housewife often submits to it in *rage . . . ;* because the maniacal housewife detests having negativity, dirt,

---

81. Simone de Beauvoir, *The Second Sex* (trans. Constance Border and Sheila Malovany-Chevallier; New York: Knopf, 2010), 474 (emphasis added). Cf. Pat Mainardi, "The Politics of Housework," in *Dear Sisters: Dispatches from the Women's Liberation Movement* (ed. Rosalyn Baxandall and Linda Gordon; New York: Basic Books, 2000 [original article, 1968]), 255-57.

and evil as her lot, she furiously pursues dust, accepting a condition that revolts her.[82]

Notably, while Beauvoir vividly rubs our noses in the drudgery of women's daily nose-to-the-grindstone, floor-scrubbing toil, she, too, spins a moral metaphor from this work. The housekeeping woman engages in nothing less than a constant battle against sin, Satan, and evil in the domestic materials of dust, dirt, and disorderliness. And it is a battle she does not — cannot — win. House*keeping*, we might say, is a cruel misnomer; the job is more like house-*losing*, losing the battle against ubiquitous and irrepressible grime. Beauvoir insists that, while housewives routinely facilitate their husbands' "transcendence" in the world, the women themselves fail to surmount their confining, "immanent" situations. Moreover, this "immanent" imprisonment well nigh drives them insane, fueling within housekeepers boiling cauldrons of frustration and rage. To twist a sports metaphor, we might say there is no joy in the Mudville of trying to clean mud-packed floors!

By introducing Beauvoir's searing exposé of women's housecleaning at the end of this study, we seem to have lost our way and become totally mired in the muck of doubt and suspicion with no faith, hope, love, or joy to be found. But she has a point that keeps us — especially those of us in our comfortable lives of supercharged vacuums, fancy steam-mops, and all sorts of other cleaning gadgets and, even more so, the still myriads of *men* who make most of the mess and expect women to clean it up — from romanticizing the sheer hard, mind-numbing work of poorer women's daily sweeping, like that performed by the housekeeper in Jesus' parable. Nevertheless, is Beauvoir's sweeping indictment of women's housecleaning entirely justified? The happy Yemeni Christian homemakers interviewed by Schersten LaHurd would likely think Beauvoir herself was bordering on the insane.

On the academic side, feminist political philosopher Iris Marion Young grants Beauvoir's observation "that much of what we call housework is drudgery, necessary but tedious, and . . . that a life confined to such activity is slavery." But such "an entirely negative valuation of . . . [women's] activity of giving meaning to and maintaining a home" does not reflect the whole picture. In fact, it manifestly "flies in the face of the experience of many women, who devote themselves to care for house and

---

82. Beauvoir, *The Second Sex*, 476 (emphasis added).

children as a meaningful human project. . . . [I]t seems too dismissive of women's own voices to deny entirely the value many give to 'homemaking.'"[83] Young then expounds a fourfold "critical value" of home building and maintaining in the areas of (1) safety, (2) individuation, (3) privacy, and (4) preservation.[84] This last sphere, preservation — described as "the activity of safeguarding the meaningful things in which one sees the stories of one's self embodied, and rituals of remembrance that reiterate those stories"[85] — resonates with the woman searching for her lost coin and summoning her women neighbors when she finds it: she rediscovers a "meaningful thing," perhaps a source of her livelihood, within her household and shares the story with her friends, which becomes part of community lore (Luke 15:9).

Far from seething with rage, as Beauvoir would have it, the woman in Jesus' parable is shouting for joy at her housecleaning find and sharing this joy with the women in her neighborhood (15:9). It's party time — breaking the tedium of housework, but also resulting directly from it. It's bringing a bit of heavenly joy (15:10) into earthly toil, which is analogous to the work of biblical hermeneutics: struggling to find glimpses of God's truth and heavenly bliss in the midst of raw human experience and mundane employment.

---

83. Iris Marion Young, "House and Home: Feminist Variations on a Theme," in her *Intersecting Voices: Dilemmas of Gender, Political Philosophy, and Policy* (Princeton: Princeton University Press, 1997), 148-49.

84. Young, "House and Home," 160-64; cf. 149-59. While Young focuses on women's typical involvement in housework, she would certainly agree that men should fully share in this labor.

85. Young, "House and Home," 163-64.

3. A Woman's Right to Choose?
Mother Mary as Spirited Agent and Actor
(Luke 1–2)

When the biblical God "elects" someone for special service through some form of audiovisual revelation, negotiation seems fatuous; resistance is futile. It is better for everyone, including God, presumably, if the "chosen one" embraces the divine call with joyful obedience from the outset. But that's not necessary: God always gets God's "man" in the end. God's authority prevails to enlist God's agents.

This is not to say that God totally runs roughshod over human free will. The geriatric Abraham and Sarah are free to laugh at God's absurd childbearing promise and to scheme for an alternative plan (through Hagar) to help God out, but God gets the last laugh with the miraculous birth of Isaac ("laughter") (Gen 16:1-6; 17:1-8; 18:9-15; 21:1-7). The ambushed Moses can hem and haw all he wants on holy ground about his perceived inadequacies to lead Israel out of slavery; God listens but does not relent for a second: Moses *will* lead God's people with God's help, whether Moses likes it or not (Exod 3). No one is more determined than Jonah to resist God's call, and God allows the stubborn prophet enough slack to think he's escaped to the Spanish Riviera before reeling him back in for his onerous mission to Nineveh: Jonah *will* preach in the Assyrian capital (successfully!), though he chokes on every word. Finally, Saul/Paul's zealous terrorist campaign against the early church comes to a screeching halt with his world-shattering "revelation" *(apokalypsis)* of the living Jesus, who like a commander in chief launches Paul on a new apostolic career with no regard for Paul's opinion on the matter. On later reflection, Paul realizes he never really had a chance to chart his own course, since "God . . . set me apart before I was born and called me through his grace" (Gal 1:15). So also said Jeremiah, which is probably where Paul got the idea (Jer 1:4-5). In short, while the biblical challenges to "choose this day whom you will serve" (Josh 24:15; cf. Deut 30:19-20; 1 Kings 18:21) ring loud and clear, if God chooses you first, you can pretty much consider it a done deal.

If God always gets God's man, despite men's protestations and procrastinations, how much more, we might ask, does God commandeer *women* into God's special service, assuming ancient stereotypes of female passivity and complicity? Of course, we first face the stark reality that throughout the Bible God *rarely bothers at all* to call women to special vocations. Prophetesses, like Miriam, Deborah, Huldah, and Noadiah, do emerge now and again in the OT, but typically *not* as a result of narrated visions or dramatic commissions. Oddly enough, Deborah, who serves as Israel's judge as well as prophet, stands out from the other judges not only by her gender, but also by her *lack of explicit divine recruitment.* Whereas "the LORD raised up" Othniel and Ehud before Deborah as "deliverer[s] for the Israelites" (Judg 3:9, 15) and an "angel of the LORD appeared" to Gideon after her (6:12), we are simply told that "Deborah, a prophetess, wife of Lappidoth, was judging Israel" or "arose as a mother in Israel" (4:4; 5:7). While she more than holds her own as an honorable ruler of God's people, how she came to her position is never reported.

In a few exceptional cases God calls women to carry out some significant duty, but these tend to be older, "barren" subjects selected to bear children (at last) — specifically, important sons in Israel's history.[1] The anonymous wife of Manoah receives a personal angelic visitation, announcing her blessed vocation to birth Israel's next judge (Samson) and raise him as a strict "nazirite to God" (Judg 13:3-5). The postmenopausal Sarah and Elizabeth and the unfortunate cowife Hannah, who produce Isaac, John the Baptist, and Samuel, respectively, represent similar cases,

---

1. Hagar represents a separate, unique case of divine revelation to a mother (though not formerly barren woman) and her son. Twice the Lord's angel appears to Hagar in an isolated, distraught condition, promising divine care and blessing for her and her boy Ishmael. She complies with the Lord's instruction with no fuss (even when it directs her back to her harsh mistress's house) and exults in the Lord's provision (Gen 16:7-14; 21:15-21). Of course, her "foreign" legacy and that of Ishmael remain in conflict with covenant people of Israel. On women's experiences of special revelation in Hellenistic-Jewish writings, namely, those of Rebekah in *Jubilees,* Job's wife and daughters in *Testament of Job,* and Aseneth in *Joseph and Aseneth,* see Randall D. Chestnutt, "Revelatory Experiences Attributed to Biblical Women in Early Jewish Literature," in *"Women Like This": New Perspectives on Jewish Women in the Greco-Roman World* (ed. Amy-Jill Levine; Atlanta: Scholars, 1991), 107-25. We will explore Aseneth's case in chapter 6.

though not triggered by direct angelic revelations.[2] In any event, all these women *want* to have children and be rid of the cultural "disgrace" they have long suffered (cf. Luke 1:25). If they have any complaint about their promised pregnancy, it's that God didn't so bless them sooner or might not be able to pull it off at this late date. Sarah's mocking laughter at the prospect of bearing a son has everything to do with her old age and nothing to do with a personal choice not to have children. Even in her cynicism, she regards childbearing as a joyous gift ("After I have grown old . . . shall I have pleasure?" [Gen 18:12]); and once Isaac is born, any residual trace of bitterness is transformed into true mirth (21:1-7).

In short, the few biblical women God elects for a special son-bearing vocation happily accept this role as a blessing. We might say they choose to embrace God's choice of them, except that the whole idea of human "choice" falters on the notion that God doesn't really give these women an option; and even if they had a vote on the matter, would they — *could* they — have chosen otherwise, given the heavily maternal-oriented constructions of female identity in biblical society? While the men God calls often engage in considerable deliberation and remonstration before complying with God's will, the women accede with minimal fuss.

However, against this pattern of women's limited agency in the Bible, one figure stands out in relief: Mary of Nazareth, dramatically called through archangel Gabriel to bear Jesus, "Son of the Most High" and Israel's Messiah (Luke 1:26-33). Besides the uniqueness of this son's identity and destiny, two features distinguish Mary's vocation from cousin Elizabeth's and that of her biblical forebears. First, Mary is *not old and barren.* Quite the contrary, she is young and fertile, an *engaged virgin* (Luke 1:27) on the threshold of realizing her maternal potential. Her reproductive opportunities lie ahead; her womb remains open rather than closed. Theoretically, at least, she has options — not whether to try and have children with her husband (not to do so would have been virtually *inconceivable* in her culture) but perhaps, to some limited extent, *when* to have them and *how many.* Of course, God and Joseph would have the primary say in the matter; but still, at least in comparison with Elizabeth and company, Mary has *some capacity for choice* and self-determination.

---

2. Sarah overhears three divine messengers who promise Abraham that he will yet have a son by Sarah (Gen 18:9-15); Hannah receives word via the priest Eli that her prayer for a son has been answered (1 Sam 1:17-20); and it is Zechariah, rather than Elizabeth, who receives the angelic birth announcement (Luke 1:8-20).

Whether she exercises that capacity is another matter, which leads to the second point: Mary is *not entirely compliant and passive* in response to Gabriel's announcement and the surprising events that unfold thereafter in Jesus' infancy and childhood. Much is made, and rightfully so, of Mary's model response of faithful obedience: "Here am I, the servant of the Lord; let it be with me according to your word" (Luke 1:38). But these are neither her first nor her last words on the subject. To be sure, Mary chooses what God chooses for her, but she does so more determinedly than deterministically.

In *Jesus: Miriam's Child and Sophia's Prophet,* Elisabeth Schüssler Fiorenza makes a provocative observation: "I do not know of any feminist mariological reflection that theologically connects the 'free choice' of Mary with a woman's sexual 'right to choose.'"[3] She drops this little bombshell as an aside for others to pick up, lamenting that while some critics have stressed Mary's "free" and active participation in the events of Luke's birth narrative, they tend to stop short of probing the theological implications of Mary's involvement for a woman's "right to choose" her vocation, especially in regard to sexual-maternal matters. I do not aim to tackle here all the complex issues that Schüssler Fiorenza's challenge raises. Abortion, for example, would have been as inconceivable in Mary's Jewish-scriptural worldview as an intentionally childless marriage. Though working within a limited sphere of choice (God remains the Decider), Mary still emerges as a dynamic *dramatis persona,* a participatory agent in God's redemptive drama. This chapter focuses on how and to what extent Mary acts and opts in Luke 1–2. Such a study, if true to Luke's God-centered story, is inevitably fraught with theological implications for women's (and men's) God-given right to choose for or against God's will in conjunction with or opposition to self-interest, as the case may be. It's the old dogmatic tension between divine sovereignty and human responsibility, but with a new twist viewed from Mary of Nazareth's perspective and through feminist-critical lenses.

From a feminist standpoint, we explore various theoretical and theological conceptions of women's agency and divine providence, in light of which we may better track Mary's choice responses to God's compelling call in Luke 1–2.

---

3. Elisabeth Schüssler Fiorenza, *Jesus: Miriam's Child, Sophia's Prophet; Critical Issues in Feminist Christology* (New York: Continuum, 1994), 169.

Women's Agency and Divine Providence in Feminist Perspective

We have already touched on the truncated scope of *agential* self-governance conceivable to Mary within her biblically constructed culture, cropped all the more by pervasive beliefs in *providential* control of personal lives and national histories. How do feminist theory and theology negotiate these tensions between women's freedom to plan their own lives and their subjection to powerful forces of control, divine and otherwise?

Contemporary debates about women's identities and capacities often swirl around *essentialist* (nature) and *constructivist* (nurture) polarities. Essentialism assumes the primacy of various inherent, universal characteristics, shared by all members of the female sex, which determine women's "natures." Of course, opinions differ widely regarding which qualities are most "essential" to femaleness, such as reproductive organs and other biophysical features or maternal instincts and other social-psychological traits. But, whatever their particularities, essentialist perspectives accentuate stable commonalities over volatile differences among women across time and cultures; for example, more binds white middle-class North American women to their poorer sisters in the contemporary global South or to their distant foremothers in Mediterranean antiquity than divides them.

By contrast, from the constructivist standpoint, "'selves' are no longer assessed and measured by universals but are viewed as dynamic products of vast cultural forces. . . . [T]he self [is imaged] not as a stable entity but a kind of 'site,' terrain, territory or space through which cultural constructs move, often settle, and are frequently contested and changed."[4] From this angle, women's identities are more inscribed through experience than ascribed by inheritance; more forged by culture and politics than frozen by nature and genetics; and potentially more variegated among women according to their different social histories and locations.

Ironically, at both ends of this essentialist-constructivist spectrum, women's agency or capacity to choose can be severely curtailed: by *internal programming* on the essentialist side; by *external propagandizing* on the constructivist side. You can't fight Father Creator or Mother Nature; and you can't fully escape the long, strong arm of the law, the media, the economy, the state, religion, and other pervasive instruments of homogeniza-

---

4. Serene Jones, *Feminist Theory and Christian Theology: Cartographies of Grace* (Minneapolis: Fortress, 2000), 36-37; cf. 22-42 for her full and incisive discussion of the essentialist/constructivist debate.

tion and social control. You can try to resist these innate or imposed forces, but you will be largely engaging in an exercise of futility. The essentialist might say: "Which of you by worrying (or choosing) can add one inch to your height or alter one chromosome of your genetic code?" The constructivist might quip: "You can take the girl out of the country, but not the country out of the girl." You might choose to flee to the hills in protest of everything the dominant society represents, but you will hardly be free. Unless some apocalyptic sea change occurs, you will simply be defining yourself *in reaction to* the powers that be — which means they are still running your life. And historically, the powers that be have been overwhelmingly patriarchal, kyriarchal, and disinterested (because self-interested) in promoting women's authority and agency.

While honestly facing the grim reality of these limited options for women, many feminists still defy accepting these frameworks as straitjackets. Being the "weaker sex" in terms of brute strength scarcely means that women are impotent or incapable of launching effective campaigns for liberation; and being socialized into dominant constructions of "a woman's place" does not entirely squelch opportunities for consciousness-raising and self-determination. Leading feminist philosopher Martha Nussbaum adopts a nuanced essentialist stance that focuses on universal *capabilities*, rather than characteristics, shared by all humans — female and male — but rarely realized equally for women's functioning. Because of the way most human societies have been constructed, women have rarely been allowed to actualize their full capabilities. But, as Nussbaum argues, women's fundamental capabilities, however eroded by social conditions, have by no means been eradicated and persist in crying out for flourishing expression.

> Women in much of the world lose out by being women. Their human powers of choice and sociability are frequently thwarted by societies in which they must live as the adjuncts and servants of the ends of others, and in which their sociability is deformed by fear and hierarchy. But they are bearers of human capabilities, basic powers of choice that make a moral claim for opportunities to be realized and to flourish. Women's unequal failure to attain a higher level of capability, at which the choice of central human functions is really open to them, is therefore a problem of justice.[5]

5. Martha C. Nussbaum, *Women and Human Development: The Capabilities Approach* (Cambridge: Cambridge University Press, 2000), 298. In addition to this work, see Nussbaum's discussions of her capabilities approach in *Creating Capabilities: The Human Devel-*

By advocating universal capabilities for women and men, Nussbaum does not aim to flatten differences within or between the sexes. In this model, women should be free to choose *how they express and exercise* their capabilities, thus allowing for multifarious, multicultural ways of being women. But they must have the capability or right[6] to choose in the first place for women's variegated experiences to be *their* experiences, authentically and purposefully, not those saddled upon them by external agents. By the same token, essential capabilities must be conceived in broadly humanistic rather than sexist terms to ensure that they do not simply replicate normative male interests under the guise of universality. Toward this end, Nussbaum delineates ten "central human functional capabilities," the first seven of which prove most relevant to Mary's experience in Luke's infancy narratives.

1. *Life.* Being able to live to the end of a human life of normal length; not dying prematurely, or before one's life is so reduced as to be not worth living.
2. *Bodily Health.* Being able to have good health, including reproductive health; to be adequately nourished; to have adequate shelter.
3. *Bodily Integrity.* Being able to move freely from place to place; having one's bodily boundaries treated as sovereign . . . having opportunities for sexual satisfaction and for choice in matters of reproduction.
4. *Senses, Imagination, and Thought.* Being able to use the senses, to imagine, think, and reason — and to do these things in a "truly human" way. . . . Being able to use imagination and thought in connection with experiencing and producing self-expressive works and events of one's own choice, religious, literary, musical, and so forth. . . . Being able to search for the ultimate meaning of life in one's own way.

---

opment Approach (Cambridge: Harvard University Press, Belknap Press, 2011); *Frontiers of Justice: Disability, Nationality, Species Membership* (Cambridge: Harvard University Press, Belknap Press, 2006); *Sex and Social Justice* (Oxford: Oxford University Press, 1999), 29-54; "Human Capabilities, Female Human Beings" and "Emotions and Women's Capabilities," in *Women, Culture, and Development: A Study of Human Capabilities* (ed. Martha Nussbaum and Jonathan Glover; Oxford: Oxford University Press, 1995), 61-104, 360-95.

6. On the close affinity between "capabilities" and "human rights" approaches to social justice, see Nussbaum, *Creating Capabilities*, 62-68, and Amartya Sen, *Development as Freedom* (New York: Anchor, 1999), 72-110, 131-38, 227-48, 285-98; Sen, *The Idea of Justice* (Cambridge: Harvard University Press, Belknap Press, 2009), 64-66, 295-98, 355-87; David A. Crocker, "Functioning and Capability: The Foundations of Sen's and Nussbaum's Development Ethic," in *Women, Culture, and Development* (ed. Nussbaum and Glover), 186-91.

5. *Emotions.* Being able to have attachments to things and people outside ourselves; to love those who love and care for us, to grieve at their absence; in general, to love, to grieve, to experience longing, gratitude, and justified anger. Not having one's emotional development blighted by overwhelming fear and anxiety. . . .

6. *Practical Reason.* Being able to form a conception of the good and engage in critical reflection about the planning of one's life.

7. *Affiliation.* Being able to live with and toward others, to recognize and show concern for other human beings, to engage in various forms of social interaction; to be able to imagine the situation of another and to have compassion for that situation; to have the capability for both justice and friendship. Having the social bases of self-respect and non-humiliation; being able to be treated as a dignified being whose worth is equal to that of others.[7]

Christian feminist theologian Serene Jones negotiates the essentialist-constructivist continuum with a middle position she calls "strategic essentialism" or "pragmatic universalism."[8] While maintaining "a healthy dose of constructivist suspicion" about the exploitative powers that inevitably shape women's lives in oppressive ways, Jones resists the tendency of this perspective to fossilize into a rigid "cultural determinism." Hence she stresses the qualifying judgment of secular feminist constructivists like Judith Butler "that women are not *incapable* of actively and intentionally participating in processes of cultural formation."[9] Some sense of women's agency is thus retained as "an 'implicated resistance,' one that is never completely free of the constructions it contests but with enough critical distance from them to challenge the status quo and envision alterna-

7. This list of capabilities and their descriptions are cited from Nussbaum, *Women and Human Development*, 78-80. She regards "practical reason" and "affiliation" as particularly central to this list, "since they both organize and suffuse all the others, making their pursuit truly human" (82). The final three items among the ten — concerning "other species," "play," and "control over one's environment" (politically and materially) — are somewhat less relevant to Mary's case. I return to Nussbaum's entire capabilities register in chapter 8. For other places where Nussbaum delineates and discusses her decalogue, see *Creating Capabilities*, 31-45; *Frontiers of Justice*, 76-81; *Sex and Social Justice*, 39-42.

8. Jones, *Feminist Theory*, 42-48.

9. Jones, *Feminist Theory*, 38 (emphasis in original). She goes on to explain: "They [constructivists like Butler] protect the notion of agency by saying that, unlike essentialism's subject, 'woman' is shaped not by inevitable traits but by 'imaginative' products of human community and can therefore be contested and changed" (38).

tives."[10] Beyond that, however, Jones positively affirms certain "strategic essentials" of women's functional identities — like "agency, embodiment, relationality, and difference" (similar to Nussbaum's universal capabilities) — that operate in tension with diverse, constructive external forces.[11] She keeps one foot planted in the essentialist camp for both pragmatic and political reasons: *pragmatically,* she espouses the commonsense notion that "people simply cannot live without a view of human nature that includes 'essentials' or 'universals'" (the relativistic alternative is too close to nihilism for comfort); and *politically,* she acknowledges that people rally to promote a value or condition widely held to be "essential" for human flourishing (announcing a cold theoretical principle that "women exist only as a social construction" is unlikely to stir the troops).[12]

But Jones also roots her views of women's identity and agency in rich *theological* soil. On the essentialist side, Jones embraces universal claims concerning God's relationship to humanity, particularly: (1) God's love for all persons; (2) God's "good creation" of human bodies, female and male; (3) God's "fundamental" opposition to all forms of oppression and injustice against human beings; and (4) humankind's finding true identity in fellowship with God and other people.[13] But feminist theology is under no Pollyanna illusions that such essentials routinely suffuse humanity's, especially women's, experience. Quite the contrary, a hermeneutic of suspicion combined with a strong doctrine of sin, both individual and structural, exposes how much of women's lives is forcibly shaped into marred molds. Hence constructivist realism tempers essentialist idealism. Or in theological terms, "prophetic critique" unmasks deviations from "revelatory truth."[14]

But Jones's feminist theology doesn't stop with explanation. It moves to transformation — "the remaking potential of grace." Jones glosses "strategic essentialism" in terms of "eschatological essentialism" that negotiates between "normative truth," on the one pole, and "prophetic suspicion," on the other — remaining staunchly, courageously, and faithfully open to the full,

10. Jones, *Feminist Theory,* 38.
11. Jones, *Feminist Theory,* 48.
12. Jones, *Feminist Theory,* 45-46. On a more personal practical and political side, Jones persuasively argues: "If I believe women are essentially agents capable of making decisions [notice the appeal to capability, à la Nussbaum], owning their own bodies, and crafting their own lives, then I will encourage my daughter to think for herself and take on responsibilities" (46).
13. Jones, *Feminist Theory,* 51-53.
14. Jones, *Feminist Theory,* 52-55.

future realization of universal values of love, justice, and goodness through God's transformative grace.[15] "At the heart of feminist theology," Jones contends, "lies the belief that God wills that women (along with all people) flourish, and that, as people of faith, Christians are called to follow God's will and seek out conditions for that flourishing, all the while recognizing the limits of sin and the need for the Holy Spirit. Feminist theologians thus affirm that God's grace has transformative power. They believe that human beings can be converted, changed, redeemed, reborn, remade."[16]

As for the place of women's agency in this transformative enterprise, Jones draws on the doctrine of sanctification with its sanguine visions of growth, fruitfulness, and regeneration. As she describes the feminist implications of sanctification, "the woman who inhabits this doctrinal terrain is neither passive nor fragmented but is set in motion and directed toward a goal." She emerges as "the embodied agent struggling to become the ever shifting essential woman of the *future*. She does not look behind her to ossified descriptions of her nature to direct her life; rather, she looks ahead, toward an emancipatory future where her identity is defined as 'graced.'"[17] The future is wondrously open and free, but not toward anything and everything. Sanctification sets a "goal" — a liberating one, to be sure, but a particular target all the same — for the "essential woman" to reach. It marks a "terrain" — a wide and goodly space, but still hedged in — within which she may flourish in accord with God's loving purposes for her. In sum, the Christian woman "agent" lives, moves, and has her being within what Jones dialectically images as the "bounded openness" or "enveloped wonder" of God's grace.[18]

Having explored human agency from the perspective of women's self-perception and self-actualization, theological analysis must also consider the matter from God's viewpoint. Here we face the thorny problem of *di-*

15. Jones, *Feminist Theory*, 53-54. As Jones indicates on p. 186 n. 12, her eschatological emphasis builds on the work of pioneering feminist theologian Letty Russell (*The Future of Partnership* [Philadelphia: Westminister, 1979]; *Household of Freedom* [Philadelphia: Westminster, 1987]).

16. Jones, *Feminist Theory*, 52.

17. Jones, *Feminist Theory*, 64 (emphasis in original).

18. Jones, *Feminist Theory*, 42-43, 48-49, 168, 176. Jones draws her notion of "enveloped wonder" from French feminist theorist Luce Irigaray (*An Ethics of Sexual Difference* [trans. Carolyn Burke and Gillian C. Gill; Ithaca, N.Y.: Cornell University Press, 1993], 72-83, 116-32); cf. discussion of Irigaray's perspective on wonder in Iris Marion Young, *Intersecting Voices: Dilemmas of Gender, Political Philosophy, and Policy* (Princeton: Princeton University Press, 1997), 56.

vine providence, especially so-called "personal" or "particular" providence affecting individual lives. Though not a common focus of feminist theology, feminist writer-editor Kalbryn McLean tackles this problem of the "personal politics of providence" in dialogue with the king of providence, John Calvin. In his high conception of God as sovereign Creator and Father, Calvin seeks "to preserve God's utter freedom of action, God's agency," with the corollary that "nothing and no one exercise their own power except insofar as God wills them to do so." Human agency — of men and women alike — is thus wholly subsumed under God's "ceaseless activity that regulates everything that happens in absolute specificity."[19] But in McLean's reading, Calvin's pervasive view of God's providence does not eliminate human capacity for free will, as evidenced in our bent to sin — our repeated choices, which God permits, to go against God's will and pursue our own selfish interests. Even here, however, God's sovereign agency wins the day, as "God's plan 'absorbs' the resulting human behavior into the divine goodness without nullifying creaturely impetus."[20]

While acknowledging a degree of comfort flowing from the notion that an all-knowing, all-powerful God works all things out according to God's good purposes, McLean also laments, from a feminist perspective, the harmful subjugation of women that results from an anemic view of women's agency, not least one that too readily associates self-assertion with sin. How can a sweeping doctrine of providential control support a robust commitment to women's flourishing and empowerment? Seizing on the "pastoral intentions" of Calvin's thought, McLean affirms that "there is something theologically sound and empowering about holding fast to the idea that God is directly involved in our lives," both personally and politically.[21] But to safeguard women's independent agency, she hastens to imagine "the possibility that God, or particular providence, works through persons *who invite God to do so.*"[22] That is, she stresses the disposition of "hospitality toward God,"[23] actively preparing for and welcoming God's free and gracious participation in women's lives.

Moreover, for women's sake, McLean urges an intentional imaging of

---

19. Kalbryn A. McLean, "Calvin and the Personal Politics of Providence," in *Feminist and Womanist Essays in Reformed Dogmatics* (ed. Amy Plantinga Pauw and Serene Jones; Louisville: Westminster John Knox, 2006), 109.

20. McLean, "Calvin," 110.

21. McLean, "Calvin," 115.

22. McLean, "Calvin," 121 (emphasis added).

23. McLean, "Calvin," 121.

this guest-God less as dictatorial Father-Patriarch ruling the household (Calvin's main image), less as dominical Son-Lord micromanaging the Father's interests, and more as dynamic Holy Spirit, the "wild child of the divine family" — "one who does not stand over us in a controlling position but instead swirls around us, ever present and shape shifting, ready to infuse us with energy when our bodies grow weary, ready to sharpen our vision when our eyes become heavy, ready to give us tongues of fire when we need to denounce injustice and still sing God's praise."[24]

Such an "agency-empowering"[25] vision of the Holy Spirit resonates in suggestive ways with the Virgin Mary's conception of divine-human life by the "overshadowing" operation of the Spirit (Luke 1:35) and her Spirit-inspired paean of praise to the Mighty One who lifts the lowly and topples the forces of injustice (1:46-55). We now turn to explore these rich dynamics of Mary's response to God's call more fully.

Mary's Opportunity (Luke 1:26-38)

Mary's opening scene in the Lukan drama features her encounter with the angel Gabriel who, following his recent birth announcement to the aged priest Zechariah, now makes a similar promise to the young girl Mary.[26] Before recounting this annunciation, the narrator briefly sets the stage. It happens "in the sixth month," that is, the sixth month of the postmenopausal Elizabeth's (Zechariah's wife) pregnancy, intimating the close connection between Elizabeth's and Mary's experiences (Luke 1:26, 36);[27] and it takes place in the backwater Galilean town of Nazareth, which, quite unlike the Jerusalem temple setting of Zechariah's vision, has no grand social, religious, or political expectations ("Can anything good come out of Nazareth?" [John 1:46; cf. 7:52]).

We also learn of Mary's marital status as a virgin (*parthenos*, twice)

24. McLean, "Calvin," 123; cf. 122-24.

25. McLean, "Calvin," 123.

26. On the juxtaposition of angelic birth announcements to Zechariah and Mary in Luke 1:5-80, see F. Scott Spencer, *The Gospel of Luke and Acts of the Apostles* (Nashville: Abingdon, 2008), 100-105.

27. Their affinity also extends to some biological kinship bond (*syngenis* — "kinswoman," "relative," perhaps cousin [1:36]). Further, Elizabeth's "sixth month" checkup suggests the maturity of her pregnancy beyond the danger period of miscarriage, indicating that God's childbearing promise is well on its way to being fulfilled.

engaged to a man of Davidic lineage named Joseph (Luke 1:27). Her destiny and capabilities are thus linked — and limited by — her betrothed husband. To what extent she *chose* to enter into this marital contract is of no concern here; in any case, being engaged, her opportunities to chart her own life would normally be circumscribed by Joseph's patriarchal will.[28] Mary's intact virginity allows her freedom from sexual stigma (for the moment), but also presumes Joseph's right to have her at the appropriate time and have children by her. Her body is not her own. To what extent mutual love motivates this relationship is again outside the story's interest. But still we have no reason to surmise that Mary regarded her marriage to Joseph and the prospect of having children by him as anything but a normal, even blessed, opportunity. And the chance to contribute to the venerable Davidic lineage would have been no mean achievement for a Galilean girl.

The last component of Mary's introductory profile emphasizes her *name: Mariam* (1:27). This was the most common female appellation in first-century Palestine, paying homage to Moses' sister *Miriam/Mariam* (LXX), who played a key role in saving the infant Moses' life and in celebrating as a *prophet* God's redemption of Israel from slavery (Exod 15:20-21; Mic 6:4).[29] She appears free to sing and dance before the Lord, tethered to no male authority, *until* the tragic incident when Miriam questions Moses' judgment and authority and God inflicts her with leprosy and excludes her from the community (Num 12). She is never heard from again in the Torah and stands as a problematic, ambivalent example of women's agency and prophecy.[30] We must wait and see — and listen to — how Mariam of Nazareth mirrors or modifies her ancestral namesake.

---

28. Cf. Barbara E. Reid, *Choosing the Better Part? Women in the Gospel of Luke* (Collegeville, Minn.: Liturgical Press, 1996), 65: "It is striking that although Mary is introduced in terms of her relation to Joseph, she becomes the focus and active agent in the annunciation scene, and not him." We will unpack Mary's surprising role as "active agent" below.

29. See Deirdre Good, "What Does It Mean to Call Mary Miriam?" in *A Feminist Companion to Mariology* (ed. Amy-Jill Levine and Maria Mayo Robbins; Cleveland: Pilgrim Press, 2005), 99-106; Good, "The Miriamic Secret," in *Mariam, the Magdalen, and the Mother* (ed. Deirdre Good; Bloomington: Indiana University Press, 2005), 3-24; Tal Ilan, "Notes on the Distribution of Women's Names in Palestine in the Second Temple and Mishnaic Period," *Journal of Jewish Studies* 40 (1989): 186-200.

30. In addition to Good's studies cited in n. 29, see Susan Ackerman, "Why Is Miriam among the Prophets? (And Is Zipporah among the Priests?)," *Journal of Biblical Literature* 121 (2002): 47-80; Phyllis Trible, "Bringing Miriam Out of the Shadows," *Bible Review* 5 (1989): 14-25, 34; Rita J. Burns, *Has the Lord Indeed Only Spoken through Moses? A Study of the Biblical Portrait of Miriam* (Atlanta: Scholars, 1987).

Mary's exchange with Gabriel unfolds in three stages, each initiated by the angel's speech and followed, first, by the narrator's assessment of Mary's responsive mien; second, by her direct interrogation; and third, by her submissive declaration. Initially Gabriel greets Mary as one abundantly graced by the Lord's presence (Luke 1:28). From our safe observation point as distant readers, we might assume that an angelic visit signals special favor, but in the heat of the moment, Mary is not at all sure this is a blessed event. Why on earth should she be singled out? Nazareth's record of previous angelic visitations would be slim to none. Perhaps Gabriel has lost his way, misread his assignment. Even if he has the right place, does he have the right person? "Male" angels (this is not Gabriella) normally appear to male characters in the Bible, like Zechariah.[31] It is thus easily imaginable, as Serene Jones suggests, that "with women who, through the ages, have not recognized their value, Mary is looking over her shoulder to see who else Gabriel must be talking to."[32] Add to this that Mary has not, like Zechariah, been praying for divine intervention, nor is she anywhere near the temple or any other sacred place. She's caught completely off guard. Of course, for that matter, so is Zechariah, though he has fewer reasons to be surprised; in fact, more than surprised, he becomes troubled *(tarassō)* and overwhelmed with fear *(phobos)* when he first "sees" Gabriel (1:12).

In both similar and different terms, Mary's "feisty and challenging"[33] first response is described as *perplexed (diatarassomai)* and *pondering (dialogizomai)* over "the word" *(logos)* of Gabriel, not simply his appearance

---

31. Cf. Reid, *Choosing the Better Part?* 64-65, and the discussion above of the few OT cases where angels appear to select women. Moreover, at the end of Luke two dazzling male messengers *(andres duo)* will appear to a group of women at Jesus' empty tomb, but such an experience strikes the male apostles, to whom the women report, as so exceptional that it is completely dismissed as an "idle tale" until the men can confirm it for themselves (24:1-11, 22-24).

32. Serene Jones, *Trauma and Grace: Theology in a Ruptured World* (Louisville: Westminster John Knox, 2009), 115.

33. Peter J. Gomes, *The Good Book: Reading the Bible with Mind and Heart* (New York: Morrow, 1996), 232: "Moses is in some anticipation of Mary, who also receives rather unexpected tidings — hers from the angel Gabriel. Mary has been so often depicted as weak and submissive, 'the handmaiden of the Lord,' or, as one angry feminist once put it, 'the doormat of God,' that we forget the feisty and challenging nature of her initial response. . . . Rather than rushing to anticipate her humility or to make an argument about the doctrine of the Virgin Birth, we might do well to pause and ponder her wariness, her caution, indeed her reluctance to being pushed into joy."

(1:29).[34] Mary attends to the angel's message from the start, whereas Zechariah becomes stuck initially on the spectacle.[35] The two *dia*-compound verbs stress Mary's affective-cognitive thinking "through" the implications of this strange visitation.[36] The one term, an intensified form of *tarrasō* designating Zechariah's roiling distress (Luke 1:12; cf. Matt 14:26; Mark 6:50), connotes a strong, emotional "upheaval of thought,"[37] while the other indicates a more rational disputation of argument.[38] Together they resist stereotypical, dismissive caricatures of young women like Mary as hysterical or gullible. She reacts with robust emotional and intellectual engagement. No angel, even the imposing Gabriel, is going to pull one over on Mary.

Second, Mary's internal reflection becomes verbal in response to Gabriel's specific announcement: "And now, you will conceive in your womb and bear a son, and you will name him Jesus" (Luke 1:31). Such child-conceiving and naming a child would no doubt have already been in the forefront of Mary's thoughts, as with any young betrothed woman in this culture; normally it did not take an angel to jump-start that. But here he is, the Lord's mighty messenger, coming on rather strong with Mary about this birthing business — calling her to attention ("Now look here!"

34. Note two grammatical verb points based on Daniel B. Wallace, *Greek Grammar beyond the Basics: An Exegetical Syntax of the New Testament* (Grand Rapids: Zondervan, 1996), 483, concerning Luke 1:29 — "[She] pondered *(dielogizeto)* what sort of greeting this might be *(eiē)*": (1) the first verb is imperfect, suggesting continuing reflection — "she *was pondering*"; (2) the second verb is optative, only used by Luke in the NT in oblique or indirect questions (Luke 1:29; 8:29; 18:36; 22:23; Acts 17:11; 21:33; 25:20). In the present case, its indirectness may blunt some of the edge from Mary's response, but it implies a pointed, direct question in Mary's mind: "What sort of greeting *is* this?"

35. Cf. Brendan J. Byrne, *The Hospitality of God: A Reading of Luke's Gospel* (Collegeville, Minn.: Liturgical Press, 2000), 23: "Where Zechariah had been troubled by the angelic apparition, what troubles Mary is the content of this greeting (v. 29)."

36. On the affective-rhetorical dynamics ("cardiography") of Luke 1:5-56, see Karl A. Kuhn, *The Heart of Biblical Narrative: Recovering Biblical Appeal to the Emotions* (Minneapolis: Fortress, 2009), 63-95.

37. The title of Martha Nussbaum's work, *Upheavals of Thought: The Intelligence of Emotions* (Cambridge: Cambridge University Press, 2001), is borrowed (see p. vii) from a passage in Marcel Proust, *Remembrance of Things Past*. More than "mere" impulses, strong emotional reactions — like fearing a mighty angel's sudden appearance or powerful storm — remain integrally wrapped up with cognitive reflections in human experience.

38. Elsewhere in Luke, *dialogizomai/dialogismoi* refers to the crowds' deliberations about John's message (3:15), the scribes'/Pharisees' arguments with Jesus (5:22; 6:8), and the disciples' wrangling about their social status (9:46). Though the latter two examples reflect misguided disputes, they still imply engaged thinking rather than knee-jerk responses.

[*idou*]), claiming control over her womb *(gastēr)*, and dictating her baby's moniker. Her body, her life, her plans are not her own. But is not this still good news for Mary in her context, as she is promised the high honor of producing a firstborn son — and not just any son — but the "great" *mega*-Son of "the Most High" — destined to rule in perpetuity over God's people on David's throne (1:32-33; cf. 2 Sam 7:16)? In other words, the angel casts the identity of Mary's child in nothing short of messianic proportions.[39]

That's a lot for this ordinary young lady to take in. Unlike later, legendary depictions of Mary's pious childhood, where she had been given to the Lord (à la Samuel) and groomed for sacred service by parents and priests in her little nursery shrine at home and in the temple until the onset of menses at age twelve when temple residence became problematic,[40] Luke offers no trace of Mary's preparation for messianic motherhood. There was no consensus at this time regarding how the messianic age might break in, and no common, starry-eyed dream among first-century Jewish girls to nab some nice Judahite man in hopes of bearing him the once and future king of Israel. The Lukan Mary's shock and awe over Gabriel's announcement are mounting by the minute — leading her, however, not to crumble in a helpless heap, but to ask for clarification. She does not immediately give herself over to the angel's plan, however much he claims divine authorization. This is her body, and she would like to know exactly how it's going to be appropriated.

Sensing the heavy urgency of Gabriel's proposal, well in advance of her wedding night with Joseph, and by no means entertaining the pagan notion that God might find her so attractive as to impose himself upon her sexually and implant some divine seed within her, Mary asks the logical question: "How will this be, since a male *(andra)* I do not know *(ou ginōskō)* [and do not intend to know sexually until my wedding night]?" (Luke 1:34, my translation). We tense up as Lukan readers at this point, because we know from Zechariah's story that Gabriel does not take questions well. Zechariah's similar probing of the unexpected birth announcement

---

39. While no set messianic formula dominated first-century Judaism, notions of Davidic kingship and divine sonship via biblical texts like 2 Sam 7 and Ps 2 were certainly in play. See Adela Yarbro Collins and John J. Collins, *King and Messiah as Son of God: Divine, Human, and Angelic Messianic Figures in Biblical and Related Literature* (Grand Rapids: Eerdmans, 2008).

40. *Infancy Gospel of James* 6-9; see Ronald F. Hock, *The Infancy Gospels of James and Thomas with Introduction, Notes, and Original Text* (Santa Rosa, Calif.: Polebridge, 1995), 41-49.

— "How will I know *(gnōsomai)* that this is so?" (1:18) — marks the last words he says for nine months! Gabriel is not a paragon of patience. Although Mary's query is qualitatively different from Zechariah's, focusing more on process than proof and leaving more room for faith than doubt, she still displays remarkable moxie and agency in challenging Gabriel and the appropriation of her womb. Perhaps even more remarkably, Gabriel honors her personal role in God's plan by explaining what will happen to her body rather than stifling her vocal chords. Perhaps if Zechariah had been more concerned about Elizabeth's involvement than his own uncertainty — after all, it was *her* body that would be most affected — he would have merited a more sympathetic response.

Juxtaposing his forecast of John the Baptist's fetal filling with the power of the Holy Spirit in Elizabeth's womb (1:15-17), Gabriel predicts Mary's enveloping by the same divine, dynamic agency: "The Holy Spirit will come upon *(epeleusetai)* you, and the power of the Most High will overshadow *(episkiasei)* you" (1:35). These double *epi*-verbs describing the Spirit's forceful coming "upon/over" Mary counterpoint the double *dia*-verbs denoting her careful thinking "through" the situation. Does *epi* in fact trump *dia,* coercively *over*whelming and *under*cutting Mary's agency? Question all you want, but if God comes upon and over you, forget about it: your fate is sealed.

Yes, but must this divine overpowering be viewed as brute, imperious, patriarchal force? Perhaps not, if associated with the Holy Spirit, the "wild child" of God's communal being, to reprise McLean's happy image, which blows where it wills with explosive energy but always in the interest of creating and sustaining new life, whether brooding over primordial waters at the world's inception (Gen 1:2) or bringing "new birth" to God's people as part of the world's redemption (John 3:3-8). This generative role of the Holy Spirit in producing God's Son in Mary's womb apart from male sperm clearly supports Jesus' virginal conception, but *not* in two commonly "conceived" ways that undermine Mary's own spirited participation, yea partnership, with the Spirit in the creative process. For one, the Holy *(Hagion)* Spirit's productive work makes Jesus a holy son within Mary's body ("the child to be born *will be holy* [*hagion*]"),[41] not Mary a holy mother fit for Jesus. Mary's purity, sexual or otherwise, is not at issue here. She's been a virgin all her life, like scores of other girls in her society. She doesn't need to be

---

41. "Therefore" *(dio)* in 1:35 makes a direct causal connection between the Holy Spirit's coming over Mary and working within her womb to produce a holy child.

"made holy" or "made over" in any sense to become a worthy vessel of God's Son. The whole point of her being "favored" or "graced" is that God chooses her *as she is and will be* — a normal, everyday human female, not some unique, ideal figure that no other woman could approximate.[42]

Second, ascribing Jesus' conception to the divine Holy Spirit — the feminine *ruach* in Hebrew and neuter *pneuma* in Greek — subverts notions of Mary's passive body being somehow penetrated and impregnated by God the Father's "seed." Gabriel does not pick up Mary's sexual language in his response: Father God will not "know" her in that sense. The life-giving Holy Spirit will come "over/upon" her, not *within* her.[43] Mary thus retains freedom *within herself* — her spirited self, we might say — to receive and respond to the Spirit's creative initiative.

Indeed, the climax falls on Mary's classic third response to the annunciation, in which she declares: "Look, the slave of the Lord; if at all possible, let it be to me according to your word" (Luke 1:38, my translation). Though obscured in the NRSV, Mary's reaction here matches the beginning of Gabriel's report: as he exhorted Mary to "look" *(idou)* and give careful consideration to his birth announcement, now she implores the angel to "look" *(idou)* at her as a willing participant in God's redemptive plan. Ironically, however, she freely gives herself over to the Lord as his *slave (doulē)*, completely surrendering her autonomy, it seems. She then offers herself as the embodied tablet on which God's angel-mediated "word" may be inscribed. Still, however, from beginning to end, Mary has intelligently engaged Gabriel's message (*logos* [1:29]/*rhēma* [1:38]); this is no impulsive, clueless decision she makes. It is also not simply formulaic or robotic, the expected dutiful acquiescence to the divine will. The use of the optative mood for "let it be" *(genoito)*, compared with the imperative and subjunctive, carries "slightly remoter, vaguer, less assured, or more contingent" connotations.[44] In the present situation, according to van den

---

42. See the sharp critique of "the ideal-typical ecclesiological approach" to Mary in popular and academic circles in Schüssler Fiorenza, *Jesus*, 164-72; cf. Beverly Roberts Gaventa, *Mary: Glimpses of the Mother of Jesus* (Columbia: University of South Carolina Press, 1995; Minneapolis: Fortress, 1999), 73: "Certainly Luke gives no indication that he regards Mary as a type or symbol confined to women. Indeed, if Mary is a symbol at all, she symbolizes God's gift of grace to all humankind" (cf. 54-55).

43. As Reid (*Choosing the Better Part?* 68) and other commentators stress, the *epi*-verbs do not carry coital connotations here.

44. Stanley E. Porter, *Idioms of the Greek New Testament* (2nd ed.; Sheffield: Sheffield Academic, 1994), 59. He continues: "In other words, like the subjunctive, *the optative mood*

Hengel, it "expresses Mary's intense desire . . . [and] longing [that] was not blind to the obvious difficulties she also foresaw."[45]

As her prophetic song will soon make clear, Mary longs not for her personal acclaim, but for the salvation of her beleaguered people (1:46-55). If her bearing God's messianic Son will catalyze such liberation, then so be it. But she knows it will not be easy, not least because of the "impossible" scenario of virginal conception Gabriel has just sketched (cf. 1:37). Elizabeth's pregnancy by Zechariah in old age is one thing; conceiving as a virgin by the Holy Spirit is quite another. The former at least has some biblical precedent; the latter doesn't, except by a novel interpretation of Isaiah 7:14 in Matthew 1:22-23, which Luke does not promote. So Mary wants to believe, longs to believe, Gabriel's decree that nothing is impossible with God (1:37), but she's not entirely sure. If at all possible — and she hopes against hope that it is — let this miracle happen within her not chiefly for her sake, but for the advancement of God's salvific rule.

In notable respects Mary's situation resembles that which will later engulf Jesus at the end of his life. Confronting the prospect of imminent crucifixion as the goal of God's mission, Jesus recoils from this destiny and prays for a reprieve, if his Father so wills; but then he quickly adds: "Yet, not my will but yours be done" (22:42). Though using the stronger imperative expression "let it be done *(ginesthō)*," Jesus, like his mother, struggles as a human agent with life-and-death decisions and needs, no less than she, an "angel from heaven . . . [to give] him strength" (22:43).[46] The overarching divine will orchestrates the drama of salvation throughout Luke's narrative *in concert with* key players, like Mary and Jesus, who function as voluntary cooperative agents.

---

grammaticalizes the semantic feature of projection but with an element of contingency" (59-60 [emphasis in original]). Mary employs a "volitive" (or "voluntative") type of optative in Luke 1:38 typical of *prayerful petitions.* Wallace (*Greek Grammar,* 481) suggests that this "is largely a carry-over from Attic [Greek]" from a context in which "prayers offered to the semi-gods of ancient Athens could expect to be haggled over, rebuffed, and left unanswered." But he hastens to add that such contingency or doubt, signaled by the optative mood, is mitigated (though not entirely eliminated) in NT petitions to the one true, trustworthy, and gracious God: "[A]though the *form* of much prayer language in the NT has the tinge of remote possibility . . . its *meaning* often moves into the realm of expectation. If uncertainty is part of the package, it is not due to questions of God's ability, but simply to the petitioner's humility before the transcendent one" (emphasis in original).

45. John van den Hengel, "Miriam of Nazareth: Between Symbol and History," in *A Feminist Companion to Mariology* (ed. Levine and Robbins), 144.

46. Reid, *Choosing the Best Part?* 69-70.

In sum, as an ordinary young woman, Mary accepts God's claim upon her life as a willing follower — the "first disciple" in Luke and "model disciple" for others, male or female[47] — though not without doubts, desires, and demurrals appropriate to a freethinking agent. Using McLean's language, we might say that, with eyes wide open, Mary deliberately accepts the divine invitation to welcome the Spirit and cohost the birthing of God's Son in her womb. Or appropriating the enlightened perspective on women's rights of nineteenth-century philosopher John Stuart Mill in his day, we might acclaim Mary as a young "woman of spirit and capacity"[48] — that is, *a spirited, capable woman.*

But there remains this problematic slave/servant status she also assumes and the fact that she is not accorded a safe right of refusal, any more than Moses or Jonah. After all the trouble Gabriel takes to visit her and respond to her serious probing and pondering, Mary scarcely seems free to say something like . . .

> Thanks, but no thanks. I'm going to pass on this one. I'm not quite up to this whole Messiah-mothering business right now. That's a really huge responsibility as well as privilege. Maybe you could check back in a few years after I grow up a little and settle down and have a couple of kids with Joseph. Or by all means, feel free to approach someone else. Lord knows we need a Messiah now. Susannah down the road may be just the one — she's always been up for a challenge and has a bit of Messiah-complex anyway. You might check with her.

Sounds silly, doesn't it? Like a parody — almost impossible to imagine in this context. Yet if freedom of choice means anything for women, does it

47. See Gaventa, *Mary,* 51-59, 72-75; Gaventa, "'All Generations Will Call Me Blessed': Mary in Biblical and Ecumenical Perspective," in *A Feminist Companion to Mariology* (ed. Levine and Robbins), 126-29.

48. John Stuart Mill, *The Subjection of Women* (ed. Susan M. Okin; Indianapolis: Hackett, 1988 [orig. 1869]), 29. Later, Mill attributes women's spiritedness and capability to a "nervous temperament," which we would judge as sexist and condescending, but which Mill casts in more positive terms of perseverance and leadership: "It is the character of the nervous temperament to be capable of *sustained* excitement, holding out through long continued efforts. It is what is meant by *spirit.* It is what makes the high-bred racehorse run without slackening speed till he drops down dead. It is what has enabled so many delicate women to maintain the most sublime constancy not only at the stake, but through a long preliminary succession of mental and bodily tortures. It is evident that people of this temperament are particularly apt for what may be called the executive department of the leadership of mankind" (66 [emphasis in original]).

not grant the right to say, "No, not now; thanks, but no thanks," regarding major life decisions, not least those involving women's reproductive lives? We might continue to debate the extent of such freedom *after* marriage or *after* pregnancy inside or outside wedlock, but hardly in the case of adolescent girls like Mary *before* their wedding nights. By all rights, Mary should be free to decline Gabriel's offer, even though she chooses not to.

Mary's Pregnancy (Luke 1:39-55)

Having explored the process of Mary's accepting her vocation to conceive God's Son by the Holy Spirit, we now turn to chart Mary's reactions to her pregnancy. Fortunately, Luke continues to focus on Mary's actions and speech. Unlike in Matthew's narrative, Joseph's concerns with a suddenly pregnant fiancée — but not by him! (Matt 1:18-25) — never come to the fore in Luke; in fact, Joseph himself remains offstage. So how does Mary respond as the life of God's Son takes shape in her womb?

She does not simply stay quiet, keep to herself, and bide her time until she gives birth. Quite unlike her relative Elizabeth, who "remained in seclusion" for the initial five months of her pregnancy (Luke 1:24), the first thing Mary does "in those days" is head south to the hills of Judea and the house of Zechariah and Elizabeth. Here the prepositional direction shifts from *dia* (through) and *epi* (upon) to *eis* (into): "Mary set out *into (eis)* the hill country with haste *into (eis)* a city of Judea, and she *entered into (eisēlthen eis)* the house of Zechariah and greeted Elizabeth" (1:39-40, my translation). As her body is changing within, she takes it *into* different territory. Such shape- and space-shifting operations, which to some degree intimate Mary's capacity "to move freely from place to place," in Nussbaum's terms, also reflect Mary's liminal state and precarious situation in her culture. She ventures out on the first of many journeys that drive the plot of Luke and Acts. This maiden journey, as we might call it, stands out for its *hasty departure*[49] and *lonely execution* — a solo flight launched with an edgy sense of urgency, if not panic.

What possesses Mary to do such a rash thing, to risk her and her

49. Mary's leaving "with haste" *(meta spoudēs)* recalls the Israelites' hurried eating of the Passover meal on the night of their hasty exodus from Egyptian bondage (Exod 12:11; Wis 19:2) and previews the shepherds' rush to Bethlehem to see the baby Jesus (Luke 2:16) and Zacchaeus's dash home to entertain the adult Jesus (19:5, 6; both stories use the cognate verb *speudō* [hasten, hurry]).

baby's safety by traveling alone forty miles or so into hilly terrain? It no doubt has everything to do with this powerful generative Spirit that has possessed her and turned her life upside down. But what will running away accomplish? What does she hope to achieve? Though Luke doesn't say this, it's hard not to imagine Mary's desire to leave Nazareth so she can avoid the awkward questions that will surely arise about her pregnancy. The Jerusalem audience logically surmised that Zechariah had seen a vision in the temple (1:21), but the Nazareth community is unlikely to grant a similar experience to young Mary, certainly not as an explanation for a preposterous virginal conception! Implicitly, then, Mary's hasty "heading for the hills" of Judea marks the Lukan counterpart to the Matthean Joseph's decision to "put Mary away secretly" (Matt 1:19 NKJV).[50] But more clearly in Luke's story, the pregnant Mary doesn't just dash away anywhere to escape the heat at home. She doesn't wind up, like the pregnant Hagar, wandering in the wilderness until the angel of the Lord finds her (Gen 16:7-14). She intentionally heads to Judea to see Elizabeth; technically, she enters the "house of Zechariah," but it's only Elizabeth she greets and talks with at length (Luke 1:40-45). Whatever nod the narrative makes to Zechariah's patriarchal authority is quickly overshadowed by the two women's Spirit-inspired conversation. Of course, the mute old priest couldn't contribute much to Mary anyway. Mary has come seeking comfort, empathy, and insight from her elder, pregnant kinswoman. The ensuing exchange proves that Mary has made the right move.

From the moment of Mary's arrival, Elizabeth becomes "filled with the Holy Spirit" and both bodily and vocally affirms Mary's life-giving vocation (1:40-45). Way beyond the age of bounding about herself and carrying a child who has yet to crawl or take a single step, Elizabeth exults in the joyous leap she feels in her womb upon hearing the sound of Mary's greeting (1:41, 44). Such spirited activity evokes the "leaping of the lame like a deer" that Isaiah imaged for the restoration of God's people and functions as a dramatic sign in Luke that such a vision is coming to life in the sons of Mary and Elizabeth (Isa 35:5-6; cf. Luke 6:23; Acts 3:8). Moreover, enhancing this uterine dance, Elizabeth thrice blesses Mary: first, for who she is ("Blessed are you among women"); next, for who she bears ("Blessed is the fruit of your womb"); and finally, for what she has done ("Blessed is she

---

50. See Richard W. Swanson, "Magnificat and Crucifixion: The Story of Mariam and Her Son," *Currents in Theology and Mission* 34 (2007): 101-3 (under the apt heading, "'Mariam ran'").

who believed what was spoken to her by the Lord") — a dazzling affirmation of her gender (woman), generativity (mother), and spirituality (believer). It's important to note that such effusive praise focuses on Mary's independent identity and agency as much as on "the Lord" she will birth, and does not so much set her above or apart from other women as *among* them (*en gynaixin* [Luke 1:42]). Again, the preposition matters. Neither Elizabeth nor Luke sets up Mary as an idyllic icon impossible for other women to even approximate. The whole point of the Elizabeth-Mary exchange stresses their common female-maternal-spirited bond.[51]

Elisabeth Schüssler Fiorenza creatively employs Mary's hill country trek "as a hermeneutical metaphor and interpretive key for a critical feminist theology." She characterizes this long march as "an arduous intellectual journey, guided by a critical hermeneutics of suspicion."[52] This image fits nicely with Mary's portrait as an actively thinking, questioning agent. But doubt and suspicion do not override the entire train of thought. Schüssler Fiorenza stresses that the *hilly* topography typifies both "the 'ups and downs' of feminist struggles for liberation," as opposed to the more dire and desolate spatial images of *wilderness* and *minefield.* Hope still pulses in the hills where women can "meet on their own terms and in their own space" — as with Mary and Elizabeth, who share "the joyous embrace of two women pregnant with the possibilities of new life" and showcase "the protective strength and communicative power of women talking to and blessing each other."[53]

This emphasis on women's *mutual* instruction and benediction is reinforced by Mary's famous Magnificat, which immediately follows Elizabeth's blessing and, for all its soaring exaltation of God and reconfiguration of social hierarchies, is first and foremost addressed *to Elizabeth in Elizabeth's home,* where Mary remains for three months (1:56). The Magnificat solidifies the bond between God and God's female cocreators of God's prophetic agents.

But Mary also proves to be a prophet in her own right.[54] The Lord speaks through her, as he has done through Elizabeth and will do through John and Jesus. This Miriam need not fear the dreadful silencing of her an-

---

51. On this Mary-Elizabeth bond in Luke 1 viewed as a "gynocentric text," see Richard Bauckham, *Gospel Women: Studies of Named Women in the Gospels* (Grand Rapids: Eerdmans, 2002), 47-76.

52. Schüssler Fiorenza, *Jesus,* 33; cf. 33-63.

53. Schüssler Fiorenza, *Jesus,* 33-34.

54. See Gaventa, *Mary,* 55-59, 73.

cient namesake.[55] Of course, far from speaking "against [the Lord's] servant" as Miriam and Aaron did against Moses (Num 12:8), Miriam of Nazareth reinforces her own status as the Lord's "servant/slave" (Luke 1:48) and rejoices in the Lord's merciful aid to "his servant Israel" (1:54). This Miriam knows her subordinate place, indeed, accentuates it by noting the particular "lowliness" *(tapeinōsis)* of her slave position (1:48). As such she seems to settle deep into the servile mode she began to assume at the end of her encounter with Gabriel and to shrink back from any independent, self-determining agency she asserted. But three factors mitigate such a restrictive reading.

First, the role of servant/slave/minister, variously designated by *diakonos, doulos, pais* and cognates, represents for Luke the quintessential, "greatest" vocation for all of God's people — highborn or lowborn, male or female — including Jesus, who announces to his male disciples at the Lord's Supper: "The greatest among you must become like the youngest, and the leader like one who serves *(diakonōn)*. . . . I am among you as one who serves *(diakonōn)*" (22:26-27). The conjoining of *youth* with *servanthood* in this text only enhances Mary's identity as a model disciple. To be sure, women in Luke's narratives, as in society generally, accept servant roles more readily than men — often because they have little choice in male-dominated structures — but this status quo is challenged as much as defended by Luke. While the twelve apostles repeatedly jockey for lordly honor and standing typical of "the Gentiles" (22:25), their Lord Jesus exhorts them to follow a different path ("But not so with you" [22:26]), the way of sacrificial service embodied by him and his mother.[56]

Second, Mary exclaims that her "lowly" state, far from being taken for granted, is the object of the Lord's special interest: "he looked/gazed upon *(epeblepsen epi)* the lowliness of his slave-woman" (1:48, my translation). Of course, the position of being looked *upon,* of being *under* the gaze of a dominant power, is fraught with potential danger for women's welfare and freedom. However, the only other use of *epiblepō* in Luke's writings relates to a desperate father's request that Jesus "look upon" his gravely afflicted son with compassion as well as power (9:38), which Jesus does, expelling the vi-

---

55. It is perhaps worth noting that Luke introduces Elizabeth as a "daughter of Aaron" (1:5) — this same Aaron who joined with sister Miriam in speaking against their brother Moses' marriage to a Cushite woman and claiming that the Lord speaks "through us also" (Num 12:1-2). However, when the Lord angrily defends "my servant Moses," only Miriam is smitten with leprosy and shunned by the community for a week (12:9-16).

56. See chapter 4 on Joanna for further discussion of women and men's servant roles in Luke.

cious spirit that had seized the boy (9:42-43). In the OT, the prayer of Hannah provides a close parallel related to childbearing: "Adonai, Lord ... if looking you will look on the humiliation of your slave *(epiblepōn epiblepsēs epi tēn tapeinōsin tēs doulēs sou)* and remember me and give to your slave an offspring of men ... I will give him as one devoted before you" (1 Sam 1:11).[57] Here the barren Hannah *invites* the Lord's attention to and involvement in her lowly state, which results in her desired conception and delivery of Samuel. Though Mary did not request the Lord's visitation, she joyously recognizes in it the same generative grace Hannah received.[58] And though the Lord's power remains dominant over his slave, it functions in a cooperative or collaborative as much as a co-optive or coercive way. Mary marvels how "the Mighty One has done great things for me *(moi)*" — which can also mean "in me" or "through me" (Luke 1:49). The fact is: God will not act unilaterally in bringing forth his Son on earth. God will work with cocreator Mary, which is also to say that Mary will work with God and that Mary herself will do great things acknowledged by "all generations" to come (1:48).

Third and most dramatically, as Mary's song modulates from a personal memoir of God's dealings with her (1:46-49) to a political manifesto of God's purpose for the world (1:50-55), it turns established power structures upside down:

> "[God] has brought down the powerful *(dynastas)* from their thrones,
> and lifted up the lowly *(tapeinous)*." (1:52)

From her own experience and reflection, Mary reaches a stunning theological conclusion: through the "Son of the Most High" she will bear, the Savior God will "lift up," not merely "look upon," all who are lowly like her and, indeed, topple the whole high/low hierarchy. The new era of God's "uplifting" reign is dawning with Mary arising as its first exemplar, prophet, and theologian. In full voice, there is no keeping Mary down now; the lowly slave girl has busted through the ceiling and opened the way for

---

57. Translation of LXX by Bernard A. Taylor, "1 Reigns (Old Greek)," in *A New English Translation of the Septuagint and the Other Greek Translations Traditionally Included under That Title* (ed. Albert Pietersma and Benjamin G. Wright; Oxford: Oxford University Press, 2007) (hereafter *NETS*), 249.

58. On the echoes between Hannah's song in 1 Sam 2:1-10 and Mary's Magnificat, see Raymond E. Brown, *The Birth of the Messiah: A Commentary on the Infancy Narratives in the Gospels of Matthew and Luke* (2nd ed.; New Haven: Yale University Press, 1993), 302, 335-36, 357-63, 647-50; Gail O'Day, "Singing Woman's Song: A Hermeneutic of Liberation," *Currents in Theology and Mission* 12 (1985): 203-10.

other lowly ones, female and male, to rise with her to positions of robust health and honor in God's just and merciful realm.[59] Of course, all these lifted ones will continue to serve as God's subjects, but they will do so in freedom and gratitude as servant partners of the "Most High" deity and not as slaves to any earthly masters.

As many have noted, Mary's Magnificat functions as a paradigmatic agenda of Jesus' messianic ministry throughout Luke's Gospel. As such, this young virgin and village girl of twelve, let us say, demonstrates remarkable vision, insight, boldness — and yes, *agency* — to proclaim the reordering of society under God's rule. The twelve-year-old Jesus will display a similar precociousness in the temple but will give no speech or song remotely rising to that which he heard in his mother's womb (2:46-49). And afterward, he will return to Nazareth and *subject himself under (hypotassomenos)*[60] Mary for the next eighteen years (2:51)! Not until he preaches in his hometown synagogue *at age thirty* does Jesus announce his programmatic mission statement, in terms resonant with Mary's song (4:16-30; cf. 3:23). If we assume Mary's presence in the audience, we might imagine her thinking: "Well, it's about time, Son!"

Mary's Maternity (Luke 2:1-21)

Thus far we have observed Mary's proactive-cooperative participation in managing and interpreting her conception and pregnancy with God's Son. But as "the time comes" in Luke's famous Christmas story "for her to deliver her child" (2:6), Mary's agency appears to diminish precipitously. The narrative begins with another journey; this one, however, *Mary does not choose and chart on her own*. Instead she is forced to travel at the worst possible time by dominant male authorities: Emperor Augustus and Governor Quirinius launch a realm-wide census — "a penetrating symbol of Roman overlordship"[61] — requiring Joseph to register in his ancestral Judean home with his very pregnant fiancée. Luke offers not a word concerning how Joseph found out or felt about Mary's shocking pregnancy, but in any

59. The health factor emerges in the exclamation, "[God] has filled the hungry with good things" (1:53).

60. If we continue our prepositional interest, here *hypo*, signifying "under," comes into play. But it is Jesus who places himself under Mary, not the other way around. See more on Luke 2:40-52 in the last section below.

61. Joel B. Green, *The Gospel of Luke* (Grand Rapids: Eerdmans, 1997), 122.

event, he functions as traditional paterfamilias and takes Mary to Bethlehem.[62] At least he doesn't abandon her (or worse) in her precarious condition, and he has little choice himself but to comply with the census edict. But for her part, Mary seems to have skidded back to the "lowest" rung on the social ladder and lost all control of her life to kyriarchal rule (emperor, governor, groom), which has literally reduced her to a number, if she counts at all in the census records.[63]

Nevertheless, though Mary remains firmly embedded in her social world, she is not paralyzed therein. While in Bethlehem, she reemerges as an active agent of God's saving purpose. The forces that impelled her to Bethlehem at this time have unwittingly "fulfilled"[64] God's plan for the true Lord's birth in the city of David (2:11). God orchestrates the proceedings, but at the critical "time" Mary executes them. Mary is the generative subject of all the action: "*she* [1] gave birth to *her* firstborn son [no Joseph, no midwife, no other assistant] and [2] wrapped him in bands of cloth [a customary gesture of protective care], and [3] laid him in a manger [an exceptional, but in this case expedient, move] because there was no place for them in the inn" (2:7). These are all fully physical, embodied acts on Mary's part; this is all her doing — her *labor* — unmitigated by anesthetic, unaided by supernatural power.[65]

62. François Bovon stresses the "shocking" nature of this trek in *Luke 1: A Commentary on the Gospel of Luke 1:1–9:50* (trans. Christine M. Thomas; Minneapolis: Fortress, 2002), 85: "It is shocking for the readers that a bride-to-be is traveling with her fiancé and is, beyond this, pregnant. . . . The shocking character of the pregnant bride-to-be who travels with her fiancé should not be smoothed over; it is provoked by Luke."

63. "He went to be registered *with Mary*" (2:5) may imply her individual enrollment in the census, rather than simply her accompaniment of Joseph. Though he leaves the matter open, Brown (*Birth of the Messiah*, 396-97) notes that Mary's registration "is not an impossibility in Roman practice."

64. See Luke 2:6: "While they were there, the days were *completed* [or *fulfilled* (*eplēsthēsan*)] for her to give birth" (NASB). This sense of time fulfillment with the verb *pimplēmi* runs through Luke's birth narrative: see 1:23; 2:6, 21, 22; cf. 21:22.

65. In marked contrast to the miraculous, nongynecological birth of Jesus in a cave, witnessed by Joseph and a midwife, reported in the *Infancy Gospel of James* 19:15-17: "Suddenly the cloud withdrew from the cave and an intense light appeared inside the cave, so that their eyes could not bear to look. And a little later that light receded until an infant became visible; he took the breast of his mother Mary. Then the midwife shouted: 'What a great day this is for me because I've seen this new miracle!'" (cf. 11:5-7; 19:18–20:12; trans. Hock, *Infancy Gospels*, 67). On the sharp disjunction between the portraits of Mary of Luke and of the *Infancy Gospel of James*, see Mary F. Foskett, "Virginity as Purity in the *Protoevangelium of James*," in *Feminist Companion to Mariology* (ed. Levine and Robbins), 67-76.

Beyond their utilitarian function, the last two operations serve a key semiotic purpose in Luke's narrative as *the sign (to sēmeion)* for the shepherds' identification of the Christ child: "you will find a child wrapped in bands of cloth and lying in a manger" (2:12). Much could be explored concerning what the swaddling strips and feeding trough signify, but at base, from a biblical perspective, they suggest God's visitation of the world in the humblest, most common of circumstances.[66] The Davidic son figure in Wisdom of Solomon, for all his royal power and privilege, reflects on his ordinary, earthy roots:

> I also am mortal, like everyone else,
> a descendant of the first-formed child of earth;
> and in the womb of a mother I was molded into flesh,
> within the period of ten months, compacted with blood. . . .
> And when I was born, I began to breathe the common air,
> and fell upon the kindred earth;
> my first sound was a cry, as is true of all.
> *I was nursed with care in swaddling cloths.*
> For no king has had a different beginning of existence;
> there is for all one entrance into life, and one way out.[67]

Of course, common cloths are one thing for a royal infant; makeshift cribs are quite another. Mangers were scarcely the furniture of choice in prime birthing suites; they were designed for oxen, donkeys, and such, draft animals dependent on their owners for sustenance, as Isaiah observes:

> The ox knows its owner,
> > and the donkey its master's crib [or lord's manger *(phatnēn tou kyriou)*]. (Isa 1:3a)

Isaiah makes this quotidian point to set up a haunting theological contrast:

66. Cf. Byrne, *The Hospitality of God*, 32: "[Jesus'] birth takes place on the margins, beginning a pattern to be realized over and over in his life and ministry. The visitor from God [cf. 1:78], who could not find hospitality in his own city, will nonetheless institute in the world the hospitality of God. The poor, marginalized shepherds of Bethlehem will be the first to experience it."

67. Wis 7:1-6. I have omitted the phrase in 7:2b — "from the seed of a man and the pleasure of marriage" — which obviously does not apply to Jesus' supernatural conception. But otherwise Jesus' *birth* wholly follows normal human processes.

but Israel does not know [its Lord],
　my people do not understand. (1:3b)

Since Luke's writings are steeped in Isaianic language and thought,[68] it's hard not to imagine some resonance: through the manger-born Savior and Lord, God's wayward people will come to know and understand their divine Master/Lord anew.

And leading the way home is Mary, "the mother of my Lord *(kyriou)*" (Luke 1:43), who already knows God's redemptive plan and posts the signs — with messianic child, swaddling cloths, and manger-crib — for the first wave of restored exiles, as it were: a band of roving shepherds working the graveyard shift. They come "with haste," matching Mary's earlier pace (1:39), and find "Mary and Joseph, and the child lying in the manger" (notice who's listed first now, as Joseph's head!) (2:16).[69] The angelic chorus may provide the musical background for this scene, but Mary's Magnificat still reverberates loud and clear with accents on lifting the lowly and leveling hierarchies. Nomadic herdsmen, not aristocratic nabobs, first attend this king. And while the shepherds may take the lead in broadcasting the good news of God's visitation (2:17-18, 20), Mary takes precedence in delivering, nurturing, and displaying the Christ child they extol.

Moreover, though silent throughout 2:1-20, Mary's central role relative to the report of Jesus' birth becomes evident at the story's conclusion in 2:18-20.

People: And *(kai)* all who heard it were amazed at what the shepherds told them (2:18).

Mary: But *(de)* Mary treasured *(syneterei)* all these words *(rhemata)* and pondered *(symballousa)* them in her heart (2:19).

Shepherds: [And *(kai)*] the shepherds returned, glorifying and praising God for all they had heard and seen, as it had been told them (2:20).

The headline news of Israel's long-expected Savior-Messiah-Lord — conveyed by the angel/heavenly host to the shepherds and, in turn, by these

---

68. See James A. Sanders and Craig A. Evans, *Luke and Scripture: The Function of Sacred Scripture in Luke-Acts* (Eugene, Oreg.: Wipf and Stock, 2001); David W. Pao, *Acts and the Isaianic New Exodus* (Grand Rapids: Baker, 2002). On Isa 1:3 and Wis 7:4-5 as texts informing Luke's manger/swaddling clothes "sign," see Byrne, *The Hospitality of God*, 32 n. 3.

69. Green, *The Gospel of Luke*, 138.

shepherds to "all who heard" — provokes this general audience's astonishment and the shepherds' continuing adulation of God. Such responses — amazement and excitement — are well and good, as far as they go, but fall short of the deepest levels of faith and understanding, of coming to "know the [full] truth concerning the things about which you have been instructed" (1:4).[70] There is a lot to take in here that cannot be absorbed all at once. If the Christ child himself is going to have to "grow in wisdom" to grasp fully his relationship with God and people (2:40, 52), then so must every other character in Luke.

And Mary leads the way in this learning process. Spliced between the amazed auditors and awe-filled shepherds is the ever attentive and reflective mother of Jesus. Yet again, a related pair of verbs with shared prepositional prefixes characterizes Mary's response: *syntereō* and *symballō*. The *syn/sym* preposition suggests Mary's determined striving to "pull/get it all together,"[71] to interpret and integrate all the new words and events *(rhēmata)*[72] she's encountered in Bethlehem into a coherent whole. More specifically, *syntereō* connotes "keeping with concern"[73] or "receiving and retaining the event, as much the deed that one sees as the words one hears."[74] It implies a deep emotional and intellectual engagement with matters beyond what the sappy translation — "Mary treasured all these

70. On Luke 2:18, see the comment by Frederick W. Danker, *Jesus and the New Age: A Commentary on St. Luke's Gospel* (rev. ed.; Philadelphia: Fortress, 1988), 61: "Their listeners 'wondered' *(thaumazō),* a normal response to description of divine actions (cf. Luke 1:21, 63) but not necessarily indicative of faith (cf. Acts 3:12). Wonderment can even be associated with unbelief (Luke 24:41). The contrast with Mary's response (v. 19) suggests that the person of Jesus will be subject to misunderstanding (cf. 4:22-24; 8:25; 9:43-45; 11:14-16)."

71. Cf. the nuance of *symballō* as "trying to get it all together" in Danker, *Jesus,* 61, and Walter Bauer, Frederick W. Danker, W. F. Arndt, and F. W. Gingrich, *A Greek-English Lexicon of the New Testament and Other Early Christian Literature* (3rd ed.; Chicago: University of Chicago Press, 2000) (hereafter BDAG), 956; also, applied to Mary, as "tossing them together in her heart," in Joseph A. Fitzmyer, *The Gospel according to Luke I–IX: Introduction, Translation, and Notes* (New York: Doubleday, 1981), 413. The imperfect *(synetērei)* and present *(symballousa)* verb forms connote continuing contemplation on Mary's part, counterpoised with the indeterminate aspects of the aorist verbs conveying the shepherds' responses in the previous verse.

72. On *rhēma* in this context as signifying the whole word-and-act *(Wort und Tat)* complex of the angel's revelation, see W. C. van Unnik, "Die Rechte Bedeutung des Wortes Treffen, Lukas II 19," in *Sparsa Collecta: The Collected Essays of W. C. Van Unnik,* part 1: *Evangelia, Paulina, Acta* (Leiden: Brill, 1973), 86-87.

73. Brown, *Birth of the Messiah,* 406.

74. Bovon, *Luke 1,* 92.

words . . . in her heart *(kardia)*" — suggests.[75] Mary is not gushing with some sentimental maternal pride over her special boy the angels and shepherds have just exalted (she will cherish this tender moment forever). That reflects more our modern, mushy Christmas spirit than the Lukan Mary's state. Far from feeling warm fuzzies about the shepherds' revelations about Jesus, Mary holds on to them like a wrestler, probing them, mulling them, trying to wrench from them their thick meaning.

She functions as no less than a dedicated sage, described by Jesus ben Sira (though he limits the office to males), poring over God's mysterious decrees:

> How different the one who devotes himself
>   to the study of the law of the Most High!
> He seeks out the wisdom of all the ancients,
>   and is concerned with prophecies;
> he *preserves (syntērēsei)* the sayings [or narrative *(diēgēsin)*][76] of the
>   famous
>   and *penetrates (syneiseleusetai)* the subtleties of parables;
> he seeks out the hidden meanings of proverbs
>   and is at home with the obscurities of parables. (Sir 38:34b–39:3)

The parallel structure links "preserving" information with "penetrating"[77] its subtle significance — more specifically, preserving "the narrative" of heroic figures with penetrating the nuances of "parables." As it happens, Luke's opening verse identifies the entire account as a "narrative" (*diēgēsin* [1:1]), which, as it unfolds, will focus on the singular hero of the Lord Jesus and his revelation of God's wisdom through numerous challenging, and sometimes obscure, parables (cf. 8:9-10). Interpreting this Gospel thus requires patient, penetrating sifting of its subtle meanings and messages — precisely that exemplified by Jesus' mother Mary.

The second verb describing Mary's response, *symballō*, carries similar overtones of deep, delving analysis. Moreover, as van Unnik concludes, the term emerges in Hellenistic contexts stressing the quest for "the correct

---

75. See the assessment of this NRSV rendering in Gaventa, "'All Generations Will Call Me Blessed,'" 127: "So the New Revised Standard Version translates, suggesting that Mary was simply storing up sweet memories. But the evangelists are not usually sentimental, and what Mary does is not so much to 'treasure' as to 'ponder,' to 'reflect,' to 'worry.'"

76. Benjamin Wright, "Sirach," in *NETS*, 751; otherwise this citation is from the NRSV.

77. *Syneiseleusetai* (from *syneiserchomai*): another *syn-* verb plus *eis* — literally, "coming/going in together."

meaning" *(die rechte Bedeutung)* of some divine sign or message in the face of multiple, ambiguous interpretive options.[78] This is no mere meditative exercise, but rather a deliberate, determined act of problem solving and discerning the significance of God's dealings with the world. Far from day-dreaming or musing about curious events, Mary engages her mind and "heart" — the center of will and purpose as well as thought and emotion — to ascertain the solid truth.[79]

As her "dynamic" investigation of complex divine words/acts aligns Mary with *sages* like Ben Sira,[80] it also associates her with *patriarchs* like Jacob, *seers* like Daniel, and *priests* like Levi and Josephus who struggled to understand *(syntereō/symballō)* puzzling dreams and visions.[81]

- While Joseph's brothers responded with jealousy to his lofty dream, father Jacob, though perplexed at the prospect that he and Joseph's mother would bow down and serve their son, nonetheless "closely watched the matter" *(dietērēsen to rhēma)* (Gen 37:10-11).[82]
- In the wake of his tumultuous kingdom visions, culminating in the coming of "a son of man," Daniel reports: "My thoughts were greatly troubling me, and my appearance was changed, and I kept the matter in my heart" *(en tē kardia mou synetērēsa)* (Dan 7:28).[83] Such mental and physical upheaval pushes way beyond quiet reflection.
- After an angel unveils to him the enthroned "Holy Most High" and then provides a sword and shield that he must use to "perform vengeance on Shechem for the sake of Dinah, your sister," the priestly patriarch Levi remarks: "And I guarded these words in my heart" *(synetēroun tous logous toutous en tē kardia mou)* (*Testament of Levi* 5:1–6:2).[84] And

---

78. Van Unnik, "Rechte Bedeutung," 75-91.

79. Cf. Luke's purpose for writing his narrative in 1:4, which may be rendered: "that you may know the solidity/solid truth *(asphaleian)* of the things you were taught."

80. Cf. van Unnik's comment ("Rechte Bedeutung," 89) that Ben Sira promotes a study of sacred writings that is "not something static, but dynamic" *(nicht etwas Statisches, sondern etwas Dynamisches).*

81. See van Unnik, "Rechte Bedeutung," 84-90; Danker, *Jesus,* 61.

82. The verb used here, *dietēreō,* is a close cognate of *syntereō* and also designates Mary's pondering in Luke 2:51. See van Unnik, "Rechte Bedeutung," 89; Brown, *Birth of the Messiah,* 406, 429-30.

83. Theodotion's (TH) Greek text; trans. R. Timothy McLay, "Daniel," in *NETS,* 1014.

84. Translated by H. C. Kee, "Testaments of the Twelve Patriarchs," in *The Old Testament Pseudepigrapha,* vol. 1: *Apocalyptic Literature and Testaments* (ed. James H. Charlesworth; Garden City, N.Y.: Doubleday, 1983), 789-90.

straightaway, he moves to put "these words" into action by slaying Shechem. Levi's heart and hand are intimately connected.

- Hunted by Roman forces during the Jewish War, the priest and military commander Josephus recalls repeated dreams in which God predicted his people's defeat at the hands of Vespasian. With his back against the wall, Josephus proceeds "to interpret the matters ambiguously communicated by God" *(symbalein ta amphibolōs hypo tou theiou legomena) (Jewish War* 3.352; cf. 3.340-354). Clearly, the desperate situation calls for more than "throwing together" *(symbalein)* or "kicking around" a few ideas. This is a crucial time for correct decision and action. Josephus must press through the ambiguities and figure out just what God means and aims for him to do.

These last two examples intimate that the *syn/sym* verbs applied to Mary in Luke 2:19 shade beyond cognitive reminiscence toward active obedience, toward "keeping God's commandments in one's heart."[85] The intent of such Torah keeping is always productive rather than simply preservative, behavioral more than archival; not just hearing but *heeding* God's word. Later in Luke, Jesus will stress this point, interestingly enough, in juxtaposition with an anonymous woman's adulation of mother Mary: "While he was saying this, a woman in the crowd raised her voice and said to him, 'Blessed is the womb that bore you and the breasts that nursed you!' But he said, 'Blessed rather are those who hear the word of God and obey it!'" (11:27-28).

Mary's "blessedness" derives not only, or primarily, from serving as a vehicle for Jesus' birth or faucet for his nourishment, but from her active engagement with God's words and deeds. Along with her functional womb and breasts, she uses her faithful mind and heart — and indeed her whole self — to interpret the signs of the times and to act upon them. Although no angel directs her to do anything this time, Mary does not just sit around musing about the shepherds' visit and report. Her careful exegesis of the situation prompts her to action — circumcising and naming her infant son Jesus or "Savior." To be precise, Luke does not explicitly attribute the circumcision/naming ritual to Mary's initiative. But who else would have known "the name given by the angel before he [Jesus] was conceived in the womb" (2:21; cf. 1:31)? We are thus brought back full circle to the annuncia-

---

85. This usage of *syntēreō* in the context of law keeping or commandment keeping is prominent in Sirach: see 2:15; 6:26; 13:12; 15:15; 35:1; 37:12; 44:20.

tion: God chooses Mary and generates divine life in her virgin womb by the Holy Spirit. But from that point on, Mary chooses to receive this dynamic word, reflect upon it, nurture it, bring it to fruition, put it into action — and to do it all deliberately and diligently in difficult circumstances.

Mary's Destiny (Luke 2:22-40)

Within a month or so, Mary is back on the road again, heading this time to the temple in Jerusalem to fulfill the dual requirements of *purification* and *presentation,* prescribed by Jewish law (2:22). Mary continues to exhibit relative freedom of movement and resolute faithfulness to God's will. Though Luke does not do the math here, we can chart "the time" of Mary's purification (2:22), according to Leviticus, thirty-three days following her initial seven-day "unclean" period after bearing a male child (circumcised on the eighth day) or, in other words, *forty days* after giving birth (Lev 12:1-4). Otherwise, Luke accentuates momentous events for Jesus and Moses in forty-day (and forty-year) increments (cf. Luke 4:1-2; Acts 1:3-5; 7:23, 30, 36).

As with the Bethlehem journey, Mary is again accompanied by Joseph and the infant Jesus. The baby is brought for "presentation" or "dedication," consecrating the "firstborn male . . . as holy *(hagion)* to the Lord" (Luke 2:23; cf. Exod 13:1-2, 11-13; 34:19-20). Again we notice Mary's active confirmation of Gabriel's plan, in this case the stipulation that "the child to be born [to you] will be holy *(hagion)*" (Luke 1:35). However, Mary's initiative in these proceedings is blunted somewhat by Luke's report that "*they* [i.e., Mary and Joseph] brought him [Jesus] up to Jerusalem to present him to the Lord . . . and *they* offered a sacrifice" (2:22-24). Also, Luke seems to push this shared activity to the breaking point with his curious reference to "*their (autōn)* purification" (2:22).

Excuse me? *Their* purification? *Presentation* focuses on the child. *Purification* functions *only* with respect to the woman, *only* the mother who has given her own blood supply to nurture the fetus and then shed her blood, at considerable risk to her own life, to bring forth the child into the world. Her resultant "impurity" is not sinfulness in any sense. Quite the contrary, it marks her numinous and ominous proximity with sacred borders of life and death; the bleeding, birthing woman shares God's creative work in the most intimate way possible for a human being. Accordingly, such a glorious — and precarious — physical and spiritual state demands ritual representation, symbolizing the mother's set-apartness from and reconstitution (purification) of "normal" relations with the Most Holy God and God's covenant people. The baby Jesus needs no such purification: he's "the one who opened or broke through the womb" (*dianoigon mētran,* literal rendering of "firstborn" [2:23])[86] into a separate existence outside his mother; his "holy" dedication to God must simply be confessed ("every firstborn male *will be called* [*klēthēsetai*] holy to the Lord" [2:23, my translation]), rather than reconstituted and certified with an offering in the sanctuary. In other words, the baby Jesus is "presented," not "purified." As for Joseph, he's had nothing to do with Jesus' conception in or parturition from Mary's womb, and thus has no need for purification or any other act.[87] He's merely along for the rite.

So we keep asking: Why *their* purification? Some scribal variants substitute "her" or even "his" (oddly) for "their"; but the manuscript evidence strongly supports the plural reading. Perhaps Luke is a bit muddled about fine points of Jewish ritual observance.[88] In any case, the language may suggest nothing more than a general collective response: this is a devout, traditional family — (step)father, mother, and son — intent on raising the child Jesus according to Jewish law. Fine and good — nothing glaringly suspicious here. We might even interpret the situation, in Nussbaum's terms, as a positive example of Mary's capacity for *affiliation,* of "being able to live with and toward others . . . to engage in various forms of social interaction . . . having the social bases of self-respect and non-humiliation; being able to be treated as a dignified being whose worth is equal to that of others."[89] If Joseph and Jesus, then, somehow embrace Mary's purification

---

86. Clearly this indicates a normal physical birth by natural means — no mystical, miraculous escape of Jesus from Mary's body.

87. Even if Joseph has been the natural father, no purification would have been required.

88. See the careful discussion of the legal issues in Brown, *Birth of the Messiah,* 436, 447-51, 682-84; Bovon, *Luke 1,* 98-99.

89. I'm not sure, however, that Nussbaum would assess this situation in these terms, given the complication that Mary still bears the full brunt of restoring *her* purity status from the "polluting" (defiling) effects of *her* placental bleeding. For all our qualifications that impurity is not sinfulness and that Jewish purity legislation attempted to regulate the sacred borders between life and death, some degree of stigma still seems attached to impurity — with tendencies toward *disgust* even, especially related to discharges of blood and other bodily fluids. Of course, as Levitical law makes clear, this is not just a women's issue: males produce their own share of "disgusting," impure flows and oozes. On the complex issues affecting human dignity surrounding shame and disgust, see studies by Nussbaum: *Upheavals of Thought,* 200-206, 220-22, 346-50; *Hiding from Humanity: Disgust, Shame, and the Law*

as "their" own, are they not according her a certain respect and dignity by association? Maybe . . .

But then again, there was no collective declaiming of the Magnificat, delivering of Jesus, or deliberating about the shepherds' visit: these were not group projects, but rather exclusively involved *Mary's* voice, womb, and heart. Why the change from *"her"* to *"their"* now? Does this commence a subtle absorbing, and thus obscuring, of Mary's individual agency and identity into the family unit dominated by husband and son? The issue is fundamental for men's response to women's rights and feminist concerns. Do we — Luke, Joseph, Jesus, male readers today — genuinely *cooperate* with and *support* women's aspirations and actions, to the extent we can; or do we effectively *co-opt* them as our own, when convenient, and thus *abort* their fulfillment? Joseph would scarcely be the first or last man to assume more credit than he was due for producing and nurturing an exceptional son: "That's my boy!" And conversely, if things don't work out so well, the blame is quickly shifted: "Oh, he just a mama's boy" (and in Joseph's case, maybe only to himself: "he's not really *my* boy anyway").

We know, of course, that Luke's narrative trumpets Jesus above all others, including his mother Mary. But is stepfather Joseph also about to leave Mary in the shade? Before we can answer that question, another man comes into the spotlight at the Christ child's dedication: an elderly, devout, Spirit-filled prophet named Simeon, who takes the baby in his arms and breaks into song about his own and the child's destinies (2:25-32). Is this yet a further displacement of Mary's parental and prophetic roles? Not entirely. Identifying himself, like Mary, as the Lord's "slave" *(doulos),* Simeon happily signals his own imminent exit from the stage (he only makes a cameo appearance), and his Nunc Dimittis, much shorter than Mary's Magnificat, echoes Mary's accent on the fulfillment of Israel's salvation through the Messiah Jesus (2:26, 29-32).[90] It seems fair to say that Simeon more supports than supplants Mary's hymn.

This supporting role becomes clearer in Simeon's prophetic oracle fol-

---

(Princeton: Princeton University Press, 2004); *From Disgust to Humanity: Sexual Orientation and Constitutional Law* (Oxford: Oxford University Press, 2010).

90. Simeon, via Isaiah, stresses more explicitly than Mary God's shining a guiding "light for revelation to the Gentiles" (Luke 2:32; cf. Isa 49:6), though the blessing of all peoples of the earth is implied in Mary's reference to God's covenant with Abraham (Gen 12:1-3; Luke 1:55). This luminous messianic-salvation theme also resounds in Zechariah's Benedictus (Luke 1:68-79).

lowing his praise canticle. Though blessing both "the child's father and mother" (reestablishing the father's patriarchal position) who both "were amazed"[91] at what had been uttered (Mary still doesn't have it all figured out), Simeon directs his final words about the Christ child to "his mother Mary" alone, securing her attention, as Gabriel did, with the interjection "Look *(idou)!*" (omitted in NRSV [2:33-34]). And the central component of Simeon's three-part oracle pointedly concerns *Mary's destiny,* with Joseph fading again into the deep background.

> Look *(idou),* this child is destined for the falling and rising of many *(pollōn)* in Israel, and to be a sign that will be opposed.
>
> And for you, too *(kai sou de),* a sword will pierce your own soul *(psychēn),*
>
> so that *(hopōs)* the thoughts *(dialogismoi)* of many hearts *(pollōn kardiōn)* will be revealed. (2:34-35 [my translation])

Far from being isolated (marginalized) as a parenthesis (KJV; RSV) or addendum (NRSV; NIV)[92] to Simeon's prophecy, Mary stands as its centerpiece, her destiny intertwined with that of Jesus and the "many," the hoi polloi in Israel. While singled out for special mention, she is not ensconced on some unique pedestal. Her "blessedness" continues among, rather than apart from, the people, but still as an individual woman and mother with "her own soul," not as an iconic, representative figure — whether Daughter of Zion, Mother of Israel, or some other image.[93] She remains prominent and central to God's plan *as* Mariam of Nazareth, not as some idealized model of Womankind.

Moreover, it now becomes shockingly clear that Mary's "blessed" state will include experiences of conflict and suffering. Far from being cocooned in some simplistic prosperity-theology bliss, Mary will feel sharp pangs like a sword ripping through her inner being. Yet these painful experiences are

---

91. The verb is *thaumazō,* which also denoted the audience's amazement over the shepherds' report in 2:18. While, as noted above, Mary's more perceptive response in 2:19 counterpointed the people's less discriminating astonishment, we now see that Mary, too, can be overwhelmed with amazement at certain times.

92. The NRSV completely obscures the central focus of Simeon's prophecy on Mary in the Greek text by reversing the second and third components. As in 2:18-20, here in 2:34-35 Luke presents an envelope A-B-A structure with Mary in the middle slot.

93. Cf. Brown, *Birth of the Messiah,* 465: "Mary is not personifying Israel because most of Israel will fall; rather Mary here is part of Israel, to be tested like the rest" (cf. 687-88).

still somehow part of God's blessed purpose. How so? The flanking points of Simeon's oracle fill out the picture.

First, the aged prophet announces that Mary's child will represent an objectionable "sign" *(sēmeion)*, precipitating the "falling and rising of many in Israel." This is the flip side of the sign revealed to the shepherds. Jesus the Messiah bears a sandwich board, as it were, proclaiming on one side the good news of salvation for lowly shepherd-types, signified by the swaddling clothes and manger (2:12), and on the other side the more discriminating sentence of judgment and reversal, signified by a seesaw, upside-down effect. Where the first sign inspired "great joy" (2:10), the second will strike a woeful chord for some, specifically, for those who will stumble, trip, and "fall" over God's messianic plan they refuse to see. *And Mary will feel the piercing pain of their demise*, not because of her own "fall" with them, but because of her deep awareness of the piston-like mechanics of God's work, not to mention her natural maternal heartbreak over the opposition her son will face.[94] She has already vividly disclosed God's intent to *bring down the powerful* and *lift up the lowly* (1:52); while such a reordering of hierarchies and demolition of the social pyramid is ultimately for the cause of peace and justice, it is far from a smooth and painless process. Closer to home, Luke later stresses that Jesus' messianic "sword" will also cut through families and kinship groups, dividing even parents from children (12:49-53; 14:25-27).[95] The Nazareth synagogue scene at the outset of Jesus' ministry, which leads to his enraged relatives running him out of

94. Although Luke does not place Mary at the foot of cross, as we find in John 19:25-27, that does not deny the Lukan Mary's natural maternal response of pain and angst *(mater dolorosa)* over her son Jesus' sufferings. Cf. Gaventa, *Mary*, 66: "[T]he piercing of Mary at least *includes* the pain involved in the death of Jesus. . . . Mary's absence at the crucifixion does not mean that it does not concern her or that Luke is unaware of its implications for her" (emphasis in original).

95. Where the parallel Q text in Matt 10:34 states, "I have not come to bring peace, but a *sword*," Luke 12:51 reads, "No, I tell you, [I have not come to bring peace], but rather *division (diamerismon)*" — stressing the divisive, more than the destructive, force of Jesus' sword wielding. As for OT parallels, the language of the Lord's sword *"passing through"* matches Ezek 14:17, "Or if I bring a sword upon that land [Israel] and say, 'Let a sword *pass through* the land,' and I cut off human beings and animals from it . . .'" (cf. *Sibylline Oracles* 3:316). According to Brown (*Birth of the Messiah*, 464), this "image is of a selective sword of judgment, destroying some and sparing others, a sword for discrimination and not merely for punishment (Ezek 5:1-2; 6:8-9; 12:14-16)" and "is perfectly in harmony with the Lucan thought in 3:34c where the child is set for the fall and rise of many in Israel" (cf. 12:51-53). While I grant Luke's stress on the divisive/discriminating sword, I do not think that Luke presses the destructive/retributive dimension ("cutting off") as strongly as Ezekiel does.

town (4:28-30), has to break Mary's heart, though Luke does not report her response. Perhaps she already had some inkling of this darker side of the messianic "sign" as she carefully weighed the angels'/shepherds' words and deeds "in her heart" (2:19). Tidings of "great joy" and "peace on earth" will not tell the whole story.[96] Christmas is not all peace and light. Mary exhibits an intellectual and emotional range wide enough to envelop the complex whole of God's salvific project.

Finally, Simeon connects Mary's soul-searching and soul-stabbing experience with the climactic unveiling *(apokalyphōsin)* of many people's "inner thoughts" *(dialogismoi)*. The precise causal link ("so/in order that" [*hopōs*]) remains ambiguous, but in some fashion, Mary's psychic turmoil expresses and exposes others' hearts and minds. Some scholars resist any association between Mary's struggles and others' *dialogismoi*, because, they argue, this term for "inner thoughts" appears in negative contexts elsewhere in Luke, referring to dubious thoughts by either disputatious scribes and Pharisees (5:22; 6:8) or ambitious or tremulous disciples (9:46-47; 24:38). Since Mary does not entertain such questionable thoughts in Luke, she could scarcely prompt others to have them.[97] But the matter is not quite so cut and dried. In fact, as we have seen, Mary did "think through" the perplexing angelic announcement "dialogically," reflected in the close verbal form, *dialogizomai* (1:29). She had considerable doubts and questions that, however, she worked "through," with Gabriel's instructional help, to come to a position of fuller faith and understanding. There is nothing inherently wrong with engaging in theological arguments or expressing personal doubts, even when they are wrongheaded! In every case where the Lukan Jesus encounters such responses, he fires back not simply with derision or dismissal ("How stupid to reason that way!"), but with corrective counterarguments designed to change misdirected minds. Asking probing questions is a noble and necessary path to "knowing the truth" (1:4) of God's revelation, provided that one is open to fresh insight and transformation. Bland airheaded acceptance of untested claims (well, okay . . . if you say so) is no better than blind pigheaded resistance to clarified revelation (that just can't be true!). Mary sets a standard of "dia-

---

96. In fact, Jesus' announcement in Luke 12:51 — "Do you think that I have come to bring peace to the earth? No!" — poses a shocking counterpoint to the angelic host's proclamation of "peace on earth" to the shepherds in the wake of Jesus' birth (2:13-14).

97. E.g., Brown, *Birth of the Messiah*, 441, 465-66. Brown's wholly "positive" assessment of Mary's experience follows his reading of the Mary reference as "parenthetical" rather than integral or central to Simeon's oracle in 2:34-35, as I take it.

logic"[98] growth and maturity, even in her adolescence, challenging scribes, Pharisees, and disciples alike toward similar progressive thinking. Perhaps her pressing through where they bog down is how she "reveals" the deficiencies of their inner thoughts.

Following the poignant climax of Simeon's Mary-directed prophecy in 2:34-35, two brief units complete the presentation episode. First, fitting Luke's pattern of pairing male and female characters, the prophet Anna confirms Simeon's basic assessment of the infant Jesus' messianic, redemptive significance — though she utters no Spirit-inspired oracles of her own. We only hear Simeon's direct, authoritative voice throughout this incident. Ironically, however, while we hear nothing *from* Anna, we learn more *about* her than Simeon, namely: her family pedigree (daughter of Phanuel, tribe of Asher, longtime widow), age (eighty-four), and temple activity (persistent fasting and praying) (2:36-37). As Gaventa has observed, this notation of the elderly Anna's noble heritage and faithful history parallels Elizabeth's introductory profile (1:5-7), even as it *parts from Mary's.* Unlike with Elizabeth and Anna, we never learn of Mary's personal ancestry (Joseph provides the Davidic tie) or particular spiritual habits. Along with her contrasting youth, Mary's tabula rasa, so to speak, reinforces her lowly status and, as Gaventa stresses, "the inexplicable nature of her selection by God"[99] — a gesture of amazing grace. But I would also add that Mary's thin precharacterization in Luke, her lack of defining history and experience, highlights her individual agency in the story. She blossoms and develops before our eyes as a questioning, probing, prophe-

---

98. The classic formulation of dialogic processes of repeated questioning-and-answering that drive and shape all meaningful communication is that of Mikhail M. Bakhtin, *The Dialogic Imagination: Four Essays* (ed. Caryl Emerson and Michael Holquist; trans. Michael Holquist; Austin: University of Texas Press, 1981). For example: "The dialogic orientation of discourse is a phenomenon that is, of course, a property of *any* discourse. It is the natural orientation of any living discourse. On all its various routes toward the object, in all its directions, the word encounters an alien word and cannot help encountering it in a living, tension-filled interaction" (279); accordingly, "a passive understanding of linguistic meaning is no understanding at all" (281). As we have repeatedly seen, the Lukan Mary is no passive receptor of divine truth. On the implications of Bakhtin's dialogism for biblical interpretation, see Barbara Green, *Mikhail Bakhtin and Biblical Scholarship: An Introduction* (Atlanta: Society of Biblical Literature, 2000); Carol A. Newsom, "Bakhtin, the Bible, and Dialogic Truth," *Journal of Religion* 76 (1996): 290-306; L. Juliana M. Claassens, "Biblical Theology as Dialogue: Continuing the Conversation on Mikhail Bakhtin and Biblical Theology," *Journal of Biblical Literature* 122 (2003): 127-44.

99. Gaventa, *Mary,* 66.

sying, conceiving, delivering, purifying, presenting young woman, with a challenging, suspenseful destiny, tantalizingly laid out by Simeon, yet to unfold.

Moreover, in the second and final segment, the theme of character growth and development extends to the child Jesus upon the family's return home to Nazareth: "The child grew and became strong, filled with wisdom; and the favor of God was upon him" (2:40). For the first time in Luke, Jesus now becomes a thinking, acting agent in his own right. But since he remains under his parents' authority, the potential for a clash of agencies arises, especially with his mother whose agency and destiny are most wrapped up with his. And this is exactly what happens next — in the concluding episode of Luke's birth/childhood narrative — where Mary already begins to feel some of that sharp, soul-piercing distress Simeon had forecast.

Mary's Anxiety (Luke 2:41-52)

Luke flashes forward from Jesus' infancy to his puberty at twelve years old, roughly the same age as Mary when she encountered the angel Gabriel and conceived Jesus. For obvious physical reasons, this age, extending into the early teen years, marked a transition toward adulthood in ancient Jewish society, though males would not typically marry until closer to thirty.[100] It thus represents an apt time for Jesus to begin asserting his independence from his parents, even in a culture that highly valued family solidarity and lifelong honoring of one's mother and father. Jesus has now "grown and become strong" (2:40) enough to pit his will against theirs.

Not surprisingly, Jesus' growth coordinates with yet another journey from Galilee to Judea, this one a Passover pilgrimage from Nazareth to Jerusalem, as was the annual custom of Jesus' family (2:41-42). Of course, Jesus now walks on his own two feet, being carried neither in Mary's womb nor in her arms; on the return trip he opts not to walk with his parents at all, but rather to stay behind in the temple without informing them of his whereabouts (2:43). Assuming, reasonably, that Jesus was among the larger

---

100. See Philo, *On the Creation* 103-5 (cf. *Cherubim* 113). Philo draws on Solon and Hippocrates in dividing male development into seven-year stages. The second stage, ages seven to fourteen, culminates in puberty; the fifth stage, twenty-nine to thirty-five, is "the season of marriage."

caravan of kin and friends heading back to Galilee, Mary and Joseph do not worry about his "missing" status until a day into the journey.[101] On "amber alert," they launch a protracted, panicky search that ends "after three days," when they find the adolescent Jesus sitting in a seminar with the temple teachers (2:44-46). Consonant with the audience's "amazement" *(existēmi)* at Jesus' precocious "understanding" *(synesis)* of and responses to the scholars, his parents react with "astonishment" *(ekplēssō)* upon discovering their absent son (2:47-48).

Though such a reaction is often romanticized into a wide-eyed, awe-filled admiration of young Jesus' phenomenal wisdom (his parents must be so proud!), the ancient cultural context suggests a very different scenario. Respecting and submitting to one's parents and teachers constituted a basic tenet of the Jewish legal and wisdom tradition.[102] Yet in this case, an independent young man separated from his family, without their knowledge or permission, dares to take a seat among the distinguished religious elders and engage them in dialogue. Unlike Saul of Tarsus, who was formally "brought up in [Jerusalem] at the feet of Gamaliel," a venerated teacher of the Jewish law (Acts 22:3; cf. 5:34), the twelve-year-old Jesus seems to be more of an audacious interloper than an authorized student. In fact, he appears to be flouting the authority of both parents and teachers. Accordingly, his parents' "astonishment" *(ekplēssō)* upon finding him tilts more toward being "dumbfounded" or "shocked"[103] — even ashamed — at their son's behavior than being spellbound and overjoyed. A displaced son was a disgraced son, who brought shame on his family. Better that Jesus is "lost" in the temple with the scholars than in a "far country" with the pigs (cf. 15:11-32) — but not as much better as we might think.

That Jesus' parents are truly beside themselves with frustration rather than admiration is confirmed by Mary's response, speaking on behalf of both her and Joseph. It's nice to hear from Mary again and notable that she continues to assume a prominent role in the family. But Mary's brief speech here raises some concerns from a feminist perspective as the first words she speaks, after a long hiatus, since her substantial Magnificat, and as the last words she will utter in Luke's narrative. Put another way, these words — scarcely on the level of her powerful song — constitute Mary's

---

101. I build here on my discussion of this incident in F. Scott Spencer, *What Did Jesus Do? Gospel Profiles of Jesus' Personal Conduct* (Harrisburg, Pa.: Trinity, 2003), 32-36.

102. See, e.g., Exod 20:12; 21:15, 17; Lev 19:3; 20:9; Deut 5:16; 21:18-21; Prov 4:1-4; 19:26; 28:24; Sir 3:1-16; Mark 7:9-13; Luke 18:20.

103. BDAG, 308.

swan song in Luke, the final message left ringing in our ears.[104] Applying a "hermeneutics of conspiracy," feminist scholar Brigitte Kahl observes a marked tension between Mary's portraits in Luke 1 and 2, with the latter chapter muffling her former testimony and influence, "relegat[ing] [her] back into the old assignment to and submission under the acting and speaking men. Mary is no longer the one who believes, sets forth, and speaks; she is one who accompanies, listens, remembers."[105]

But this inner-textual "conspiracy" is not as patent as Kahl avers.[106] Mary's direct speech in Luke 2:48 evinces that she does not remain entirely mute after Jesus' birth, and these few final words, though more personal than prophetic, pack their own punch. She offers her own pointed opinion on Jesus' conduct: "Child *(teknon)*, why have you treated us like this? Look *(idou)*, your father and I have been searching for you in great anxiety" (2:48). These are not the words of a passive, submissive woman who has surrendered her will and agency to her son, however grown up and accomplished he may be. As Jesus begins to assert himself, Mary asserts back. He may be on the brink of manhood, but he remains her "child" *(teknon)*, obliged to give due attention *(idou)* to her, his mother, as she had given to the angel Gabriel and the prophet Simeon. He may be destined to be Lord and Christ, but that doesn't give him the right at age twelve to go and do as he pleases without consulting Mom and Dad. For all the differences between first-century Middle Eastern and twenty-first-century Western family values, parental angst about a missing child needs little translation. Jesus had no phone with which to call or text Mary about his independent plans, but he could have certainly gotten word to her somehow.

Mary responds as a fully embodied human agent: *intellectually,* asking for a rational explanation ("why [*ti*]?"); *actively,* "searching" three days for Jesus; and *emotionally,* "in great anxiety." The last component is particu-

104. Jesus' mother makes brief cameo appearances in Luke 8:19 and Acts 1:14 (only by name) and is alluded to by a woman in the crowd in Luke 11:27 — but Mary utters no words in the two-volume narrative after Luke 2:48.

105. Brigitte Kahl, "Reading Luke against Luke: Non-Uniformity of Text, Hermeneutics of Conspiracy and the 'Scriptural Principle' in Luke 1," in *A Feminist Companion to Luke* (ed. Amy-Jill Levine and Marianne Blickenstaff; London: Sheffield Academic, 2002), 84.

106. Cf. Turid Karlsen Seim, "The Virgin Mother: Mary and Ascetic Discipleship in Luke," in *A Feminist Companion to Luke* (ed. Levine and Blickenstaff), 95: "The concluding story in Lk. 2.41-51 about the 12-year-old Jesus . . . represents a major problem in Kahl's otherwise intriguing interpretation. It is the mother who at this point carries the voice of the parents and, furthermore, the introduction of a divine father and the belonging to this father's house happen at the cost of the father."

larly poignant: elsewhere in Luke's writing, the term for "great anxiety" *(odynaomai)* describes the rich man's "agony" in the flames of Hades (Luke 16:24-25) and the Ephesian elders' deep "grieving" over the departing Paul whom they thought they would never see again (Acts 20:38). We may thus capture the intensity of Mary's distress with the paraphrase: "Child, why have you put us through hell? We feared we may never see you again!" This is not some hysterical reaction on Mary's part. Again, any parent can easily sympathize. This simply reinforces Mary's profile in Luke as a full-blooded thinking, feeling, and acting subject, rather than a porcelain statue or iconic figure. The fact that she freely expresses such vigorous agency to Jesus at a stage where he begins to manifest his christological potential confirms a dynamic, dialogic dimension to her faith and understanding of God's will.

But where we might support Mary's impassioned challenge to her lost-and-found son, Jesus is not so congenial in return. He coolly counters his mother's question with two of his own: "Why *(ti)* were you searching for me? Did you not know that I must be *(dei)* about my Father's interests?" (Luke 2:49).[107] This retort represents the first words Jesus utters in Luke's Gospel. On one level, it reflects a typical adolescent chafing against parental authority — something like "You're not the boss of me," in today's lingo. But on another level, it introduces Jesus' self-conscious loyalty to a higher power and wider family, namely, that of his Father God.[108] This initial use of "must" *(dei)* in Luke stresses the inexorable divine mandate on Jesus' life,[109] and the reference to "my Father [God]" and "his interests" all but erases stepfather Joseph and puts mother Mary in a firmly subordinate place under Jesus' heavenly Patriarch. Moreover, the heretofore perceptive Mary seems to be no longer as "in the know" as she should be ("Did you not know!"), confirmed by the narrator's comment that Mary (and Joseph) "did not understand *(synēkan)* what [Jesus] said to them" (2:50). In fact, up to this point in the episode, only Jesus displays true "understanding" *(synesis* [2:47]). Suddenly, Mary's passionate exercise of agency and

107. Alternative NRSV reading in footnote — much preferable to the more traditional "in my Father's house." The Greek literally and vaguely reads, "I must be in/about the things of my Father *(en tois tou patros mou)*." There is no reference to "house."

108. Jesus' self-assertive rebuff to his mother here is somewhat similar to his cool rejoinder at the wedding at Cana in John 2:4: "Woman, what concern is that to you and to me?"

109. See Charles H. Cosgrove, "The Divine *Dei* in Luke-Acts: Investigations into the Lukan Understanding of God's Providence," *Novum Testamentum* 26 (1984): 168-90.

humanity — in challenging her disrespectful son — seems reduced to a pathetic exercise of ignorance and futility. Are we not driven back, then, to Kahl's suspicion of inner-Lukan conspiracy against Mary?

Not entirely. Human knowledge is never omniscient. As we have traced Mary's developing portrait in Luke, she has *grown* in knowledge through asking probing questions and deliberating about mysterious words and events; and even then, such deep reflection does not shut down the learning process, as if she has solved all the problems and secured all the answers, but rather leaves open rich possibilities of fresh insight and understanding. This is no slap at Mary's faithfulness, provided she persists in seeking the truth; quite the contrary, "growing in wisdom" or pursuing what we might call a lifelong journey in faith seeking understanding stands as a hallmark of discipleship in Luke's narrative. As noted above, the statement immediately preceding the account of the twelve-year-old Jesus' encounter with the temple teachers accents *his experience* of growing in wisdom (2:40). And even more remarkably, a similar assessment of Jesus' developing character also *concludes* this incident, in conjunction with *his obedient return to Nazareth* and *Mary's ongoing interpretation of "all these things"* (2:50-52). As Luke structures these final elements of the birth/ childhood stories, for the third time now we see Mary featured in a *central* position surrounded by others, in this case, Jesus.

> *Jesus:* Then he went down with them and came to Nazareth, and was obedient *(hypotassomenos)* to them (2:51a).
>
> *Mary:* His mother treasured *(dietērei)* all these things in her heart *(kardia)* (2:51b).
>
> *Jesus:* And Jesus increased in wisdom and in years, and in divine and hu-man favor (2:52).

As it comes on the heels of Jesus' brash self-assertion of independence from his parents and supreme obligation to his Father-God, it is stunning to see him returning home with his parents and, even more, placing him-self obediently under their authority *(hypotassomenos)*! For all his preco-ciousness before the temple teachers, he obviously still has much to learn (as 2:52 confirms) from his parents, no less, who "did not understand" what he had said or done in the temple. Clearly, they will not remain in the dark — especially Mary, who once more is touted as holding all these words and deeds deep inside, sifting "through" *(diatēreō)* their implications, and searching for the right meanings and applications.[110] Evidently, Jesus will have much to think and work through *with her* concerning his mission, which will not commence, according to Luke, for eighteen more years, at age thirty (3:23)!

It is unfortunate that Luke does not provide further details concerning these formative "hidden" years of Jesus' life, but he leaves the strong impression that Mary was actively, intellectually, and theologically engaged in them in a significant way — and in some measure, a *self-differentiating* way as well. Luke does *not* preface Jesus' return to Nazareth with the temple leaders' stress on Mary's blessed role as Jesus' mother, as we find in the *Infancy Gospel of Thomas:*

> Then the scholars and the Pharisees said, "Are you the mother of this child?"
>
> She said, "I am."
>
> And they said to her, "You more than any woman are to be congratulated, for God has blessed the fruit of your womb! For we've never seen nor heard such glory and such virtue and wisdom." (19:8-10)[111]

Luke agrees with this affirmation of Mary's blessedness as the bearer of the Christ child, as already voiced through Elizabeth and Mary herself (Luke 1:42-45, 48). But the Lukan Mary is not reduced simply to a womb-container that carried and delivered God's Son; and her identity, though inextricably bound up with Jesus', is not totally subsumed by him. Once he is born, she becomes no inert, passive mother figure merely basking in Jesus' glory. Mary's blessedness, from Luke's perspective, includes how she blesses Jesus — and thereby the world which God will save through Jesus — as much as how he blesses her. And she blesses Jesus and the world throughout Luke 1–2 as a fully embodied agent of and partner with God in her own right, freely exercising her own thoughts, feelings, and actions in probing and practicing God's will.

---

110. See the discussion above of the cognate verb *syntēreō*, in 2:19, with similar connotations of a concerted quest for understanding leading to faithful action.

111. Translated by Hock, *Infancy Gospels*, 143.

4. The Quest for the Historical Joanna: Follower of Jesus, Friend of Mary Magdalene, and Wife of Herod's Official (Luke 8:1-3; 24:10)

In assessing Jesus' attitudes toward and associations with women, scholars have reached a consensus regarding untenable, extreme positions. On the one end, despite his celibate lifestyle and close relationship with a dozen male companions, Jesus was no misogynist. He welcomed any woman, old or young, who pursued God's will as his intimate "mother" or "sister" (Mark 3:35); he ministered to women in need, especially those afflicted by illness and bereavement; and he exchanged hospitality, both feeding women and being hosted by them (Matt 14:21; 15:38; Luke 8:2-3; 10:38-42).[1] But, on the other end, Jesus was no feminist. However much he might have been ahead of his time, he did not jump two millennia on gender equality. He called God "Father" and twelve men to be his apostles and future judges of Israel (Matt 19:28//Luke 22:28-30); he rarely initiated contact with women and never explicitly called women to follow him;[2] and however much he might have laid the groundwork for an inclusive, servant-driven

1. In the Synoptic feeding miracles, only Matthew specifies that the multitudes included "women and children" (14:21; 15:38). Such an observation is reasonable: if thousands of men flocked to Jesus for feeding, healing, and teaching, surely many of their wives and children, as well as other needy women, also came.

2. In the Gospels, the only women Jesus reaches out to — without some prompting — are the widow at Nain and the bent-over woman in the synagogue in Luke 7:13-14 and 13:12-13, respectively, and the Samaritan woman at the well in John 4:7; and he is not beyond displaying some annoyance or resistance to women who seek him out, as with the hemorrhaging woman (Mark 5:27-32), the Syrophoenician/Canaanite mother (Mark 7:24-27//Matt 15:21:26), the mother of James and John (Matt 20:20-23), and even his own mother (John 2:3-4).

Many thanks to Amy-Jill Levine for her trenchant critique of an earlier draft.

community, it was insufficient to keep his followers from furthering patriarchal, hierarchical, and "kyriarchal" ecclesiastical structures in his name.[3]

Of course, between the poles of callous misogyny and radical feminism lies a wide range of options. Granting that Jesus' movement had a place for women but fell short of offering "equal opportunity" for leadership — the fact that Jesus was the charismatic head of this movement restricted "democratic" enterprise for both men and women[4] — I seek to clarify the roles women played in his mission under two categories:

Master-Disciple Relations

- Did Jesus attract women to follow him "on the road" as well as "in their hearts"? If so, what kind of itinerary did Jesus and women share (local excursions, day trips, overnight missions)?
- Did Jesus precipitate women's separation from their husbands and households in order to follow him? Alternatively, did Jesus' calling men leave women as householders?

Patron-Client Relations

- What did women receive from Jesus by way of aid or assistance? What did Jesus do for women? Why were women attracted to Jesus?

3. In numerous writings, Elisabeth Schüssler Fiorenza has exposed the biblical world's (and our own) "patriarchal, or better kyriarchal (i.e., lord, slave-master, father, elite male domination), values and visions" (*Wisdom Ways: Introducing Feminist Biblical Interpretation* [Maryknoll, N.Y.: Orbis, 2001], 1; cf. 117-24).

4. Elisabeth Schüssler Fiorenza (*Jesus and the Politics of Interpretation* [New York: Continuum, 2000], 65) challenges reconstructions of the historical Jesus featuring "the exceptional man, charismatic leader, and superhuman hero" as excessively romantic, male-centered ideals that betray "anti-Jewish . . . antidemocratic and antifeminist" biases. In contrast, she accentuates traditions focused more on the "discipleship of equals" in the community surrounding Jesus than on the "great man" Jesus himself. I agree that assessments of his extraordinary uniqueness wrench the historical Jesus out of his formative Jewish context and foster anti-Jewish triumphalism. But seeing Jesus as a "charismatic leader" (which is not the same thing as a "superhero") fits both a well-known Jewish model (judges, prophets, and some kings) and the earliest Gospel evidence, such as the audacious "follow me" calls in Mark and Q (Mark 1:16-20; 2:13-17; 8:34-37; 10:17-31; Matt 8:18-22/Luke 9:57-60). Jesus does not negotiate with disciples (see F. Scott Spencer, "'Follow Me': The Imperious Call of Jesus in the Synoptic Gospels," *Interpretation* 59 [2005]: 142-53). We must also acknowledge that "democracy" or a "discipleship of equals" is as much a modern romantic ideal as "heroic individualism." To be fair, Schüssler Fiorenza does recognize "the tensions and struggles," represented in the Jesus traditions, "between emancipatory understandings and movements inspired by the democratic logic of equality, on the one hand, and the dominant kyriarchal structures of society and religion in antiquity, on the other" (78).

- What did women give to Jesus by way of aid or assistance? What did women do for Jesus? Did women followers function as Jesus' "support staff," or something more?

Unfortunately, the Gospels do not provide abundant evidence for answering these questions. As highly selective portraits of Jesus' life and work, these narratives are even more selective in covering the people around Jesus. And written from an androcentric perspective, the Gospels' interest in women is sketchy at best, suspect at worst. But a few women in Jesus' life periodically emerge from the shadows, including multiple Marys (Jesus' mother, Martha's sister, Mary Magdalene, and others)[5] and one *Joanna*, who, though mentioned briefly in just two Lukan texts in tandem with Mary Magdalene (8:3; 24:10), has recently spawned something of a cottage industry of special studies.[6] Apart from her unique name in the Gospels (though there are plenty of "Johns," her masculine counterpart)[7] and this burgeoning interest in her contribution to early Christian history, Joanna provides a useful test case for investigating Jesus' dealings with women.

First, Joanna appears in the *only* passage in the Gospels' early segments (not flashbacks from passion/resurrection accounts) indicating that women accompanied Jesus in Galilee (Luke 8:2-3). Second, in this same text, Joanna emerges as one of only a few women functioning as both *recipient* (healing) and *benefactor* (helping) of Jesus' ministry. In one sense, her "serving" Jesus reflects the standard response of a grateful client; in another sense, its apparent material-financial dimension — underwriting a traveling charismatic preacher — shades into patronage. These first two points regarding Joanna apply equally well to Mary Magdalene, Susanna (mentioned only here in the NT), and miscellaneous "other women" (*heterai* [8:3]). But additional features distinguish Joanna from these other women.

Third, Joanna is introduced as *married* — the wife of Chuza — in contrast to the vast majority of Gospel women who appear as single or un-

---

5. Over a quarter of all Jewish girls born in first-century Palestine were named Mary (Miriam). See Tal Ilan, "In the Footsteps of Jesus: Jewish Women in a Jewish Movement," in *Transformative Encounters: Jesus and Women Re-viewed* (ed. Ingrid Rosa Kitzberger; Leiden: Brill, 2000), 122; Ilan, "Notes on the Distribution of Women's Names in Palestine in the Second Temple and Mishnaic Period," *Journal of Jewish Studies* 40 (1989): 186-200.

6. Five such studies are discussed below under the heading "Interpretive Mixes."

7. Although unique in the Gospels, "Joanna" was the fifth most common girl's name in first-century Palestine, according to Ilan, "In the Footsteps," 123.

attached. Mothers like the Canaanite woman and the bearer of Zebedee's sons (Matt 15:21-28; 20:20-23) meet Jesus, as do widows like Anna and the woman at Nain (Luke 2:36-38; 7:11-17), but their encounters with Jesus are direct and personal, unencumbered by husbands and fathers. Apart from Mary and Joseph in the birth narratives, the only married couple that has anything to do with Jesus is Jairus and his unnamed wife (Mark 5:40),[8] and there is no indication that they, individually or together, follow or support Jesus after he resuscitates their daughter. Joanna, then, represents an intriguing example of a married woman who followed Jesus, perhaps even leaving her husband to do so.[9]

Fourth, Luke discloses Joanna's tie to the Herodian household through her marriage to Antipas's *epitripos* (foreman, steward, estate manager) (Luke 8:3). Joanna's connection to the tetrarch's court at Tiberias was unique among Jesus' followers, female or male. Her possible access to wealth and privilege put her in a prime, yet potentially precarious, position for offering support to Jesus (precarious because of Jesus' critique of Herod in 7:24-30; 13:31-33). Others who contributed financially to Jesus' mission (Mary Magdalene and Susanna) and/or provided hospitality to Jesus and his followers (Martha and Mary) *may* have been women of some means and status, but only Joanna had official ties to the Herodian family. Most women in Jesus' world had little to offer Jesus materially. The hemorrhaging woman healed by Jesus likely enjoyed some opulence — enough to pay every doctor in town for twelve years — but by the time she met Jesus her cash flow had run dry (Mark 5:25-26),[10] and obviously, the poor widow who donated her last two "coppers" to the temple treasury had nothing to give Jesus (and she was not a follower of Jesus, as far as we know; Jesus simply used her as an object lesson [Mark 12:41-44//Luke 21:1-

---

8. Jesus has no encounter with Herod and wife Herodias together, and he never meets Pilate's wife (Matt 27:19).

9. Other possible examples include Mary, "the wife of Clopas," placed with other women at the cross in John 19:25, and the mother of Zebedee's sons in Matthew. In the latter case, the fact that Zebedee's sons (James and John) leave their father to follow Jesus in Matt 4:21-22 raises the possibility that their mother did likewise. However, in the two scenes where she appears — interceding for her sons in 20:20-24 and at the cross in 27:56 — she is identified not as "the wife of Zebedee," but simply as the mother of his sons, perhaps suggesting that she was no longer married to Zebedee (widowed?).

10. Some scholars assume the relative wealth and privilege of the Syrophoenician woman who pleads with Jesus to heal her demon-possessed daughter; but I see no direct evidence of this in Mark 7:24-30. See the discussion in Spencer, *Dancing Girls, "Loose" Ladies, and Women of "the Cloth": The Women in Jesus' Life* (New York: Continuum, 2005), 62-63.

4]). So Joanna appears to stand out among the women around Jesus as a court-connected financial contributor.

In probing Joanna's significance for understanding Jesus' associations with women, I first assess the limited data we do possess, with a particular focus on the *historical roots* of Joanna's appearance (where did she come from?) and the *vocational tasks* she carried out for Jesus and his followers (what did she do?). I then evaluate several recent *interpretive mixes* of this information about Joanna with a variety of other items — literary and material — to reconstruct the historical Joanna. Finally, I venture some tentative answers to the questions posed above about Jesus' master-disciple and patron-client connections with women.

Historical Roots

Mark's Gospel places in the background ("looking on from a distance") of the crucifixion scene a retinue of Galilean women, including Mary Magdalene, Mary the mother of James and Joses, Salome, and "many other women" who had accompanied Jesus to Jerusalem (Mark 15:40-41). This marks the first appearance of these women in the narrative. However, mitigating the impression that they are merely tacked on at the end, the narrator flashes back to Jesus' early ministry with the summary report: "these [women] used to follow (*ēkolouthoun*) him and provided for (*diēkonoun*) him when he was in Galilee" (15:41). The imperfect verbs suggest a customary pattern of activity. After this brief retrospective at Golgotha, Mark locates the named women at the tomb, where a white-clad young man informs them of Jesus' resurrection and instructs them to relay Jesus' plans for a Galilean rendezvous with Peter and the disciples — an assignment the fearful women fail to perform (16:1-8).

Luke shifts Mark's incidental flashback to the women's former service in Galilee to the actual Galilean phase of the story.[11] The same verb describing the women's ministry (*diēkonoun* [provided for/served]), along with a common accounting for "many others" *(heterai/allai pollai)*, links Luke 8:2-3 with Mark 15:41 and supports a hypothesis of literary dependence. But the *dramatis personae* differ.

---

11. See the discussion in Turid Karlsen Seim, *The Double Message: Patterns of Gender in Luke and Acts* (Nashville: Abingdon, 1994), 25-40.

Galilean Women in Mark	Galilean Women in Luke
	In Galilee (8:2-3)
	Mary Magdalene
	Joanna
	Susanna
	"Many others"
At the Cross (15:40-41)	**At the Cross (23:49)**
Mary Magdalene	Unspecified company of
Mary the mother of James the	Galilean women
younger and of Joses	
Salome	
"Many others"	
At the Tomb (15:47; 16:1)	**At the Tomb (23:55-56; 24:10)**
Mary Magdalene	Mary Magdalene
Mary the mother of	Joanna
James and Joses	Mary the mother of James
Salome	"Other women"

- Luke retains Mary Magdalene and Mary the mother of James at the cross (implicitly) and tomb (explicitly).
- Luke drops Salome altogether.
- Luke keeps Mary Magdalene in the early list of Jesus' followers but not Mary the mother of James/Joses.
- Luke 8 replaces Mary the mother of James/Joses with Joanna and Susanna, who do not appear at all in Mark.
- Luke 24:10 places Joanna (but not Susanna) at the tomb with the two Marys.

Thus, the main figure that Luke adds and identifies by way of marital status is Joanna, "the wife of Herod's steward Chuza" (8:3). The fact that she and her husband are both named and affiliated with Herod Antipas's court perhaps suggests that they were well-known historical figures to elite members of Luke's audience (like "most excellent" Theophilus [1:3]).[12] But Luke has a special interest in Herodian officials and affairs,[13] which com-

12. Cf. Carla Ricci, *Mary Magdalene and Many Others: Women Who Followed Jesus* (Minneapolis: Fortress, 1994), 70-71.

13. See Luke 3:18-20; 9:7-9; 13:31-35; 23:6-12; Acts 4:27; 12:1-6, 20-23; 13:1; John A. Darr,

plicates assessing Joanna's identity. On the one hand, some scholars posit Joanna as a likely source for Jesus' interrogation by Herod, an episode unique to Luke's passion account (23:6-12).[14] This theory presumes that Joanna was invited to the "trial" or otherwise knew how to get the gossip on Herodian business. But, on the other hand, a figure like Joanna (or Manaen in Acts 13:1) — sympathetic to Jesus with ties to Herod's court — might serve a Lukan tendency to demonstrate the Jesus movement's legitimacy, or at least innocuousness, in high places.

Another argument commonly advanced for the historicity of female disciples like Joanna trades on their supposed *discontinuity* with first-century Mediterranean (especially Jewish) practice. According to this opinion, good, respectable ladies did not wander around with an itinerant male teacher and his merry band of men. A woman's place was in the private, protected home, not in the public arena or on the open road; any religious or political movement that lured women away from the house would be considered scandalous. Thus, the logic runs, it is unlikely that Mark or Luke would have fabricated this feature of Jesus' mission.[15]

Recent studies, however, have demonstrated that ancient Mediterranean women were not as restricted in their movements as is often assumed. Customs varied somewhat between upper and lower classes in both the more "progressive" Roman-dominated West and the more "conservative" Greek-influenced East.[16] Promoting women's segregation in

---

Herod the Fox: Audience Criticism and Lukan Characterization (Sheffield: Sheffield Academic Press, 1998), 137-212; *On Character Building: The Reader and the Rhetoric of Characterization in Luke-Acts* (Louisville: Westminster John Knox), 127-68.

14. E.g., Ben Witherington III, *Women in the Ministry of Jesus: A Study of Jesus' Attitudes to Women and Their Roles as Reflected in His Earthly Life* (Cambridge: Cambridge University Press, 1984), 118-21; Ricci, *Mary Magdalene,* 69.

15. See, e.g., Joseph A. Fitzmyer, *The Gospel according to Luke I–IX* (New York: Doubleday, 1981), 696: "[T]he episode of 8:1-3 . . . indicate[s] . . . a recollection about Jesus which differed radically from the usual understanding of women's role in contemporary Judaism"; Robert C. Tannehill, *The Narrative Unity of Luke-Acts: A Literary Interpretation,* vol. 1: *The Gospel according to Luke* (Philadelphia: Fortress, 1986), 138: "[T]raveling around with a religious teacher conflicts strongly with traditional female roles in Jewish society. Such behavior neglects a husband's rights and a wife's responsibilities to her family. It would probably arouse suspicion of illicit sexual relationships"; Witherington, *Women,* 117: "There is little reason to question the authenticity of the information that women traveled with and served Jesus and the disciples as this was conduct which was unheard of and considered scandalous in Jewish circles"; and Ricci, *Mary Magdalene,* 85: "[T]he fact that Jesus accepted women among his following was for his time and its historical-cultural environment both unusual and scandalous."

16. See the carefully researched and nuanced studies, drawing on both material and lit-

separate domestic quarters, away from the public marketplace, only made sense for the aristocratic minority wealthy enough to own multiroom residences and slaves to do the shopping and run errands. Philo of Alexandria thought that elite women "are best suited to the indoor life which never strays from the house, within which the middle door is taken by the maidens as their boundary, and the outer door by those who have reached full womanhood." But as he endorsed a woman's "life of seclusion [in which] she should not show herself off like a vagrant in the street before the eyes of other men," Philo also acknowledged that "a free-born lady worthy of the name" would still venture out "to go to temple" (albeit "not when the market is full").[17] The vast majority of the population — belonging to peasant and artisan families cohabiting cramped, single-room dwellings or small tenement apartments and barely eking out a living — had little time and use for fine distinctions, gendered and otherwise, regarding "personal space" and "division of labor." The Gospels themselves provide ample evidence for women's freedom of movement in Roman Palestine, including the freedom to hear and host a teacher like Jesus, and Jesus' critics do not target his association with women *qua* women as a major issue.[18]

---

erary evidence, of Carolyn Osiek and David L. Balch, *Families in the New Testament World: Households and House Churches* (Louisville: Westminster John Knox, 1997), 24-32, 36-64; Eric M. Meyers, "The Problem of Gendered Space in Syro-Palestinian Domestic Architecture: The Case of Roman-Period Galilee," in *Early Christian Families in Context: An Interdisciplinary Dialogue* (ed. David L. Balch and Carolyn Osiek; Grand Rapids: Eerdmans, 2003), 44-69; Ross Shepard Kraemer, "Jewish Women and Christian Origins: Some Caveats" and "Jewish Women and Women's Judaism(s) at the Beginning of Christianity," in *Women and Christian Origins* (ed. Ross Shepard Kraemer and Mary Rose D'Angelo; New York: Oxford University Press, 1999), 35-79; Kraemer, *Her Share of the Blessings: Women's Religions among Pagans, Jews, and Christians in the Greco-Roman World* (New York: Oxford University Press, 1992), 93-127; Tal Ilan, *Jewish Women in Greco-Roman Palestine* (Peabody, Mass.: Hendrickson, 1996), 126-29, 176-204; Luise Schottroff, "Toward a Feminist Reconstruction of the History of Early Christianity," in Luise Schottroff, Silvia Shroer, and Marie-Theres Wacker, *Feminist Interpretation: The Bible in Women's Perspective* (Minneapolis: Fortress, 1998), 184-90.

17. Philo, *Special Laws* 3.169-171. See the citation and discussion of Philo's text that "allows for some destabilization of the public/private binary" in Shelly Matthews, *First Converts: Rich Pagan Women and the Rhetoric of Mission in Early Judaism and Christianity* (Stanford: Stanford University Press, 2001), 84-85; cf. Spencer, *Dancing Girls*, 149-50.

18. See Jane Schaberg, "Luke," in *Women's Bible Commentary* (ed. Carol A. Newsom and Sharon H. Ringe; Louisville: Westminster John Knox, 1998), 375: "Scholars often remark that the practice of including women in such a ministry [of Jesus] was scandalous. If this is true,

The only Gospel text that registers any critique of Jesus' association with women (John 4:27) places the question in the minds of his *disciples,* not his opponents, with respect to the unique case of Jesus' conversation with a woman who is *Samaritan, alone,* and *beside a well* — the last two items evoking suggestive biblical images of marriage transactions.[19] Moreover, one could read the disciples' query as evidence that Jesus did not customarily talk with women. If Jesus had made a habit of meeting and recruiting single women at well sites across Palestine, then we might have the makings of true scandal.[20] But he didn't, and we don't. As for the women in Luke 8:2-3, it is not clear what or whom they might have left to follow Jesus. The emphasis in Luke 14:26 and 18:29 on forsaking *wife,* with no corresponding mention of husband, may not so much exclude or ignore women disciples as intimate that Jesus only summoned unmarried women and

---

why did that scandal leave no mark on the traditions, and why was the practice never explicitly defended?"

In Matt 21:31-32, Jesus announces to the temple authorities his acceptance of prostitutes, along with tax collectors, in God's kingdom (although he credits *John the Baptist,* not himself, most directly with reaching out to such marginal types). The polemical context implies, but does not spell out, that the rulers would hardly be thrilled with such a social agenda; but prostitutes represented a particular, deviant class of women, not all womankind. In Luke's story of the woman who anoints Jesus' feet, Simon the Pharisee objects not to her as a woman per se, but as a peculiar "kind of" woman ("sinner") engaged in some peculiar activity ("touching" Jesus). Moreover, reversing the usual dichotomy, the trouble with "this woman" surrounds her location *inside* the house, *within* domestic space, rather than outside, "in the city" (Luke 7:37), where she belongs.

Sean Freyne's attempt to link Jesus' association with women with the accusation that he was "a drunkard and friend of sinners" is based on external evidence surrounding women's involvement in Dionysiac cults and practices in Galilee and elsewhere, not on any direct Gospel connection ("Jesus the Wine-Drinker: A Friend of Women," in *Transformative Encounters: Jesus and Women Re-viewed* [ed. Ingrid Rosa Kitzberger; Leiden: Brill, 2000], 162-80). Gospel "sinners" may be male or female, and there is no indication that Jesus' friendship with women — sinful or otherwise — was singled out for criticism.

19. See Spencer, *Dancing Girls,* 88-92; Spencer, "Feminist Criticism," in *Hearing the New Testament: Strategies for Interpretation* (ed. Joel B. Green; Grand Rapids: Eerdmans, 2010), 314-16.

20. Even the Samaritan woman does not journey with Jesus and the disciples, but rather returns to her hometown and bears witness to Jesus there. Barbara Reid (*Choosing the Better Part? Women in the Gospel of Luke* [Collegeville, Minn.: Liturgical Press, 1996]) further cautions regarding the supposedly scandalous nature of Jesus' well-side encounter with this woman: "In scenes very similar to that of John 4 . . . the patriarchs or their male servants approach a woman as a prospective bride at a well (e.g. Gen. 24:10-49; 29:4-14; Exod. 2:15-22). It is never hinted that their ensuing conversation is disapproved" (150).

that any wives who did follow were accompanied by their husbands or sons. We know nothing about the marital or parental status of Mary Magdalene, Susanna, or the "many others." If they were single or unattached women (virgins, widows, divorcées, childless women, slaves?), their association with Jesus' movement would not have been considered extraordinary or suspicious. Women affiliated, in various ways, with Pharisaic and Therapeutic "parties" within Judaism and with Cynic and Epicurean branches of Greco-Roman philosophy — why not with Jesus?[21] However, it is at this point that the distinctive *wife of Chuza* poses a more provocative case. Had Joanna abandoned her prominent husband to follow a folk healer — that might well have raised eyebrows and set tongues wagging![22] But we know nothing about Chuza's response to Jesus or the state of his marriage to Joanna. Perhaps Chuza was dead by the time Joanna met Jesus.[23] Or perhaps he also sympathized with Jesus (like Manaen in Acts)

21. The Pharisees and Therapeutae were not primarily traveling movements, however. On women's affiliations with the Pharisees, see Tal Ilan, "The Attraction of Aristocratic Women to Pharisaism during the Second Temple Period," *Harvard Theological Review* 88 (1995): 1-33; Ilan, *Integrating Women into Second Temple History* (Peabody, Mass.: Hendrickson, 1999), 11-42. On women's involvement with the Therapeutae referred to by Philo, see Joan E. Taylor, "The Women 'Priests' of Philo's *De Vita Contemplativa*: Reconstructing the Therapeutae," in *On the Cutting Edge: The Study of Women in Biblical Worlds; Essays in Honor of Elisabeth Schüssler Fiorenza* (ed. Jane Schaberg, Alice Bach, and Esther Fuchs; New York: Continuum, 2003), 102-22; and Kraemer, *Her Share*, 113-17, 126-27. On Epicurean and Cynic inclusion of women in their itinerant missions, see Kraemer, *Her Share*, 89-92, and Richard I. Pervo, "Unnamed Women Who Provide for the Jesus Movement," in *Women in Scripture: A Dictionary of Named and Unnamed Women in the Hebrew Bible, the Apocryphal/Deuterocanonical Books, and the New Testament* (gen. ed. Carol Meyers; Grand Rapids: Eerdmans, 2000), 442-43.

22. Apart from being a married woman, Joanna's aristocratic status may have also rendered her wandering about with a popular prophet and healer suspicious. Because wealthy women had large houses and multiple servants, they could afford to be more withdrawn from the public. On the other hand, their high standing and opulence gave them more freedom than lower-class women for traveling about, if they so chose. Pervo, "Unnamed Women," 442, offers a sober opinion on the matter: "Behind Luke 8:1-3 appears to lie a somewhat scandalous but not unthinkable tradition that the followers of Jesus included some relatively well-off women."

23. This option, while historically possible, is mitigated by Luke's frequent references to widows elsewhere. If Luke knew that Joanna was a widow, he likely would have said so. On the other hand, Luke tends to reserve the *chēra* designation for especially *poor, destitute* widows, which obviously would not fit Joanna. See Luke 4:26; 7:11-17; 18:1-8; 21:1-4; Acts 6:1-7; 9:39-41; F. Scott Spencer, "Neglected Widows in Acts 6:1-7," *Catholic Biblical Quarterly* 56 (1994): 714-33. For a different view, see Reid, "The Power of the Widows and How to Sup-

and supported, or at least tolerated, his wife's actions. Is it even possible that Joanna and Chuza were among the "seventy others" dispatched by Jesus "in pairs" in Luke 10:1-2 and thus a traveling missionary couple like Priscilla and Aquila (Acts 18:18-26; Rom 16:3; 1 Cor 16:19) or Peter and his wife (1 Cor 9:5)? Possible, yes, but it is impossible to be certain in the absence of evidence.

Finally, concerning the putative scandalous nature of Joanna and other women following Jesus, being "with him" and "providing for him/ them out of their resources" need not imply *constant* accompaniment of Jesus, *always* out on the road, *never* sleeping in one's own bed, and *total abandonment* of family. These women may well have journeyed with Jesus on a *limited, selective* schedule, especially since his "circuit" was confined to a small region in the lower Galilee.[24] Perhaps their primary way of being "with" Jesus was through financial support ("providing for him"), bankrolling the mission. In any case, the complete disappearance of Joanna and company after Luke 8:1-3 — until they suddenly reappear almost sixteen chapters later at Calvary, having "followed him [Jesus] from Galilee" (23:49, 55) — at least opens the possibility that these women were occasional and intermittent, though still dedicated and valuable, followers of Jesus in the physical sense.[25]

While nothing in the Gospel accounts raises serious doubt concern-

---

press It (Acts 6.1-7)," in *A Feminist Companion to the Acts of the Apostles* (ed. Amy-Jill Levine and Marianne Blickenstaff; London: T. & T. Clark, 2004), 71-88. While acknowledging that Luke characterizes many widows as poor, Reid argues that such portraits mask underlying power, both economic and ministerial, that widows possessed in early Christianity. In particular, Reid suggests that the neglected *diakonia* in Acts 6 had to do with financial help provided *by* the Hellenist widows, not food service given *to* them; hence, "the widows in Acts 6 may have been exercising a ministry akin to that of Mary Magdalene, Susanna, and Joanna, who ministered to Jesus and his followers out of their own financial resources" (84).

24. As Schaberg, "Luke," 375, queries (as a real possibility): "[S]ince the area [Galilee] is small, and since only the male disciples are said to have left their homes to follow Jesus (18:28), did the travel for the women consist of day trips from home bases?"

25. Robert J. Karris ("Women and Discipleship in Luke," in *A Feminist Companion to Luke* [ed. Amy-Jill Levine and Marianne Blickenstaff; London: Sheffield Academic, 2002], 23-43) stresses the summary nature of Luke 8:1-3 as describing a regular, ongoing practice of Galilean women's traveling as disciples with Jesus, substantiated by the links in 23:55 and 24:6-7 ("Remember how he told you . . .") back to the earlier Galilean mission and passion predictions. However, apart from whether Luke's narrative accurately portrays the historical circumstances of women following Jesus, the summary (8:1-3) and flashbacks (23:55–24:10) are quite brief and the gap between them rather large, thus leaving a lot of questions unanswered about the extent and modes of women's attachments to Jesus.

ing the historical existence of Joanna, Mary Magdalene, and other female followers of Jesus, dubious judgments about Jesus' uniqueness or "dissimilarity" do not strengthen the case. In addition to anachronistic, anti-Judaic polemic isolating Jesus from his Jewish environment, perhaps part of the modern mania for making Jesus appear to be a singular pro-woman activist stems from a guilty conscience regarding how Christianity has oppressed women. If we accentuate how revolutionary Jesus was to welcome women, we exonerate him from bad behavior done in his name. But such a tack only compounds bad history with bad psychology. Feminist interests are better served by acknowledging the *matter-of-factness* of Jesus' association with women in conjunction with other movements of his time.[26] The presence of women around a charismatic figure like Jesus is what we would expect, unlike the more reclusive and exclusive Essene sect comprised of celibate males, for example, identified by Pliny, Philo, and Josephus.[27]

Having affirmed the likelihood that women followed Jesus in some capacity (as Luke 8:1-3 claims), we still must account for *why these particular women* became attracted to Jesus' movement. No specific call or commissioning introduces Joanna or Mary Magdalene, as we find with fisherman Simon Peter (along with James and John, 5:1-11), tax collector Levi (5:27-28), and the other twelve apostles (6:12-16). But their neighboring places of origin — Tiberias, in Joanna's case (assuming she resided in Herod's capital), and Magdala, in Mary's case — on the western bank of the Sea of Gali-

26. On this matter-of-factness of women following Jesus, see the comments of Luise Schottroff, *Let the Oppressed Go Free: Feminist Perspectives on the New Testament* (Louisville: Westminster John Knox, 1993), 92 (emphasis added): "One need not doubt . . . that already during the Jesus movement in Palestine, women joined Jesus' disciples on their journeys. The *self-evident and casual mentioning* of this occurrence in Mark 15:40-41 and Matt. 27:55-56 speaks for that." Moreover, "Luke also agrees with Mark and Matthew that neither the women nor the disciples in general are to be made heroes. The underlying reason for this *quite relaxed and altogether non-patriarchal reporting* about the role of women is the practice of the Christian communities of the first century. The women were, as we also know from Paul, partakers in the prophetic proclamation of the gospel" (193 [emphasis added]).

27. Pliny, *Natural History* 5.73; Philo, *Hypothetica* 11.14-17; Josephus, *Jewish War* 2.120-121; *Antiquities* 18.21. Josephus also, however, refers to other Essene groups that did marry (*Jewish War* 2.160-161); thus, even among the Essene "party," there seems to have been variable viewpoints regarding women. On the continuing debate about the presence and role of women at the Qumran community (Essene?) associated with the Dead Sea Scrolls, see James C. VanderKam, *The Dead Sea Scrolls Today* (Grand Rapids: Eerdmans, 1994), 14-15, 90-91; Jodi Magness, *The Archaeology of Qumran and the Dead Sea Scrolls* (Grand Rapids: Eerdmans, 2002), 163-87.

lee, were in the vicinity of another lakeside town, Capernaum, where Jesus meets Simon and (probably) Levi (cf. 4:31, 38). Although the Gospels record no trip made by Jesus to Magdala or Tiberias, he operates in the area. Joanna, Mary, and other women may have been among the curious Galilean crowds that gathered around him, perhaps because of his reputation as a healer.

Luke's profile of these women's medical history provides a vital clue to what lured them into Jesus' movement: they were "cured of evil spirits and infirmities" (8:2). Mary Magdalene, we are told, had been delivered of seven devils; however, beyond this demonic enumeration and its hint of a rather severe condition (cf. 8:30; 11:26),[28] we know nothing about the nature of these women's afflictions. Suffice it to say that Mary, Joanna, and other women needed relief from various maladies and Jesus provided it. A glance back at Luke 4:38-44 uncovers a plausible historical setting for these women's discipleship. In Simon Peter's house in Capernaum, where Jesus had just cured Peter's mother-in-law of a high fever, he spends the entire night, receiving "all those . . . who were sick with various kinds of diseases . . . and he laid his hands on each of them and cured them. Demons also came out of many" (4:40-41). Such curative ministry Jesus brings "to the other cities also" (4:43). While not all, or even most, beneficiaries of Jesus' healing, male or female, became active followers or supporters, surely some did. By affiliating "with him" and providing for him "out of their resources" (8:1-3), the women demonstrate their gratitude for Jesus' healing services through patronage.[29]

Vocational Tasks

The report of Joanna and other women being "with Jesus" (*syn autō* [8:1]), while indicating a measure of commitment, does not take us very far in understanding the relationship. There are myriad ways of being "with" someone, from casual association to fervent devotion. A more promising clue to the women's participation in Jesus' movement emerges in the final statement in Luke 8:3 that "they were [1] serving/ministering to/providing for [2] him/them out of [3] their possessions/the things belonging to

---

28. See Seim, *The Double Message*, 33.

29. On the women of Luke 8:1-3 as both patrons (benefactors) and clients (beneficiaries) of Jesus, see Pervo, "Unnamed Women," 441-43.

them." However, the variable readings (indicated by slash marks) demonstrate how slippery this evidence, too, can be.

Amazingly, traditional gendered roles of domestic occupation (who serves whom and at what cost?) and economic distribution (who provides for whom and controls the purse strings?) — with women typically assuming service functions with limited personal resources — still pervade modern Western societies. The philosopher and political scientist Susan Moller Okin trenchantly exposes in the American scene "the gulf that exists between the continued *perception* of most men and women that it is still the primary responsibility of husbands to 'provide for' their wives by participating in wage work and of wives to perform a range of unpaid 'services' for their husbands, and the *fact* that most women . . . are both in the labor force *and* performing the vast majority of household duties."[30] Joanna's unique role as both wife of a Herodian official and disciple and benefactress of an itinerant preacher and miracle-worker raises provocative questions about women's "serving" and "providing" capabilities in our day as much as in the first century.

Services

The verb *diēkonoun*, an imperfect form of *diakoneō*, variously translated as "serve," "provide for," "minister," or "help," is the only indicative verb in the single sprawling sentence of Luke 8:1-3 other than *diōduen* in the first line, denoting Jesus' practice of "traveling/roving through" cities and villages.[31] Structurally, Luke frames the sentence with Jesus' "roving" (8:1) and the women's "serving" (8:3), highlighting that the women's ministry helped make Jesus' mission possible: that is, they helped the movement move. Luke further defines Jesus' activity, however, unlike the women's, with a pair of related participles *(kēryssōn/euangelizomenos)* that doubly stress his heralding/preaching. Thus far, such proclamation has been limited to Gabriel, John the Baptist, and Jesus.[32]

---

30. Susan Moller Okin, *Justice, Gender, and the Family* (New York: Basic Books, 1989), 139 (emphasis in original).

31. On the two main verbs in Luke 8:1-3, linked with the activity of Jesus and the women, respectively, see Esther de Boer, "The Lukan Mary Magdalene and the Other Women Following Jesus," in *A Feminist Companion to Luke* (ed. Levine and Blickenstaff), 144.

32. See 1:19; 2:10; 3:3, 18; 4:18-19, 43-44; 7:22. As we noted in the previous chapter, Elizabeth, Mary, and Anna speak as instruments of the Holy Spirit in the birth narrative (1:39-56;

In Hellenistic Greek, the *diakon-* stem[33] often characterized a "go-between" or "messenger," allowing for an ambassadorial, hortatory form of service.[34] But it also carried multivalent connotations appropriate to a range of domestic duties and other types of manual labor. That does not mean, however, that all possible meanings can be poured into every usage. A cardinal rule of lexical study establishes *context* as the primary determinant of semantic content.[35] In the present case, it seems prudent to focus on *diakon-* in Luke's principal source (Mark) and in the context of Luke's own writings (his Gospel and Acts) rather than on selected examples from the rest of the New Testament and the larger Hellenistic corpus.[36]

In Mark, the only *diakon-* reference applied to women, other than 15:41, describes the action of Simon's mother-in-law after her fever broke: "and she began to serve *(diēkonei)* them" (1:31). While no particular service is indicated, the domestic setting ("the house of Simon and Andrew") intimates some form of table service or hospitality. Earlier in Mark 1, a company of angels "waited on" *(diēkonoun)* Jesus during his wilderness altercation with Satan and the wild beasts (1:12-13). While biblical angels routinely function

2:36-38), but Luke never describes their proclamation in "kerygmatic" *(kēryssō)* or "evangelistic" *(euangelizō)* terms.

33. Three main *diakon-* terms appear in the NT: the verb *diakoneō* (serve/minister) and nouns *diakonos* (servant/minister) and *diakonia* (service/ministry).

34. This usage is demonstrated in John N. Collins, *Diakonia: Re-interpreting the Ancient Sources* (New York: Oxford University Press, 1990) — a study heavily depended on in Karris ("Women and Discipleship," 30-33) and Warren Carter, "Getting Martha out of the Kitchen: Luke 10:38-42 Again," in *A Feminist Companion to Luke* (ed. Levine and Blickenstaff), 218-27 — to stress the status of women portrayed in Luke as full disciples, leaders, and ministers (not menial "servants"). In a later article, however, Collins ("Did Luke Intend a Disservice to Women in the Martha and Mary Story?" *Biblical Theology Bulletin* 28 [1998]: 104-11) clarifies, against Karris, Carter, and others, that *diakon-*, generally, and in Lukan literature, particularly, includes service activities of meal provision and table waiting — but without either derogatory "notions of lowliness or servitude" or any necessary implications concerning "ecclesial ministry."

35. Cf. Collins, "Did Luke Intend?" 110: "The overriding principle of interpretation is to read words in their context. Because the *diakon-* words have no determinate or constant reference, the referent can be determined only with each particular context." See Moisés Silva, *Biblical Words and Their Meaning: An Introduction to Lexical Semantics* (Grand Rapids: Zondervan, 1983).

36. Oddly, and without warrant in my judgment, Karris ("Women and Discipleship," 29-31) dismisses the immediate *diakon-* parallels in Luke's Gospel ("because of their [meal service] context") as irrelevant to the case in 8:3 in favor of isolated examples in Acts and Matt 25:44 (building on Ricci's work).

as "messengers," they deliver no word in this scene. Their service to Jesus again is unspecified, but an angel's strengthening of a beleaguered, wilderness-weary Elijah by *catering a meal for him* provides a suggestive parallel (1 Kings 19:5-8). Thus Mark's angels may be viewed as fellow "waiters" with Simon's mother-in-law. The remaining occurrences of *diakon*-cluster in Mark 9–10, where Jesus propounds the paradox to his disciples that true greatness — ranking "first" in his community — demands being "last of all and servant *(diakonos)* of all" (9:35). By exhortation and personal example, Jesus illustrates two special forms of such "diaconal" service: receiving a little *child* in his name (9:33-37) and forfeiting one's life, like a powerless *slave* (10:41-45). There is nary a whisper of proclamation in any of these *diakon-* references. The ministry both received and exercised by Jesus values menial tasks commonly associated with angels, women, and slaves as honorable expressions of "spiritual" service.

Luke happily endorses Mark's emphasis on the priority of *diakonia* within the Jesus movement — extending to Jesus himself as the "one who serves *(diakonōn)*" at table (Luke 22:27) — and enlarges upon it with additional references to food service. With respect to women, Luke reprises the story of the feverish mother-in-law's posthealing ministrations to Jesus in "Simon's house" (4:38-39) and adds the report of Martha's "much service" *(pollēn diakonian)* to Jesus in her home (10:38-40). Again, such domestic work likely includes some form of table service, perhaps along with other hospitable acts such as anointing.[37] But hospitality is by no means circumscribed as exclusively "women's work" in the community surrounding Jesus. Three Lukan passages directed to recalcitrant, honor-seeking *male* disciples underscore Jesus' insistence that everyone in God's realm, from the highest to the lowest, must gird their belts, don their aprons, and serve one another at table.[38]

> "Blessed are those slaves whom the master finds alert when he comes; truly I tell you, he will fasten his belt and have them sit down to eat, and he will come and serve *(diakonēsei)* them." (12:37; cf. 12:35-48)

> "Who among you would say to your slave who has just come in from plowing or tending sheep in the field, 'Come here at once and take your place at the table'? Would you not rather say to him, 'Prepare supper for

37. On Martha's service, see chapter 5 of this study.
38. For fuller discussion of these texts, see Spencer, *The Portrait of Philip in Acts: A Study of Roles and Relations* (Sheffield: Sheffield Academic, 1992), 199-206.

me, put on your apron and serve *(diakonei)* me while I eat and drink'?" (17:7-8; cf. 17:1-10)

"The greatest among you must become like the youngest, and the leader like one who serves *(diakonōn)*. For who is greater, the one who is at the table or the one who serves *(diakonōn)?* Is it not the one at the table? But I am among you as one who serves *(diakonōn)."* (22:26-27; cf. 22:24-30)

In both Luke and Mark, then, *diakon-* refers to domestic service, chiefly involving food, not to public witness or proclamation. Jesus does both — speaks and serves — and regards them as complementary forms of ministry for himself and his followers. In God's household, men must serve as well as speak: they must not leave women to tend to the table by themselves. At least that seems to be the ideal conveyed in Jesus' rhetoric. But in terms of practice, apart from the incidents where Jesus and the apostles (reluctantly) feed the thousands, we have no Gospel reports of men catering to women.[39] While Jesus "serves" the last Passover to the apostles in the upper room (22:7-30), he does not any more hop up to share Martha's *diakonia* than he commands sister Mary to help (10:38-42). If women are present at mealtime, they shoulder the burden of service.

In Luke's second volume, we begin to see both a wider and a narrower usage of the noun *diakonia* designating the overall ministry — material and spiritual, diaconal and oracular — of the church's male apostles and missionaries, chiefly, Peter and the Twelve, Stephen and the Seven, Paul and Barnabas (Acts 1:17, 25; 6:1, 4; 11:29; 12:25; 20:24; 21:19). But *diakon-* is never applied to *women's* active service in Acts. Hungry Hellenistic widows are the objects of men's benevolent *diakonia* in Acts 6:1-6, but not the subjects (actually, they are only the *designated* objects of such aid; we never *see* the men serving the women). This passage also stands out as the one place in Luke and Acts where an attempt is made to link *diakon-* explicitly to both preaching and feeding ministries. But the situation betrays a persisting tension between the two forms of service. "Serving the word" *(diakonia tou logou* [6:4]) and "serving tables" *(diakonein trapezais* [6:2]) are both important, but not equally so for the twelve apostles who are unwilling to leave the former to tend to the latter ("It is not right that *we*

---

39. Mark 6:44 and Luke 9:14 identify the crowd as five thousand *males (andres)*. However, other references depict a more plausible, diverse scenario: Mark 8:8-9 describes the throng as four thousand "people," while Matt 14:21 and 15:38 specifically acknowledge "women and children" (albeit as an afterthought).

should neglect the word of God in order to wait on tables" [6:2]) and who allowed the widows' food crisis to arise in the first place. No one was complaining, "We're not getting enough teaching around here!"[40]

What, then, shall we conclude about the women's "serving" in Luke 8:3? In its Lukan context, *diakon-* suggests a type of table service these women were no doubt used to performing, although with considerable more dignity because of the honor Jesus ascribed to such work, not least by participating in it as well as benefiting from it. However, while more accustomed to food preparation (baking [13:20-21]; milling [17:35]) and table waiting than Jesus' male followers, the women were not to be solely or even primarily responsible for such duties in Jesus' community. The men of God's household must also serve one another at table. Still, in 8:2-3, while the twelve apostles and the women are both "with" Jesus, only the women are said to serve. Then again, the Twelve are not reported as doing *anything* but hanging around Jesus. They are not preaching or miracle working at this stage any more than they are table waiting.[41] Soon Jesus does send them out "to proclaim the kingdom of God" and "bring good news" to the villages of Galilee (9:1-6), but upon their return, they display an alarming streak of ineptitude and misunderstanding — including an initial failure to appreciate Jesus' commitment to *nourishing* the needy as well as teaching and healing (9:12-17; cf. 9:18-22, 32-36, 38-41, 44-50, 54-55). He then dispatches a larger posse of seventy (-two) paired delegates, possibly including women; but after this mission, the Lukan Jesus does all preaching and teaching himself until he transfers the work to his followers just before his ascension (24:44-49).

Is Luke thereby suppressing the vocal, prophetic service of the women who walked with Jesus, or is he simply reflecting the situation in Jesus' life *(Sitz im Leben Jesu)?* A strong case can be made for Luke's muffling of women's voices *in his own setting.*[42] The apostles' dismissal of Joanna and

---

40. See Spencer, "Neglected Widows in Acts 6:1-7."

41. See Joel B. Green, *The Gospel of Luke* (Grand Rapids: Eerdmans, 1997), 319 n. 13: "[I]t is best to major on what is clear from the text [Luke 8:1-3] — namely, the identification of these women as 'with' Jesus (in the same way that the twelve were 'with' him, for neither group with the larger company of disciples is regarded as actively engaged in preaching or healing) and as exemplars (more so than are the twelve at this point in the narrative) of Jesus' message."

42. E.g., Mary Rose D'Angelo, "Women and Luke-Acts: A Redactional View," *Journal of Biblical Literature* 109 (1990): 441-61; Spencer, "Out of Mind, Out of Voice: Slave-Girls and Prophetic Daughters in Luke-Acts," *Biblical Interpretation* 7 (1999): 133-55.

Mary Magdalene's resurrection report as an "idle tale" (24:11) and the utter absence of women's "sermons" or speeches in Acts, despite the early tease that "your daughters shall prophesy" (Acts 2:17-18), seem ample proof of some discomfort with women's proclamation in Luke's context. But the extent to which Luke tendentiously injects this concern back into Jesus' lifetime remains questionable. Beyond the limited cases of Mary's hymn uttered in Elizabeth's house (Luke 1:39-56) and the Samaritan woman's witness delivered to the village of Sychar (John 4:27-30, 39-42), the Gospels contain no evidence of women testifying about Jesus. Thus Luke may be appealing to women's more modest and quiet contributions to Jesus' movement as grounds for restricting their more public and vocal leadership in the early church.

This is not to assert that Jesus was against women or thought they had nothing useful to contribute beyond food service. But the reality may have been that Jesus was hesitant to entrust his message to any of his followers — male or female — until his imminent departure necessitated a succession strategy. Jesus was the one — not his deputies — who spoke with uncanny authority and eschatological urgency, the charismatic teacher whom people clamored to hear. Whatever other agendas lay behind the Synoptic pattern of Jesus' repeated silencing of his (male) disciples, this so-called messianic secret may reflect a genuine desire on Jesus' part to control the message. So while it remains doubtful that Joanna, Mary Magdalene, or any other woman campaigned very much for Jesus during his earthly ministry beyond their own close kinship and friendship networks, *the same could be said for Peter or John or any other man.* The missions in Luke 9:1-6, 10 and 10:1-20 offer isolated, skeletal reports of the disciples' early evangelistic activities — nothing on the scale depicted in Acts.[43]

Beneficiaries

Whom the women serve in Luke 8:3 hinges on whether the text says "him" — Jesus alone — or "them" — Jesus, the Twelve, and possibly a larger group including other women. Both readings have good manuscript evidence, and both include Jesus as a beneficiary of women's ministry. But the plural might be taken as diminishing Jesus' authority, and so, as Metzger

---

43. In fact, the mission reports in Luke 9 and 10 may function more as literary previews of developing evangelistic activity in Acts than as historical reminiscences.

contends, scribes might have been tempted to introduce the singular "him" as a "Christocentric correction."[44] Substituting a singular pronoun would also harmonize with Mark 15:41 — "These [women] . . . *provided for him [diēkonoun autō]* when he was in Galilee." These reasons, along with the parallel in Luke 4:39 — "She got up and began *to serve them [diēkonei autois]*" — support the plural "them" as more original.

This reading, however, does not necessarily subordinate the women in Jesus' movement to the male disciples ("them"), and it does not relegate the women to KP duty while the men attend to more important business. As we have seen, according to Lukan values, food service is noble, not negligible, work performed by the "greatest" in the community, at least when men do it, including Jesus himself. If the Twelve are present only as leisured recipients of women's catering efforts — that is not to their credit in God's empire. Moreover, the plural indirect object "them" need not be read in terms of male-female hierarchy or differentiated labor. Although a masculine pronoun *(autois)*, "them" may refer generically to the whole coterie of Jesus' followers, male and female. The women in the group would require care and feeding, too. So the women wait on each other as well as on Jesus and the Twelve and thus model the *mutual service* that the entire company is called to enact. As Esther de Boer stresses in her careful grammatical analysis, the women in 8:2-3 should not be indiscriminately lumped together, apart from Jesus and the male apostles, as a separate servant class. The narrator carefully distinguishes three named women followers — Mary Magdalene, Joanna, and Susanna, an inner triad, perhaps, comparable to Peter, James, and John — from "many others" (feminine *heterai*); such a distinction allows for multiple, diversified roles *among women:* they may be viewed both/either as patrons and/or clients, benefactors and/or recipients.[45]

---

44. Bruce M. Metzger, *A Textual Commentary on the Greek New Testament* (2nd ed.; Stuttgart: Deutsche Bibelgesellschaft, 1994), 120-21.

45. De Boer ("Lukan Mary Magdalene," 158) specifically surmises that the many *anonymous* women are the primary providers for both the Twelve and the three prominent *named* women. She views this named trio primarily as "healed ones," not benefactors. Though I think de Boer defines Joanna's role too narrowly (I see no reason not to allow her a dual role as client and patron, "healed one" and provider), I take the point about the probability of women contributing to Jesus' movement in different ways at different times.

Resources

Further insight into women's contributions emerges from unpacking the last phrase in Luke 8:3 *(ek hyparchontōn)*, disclosing the means "out of" *(ek)* which they carried out their serving. *Hyparchō* typically means "be" or "exist," a virtual synonym for the more common "be" verb, *eimi*. In its plural participial form followed by a dative noun or pronoun, it denotes "the things which be[long] to someone," and by extension, often carries a primary *economic* sense of "possessions," "property," or "material resources." At a basic level, then, the women materially aided the Jesus group with whatever "belonged to them," however meager or munificent. This inclusive reading allows for women of all classes, not just the wealthy (like Joanna), to support Jesus.[46] The presence in the movement of some impecunious women who freely gave of themselves and their limited resources is suggested by Jesus' affirmation of the poor among God's people ("blessed are you who are poor, / for yours is the kingdom of God," 6:20).[47]

While Luke supplies ample evidence of the poor helped and honored by Jesus,[48] he also relishes examples of rich patrons commended by Jesus, especially two model men of means: first, a Roman centurion who finances the construction of a synagogue in Capernaum, seeks Jesus' aid for his dying slave, and captures Jesus' attention for his "amazing" faith (7:1-10); and second, a Jewish "chief tax collector" named Zacchaeus who hosts Jesus in his Jericho villa, claims to give half of his possessions *(hyparchonta)* "to the poor," and draws Jesus' affirmation as a true "son of Abraham" (19:1-10). In the book of Acts, two women of means also emerge as church benefactors: Mary the mother of John Mark, who hosts the Jerusalem congregation in her substantial residence (Acts 12:12-17); and Lydia the purple-dealing businesswoman, who welcomes missionaries Paul and Silas and the Philippian "brothers" in her home (16:11-15, 40).[49]

---

46. Schottroff prefers the translation, "according to what was possible for them in their circumstances." See her "Toward a Feminist Reconstruction," 186-87; Schottroff, *Lydia's Impatient Sisters: A Feminist Social History of Early Christianity* (Louisville: Westminster John Knox, 1995), 210-11.

47. Though the poor widow who contributes her last two coins to the temple treasury is not directly affiliated with Jesus' movement, his commendation of her action suggests that she models true disciple behavior and represents some actual followers of Jesus (21:1-4).

48. See L. John Topel, *Children of a Compassionate God: A Theological Exegesis of Luke 6:20-49* (Collegeville, Minn.: Liturgical Press, 2001).

49. Lydia's dealing in expensive purple cloth worn by elites likely brought her a mea-

Mary, Lydia, and other well-to-do women in Acts could provide a parallel for some of the women in Luke 8 as wealthy matrons of the Jesus enterprise. Joanna's connection to the Herodian court suggests access to considerable financial resources and residential space,[50] and more speculatively, Mary's identity as a "Magdalene" may signal her success in Magdala's prosperous fish-processing industry. Perhaps, then, these women's main support for Jesus' Galilean mission entailed not so much their traveling with him and his followers as providing an economic and domestic base of operations for the movement. While billeted in these women's homes, Jesus and his lieutenants would be planning their next moves, and as hosts of this troop and financiers of the mission, the women may well have occupied an influential seat at the conference table as well as supervised the stocking and serving of the dinner table.[51]

---

sure of wealth, but did not mean that she shared her customers' status. On Lydia's social standing, see Spencer, *Dancing Girls*, 177-81; and "Women of 'the Cloth' in Acts: Sewing the Word," in *A Feminist Companion to the Acts of the Apostles* (ed. Levine and Blickenstaff), 146-50. Luke also references "leading" Greek women "of high standing" who endorse Paul's Macedonian mission (Acts 17:4, 12); see Matthews, *First Converts;* Matthews, "Elite Women, Public Religion, and Christian Propaganda in Acts 16," in *A Feminist Companion to the Acts of the Apostles* (ed. Levine and Blickenstaff), 111-33.

50. Access to wealth and privilege placed Joanna substantially above the peasant majority but not necessarily at the highest echelon of society. She was married to Herod's business manager (who might have been a slave), not to a member of the ruling family. James Arlandson locates Joanna and her husband in the retainer class managing Herodian affairs ("Lifestyles of the Rich and Christian: Women, Wealth, and Social Freedom," in *A Feminist Companion to the Acts of the Apostles* [ed. Levine and Blickenstaff], 167-69, and Arlandson, *Women, Class, and Society in Early Christianity: Models from Luke-Acts* [Peabody, Mass.: Hendrickson, 1997], 131-34).

51. Amy-Jill Levine ("Who's Catering the Q Affair?: Feminist Observations on Q Paraenesis," in *Paraenesis: Act and Form* [ed. Leo G. Perdue and John G. Gammie; Atlanta: Scholars, 1990], 145-61) argues that Q instruction represented in Luke 10:2-12 divides Jesus' followers into two groups: "mendicants" and "supporters" — the former comprised of male (certainly) and female (possibly) disciples accompanying Jesus on the road, the latter including women who feed and fund the itinerants. Both were important to the Jesus movement, but not in the same way and not necessarily enjoying "equal" status: "[S]ome — those closest to the paradigm of Jesus — take to the road; others, the ones to be harvested (10:2) and the children of peace (10:6), provide them support. While the early Jesus movement may have been discipleship of equals, that equality should be qualified: the mendicants are all equal on one level, and those who comprise the supporting network are equal on another" (150). While Levine grants that women "supporters" may have exerted considerable influence in the early Jesus movement, she suggests that Luke has blunted this effect in the case of Joanna and the other women of 8:1-3: "Luke has coopted the potentially egalitarian

The historical likelihood of Joanna contributing funds to the Jesus movement is bolstered by evidence of women's control over independent resources, with or without their husbands' approval.[52] Documents from the Bar Kokhba era discovered in Judean caves contain records of financial investments and transactions executed by a woman named Babatha, including a loan of 300 denarii to her second husband, Judah, subject to strict terms of repayment.[53] Josephus recounts the subversive activity of the wife of Herod the Great's younger brother, Pheroras, including her paying the stiff fine Herod had levied against 6,000 Pharisees who resisted his loyalty oath to Caesar; consequently, the Pharisees endorsed her immediate family's right to rule in place of the treacherous Herod (*Antiquities* 17.32-45). Herod urged that Pheroras divorce his wife for her meddlesome behavior, but Pheroras chose to keep her (17.46-51). Tal Ilan argues that the wife of Pheroras and other women of means were drawn to resistance parties like the Pharisees, not because their teachings were particularly liberating for women, but because they welcomed those with limited involvement in the dominant system, such as women caught in the web of Herodian politics.[54] Like the Pharisees, the antiestablishment movement launched by Jesus embraced women's participation and patronage; and as the wife of Pheroras materially assisted the Pharisees against Herodian interests, so Joanna the wife of Herod's treasurer Chuza funded the Jesus movement, with or without Chuza's endorsement. Ilan concludes:

> Opposition movements . . . rallied support where they could, and thus adopted a more democratic attitude [than ruling parties]. Wealthy

---

rhetoric of Q to support a more patriarchal agenda. . . . Luke does not represent Joanna or the other women as equivalent to the disciples [but] rather . . . establishes them as the model for the support network" (152).

52. Contra David C. Sim, "The Women Followers of Jesus: The Implications of Luke 8:1-3," *Heythrop Journal* 30 (1989): 52: "Joanna, despite her apparently wealthy background, was probably not in a position to contribute financially to the ministry of Jesus. As a married woman the right to dispose of her goods lay not with her but with her husband" (cf. 53-55).

53. See Naphtali Lewis, Yigael Yadin, and Jonas C. Greenfield, eds., *The Documents from the Bar Kokhba Period in the Cave of Letters: Greek Papyri* (Jerusalem: Israel Exploration Society, 1989), 24, 71-75; Ross Shepard Kraemer, ed., *Women's Religions in the Greco-Roman World: A Sourcebook* (Oxford: Oxford University Press, 2004), 143-52; Arlandson, "Lifestyles," 164-69. I discuss the Babatha documents much more fully in chapter 7.

54. See Ilan, "The Attraction of Aristocratic Women to Pharisaism during the Second Temple Period"; *Integrating Women*, 11-42; "In the Footsteps of Jesus."

women would support opposition movements over and against their husbands' political leanings, thus maintaining financial independence by supporting charities of their choice. Through their monetary contributions, such women may have influenced decision and policy making in the opposition parties they chose to support. Such a reconstruction is certainly probable for early Christianity, and is just as plausible for the Pharisee movement.[55]

Interpretive Mixes

When limited, direct literary evidence pertaining to a distant figure like Joanna is exhausted, scholars draw on other interpretive tools — notably archaeological and additional textual data illuminating first-century Mediterranean society mixed with informed historical imagination. As a result, Joanna has begun to be fleshed out in considerable detail beyond her Lukan cameo. The following five profiles contribute to an intriguing and remarkably multidimensional dossier, prompting us to query, "Will the real Joanna please stand up?"

Champion of the Poor

Gerd Theissen's *Shadow of the Galilean* is a historical novella about the life of Jesus deeply rooted in ancient sources but written as a detective story.[56] The main character is Andreas, a fictional Galilean produce merchant blackmailed by Pontius Pilate into spying on Jesus and his movement. Andreas never quite catches up with Jesus directly, but he learns a great deal from interviewing several of Jesus' followers, including, Andreas surprisingly discovers, Joanna, the wife of a chief Herodian official.[57]

As a government operative, Andreas is warmly welcomed into the couple's large, stylish home in Tiberias, Herod Antipas's glistening new capital on the shore of Lake Gennesaret. While Chuza is out auditing Herod's estates, Joanna informs Andreas that she regularly sends "money and food"

55. Ilan, "Attraction of Aristocratic Women," 24.

56. Gerd Theissen, *The Shadow of the Galilean: The Quest of the Historical Jesus in Narrative Form* (Philadelphia: Fortress, 1987).

57. The encounter with Joanna appears in chapter 13 under the title "A Woman Protests" (Theissen, *Shadow of the Galilean*, 119-27).

to Jesus without her husband's knowledge. She says nothing about her traveling with Jesus (the most she admits is: "When it's possible, I look for Jesus in order to listen to him"), but the material support she and other wealthy women provide guarantees the movement's survival and accounts for some of its reputation. Jesus' redistribution of the women's generous philanthropy sparks as much amazement as gratitude. As Joanna observes, "These poor people have often never seen so much food all at once. If you like, it's indeed a miracle."[58]

As for Joanna's motivation in supporting Jesus, Theissen focuses on her sympathy with Jesus' compassion for the "little people," not on any personal healing she might have received. When Chuza returns home, joins the conversation, and ridicules Jesus as a peddler of false hopes, Joanna finally admits to underwriting Jesus' mission. She retorts: "See here, Chuza. I won't stand for that. Perhaps we women understand the dreams and hopes of the little people more than you do. What you say is wrong."[59] In the ensuing argument, Joanna points out that Jesus' vision of a messianic age is not as far-fetched as Chuza thinks. In fact, signs of God's restored kingdom are already being realized in Jesus, and liberation from worry and tyranny — normally the luxury of elites — is starting to energize the poor through Jesus' nourishing work and instruction about their value as children of the heavenly Father (cf. Matt 5:44-45; 6:25-26).[60] At the end of the day, Chuza does not embrace his wife's viewpoint, but neither does he peremptorily dismiss her as a flighty, "eccentric woman." Indeed, with perhaps a tad too much romanticism, Chuza assures Joanna, "If you value him — I would rather change my views about Jesus than despise you."[61]

This bit of melodrama aside,[62] I see nothing historically implausible in Theissen's reconstruction. However, two items from Luke's account that Theissen omits (intentionally? inadvertently?) seem equally feasible: (1) Joanna's experience of Jesus' healing as the catalyst for her discipleship

---

58. Theissen, *Shadow of the Galilean*, 119-20.

59. Theissen, *Shadow of the Galilean*, 122.

60. Theissen, *Shadow of the Galilean*, 122-24.

61. Theissen, *Shadow of the Galilean*, 125.

62. However, Josephus's account of Pheroras's refusal to divorce his wife, as Herod desired, also plays up the romantic element: "But Pheroras, though greatly moved by the force of these words [Herod's divorce plea], said that it would not be right for him to give up any part either of his attachment to his brother or of his devotion to his wife and that he would prefer death rather than endure to live without a wife so dear to him" (*Antiquities* 17:48-49).

and patronage; (2) the possibility of Joanna leaving home, at least periodically, to journey with Jesus.

Independent Lady

Being healed by Jesus and leaving home to follow Jesus are central to Joanna's story sketched by Elisabeth Moltmann-Wendel in *The Women around Jesus*.[63] Moltmann-Wendel regards Joanna as an "explosive," "scandalous figure in the New Testament" precisely because she was a privileged court "lady" who "gives up a rich, secure life at the side of an influential man and shares in the risky and penurious life of a popular figure and social revolutionary." "What material for romances!" Moltmann-Wendel exclaims, although she esteems Joanna's experience as hard, historical reality.[64] The tendency toward soft, starry-eyed interpretation marks the sweep of Christian tradition that either ignored Joanna ("hardly anyone knows Joanna," Moltmann-Wendel laments)[65] or, when it did glance her way, quickly made her out to be a kindly, generous widow toting her flask of oil (in the few paintings where she appears)[66] and supplying goods and services to the ascetic Jesus, including the garment he wore (and lost to the gambling soldiers) and the upper room where he ate his final meal. In short, Joanna "was reduced to the loving, caring woman, whom people needed."[67]

Never entertained in this reimaging was the prospect of Joanna abandoning husband and family to run after Jesus — hence the presumption of her widowhood or her husband's permission to follow Jesus. But, Moltmann-Wendel opines, Joanna may have had ample reason to leave her husband and the decadent Herodian palace with its "atmosphere of lust, caprice, wealth and whim, indifference and open curiosity," evidenced in

---

63. Elisabeth Moltmann-Wendel, *The Women around Jesus* (New York: Crossroad, 1997). Her treatment of Joanna appears in chapter 7, "Joanna: A Lucan Lady," 130-44.

64. Moltmann-Wendel, *The Women around Jesus*, 133-34.

65. Moltmann-Wendel, *The Women around Jesus*, 133.

66. Moltmann-Wendel, *The Women around Jesus*, 134; cf. reprint of engraving by Adrian Collaert (130). See also reproduction of *Saint Joanna, the Myrrhbearer* by Orthodox iconographer Luke Dingman, in *Bible Review* 21, no. 2 (Spring 1995): 12 (illustrating the article by Ben Witherington III, "Joanna: Apostle of the Lord — or Jailbait?"), which features Joanna holding a bottle of myrrh.

67. Moltmann-Wendel, *The Women around Jesus*, 134-35.

the "serving" of John the Baptist's severed head at Herod's lavish birthday party (Matt 14:1-12; Mark 6:14-29; cf. Luke 9:9).[68] In Moltmann-Wendel's judgment, "Joanna's encounter with Jesus and her healing introduced her for the first time to something else: an independent life without whim, with a purpose; a community of men and women from different levels of society who dealt with one another in complete freedom and from whom healing powers emanated. Joanna left her husband to begin a new life of her own."[69] At this point of Joanna's interest in Jesus' diverse and inclusive community, Moltmann-Wendel's imagination merges with Theissen's, but Moltmann-Wendel also underscores the motivational factor of Jesus' "healing powers" and regards Chuza's role in Joanna's discipleship as wholly contrasting and constraining, not supportive or sustaining. Chuza may have gone along with Antipas's initial "half-sympathy" and dilettantish curiosity in the wonder-working Jesus, which in any case eventually "turns from laxity and indecision into the opposition which forces the execution of Jesus." But it is Joanna alone who "embodies a *total sympathy* [with Jesus] which risks everything."[70] She stands out as the lone member of Herod's court who dared "identifying herself with a traitor of the state" at Golgotha.[71]

If ever there were a true, faithful disciple who sacrificed family, position, security, and wealth to follow Jesus, Joanna was it. So why has she not received her due recognition? Moltmann-Wendel lays much of the blame at Luke's feet. In a Gospel that clearly asserts, "none of you can become my disciple if you do not give up all your possessions" (14:33), well-to-do women like Joanna do not measure up to "disciple" *(mathētēs)* status. Since they retained possessions to help Jesus rather than relinquished all *before* following him (as was demanded of the rich ruler in 18:22), these women did not — indeed, could not — fully attain the "ascetic, monastic, masculine ideal [that] slipped into the church" with Luke's endorsement. In Luke's book, "the women were not female disciples."[72]

While I concur with Moltmann-Wendel's stress on Joanna's attraction

---

68. Moltmann-Wendel (*The Women around Jesus*, 135) speculates that Joanna might have been "a spectator" at this party.

69. Moltmann-Wendel, *The Women around Jesus*, 136.

70. Moltmann-Wendel, *The Women around Jesus*, 139 (emphasis added).

71. Moltmann-Wendel, *The Women around Jesus*, 139.

72. Moltmann-Wendel, *The Women around Jesus*, 141. Of course, the NT overall rarely speaks of "female disciples." In fact, there is one lone NT reference to a feminine form of "disciple" *(mathētria)*, applied — by Luke! — to Tabitha/Dorcas in Acts 9:36.

to Jesus' healing ministry and the *possibility* of her leaving Chuza to become a disciple of Jesus, I am less sanguine about the further motivation she attributes to Joanna. I grant that, in the interest of assuring Theophilus and like-minded readers that Jesus' movement was not utterly antifamily and socially disruptive, Luke might have soft-pedaled how far respectable ladies like Joanna were willing to go to follow Jesus. But Luke still exposes more than enough of Jesus' antiestablishment comments and actions to keep the powers that be on alert,[73] and while he circumscribes women's roles (especially concerning leadership), he continues to showcase numerous women's (though not many wives') involvement with Jesus and the early church. Luke *may* know more about Joanna's "discipleship" than he is willing to tell; nevertheless, gratitude to Jesus for healing her provides reasonable, sufficient explanation for Joanna's role, irrespective of her political views or marital situation. The fact is: we do not know how Joanna felt about tetrarch or husband. We only know how she felt about Jesus; and while Jesus was no fan of "that fox" Herod in his luxurious den (7:24-26; 13:31-32), that may have mattered little one way or the other to Joanna. When faced with a serious illness, most people seek out doctors with the best *medical* credentials, regardless of their political or religious persuasions.

Chaste Devotee

Unlike Moltmann-Wendel, Robert Price does not envision women flouting their husbands to follow Jesus, much less making a total break to do so.[74] Querying, as we did above, how "scandalous" women's attachment to Jesus was (given the absence of calumnies and defenses to this effect), Price seems to accept Schaberg's conjecture that "perhaps the radius of Jesus' travels was not great and that the women came out from their homes to meet him each day, rather, I [Price] should imagine, like well-wishers sta-

---

73. See, e.g., Jesus' critique of "those who put on fine clothing and live in luxury . . . in royal palaces," in contrast to rougher but "greater" prophets of God, like John the Baptist (7:24-30); his defiance of Herod Antipas's predatory, "fox"-like schemes against him (13:31-35); and his disruptive demonstration in the temple and predictions of its destruction (19:41-48; 21:5-24).

74. Robert M. Price, *The Widow Traditions in Luke-Acts: A Feminist Critical Scrutiny* (Atlanta: Scholars, 1997). His treatment of Joanna appears in chapter 6, "Chaste Passion: The Chastity Story of Joanna," 127-51.

tioned with cups of lemonade for the runners in a marathon."[75] Though trivializing the women's contribution (a "cup of water" [or lemonade] was a pretty big deal with Jesus [cf. Matt 10:42; Mark 9:41], and Joanna's largesse no doubt extended well beyond refreshments), the point about the women's more occasional and variegated modes of being "with Jesus" remains viable.

But what was "not likely"[76] during Jesus' time became more common in the early church. Here, Price avers, it became fashionable for women to leave their unbelieving husbands to follow a Christian apostle. Such a trend emerges in early Christian apocryphal stories, such as the *Acts of Thomas* and *Acts of Paul and Thecla*, in which (1) a married woman hears a visiting apostle, becomes devoted to him, and vows chastity; (2) the woman's husband/governor resists and persecutes both wife and apostle; (3) the woman and apostle are rescued and/or vindicated, the husband/ governor is bested (through conversion or punishment), and the woman remains chaste.[77]

According to Price, the earliest Joanna traditions represented just such a chastity story, which Luke, writing closer to the apocryphal acts than is often assumed, retrofitted into Jesus' life and "rudely handled" for his own aims.[78] Since Luke did not want to encourage Christian women to abandon their husbands and families, he domesticated Joanna into Jesus' donor instead of his disciple. Philanthropy is good; divorcing or deserting the paterfamilias, not. Nonetheless, in attempting to manage Joanna's troubling tradition, Luke leaves some tantalizing traces of the original story.[79] In particular, Price notices the unique part Luke assigns to Herod Antipas (Luke 13:31-33; 23:6-12) and Joanna (23:49; 24:10) in Jesus' passion. He sees the Herodian segment of Jesus' trial scene as a vestige of Joanna's chastity tale, with husband Chuza originally playing a key role. Peering behind the Lukan curtain, Price spies a jealous Chuza fulminating over his wife's sud-

---

75. Price, *Widow Traditions*, 135.

76. See the section headed "Not Likely" in Price, *Widow Traditions*, 132-36.

77. Price, *Widow Traditions*, 136-38. Here I have synthesized Price's fourteen points (137) into three primary ones. Price builds heavily on the studies of Ross Shepard Kraemer, "The Conversion of Women to Ascetic Forms of Christianity," *Signs: Journal of Women in Culture and Society* 6 (1980): 298-307, and Virginia Burrus, *Chastity as Autonomy: Women in the Stories of Apocryphal Acts* (Lewiston, N.Y.: Edwin Mellen, 1987).

78. Price, *Widow Traditions*, 137.

79. See Price, *Widow Traditions*, 150: "But why would Luke have included a vestige of a tradition so odious to him? Simply in order to refute it!"

den, "long, unexplained absences" in the company, so he has heard, of some backwater itinerant preacher and "wizard."[80] The powerful Chuza, used to getting — and keeping — what he wants, will not give up his wife without a fight. So "we must surmise," according to Price, "that Chuza sought his royal friend's [Herod's] help in bringing his wife back into line, as well as settling the score with the troublemaker who took her away from him."[81] Ultimately, in this scheme, Chuza incited Antipas to have Jesus tried and executed[82] on the grounds — attested in Marcionite and Old Latin texts of Luke 23:5 — that Jesus "led astray/alienated our sons and wives from us."[83] Following the chastity script's typical ending, jilted husband and ruler endeavored to eliminate the competition, but to no avail, in light of Jesus' putative resurrection — *first recognized and reported by Joanna and other women.*

I do not think that Luke-Acts so readily betrays an apologetic assault against chastity stories generally, still less against a particular one featuring Joanna, back-shifted into Jesus' context. If Luke wanted to demonstrate that Jesus posed no threat to marital stability and never compelled (seduced) married women to defy their husbands' authority to follow him, it seems that Luke would have populated his Gospel with a few more happy couples or faithful (to their husbands!) married women. Luke does a little better in his second volume, but neither of the more extended treatments of Christian married couples perfectly fits Price's theory. The story of Ananias and Sapphira is hardly a positive one, and it strongly suggests that the wife *should have parted ways with her husband;* in fact, Sapphira's continuing alliance with Ananias leads to her death![84] Paul's associates, Aquila and Priscilla, appear to counter the chastity traditions more effectively: here a missionary couple works *together* to spread the gospel. Still, after their introduction in Acts 18:2, Priscilla is always named *before* Aquila

80. Price, *Widow Traditions,* 140, 149.

81. Price, *Widow Traditions,* 140.

82. Price (*Widow Traditions,* 141-47) partly builds his case on the questionable assumption that the *Gospel of Peter* — betraying "tell-tale signs of a counter-Passion in which Herod Antipas played the villain, not Pilate" (146) — preserves a more primitive passion tradition than do the canonical Gospels.

83. Price, *Widow Traditions,* 148-49. Metzger, *Textual Commentary,* 152, discusses this variant (the Marcion reading is attested in Epiphanius), but it is not deemed worthy of a notation in the Greek UBS text (4th ed.).

84. Acts 5:2 stresses Sapphira's active role in the couple's shady transaction ("with his wife's knowledge") and 5:7-10 gives her individual responsibility — and opportunity — for making things right.

(18:18, 26), intimating some independence from her husband and closer bond to Paul. To be sure, she does not leave her husband for Paul, and we know nothing about her sex life, but the mention of Philip's four *virgin* prophetic daughters (21:9) shows that Luke is by no means opposed to female asceticism.[85] Nor has Luke a text comparable to 1 Corinthians 7:1-5 arguing *for* conjugal rights.

If the quest for the historical Joanna is hampered by skimpy evidence, the quest for the historical Chuza is even more dubious. Whereas Theissen grants Chuza a somewhat supportive, romantic role, Price assigns him the vindictive, antagonistic part. But in both cases, these *male* scholars, however feminist-sensitive they may be,[86] give Chuza much more play than does Moltmann-Wendel, who cares not a whit for Chuza except as a representative of a profligate and oppressive Herodian court.

Double Agent

Marianne Sawicki offers a creative reconstruction of Joanna's and Mary Magdalene's intertwined histories, based upon archaeological as well as textual clues to first-century Palestine's geopolitical and socioeconomic landscape.[87] In particular, she mounts a case for their friendship, even partnership, *prior to* meeting Jesus. First, these women bear two of the most common names used in the Herodian era by families who maintained strong ties to the Hasmonean (Maccabean) dynasty that ruled Judea and Galilee in the century before Jesus' birth. In 42 B.C.E. the Hasmonean princess Mariamme married the Idumean Herod ("the Great"), who took the throne in 37 B.C.E. and launched decades of Herodian control in the region, perpetuated in Galilee by his son Antipas (4 B.C.E.–39 C.E.). A paranoid and ruthless ruler, Herod the Great severely curtailed Hasmonean influence by a series of murders: the high priest and

85. See Seim, *The Double Message*, 185-248; Seim, "The Virgin Mother: Mary and Ascetic Discipleship in Luke," in *A Feminist Companion to Luke* (ed. Amy-Jill Levine and Marianne Blickenstaff; London: Sheffield Academic, 2002), 89-105.

86. Both Theissen and Price endeavor to be "pro-women" in their scholarship. Price even subtitles his study *A Feminist-Critical Scrutiny*.

87. Marianne Sawicki, *Crossing Galilee: Architectures of Contact in the Occupied Land of Jesus* (Harrisburg, Pa.: Trinity, 2000), 135-53, 179-84, 191-98; Sawicki, "Magdalenes and Tiberiennes: City Women in the Entourage of Jesus," in *Transformative Encounters* (ed. Kitzberger), 181-202.

brother of Mariamme, Aristobulus (35 B.C.E.); Mariamme herself (29 B.C.E.); and her two sons by Herod (7 B.C.E.). Such tyranny did not soon fade from Hasmonean view: many kept Mariamme's memory alive by naming their daughters after her ("Mary" is a common variant) and by using other popular Hasmonean appellations, like Joanna/John, after Jonathan, the brother of Judah "the Maccabee," John Hyrcanus, and others. What's in a name? In this case, not only honoring the past, but also fanning the flame of nationalist freedom.[88]

Beyond these possible geopolitical ties between the families of Joanna and Mary Magdalene, Sawicki also posits a close socioeconomic bond. They resided in the neighboring lakeside cities of Magdala and Tiberias (only three miles apart) that became booming trade and tourist centers during the tetrarchy of Herod Antipas. Joanna appears to have followed in Mariamme's footsteps, marrying into the Herodian system as the wife of Antipas's "chief of staff" Chuza.[89] In this position, Sawicki surmises, Joanna would have had major responsibility for hosting the wives of prominent traveling merchants and dignitaries en route from Syria, Babylon, and other regions to Jerusalem for commerce and/or pilgrimage.[90] Antipas had moved his capital to seaside Tiberias precisely to "Mediterraneanize" his realm, in good Roman style, and to attract foreign visitors who had previously skirted the area to the east.

The Herodian economy in first-century Galilee was further boosted by an expanding international industry of salted fish and fish sauces — products harvested from the Sea of Galilee, processed in local ports, and then exported across the lake and overland throughout the empire.[91] Here is where Mary Magdalene fit in, as Magdala — from the Aramaic Migdal meaning "(Fish) Tower" — served as an important hub for Galilean fish works.[92] She no doubt traveled throughout the region promoting the industry, because, as Sawicki quips, "No one calls you 'Magdalene' *in* Magdala."[93] In the process Mary likely made her way to Joanna's nearby

---

88. Sawicki, "Magdalenes and Tiberiennes," 183-86.

89. Sawicki, "Magdalenes and Tiberiennes," 183.

90. Sawicki, *Crossing Galilee*, 180.

91. On the Galilean fishing industry, see Sawicki, *Crossing Galilee*, 27-30, 140-47, and K. C. Hanson, "The Galilean Fishing Economy and the Jesus Tradition," *Biblical Theology Bulletin* 27 (1997): 99-111.

92. Josephus identified the town as Tarichaeae, suggesting "Picklesville" or "Pickleworks" connected with the pickling of fish for export.

93. Sawicki, "Magdalenes and Tiberiennes," 192-93 (emphasis added).

home in Tiberias, to hobnob with foreign elites (potential customers), and she may also have hosted Joanna and her guests for tours of the Magdala packing houses.

How, then, did Jesus attract the attention — and financial backing — of these sophisticated businesswomen? Sawicki appreciates the appeal of Jesus' curative powers, as Luke suggests, but she doubts that Mary and Joanna were healed of any infirmity or, initially at least, had any particular spiritual devotion to Jesus. Her admittedly "secular" hypothesis builds on the premise that a budding international resort center like Tiberias had to provide abundant opportunity for refreshment and entertainment. Just as it had its hot springs and health spas, it courted successful magicians, exorcists, and healers — like Jesus.[94] So, Sawicki theorizes, Joanna (especially) and Mary may have first sponsored Jesus' career as something of a headlining wizard in Herod's palace (think David Copperfield at Caesars Palace in Las Vegas). This scenario assumes, of course, that Jesus and Antipas were not always enemies, that Jesus did not immediately and/or totally endorse John the Baptist's critique of Antipas's marriage, and that Antipas was more curious to see Jesus' act (as Luke 23:8 confirms) than he was intent to kill him (as the Pharisees warn in 13:31). Eventually, however, Jesus did begin to annoy Antipas, and so he needed protection. And who better to provide a buffer, according to Sawicki, than Joanna? In fact, Joanna may have played something of a "double agent" role, keeping Antipas apprised of Jesus' movements, but in a selective fashion that preserved Jesus' freedom.[95]

Jesus was less fortunate in Jerusalem, however, when he ran afoul of the Roman authorities in the powder keg environment of Passover. At this point, like Price, Sawicki focuses on the role of Herod Antipas in the hasty judicial proceedings surrounding Jesus' death (23:6-12), in collaboration not only with Pilate but also with Herod's staff. However, unlike Price, Sawicki highlights *Joanna's part* in Jesus' passion, not Chuza's (though Luke does not place her or her husband at Jesus' trial). Perhaps, Sawicki imagines, Joanna tried to use her Herodian connections to intercede on Jesus' behalf, but she could only go so far without crossing a traitorous line herself. In any case, Joanna continued her double agent act, conducting a "stakeout at Calvary"[96] to gather information for Antipas regarding Jesus' fate while also leading women sympathizers with Jesus to the sites of his

---

94. Sawicki, *Crossing Galilee*, 147-49.
95. Sawicki, *Crossing Galilee*, 147-53.
96. Sawicki, *Crossing Galilee*, 151.

crucifixion and burial. It is thus highly plausible that Joanna and Mary Magdalene were among the first witnesses to Jesus' empty tomb, just as Luke reports. Moreover, Sawicki contends, their post-Easter witness to Jesus doubtless extended beyond local environs to the empire-wide network in which they were embedded. These women thus jump-started the gospel's spread to the "ends of the earth" (Acts 1:8), prior to the activities of Peter, Paul, and other missionaries presented in Acts.

> For the international mobilization of the Gospel movement to get going *after Calvary,* as it did, there had to be people close to Jesus who knew something of the world beyond Galilee. Joanna and Mary are the only figures in Jesus' immediate circle who did, according to the circumstantial evidence of their involvement with international trade and their contacts in far-flung Diaspora communities. These likely provided the bridge for the Gospel to travel up to Jerusalem and out to the cities of the eastern and western worlds. No other hypothesis fits the archaeological, geographical, and textual evidence so well.[97]

Although making a number of inferential leaps from a limited cache of evidence, as she freely admits, Sawicki has meticulously sifted these materials to produce a lively portrait of Joanna Tiberienne and Mary Magdalene that is both reasonable and provocative. The case proves stronger for Joanna (because of her explicit Herodian ties in Luke 8:3) than for Mary (personal names and place-names offer meager evidence), but the prospect of their mercantile and missionary partnership fits the pattern of paired women associates in early Christianity, like Euodia and Syntyche, Tryphaena and Tryphosa, and Martha and Mary.[98] The profiles of Joanna and Mary as independent, married (Joanna), mobile, prosperous, "connected" businesswomen resist the tendency to reduce women's participation in the early Jesus movement to a single model. Some women likely journeyed with Jesus and the Twelve some of the time as well as fed and financed the movement in their homes. And some, like Joanna and Mary, probably helped with the planning and promoting of the movement as well as its sustenance and succor.

One critical flaw, however, in Sawicki's proposal is its own reductionist

---

97. Sawicki, "Magdalenes and Tiberiennes," 196.

98. See Phil 4:2-3; Rom 16:12; Luke 10:38-42; John 11:1–12:8; Mary Rose D'Angelo, "Women Partners in the New Testament," *Journal for the Feminist Study of Religion* 6 (1990): 65-86.

fallacy, concentrating on "secular" and sociopolitical factors at the expense of religious elements. Admittedly, the latter is much trickier to prove, but the fact remains that religion and politics were inextricably intertwined in first-century Palestine. I thus give more weight than Sawicki to the inspirational factor of Jesus' healing and exorcising ministry, not merely as a tourist attraction or novelty act, but as a sign of the in-breaking kingdom of God.[99] We have no way of probing the precise nature of Joanna's or Mary's illnesses or how they might have felt about Jesus' "treatment" of their afflictions, if in fact he did treat them. But there is no reason, beyond a narrow empiricist grid, to diminish the possibility that Joanna and Mary were cured by Jesus' powerful word or touch (like Simon's mother-in-law and others with "various kinds of diseases" [4:38-41]),[100] as Luke implies,[101] and that this personal transformative encounter — and the hope it generated for a renewed society, for the poor as well as the elites (cf. Theissen)[102] — was a principal reason for their supporting Jesus' mission.

Aiding and abetting Jesus' popular movement might have made Joanna's "double agent" role even more precarious than Sawicki suggests. According to Josephus, Herod Antipas executed John the Baptist because he stirred up the crowds with his fiery sermons and thus posed a potential security threat (*Antiquities* 18.116-19). Gospel reports of the apocalyptic thrust of John's preaching and public critique of Herod's unlawful marriage to Herodias add further fuel to the tetrarch's suspicions (Mark 6:17-18; Matt 3:1-12; 14:3-4; Luke 3:1-20). Although not a permanent disciple of the Baptist, Jesus submitted to John's baptism (Mark 1:9-11), defended the "greatness" of John's work (Matt 11:7-19; Luke 7:24-35), continued John's proclamation of God's imminent kingdom (Mark 1:14-15), decried divorce and adultery (though not Herod's specifically [Mark 10:1-12; Matt 5:27-32; 19:1-12; Luke 16:18]), and attracted large crowds, perhaps including some of

99. "But if it is by the finger of God that I cast out the demons, then the kingdom of God has come to you" (Luke 11:20; cf. Matt 12:28).

100. For a balanced, reasoned assessment of Jesus' miraculous ministry in its ancient historical and literary context, see Justo L. González, *Luke* (Louisville: Westminster John Knox, 2010), 82-84.

101. Luke 8:2 states that "some women . . . had been cured of evil spirits and infirmities" without specifying that such healings had been effected *by Jesus*. But the preceding report in 8:1 of Jesus' "bringing the good news of the kingdom of God," together with evidence in 4:38-44 and 7:21-22 that such "good news" featured Jesus' healings and exorcisms, strongly suggests Jesus as the agent of Mary's and Joanna's cures.

102. Cf. the connection in 7:21-22 between Jesus' curative ministry and bringing good news to the poor.

John's former enthusiasts among his closest followers (cf. John 1:35-42). Herod became "perplexed" by these strange affinities between Jesus and John (even fearing that Jesus was John *redivivus* [Luke 9:7-9]), prompting plans to investigate Jesus further (9:9; 23:8-9) and eventually have him killed (13:31; 23:11-12).[103] As connected as Joanna was, she had to know about Herod's consternation about Jesus; yet she supported him anyway.

Prominent Apostle

Richard Bauckham offers the most extensive study of Joanna to date, running to almost a hundred pages.[104] Bauckham agrees that Joanna was an aristocratic woman of means, but he doubts Sawicki's conjecture that she came from a Hasmonean family that retained nationalistic, anti-Herodian sympathies: as Bauckham puts it, such a heritage "would make the marriage [to a Herodian officer] a little difficult to explain."[105] However, in the complicated political tug-of-war in first-century Palestine, shaky marital alliances between competing factions were commonly forged. Such arrangements were doubtless "a little difficult" to *maintain* (remember Mariamme) but not to explain. In any case, we know nothing about the circumstances that brought Joanna and Chuza together or the quality of their marital relationship. There *may* have been tensions between the two and their kinship networks, but again we know nothing about Joanna's

103. Cf. Steve Mason, *Josephus and the New Testament* (2nd ed.; Peabody, Mass.: Hendrickson, 2003), 160-61: "In the case of Herod Antipas . . . much of the gospel material is well complemented by Josephus's account. In particular, the gospels' notice that the Baptist was imprisoned for criticizing the tetrarch's marriage to his sister-in-law Herodias (Mark 6:17) makes abundant sense. Josephus says only that John was imprisoned because he had a large following and therefore was suspected of revolutionary motives; however, in view of what was going on at the time of John's arrest, it would not contradict Josephus's point if the preacher had also said of Herodias: 'It is not lawful for you to have her' (Matt 14:4). Also compatible with Josephus's portrayal is Luke's account of Antipas as 'that fox' who was seeking to kill Jesus (Luke 13:31) and participated in his trial (23:6-12)." There is a tension between the Pharisees' report in Luke 13:31 that "Herod wants to kill you [Jesus]" and Pilate's judgment in 23:15 that both he and Herod think Jesus "has done nothing to deserve death." But, of course, neither Pilate nor Herod prevents Jesus' crucifixion, and according to Luke, they "became friends" at Jesus' trial, joining hands in having Jesus mocked, beaten, and "treated with contempt" (23:15, 22-25).

104. Richard Bauckham, *Gospel Women: Studies of the Named Women in the Gospels* (Grand Rapids: Eerdmans, 2002), 109-202.

105. Bauckham, *Gospel Women*, 144.

family history. Here Bauckham rightly challenges Sawicki's dependence on Joanna's Hasmonean name as a marker of anti-Herodian sentiment: once a name becomes popular, it may be used by a variety of families with no political overtones.[106]

Bauckham also questions the social and economic affinity between Joanna and Mary Magdalene, assumed by Sawicki. True, they are grouped in Luke 8:2-3 and 24:10, but Bauckham correctly observes that we have no statement regarding Mary's financial portfolio, and he speculates that her priority in the women's list owes more to her prominence in the Jesus tradition than in the business world.[107] Moreover, her history as a desperate demoniac may suggest that she had never been married or had been spurned by a former husband, thus placing her lower in status than the married socialite Joanna.[108] While Bauckham's point about the uncertainty of Mary Magdalene's finances is well taken, his implicit link between her demonic misfortune and inferior class is less convincing. Luke assumes a close connection between the demon-possessed and the diseased "cured" by Jesus ("Jesus had just then cured [*etherapeusen*] many people of diseases, plagues, and evil spirits" [7:21; cf. 4:40-41; 10:9, 17-20; 13:11-13, 16]), and elites got sick as surely, though not as often, as peasants. The woman with enough resources to pay a dozen years' worth of doctor bills battled an incurable bleeding disorder (8:43); Joanna herself struggled with a malady — an unspecified condition, but one serious enough to cause her to seek help beyond "professional" physicians.

In terms of Joanna's situation, Bauckham presses the case that her commitment to follow Jesus and finance his mission[109] may well have triggered a marked *reversal* of status and *loss* of prestige — nothing less than a "conversion to the poor" who thronged to Jesus' movement.

[I]t was a radical step right outside the Herodian establishment to which she had belonged and into the life of the ordinary people of Gali-

---

106. Bauckham, *Gospel Women*, 144: "The masculine name John was popular because it had been a Hasmonean name, but, once popular, it would not have been used only by families wishing thereby to proclaim their nationalist loyalties."

107. Bauckham, *Gospel Women*, 117 n. 19.

108. Bauckham, *Gospel Women*, 118-19.

109. On the basis of the Babatha archives and other evidence, Bauckham concludes that "even as a married woman, she [Joanna] could very plausibly have economic resources of her own from which to support Jesus and his band of followers" (*Gospel Women*, 134; cf. 117, 121-35).

lee and of the marginalized and rejected of society whom Jesus often attracted and sought out. The kind of people she would now come to know (probably as never before) were accustomed to resenting the luxury of her former lifestyle, the burden of taxation that financed it, and the pagan domination of their land that the Herodian court she belonged to represented for them. In a certain sense her following of Jesus was also a *conversion to the poor*. She may have seen her financial contribution to Jesus' ministry as putting to rights some of the economic wrongs in which she had been involved as Chuza's wife.[110]

While affirming Ilan's analogy between the wife of Pheroras paying the Pharisees' fine and Joanna's support of the Jesus movement, Bauckham also perceives a fundamental difference in the level of commitment (conversion) of these two women: "What is unprecedented in Joanna's case . . . is that she not only financed Jesus' mission but herself joined the itinerant followers in their countercultural lifestyle. Pheroras's wife and the other Herodian women who supported the Pharisees did not cross the social gulf in the way that Joanna did."[111] Moreover, while acknowledging that "as a devout Jewish woman, Joanna had always made a practice of charitable giving to the poor," Bauckham further contends that her "joining the disciples required a more radical step."[112] Evidently Bauckham's Joanna sensed something lacking in her traditional Jewish upbringing as well as her Herodian lifestyle that she found supplied in Jesus.

Recognizing the high cost of Joanna's commitment to Jesus and the rift it might have created with her Herodian friends bolsters my critique of Sawicki. But if Sawicki risks underplaying Joanna's devotion to Jesus as well as Jesus' conflict with Herod, Bauckham overplays his hand. The loaded language of "conversion," "righting wrongs," adopting a "countercultural lifestyle," and taking "a radical step" too readily evokes the image of the misguided "sinner" repenting from her wicked ways in order to follow Jesus.[113] Bauckham never calls Joanna a "sinner" as such, but his supposition that she must "convert" *to* the poor beloved by Jesus *from* an exploitative Herodianism — and, apparently, also *from* a deficient Judaism in

---

110. Bauckham, *Gospel Women*, 150 (emphasis added).

111. Bauckham, *Gospel Women*, 162.

112. Bauckham, *Gospel Women*, 196.

113. For a nuanced and inclusive approach to conversion by a leading evangelical NT scholar, see the welcome study by Scot McKnight, *Turning to Jesus: The Sociology of Conversion in the Gospels* (Louisville: Westminster John Knox, 2002).

some sense (even though, as Bauckham admits, nurturing the poor is fundamental to Jewish piety) — tilts in that direction.

Luke is no stranger to the "conversion" model of the "repentant sinner"; indeed, he is largely responsible for it. Luke hammers the call to "repentance" *(metanoia)* more than any NT writer.[114] For example, Luke redacts Jesus' pronouncement against critics of his table fellowship with tax collectors and other sinners to include repentance: "I have come to call not the righteous but sinners *to repentance (eis metanoian)*" (5:32). And only Luke concretely illustrates the *economic* bedrock of such repentance for tax collectors — demanding that they "collect no more than the amount prescribed" (3:13), share their "possessions" *(hyparchonta)* with the poor, and make restitution for any fraudulent business practices (19:1-10) — and the hellish penalty that awaits the rich who ignore the plight of the poor (16:19-31). But such a strong stance against exploiting the poor does not compel us to judge all wealthy Lukan characters as oppressive sinners who must repent. Recall the examples of the faithful centurion (7:1-10) and the generous tax collector Zacchaeus (19:1-10). The crowd, not Jesus, labels Zacchaeus a "sinner" (19:7), and Jesus never exhorts him to "repent." Jesus invites himself to Zacchaeus's house and affirms his *voluntary* contribution of half of his estate to the poor (unlike the stingier rich ruler in 18:22).

We must not assume, then, Joanna's "conversion to the poor" or her guilty association, as the wife of Herod's business manager, in the government's abuses of power. While Luke does not directly attack Herod's burdensome tax system or other economic injustices, his sympathy for John the Baptist — who did oppose extortionist practices of political operatives (3:12-14) — in contrast to "someone dressed in soft robes [and] fine clothing and liv[ing] in luxury . . . in royal palaces" (7:25; cf. 7:24-30), implies some critique of Herodian opulence.[115] But whatever Luke's assessment of the Herodian economy, he says nothing about Joanna's complicity in any exploitation. Maybe she resisted the regime's oppression of the "little people," as Theissen suggests, and supported them before meeting Jesus, or maybe she trod a thin line on both sides of the sociopolitical fence, as Sawicki imagines. Maybe, but both proposals outrun the hard evidence. The most we can infer from Luke's sparse account is that Joanna was

114. See Guy D. Nave Jr., *The Role and Function of Repentance in Luke-Acts* (Atlanta: SBL, 2002).

115. The description of the well-heeled ruler living in luxury resonates with the "rich man who was dressed in purple and fine linen and who feasted sumptuously every day" — and who couldn't care less about the poor beggar Lazarus who lay at his gate (16:19-21).

drawn to Jesus because she was sick, not a sinner — and the two labels are not the same. She experienced a physical restoration through Jesus that she may have taken as a sign of God's restored kingdom, but not, as far as we know, a religious conversion from or to anyone or anything.

The most innovative element in Bauckham's reconstruction is also the most speculative, as he stretches Joanna's story into the post-Easter period.[116] Beyond the reasonable suggestion (cf. Sawicki) that Joanna played some formative role in spreading the Christian message, even though she never appears outside Luke's Gospel, Bauckham pushes to trace the contours of Joanna's mission. His case hinges on Romans 16:7, where Paul concludes his correspondence with greetings to "Andronicus and Junia, my relatives [or compatriots] who were in prison with me; they are prominent among the apostles, and they were in Christ before I was." Since Junia is a Latinized variant of Joanna, Bauckham posits that Paul refers to none other than the Lukan Joanna, wife of Chuza. In fact, Chuza is still very much in the picture, too. Just as Joanna adapted her name to her new Roman residence, so Chuza may have *changed* his Nabatean name to the more amenable Greek moniker, Andronicus (why Chuza chose *this* popular Greek name over another is not clear). Working backward from this premise, Bauckham hypothesizes that Chuza adopted Joanna's faith in Jesus soon after the crucifixion (thus becoming "in Christ" before Paul), and then, together, they became an influential missionary team, like Aquila and Priscilla (Rom 16:3-4) and Peter and his wife (1 Cor 9:5), using their political contacts and cosmopolitan background to promote the gospel in the imperial capital.[117]

This makes for a wonderful story, but one with too many conjectural shifts in identity and itinerary to be credible.[118] Playing the name game is

---

116. Bauckham, *Gospel Women*, 165-98.

117. While Bauckham, *Gospel Women*, 186, admits that the Chuza-Andronicus identification is only one possibility (the other being that Joanna had been widowed from Chuza and thereafter married Andronicus), his concluding "sketch" of the historical Joanna (194-98) develops Chuza a.k.a. Andronicus as the most interesting (plausible?) option. Witherington, who otherwise follows Bauckham, suggests that Chuza divorced Joanna because "she was using his money to chase after a radical prophet who had insulted his boss. . . . Herod Antipas would hardly have retained Chuza as estate agent if Chuza retained Joanna as a wife." Joanna then "remarried a Christian named Andronicus and started on a life of missionary work that took her to the heart of the empire" ("Joanna," 14, 46).

118. Ironically, Bauckham (*Gospel Women*, 194 n. 356) summarily dismisses Sawicki's reconstruction of the historical Joanna as "too speculative and not sufficiently restrained by the most probable conclusions that can be drawn from the evidence about Joanna." A case of

risky business ("Scott Spencer" is the American author of several critically acclaimed novels, including *Endless Love* and *A Ship Made of Paper,* but, unfortunately, *not* the writer of this book). In Junia's case, she has had a hard enough time being recognized as a bona fide female apostle.[119] Though not his intention, Bauckham effectively effaces Junia by identifying her with Joanna on the flimsy basis of name correspondence (a popular name at that) and speculative relocation from Tiberias and Jerusalem to Rome. At least Bauckham does not transform Junia into a man, as the RSV and NIV do, but the net result is still the loss of one apostolic woman.[120] As for Chuza, it seems as if male interpreters cannot resist giving him a bigger part in Joanna's (and Jesus') story than Luke does, whether as open conversation partner (Theissen), jealous vindictive cuckold (Price), or converted missionary partner (Bauckham). Female interpreters (Moltmann-Wendel and Sawicki) more easily leave Chuza behind, as Joanna herself may well have done.

Tentative Results

After investigating the historical Joanna from various angles, I propose some tentative answers, based on Joanna's example, to the questions regarding Jesus' relationship with women posed in the introduction. With respect to *master-disciple relations,* Jesus probably attracted women like Joanna to follow him "on the road," but I also think that the *extent* of their

---

the pot calling the kettle black? Witherington ("Joanna"), who credits Bauckham with supplying "the inspiration for this brief essay" (47 n. 8), nonetheless admits that "it takes a great deal of detective work (some will say speculation!) to connect Joanna with Junia" (46).

119. On the assumption that the early church would not have sanctioned a female apostle, modern editions of the Greek NT (followed by the RSV and NIV) inflect the name Iounian with a circumflex accent over the last syllable, denoting the masculine Junias, rather than with an acute accent, denoting the feminine Junia. However, the earliest manuscripts contain no accents, and the early church father John Chrysostom had no qualms extolling Junia as a female apostle. The NRSV changed its predecessor's reading to "Junia" in the main text, while still, however, retaining the possibility "or *Junias*" in a footnote. See Florence M. Gillmann, *Women Who Knew Paul* (Collegeville, Minn.: Liturgical Press, 1992), 66-70; Bernadette M. Brooten, "Junia," in *Women in Scripture* (ed. Meyers), 107; and the definitive discussion in Eldon J. Epps, *Junia: The First Woman Apostle* (Minneapolis: Fortress, 2005). We might also note that Epps only mentions Bauckham's "conjecture" of the Lukan Joanna's identification with the apostle Junia in an endnote (94 n. 23).

120. I owe this point to correspondence with Amy-Jill Levine.

following was variable. Some women may have formed part of Jesus' "permanent retinue," as Freyne contends,[121] but others — especially married, well-to-do women like Joanna — may have traveled with Jesus more intermittently while being devoted to him no less enthusiastically.

I see no evidence that Jesus summoned Joanna or other wives to desert their husbands and children and follow him. All the "drop everything and follow me" call stories in the Gospels feature men, and even their forsaking of hearth and home may not have been as final as is often assumed. For example, no sooner did Jesus call brothers Simon/Andrew and James/John to leave their fishing business than he appeared in Simon's home to serve and be served by Simon's mother-in-law. In James and John's case, while "they left their father Zebedee in the boat" (Mark 1:20//Matt 4:22), they did not (entirely) forsake their mother: on one occasion Mrs. Zebedee came "with her sons" to ask Jesus a favor (Matt 20:20-23).[122] After Jesus summoned Levi to leave his tax booth and join his disciples, the first thing they did was gather for dinner *in Levi's house* (Mark 2:13-17; Luke 5:27-32). Leaving one's job seems more critical for discipleship than leaving one's home.[123]

This is not to say that Jesus did not spark divisions in some households (cf. Matt 10:34-39; Luke 12:49-53; 14:25-27) or that some men and women did not leave their spouses and children, by choice or by force, to follow Jesus;[124] as silent as the Gospels are about Jesus' calling a wife away from her husband, they are equally mute about Jesus' sending a woman *back home* if she chose to journey with him. But the evidence for Jesus as a home-wrecker should not be exaggerated.[125] Often forgotten in such dis-

---

121. Freyne, "Jesus the Wine-Drinker," 176.

122. The "mother of the sons of Zebedee" also appears in Matt 27:55-56 among those women who accompanied Jesus from Galilee and supported him. Her leaving husband Zebedee to follow Jesus is implied but never specified. In any event, Jesus does not *call* her to leave and does not treat her with great respect in 20:21-23; he denies her request and addresses his response to her sons.

123. In 1 Cor 9:5, Paul suggests that Cephas/Peter and other apostles, including "brothers of the Lord," were accompanied by a "sister-woman/wife." Might some such missionary coupling go back to the historical Jesus? At least occasionally, might Peter's wife have tagged along with Jesus' traveling Galilean band, especially since her mother was well enough to look after the household?

124. See Sim, "What about the Wives and Children of the Disciples? The Cost of Discipleship from Another Perspective," *Heythrop Journal* 35 (1994): 373-90.

125. For a survey of the mixed Gospel evidence, suggesting both conflict and conciliation, surrounding Jesus' personal relations with his own family, see Spencer, *What Did Jesus Do? Gospel Profiles of Jesus' Personal Conduct* (Harrisburg, Pa.: Trinity, 2003), 25-50.

cussion is Jesus' treatment of *children*, which militates against a supposed agenda that tore mothers (or fathers) away from parental duties. The Gospels report Jesus' welcome and blessing of little ones to whom "the kingdom of God belongs" (Matt 18:1-14; 19:13-15; Mark 9:33-37; 10:13-16; Luke 9:46-48), but they give no examples of Jesus' summoning small children to follow him, with or without parents, or any information about children of the Twelve.[126] Jesus heals or resuscitates children on multiple occasions, and each time restores the parent-child bond ("'Young man, I say to you, rise!' . . . and Jesus gave him to his mother" [Luke 7:14-15; cf. Mark 5:35-43; 7:24-29; 9:14-29]). Further, although featuring older offspring, Jesus' parable of the lost son in Luke 15:11-32 reflects a goal of family reconciliation, not alienation. There is also the fact that, for all their emphasis on Jesus' servant ministry and the "slave" *(doulos)* as the "greatest" model of discipleship, the Gospels supply no case of Jesus' calling *slaves* to escape their households. They do, however, recount multiple parables and a healing story about slaves that reflect conventional social arrangements.[127] These observations fit with what I have repeatedly stressed in this investigation of Joanna; namely, while her forsaking husband and household for Jesus (temporarily or permanently) remains a possibility, the scant evidence does not allow us to develop an adequate family case history and assessment of Jesus' impact upon it.

In terms of *patron-client relations*, I start with Luke's statement that

126. Sim, "What about the Wives?" 380-82, assumes that the disciples would have had multiple children, some of them still young and dependent when Jesus called their fathers away. However, apart from never identifying any of the disciples' offspring, the Gospels do not even specify that they had children. Jesus' statement concerning "no one who has left house or brothers or sisters or mother or father or children or fields, for my sake and for the sake of the good news" (Mark 10:29; Luke 18:29), presents a broad range of *possible* sacrifices made by disciples, but not a catalogue that applied to all (e.g., did all the disciples have sisters or fields to leave?).

127. Parables: Mark 12:1-12; 13:32-37; Matt 25:14-30; Luke 12:35-48; 19:11-27; healing of the centurion's slave: Matt 8:5-13; Luke 7:1-10. This is not the place to engage in a full discussion of Jesus' social program (or whether indeed he had one). But it is worth noting that, for all the different people Jesus embraced, he never made, as far as we know, a definitive announcement à la Gal 3:28, declaring an obliteration of boundaries (on any level) between Jews/Greeks, slaves/free, and women/men. Along with his apparent tolerance of the institution of slavery, his outreach to Gentiles is minimal and never extends to their homes or permanent companionship: Jesus heals the Roman centurion's servant and Hellenistic Syrophoenician woman's daughter *without* going to their residences or ever meeting the afflicted parties; and while he liberates the Gerasene demoniac, he spurns the man's request to follow after him.

women were primarily indebted to Jesus in a positive sense — and hence attracted to him — because he healed them from various afflictions. The fact that Jesus also "freely" healed many others — free of charge and free of gender, class, and age distinctions[128] — may have further appealed to women concerned with "little people" on the margins of society. But if an affluent, well-connected woman like Joanna did support Jesus not only for her personal healing but also for his wider "charity work" in Galilee, that does not mean she necessarily underwent a marked "conversion" to Jesus and the poor or a complete "divorce" from her Herodian husband and his court with their considerable social and material benefits.

Although their healing was "free," many women whom Jesus restored voluntarily "repaid" him as grateful clients, chiefly in the form of hospitality and money. The wealthier the woman like Joanna, the more she could — and probably did — give. While these women may well have spoken about Jesus to their friends and offered Jesus advice about the direction of his movement, especially when he was in their homes, there is no indication that they engaged in organized preaching missions or exerted formal leadership during Jesus' life. But the proclamation and authority of the male disciples was also limited. This was *Jesus'* movement, not just because it rallied around him, but because he ran it as Lord and Master: though exemplifying the mutual service all his followers had to display, Jesus still brokered God's eschatological empire to men and women with audacious, even imperious, sovereignty.[129]

128. That is, Jesus healed women as well as men, isolated lepers as well as officials' servants, children as well as adults. I borrow the notion of Jesus' "free healing" (typically paired with "open eating") from John Dominic Crossan. See, e.g., his discussion of Jesus' advancement of a "brokerless kingdom" focusing on "magic and meal" in *The Historical Jesus: The Life of a Mediterranean Jewish Peasant* (New York: HarperCollins, 1991), 303-53; *Jesus: A Revolutionary Biography* (New York: HarperCollins, 1994), 66-101.

129. For hints of the imperious/imperial nature of Jesus' vocation, see Spencer, "'Follow Me,'" *Interpretation* 59 (2005): 142-53.

5. A Testy Hostess and Her Lazy Sister? Martha, Mary, and the Household Rivals Type-Scene (Luke 10:38-42)

In Luke's narrative, the household represents contested space, a fragile entity subject to conflict and division. In the familiar domestic snippet in 10:38-42, busy Martha becomes rankled by lazy sister Mary's neglect of household duties. Rather than confronting Mary directly, however, Martha vents her frustration to a third party guest, namely, Jesus: "Lord, do you not care that my sister has left me to do all the work by myself?" (10:40). This complaint is particularly apt in light of Mary's parking at Jesus' feet and hanging on his words. Jesus' presence precipitates the problem: Mary's rapt attentiveness to his teaching causes her rank inattentiveness to household service. As Martha sees it, Jesus needs to break the spell and put her sister to work.

This incident sets the stage for Jesus' varied comments about divided households (oikoi) in Luke's subsequent two chapters. Answering the calumny that he expels demons by the power of the demonic prince Beelzebul, Jesus reminds his critics that any kingdom divided against itself will self-destruct into a wasteland as its houses fall in on one another (oikos epi oikos). Jesus thus drives out evil spirits from their "houses" (hosts) as the instrument ("finger") of God, not of Satan, who would scarcely expel himself (11:15-20). But a problem remains. If the exorcised "house" (oikos) remains unoccupied and unmanaged by godly tenants, then the original wicked invader will return with seven nefarious cohorts and wreak more havoc than before (11:24-26). Whether inhabited by spirit forces or human beings, houses are precarious battlegrounds that must be tended and defended; homeowners and household servants must remain ever vigilant in both welcoming honored guests and warding off harmful intruders at all hours (cf. 11:5-8; 12:35-39).

To complicate matters further, Jesus himself does not always play a congenial role in household affairs. Sometimes, as with Martha and Mary, he's in the middle of the mess. Also, as Son of Man, he threatens to come as an intrusive thief in the night to unguarded, unsuspecting homes (12:39-40). Despite the angelic carol heralding "peace on earth" at Jesus' nativity (2:14), the mature Jesus announces that in fact he has *not* "come to bring peace to the earth . . . *but rather division!*": specifically, *household (oikos)* division between fathers/sons, mothers/daughters, and mothers-in-law/daughters-in-law (12:51-53). The latter two examples extend Jesus' divisive potential among *female* relatives: as he set sister against sister in Martha and Mary's home, he also drives a wedge between natural and in-law mothers and daughters.

On a larger scale, beyond providing an introit to Jesus' remarks about discordant households in Luke 11–12, the Martha/Mary story also fits a conventional biblical plot pattern that we may label a "household rivals" type-scene. Typical elements of this paradigm include:

1. A pair of women share a domicile in some household relation, such as sisters, cowives, mothers and daughters, mothers-in-law and daughters-in-law, or mistresses and maidservants.
2. The two women occupy different social positions, relating to each other in some hierarchical fashion — such as elder/younger, owner/servant, or favored/neglected.
3. The two women are further differentiated from each other in terms of distinctive characteristics, abilities, and interests.
4. A tense household situation arises, prompting one woman's complaint (to someone) about being treated unfairly (by someone) compared to the other woman.
5. The contested situation involves matters of hospitality, such as hosting, feeding, serving, entertaining, and accommodating.
6. The women's rivalry in the contested situation revolves around distinct-yet-similar triangular relations with a male authority, typically regarded as household "lord" (master, owner) *(kyrios)*.
7. In biblical narratives, standing out above all "lords" affecting the women's lives is the divine "Lord," sovereign over all the households of the earth. In its Lukan context, Martha's addressing Jesus as "Lord" *(kyrie)* stretches beyond a conventional term of respect ("Sir") toward a confessional faith in Jesus' divine vocation.[1]

---

1. See a full discussion of text-critical, grammatical, and theological issues surrounding

8. The domestic and/or divine "lord" adjudicates the women's rivalry on a continuum from equality and reconciliation, on one end, to favoritism and separation, on the other.

This last point marks an interpretive crux in the Martha and Mary story. Does Lord Jesus unequivocally deny Martha's plea and settle the case in favor of Mary's "better" choice? Among other details in the narrative, the fact that the NRSV's "the better part" in 10:42 may be more simply (and better) rendered "the good part" *(tēn agathēn merida)* complicates Jesus' preferential verdict. Perhaps he affirms Mary's "part" without denigrating Martha's. To help us "better" understand this and other features of the Martha/Mary incident, we undertake a comparative, intertextual analysis with other samples of the household rivals biblical type-scene in the Hebrew Bible and Gospel of Luke. Although Luke's story of Martha and Mary has received considerable scholarly attention in recent years, far out of proportion to its brief five-verse compass, little interest has been shown in its wider biblical literary context and generic framework. Projecting this familiar vignette against a wider canvas promises to offer a fresh angle of vision on Luke's (and Jesus') view of sisterhood, sibling rivalry, and family roles and values.

In exploring several biblical household rivals scenes, we must appreciate the integrity of each example, remaining alert to peculiar deviations from the type as well as basic conformities. Literary paradigms provide general templates for creative thought, not Procrustean beds or cookie cutouts. As Robert Alter discerns from his careful study of biblical type-scenes, "What is really interesting is not the schema of convention but what is done in each individual application of the schema to give it a sudden tilt of innovation or even to refashion it radically for the imaginative purposes at hand."[2]

---

the three uses of *kyrios* identifying Jesus in Luke 10:39-41 — two nominative forms employed by the third-person narrator (10:39, 41) flanking the vocative address *(kyrie)* by Martha (10:40) — in C. Kavin Rowe, *Early Narrative Christology: The Lord in the Gospel of Luke* (Grand Rapids: Baker Academic, 2009), 142-51. I do not think, however, that "the distracted and busy Martha" uses "lord/master" simply as "an everyday term of respect" for Jesus, thus falling short of the narrator in "understanding the larger significance of her address" (149-51). Complaining to the Lord does not necessarily signal a lack of comprehending his Lordship. In fact, her appeal assumes that Jesus has the Lordly right to redeploy his followers, in this case, sister Mary.

2. Robert Alter, *The Art of Biblical Narrative* (New York: Basic Books, 1981), 52. See

Sarai and Hagar

The household of patriarch Abram includes two women: Sarai, his wife (and also half sister [Gen 12:13; 20:2, 12-13]), and Hagar, Sarai's personal slave-girl,[3] among other female slaves in Abram's house (cf. 12:16). Although closely related in the household, Sarai and Hagar are quite different; as Phyllis Trible succinctly profiles them: "Sarai the Hebrew is married, rich, and free; she is also old and barren. Hagar the Egyptian is single, poor, and bonded; she is also young and fertile. Power belongs to Sarai, the subject of the action; powerlessness marks Hagar, the object."[4] The distinctions in age and reproductive capacity prompt Sarai to urge her husband Abram to "go in to" Hagar, allowing Sarai to "obtain children" by her handmaiden (16:1-2). Further, Sarai gives Hagar to Abram not merely as a surrogate childbearer, but also "as a wife" (16:3). Sarai and Hagar thus emerge as Abram's *cowives.*

Along with Abram's central, though largely passive, part in the story — around which the two women revolve[5] — the divine being YHWH also figures prominently in a more active role, both antecedently motivating the present incident and ultimately resolving it. Stated as matter of fact, not as complaint, Sarai frankly acknowledges to Abram, and insists on his confirmation ("you see"), "that the LORD has prevented me from bearing children" (16:2) all these years, now well advanced beyond expectation. For whatever reason (none is given), the divine life-giver has not given life to

---

chapter 3 of this seminal work, "Biblical Type-Scenes and the Uses of Convention" (47-62), where Alter explores various type-scenes, such as betrothals at a well, birth annunciations of heroes to barren women, epiphanies in a field, and testaments of dying heroes. He touches on household rivals paradigms in conjunction with annunciation scenes, but does not develop these at length. For other studies of type-scenes in the Hebrew Bible, see Athalya Brenner, "Female Social Behaviour: Two Descriptive Patterns within the 'Birth of the Hero' Paradigm," *Vetus Testamentum* 36 (1986): 257-73; James G. Williams, "The Beautiful and the Barren: Conventions and Biblical Type Scenes," *Journal for the Study of the Old Testament* 17 (1980): 107-19.

3. Cf. Claus Westermann, *Genesis 12–36: A Continental Commentary* (trans. John J. Scullion; Minneapolis: Fortress, 1995), 238: "The meaning [in Gen 16:1] . . . is not simply a slave girl, but a personal servant of the wife whose power of disposition over her is restricted to this: the girl [Hagar] stands in a relationship of personal trust to her."

4. Phyllis Trible, *Texts of Terror: Literary-Feminist Readings of Biblical Narratives* (Philadelphia: Fortress, 1984), 10.

5. Cf. Trible's observation (*Texts of Terror*, 10-11) that the Hebrew order of naming in Gen 16:1, 3 situates Sarai and Hagar around the central Abram character.

Sarai's womb. To this point, the Lord's promise that elderly *Abram* will yet have a male heir from his "very own issue" (15:4) has not yet explicitly included Sarai in the bargain.[6] Furthermore, we do not know whether Abram has discussed his strange divine visitations with Sarai. In any case, if she is aware of God's covenantal promise to Abram, she assumes she is too old and sterile to play any direct, generative part in its fulfillment (cf. 18:12). But she remains determined to do what she can, protect her interests, and even help Abram and the Lord out (who both seem none too proactive) by giving her younger, more productive slave-girl to Abram. Despite her subordinate position to both Abram and the Lord — with oppressive consequences for Sarai (Abram sells her for a time to Pharaoh [12:10-15]; the Lord shuts her womb [16:2]) — Sarai now runs the show. Abram "heeds" Sarai's word and takes Hagar as his cowife (16:2), and the Lord stays out of the way until later in the story and never condemns Sarai's plan (though the Lord still has other plans).[7]

So far no conflict erupts between Sarai and Hagar. Of course, Hagar has no say or choice in the matter; as a slave, she is simply "given" to Abram, penetrated ("gone into") and impregnated by him — just as Sarai planned. But soon, as Hagar takes on a measure of independent character as the bearer of Abram's child, tension and rivalry erupt between the two women. The pregnant Hagar raises Sarai's ire by looking "lightly" or "slightly" on her barren, lightweight mistress (16:4).[8] The hierarchy of owner-slave/mistress-maid is being compromised: Sarai has "lost status"[9] in her slave-girl's eyes, as the latter gains weight in the household, both

---

6. In Gen 12:1-4 and 15:4-5, the Lord promises that "a great nation" will come from Abram, beginning with his own natural son. Sarai's role as bearer of this covenant child by Abram is not specified until 17:15-21; 18:9-15.

7. The Lord first intervenes in this surrogate birth case by appearing to the runaway pregnant Hagar, ordering her to return to mistress Sarai, and forecasting conflict between her son Ishmael ("the Lord hears") and "everyone" he encounters (Gen 16:7-14). Later the Lord also promises to bless and "make a great nation" from Ishmael, though not the chosen covenant people (21:17-21). See more below.

8. Robert Alter, *Genesis: Translation and Commentary* (New York: Norton, 1996), 68: "Her mistress seemed slight in her eyes."

9. Cf. Jacob Weingreen, "The Case of the Blasphemer (Leviticus XXIV 10ff.)," *Vetus Testamentum* 22 (1972): 119-20: In Gen 16:4-5, "the writer speaks of the deterioration in Sarah's standing in the estimation of her handmaid Hagar. . . . The writer was referring, not to Hagar's assumed arrogance toward her mistress, but to Sarah's having lost status, because of the new standing which Hagar had required through her pregnancy" (cited with approval in Westermann, *Genesis 12–36*, 240).

physically and socially. Hagar does not *speak against* Sarai in any way (Hagar only speaks to the Lord in this story [16:13], never to Sarai or in Sarai's presence). Thus, whatever disrespect she conveys toward her mistress comes through her eyes and mien.

Sarai's frustration over her apparent demotion in status prompts her sharp complaint, not to Hagar (Sarai never addresses her directly), but to Abram primarily and to the Lord implicitly. Sarai demands that the male authority figures do something to rectify "the wrong done to me." Her initiative in the scheme notwithstanding, Sarai lays the blame for Hagar's uppity demeanor squarely on Abram's head and invokes the Lord to adjudicate the matter "between you [Abram] and me" (16:5). Once Sarai gives Hagar to Abram's "embrace" (16:5), Hagar becomes his responsibility, and if he won't take action to restore Sarai's honor, she seems rather certain that the Lord will take up her cause.

As it happens, Abram responds by passing the buck, and the Lord responds *to Hagar,* but not to Sarai. Abram puts the problem back on Sarai: "Your slave-girl is in your power; do to her as you please." Accordingly, Sarai "harasses"[10] Hagar, forcing the pregnant slave-girl to flee from her abusive mistress (16:6). The household rivals' contest thus seems to be decided affirmatively, though by no means amicably, in Sarai's favor. But the Lord has yet to weigh in on the matter, and when he does it's on behalf of Hagar and restoration. Abandoned by husband and mistress, Hagar flees to the wilderness where the "angel of the LORD" meets her by a spring of water. This is the first encounter in Genesis between this mysterious divine messenger and a human being and marks the closest anyone comes to "seeing" God (as God "sees" her) and surviving, as the awestruck Hagar acknowledges: "Have I really seen God and remained alive after seeing him?" (16:13).[11] But more important than the Lord's seeing Hagar is his *hearing* her desperate cry, though she does not articulate her distress in the narrative beyond telling the Lord's messenger, "I am running away from my mistress Sarai" (16:8). The angel assures Hagar that "the LORD has given heed to [her] affliction" and will bless her with an innumerable host of de-

---

10. Alter, *Genesis,* 68.

11. Or as the new JPS translation (2nd ed.) of the Tanakh renders Gen 16:13: "And she called the Lord who spoke to her El-roi ['God of Seeing'], by which she meant, 'Have I not gone on seeing after He saw me!'" On the "angel of the LORD" figure and his close identification with YHWH, to the point of interchanging them in Gen 16:11, 13, see Westermann, *Genesis 12–36,* 242-44.

scendants, beginning with the son of Abram she is carrying whose name will be Ishmael, or "God hears" (16:11).[12]

But it will be a mixed blessing. The Lord dispatches Hagar back to Abram and Sarai's house with no illusions of bliss: "Return to your mistress and suffer harassment at her hand" (16:9);[13] moreover, Ishmael can expect a life of struggle as well,

> "with his hand against everyone,
> and everyone's hand against him." (16:12)

The Lord thus brings a measure of balance among the rival wives in Abram's household, but scarcely harmony, reconciliation, or equality, as later events will sadly confirm. When Sarai eventually (and miraculously) bears her own son, Isaac, she cannot bear the prospect of Hagar and Ishmael cosharing any part of Abram's household or inheritance. So on the occasion of the "great feast" celebrating Isaac's weaning, Sarai demands that Abram expel once and for all "this slave woman with her son" (21:8-10). Reluctantly, Abram complies again with Sarai's wish, though he scarcely shows much regret in sending Hagar and Ishmael off with only paltry provision of bread and water, a scant shadow of a "great feast." Fortunately, God steps in again, promising to watch over Ishmael and "make of him a great nation" (21:11-21).

Leah and Rachel

One fateful morning a romantic triangle was formed between Jacob and two sisters, the elder Leah and the younger Rachel. However, Jacob did not design or desire this arrangement in the slightest. His uncle Laban — and father of Leah and Rachel — pulled a fast one on Jacob and substituted Leah in the wedding-night bed when Jacob thought he was marrying Rachel. The famed trickster and "heel-grabber" was himself tricked and set back on his heels. On the "morning after," the shocked Jacob worked out (another) deal for Rachel, but only as cowife (Gen 29:21-30). He was stuck with Leah as well, and that leg (Jacob-Leah) of the tripod proved considerably weaker than the other two (Jacob-Rachel; Leah-

---

12. Up to this point of the story, only Sarai's voice has been explicitly *heard* — by Abram in 16:2.

13. Alter, *Genesis*, 69-70.

Rachel); flatly put, Jacob "loved Rachel more than Leah" (29:30). The household rivalry was on.

The distinctions between the two sisters go beyond age (elder/younger) and favor in Jacob's eyes to include matters of appearance and fertility. While Rachel is altogether "graceful and beautiful" (despite her name meaning "cow") — so much so, apparently, that Jacob is smitten by consuming love at first sight (29:9-12) — the most Leah (meaning "ewe") has going for her are striking eyes, which may have been "lovely" or "soft," on one rendering of the term *rakh,* or "weak" or "odd-looking," on a less flattering connotation (29:17).[14] In any case, she is no physical match for her little sister — at least not in terms of looks.

But fertility is another matter. The God who controls the creation and reproduction of human life in Genesis inverts Jacob's preferential treatment of his cowives: "When the LORD saw that Leah was unloved, he opened her womb; but Rachel was barren" (29:31). In fact, while the husband-favored Rachel gives Jacob no children, the divine-favored Leah blesses Jacob with four sons. Although we hear no prior complaint to the Lord lodged by a desperate Leah, responses following each birth — crystallized in the names she gives each son — reflect Leah's gratitude to God for addressing her plight: "the LORD *has looked on* my affliction . . . the LORD *has heard* that I am hated . . . this time I will praise the LORD" (29:32-35).[15] Unfortunately, neither Jacob nor Rachel adopts the Lord's viewpoint. Despite Leah's repeated hopes that her son-bearing will ignite her husband's attention and affection, Jacob remains curiously — and callously — silent.

Rachel, on the other hand, can hold back no longer. Envious of her elder sister's fecundity, she speaks for the first time in the narrative, but not to her rival Leah.[16] Rather, she vents her frustration to *Jacob* and even

14. Alter, *Genesis,* 153: "[T]here is no way confidently deciding whether the word [*rakh*] indicates some sort of impairment ('weak' eyes or perhaps odd-looking eyes) or rather suggests that Leah has sweet eyes that are her one asset of appearance, in contrast to her beautiful sister."

15. The names and meanings of the four sons are: (1) Reuben, "see/look" ("the LORD has *looked* on my affliction"); (2) Simeon, "hear" ("the LORD has *heard* that I am hated"); (3) Levi, "join/attach" ("Now this time my husband will be *joined* to me"); (4) Judah, "praise" ("This time I will *praise* the LORD") (Gen 29:32-35).

16. Cf. Alter, *Genesis,* 158: "It is a general principle of biblical narrative that a character's first recorded speech has particular defining force as characterization. Surprisingly, although Rachel has been part of the story for more than a decade of narrated time, this is the first piece of dialogue assigned to her."

blames him for her barrenness: "Give me children, or I shall die!" (30:1). The theatrical flourish — "or I shall die" — recalls Esau's earlier desperate plea for Jacob's red stew (25:30-31),[17] but with much higher stakes. Whereas famished Esau in fact would not have died if he had skipped or delayed one lunch, infertile Rachel — unable to produce life and thus fulfill the basic duty of women in this culture — had already endured a kind of social death. And for Jacob's part, whereas he easily satisfied Esau's desire for food (indeed, he staged the whole scene to swindle Esau out of his birthright), he takes great offense at Rachel's accusation that he has somehow withheld children from her. He can shower her with all kinds of love, but childbearing is out of his hands. This is God's business and, frankly, God's fault, if anyone is to be blamed: "Am I in the place of God," Jacob retorts to Rachel, "who has withheld from you the fruit of the womb?" (30:2).

Suddenly no one seems happy with anyone in the family, and except for granting four sons to Leah, the Lord does not seem to be helping much; in fact, by blessing Leah he upsets Rachel. But à la Sarai, Rachel presses on to help herself, proposing surrogate maternity through her handmaid Bilhah. After Bilhah bears Jacob a second son (Naphtali) on Rachel's behalf, Rachel declares victory in the grudge match with Leah: "With mighty wrestlings I have wrestled with my sister, and have prevailed" (30:8).[18] However, the rivalry is not so neatly settled. For one thing, Rachel's scoring system is suspect: Leah's four natural, elder sons still trump Rachel's two younger surrogates. And furthermore, Leah is not through wrestling. Though she has ceased bearing her own children, she can play Rachel's game, too, and adds two additional sons to her team through her handmaid Zilpah (30:9-13).

Still, at the point where any hope of reconciliation or solidarity be-

17. Alter, *Genesis*, 158. Note, too, Alter's vivid translation ("Give me sons, for if you don't I'm a dead woman!") and apt evaluation of Rachel's comment: "It is a sudden revelation of her simmering frustration and her impulsivity."

18. Instead of NRSV's "mighty wrestlings," Alter's translation of Gen 30:8 refers to Rachel's "awesome grapplings," though he notes the interesting link with Jacob's wrestling matches, including his "heel-grabbing/grappling" contests with his elder brother Esau from the womb (*Genesis*, 159). Cf. the connection with Jacob's later wrestling with God, observed by Ilana Pardes, *Countertraditions in the Bible: A Feminist Approach* (Cambridge: Harvard University Press, 1992), 65: "Just as Jacob 'prevails' (note the recurrence of the word) in his wrestling with 'God and men' (Gen 32:28), so Rachel, in an extremely condensed version of her counterpart's struggle, claims to have overcome her sister 'with great wrestlings,' wrestlings of God. Once again, Rachel is supposedly in Jacob's position, but not quite so."

tween the sisters seems lost, they finally speak to each other (something Hagar and Sarai never do) and cut a mutually beneficial deal between them. Although by no means a recipe for happy family relations ever after, this pact at least triggers, as Pardes observes, "a momentary change in triangular dynamics," a "brief truce" among household rivals.[19] Rachel opens the discussion, asking Leah for some of the lucky mandrakes[20] her son had found and given her; Leah bitterly objects to Rachel's greedy effrontery, since Rachel has already "taken away my [Leah's] husband"; Rachel then proposes to trade Leah a night in Jacob's bed for the mandrakes; Leah agrees, and the deal is done. Both Jacob and God comply with the women's scheme without a fuss: Jacob sleeps with Leah again (apparently after a long hiatus); God "heeds" Leah again and grants her two more natural sons and a daughter; but God also "remembers and heeds" Rachel and finally "opens her womb" to bear Joseph, with the blessed hope of "adding"[21] yet another son (30:14-24).

This temporary détente between rival sisters/cowives seems to be strengthened later by their solidarity in leaving their father Laban, who had shamelessly exploited both sisters, and following husband Jacob to his homeland (31:14-16). But we can scarcely speak of a close-knit, mutually supportive sisterhood. Rachel and Leah — always mentioned now in that inverted age order — never speak to one another again in the narrative, and Rachel still connives to advance her household position by stealing her father's household gods (teraphim) (31:19, 30-35). Moreover, Jacob's favoritism toward Rachel never abates; however fruitful Leah has been, Jacob places her and all her children ahead of Rachel and her son *only when meeting the (supposedly) murderous Esau;* Rachel (and Joseph) must be protected at all costs (33:1-2).

Hannah and Peninnah

Another inverted situation of favored/barren and unfavored/fertile cowives presents itself with Elkanah, Hannah, and Peninnah. Hannah, whose name means "charming" or "attractive," feels anything but what her name signifies. Although apparently the first and older wife and definitely

---

19. Pardes, *Countertraditions in the Bible,* 105.
20. Mandrakes were thought to have aphrodisiac powers and to stimulate fertility.
21. Joseph's name evokes the Hebrew for "he adds" (30:24).

loved by husband Elkanah, she remains barren.[22] The younger cowife, Peninnah, meaning "prolific" or "fertile," fully lives up to her name, but not enough to supplant Hannah in Elkanah's heart (1 Sam 1:1-2).

Among the household rival figures observed to this point, Peninnah is the least developed and least sympathetic. Besides her name and basic marital and maternal status (we are not told how many children she has or any of their names), Peninnah is identified as Hannah's "rival" *(sārâ)*, a term typically associated with Israel's or David's enemies and persecutors (cf. 1 Sam 10:18-19; 26:24; 2 Sam 4:9).[23] She mocks Hannah's divine disfavor ("because the LORD had closed her womb") more out of meanness ("to irritate [Hannah]") than her own sense of mistreatment (1 Sam 1:6). Peninnah never complains to Elkanah or to the Lord, and Hannah says or does nothing to provoke her cowife's ire. Elkanah does give a "double portion" of the sacrificial feast to Hannah "because he loved her" (1:5), but this gracious gesture seems to be more an act of compensating Hannah's barrenness than denigrating Peninnah's status. Elkanah suitably cares for Peninnah, providing normal portions for her and "all her sons and daughters," though the narrative never explicitly cites his "love" for them (1:4). Still, it is likely that Peninnah's bitterness toward Hannah is tinged with jealousy over Elkanah's repeated, special attention to Hannah at the Shiloh festival "year by year" (1:3, 7).[24]

For her part, while Hannah is deeply distressed over her cowife's taunts — "therefore Hannah wept and would not eat" — she never lashes out at or about Peninnah, who quickly drops out from the narrative altogether (1:7). Hannah bears her burden before (1) husband Elkanah, (2) priest Eli, and (3) the Lord, but never in the form of a direct complaint

---

22. See Bruce C. Birch, "The First and Second Books of Samuel: Introduction, Commentary, and Reflections," in *The New Interpreter's Bible*, vol. II (ed. Leander E. Keck et al.; Nashville: Abingdon, 1998), 974.

23. See Robert Polzin, *Samuel and the Deuteronomist: A Literary Study of the Deuteronomic History*, part 2: *1 Samuel* (New York: Harper and Row, 1989), 26; Birch, "First and Second Books of Samuel," 975.

24. Polzin (*Samuel and the Deuteronomist*, 20) observes that in 1 Sam 1:1-8, "information is packed and condensed through the description of repetitive or habitual behavior indicated by imperfective verb forms. . . . So, we are told, these things went on year by year, Peninnah habitually provoking the barren Hannah so that the latter would weep and refuse to eat." See also Alter, *Art of Biblical Narrative*, 83: "This places the action reported in these verses in what one might call a pseudo-singulative tense. Momentarily, that is, we might have assumed that the barren Hannah's ordeal by taunting took place just once, but then it becomes evident, alas, that she has to suffer this torment year after year."

or lament about Peninnah or her own condition. Elkanah's pathetic, narcissistic attempt to comfort his distraught wife — "Am I not more to you than ten sons?" (1:8) — receives no verbal rejoinder from Hannah, but after the festival banquet where Elkanah utters his supposedly encouraging words, she leaves the table to "weep bitterly" alone before the Lord in the sanctuary (1:9-10). If she were to speak to her clueless husband, it would be something like, "Are you kidding me? *One son* would be worth more than you, you self-centered man!"[25] Conversely, Eli's undiscerning, snap judgment of Hannah's silent praying ("only her lips moved") as inebriation receives a swift retort: "I have been pouring out my soul before the LORD" (1:13-15). The priest, of all people, should have known this. The authoritative men in Hannah's life provide paltry relief or understanding.

Fortunately, Hannah's outcry to the Lord proves more fruitful. Although Hannah's cry is formulated more as commitment than complaint, she pledges — if the Lord would consider "the misery of your servant" and grant her a son — to consecrate this offspring wholly to the Lord's service (1:11). After Hannah breaks her silence and explains this extraordinary vow to Eli, the misguided priest finally kicks in and vouches that God will grant her petition (1:17). That's good enough for Hannah, who perks up, breaks her fast, and "in due time" conceives and bears Samuel (1:18-20). Where others may aggravate (Peninnah), trivialize (Elkanah), or misdiagnose (Eli) her distress, the Lord attends to Hannah's plight and gives her what she "asks."[26]

25. Further demonstrating Elkanah's insensitivity, see Birch, "First and Second Books of Samuel," 975: Elkanah "significantly does not tell Hannah that *she* is worth more to *him* than ten sons" (emphasis in original). For a trenchant critique of attempts by many male scholars to defend Elkanah's sympathy and "true love" for Hannah, see Yairah Amit, "'Am I Not More Devoted to You Than Ten Sons?' (1 Samuel 1.8): Male and Female Interpretations," in *A Feminist Companion to Samuel and Kings* (ed. Athalya Brenner; Sheffield: Sheffield Academic, 1994), 68-76. From Hannah's and most women's perspectives, Amit argues that "Elkanah's words reveal him to possess the egocentricity of a child who perceives himself as the centre of his world and is disappointed when his behavior fails to receive the attention he expects. Elkanah is revealed as one who cannot accept the fact that Hannah wants to be mother to her children and not mother to her husband. . . . Elkanah is thus indifferent to Hannah's pain, and he finds it easy to decide for her that his closeness to her is more important for her than her own children would be. It would seem that his self-esteem knows no bounds" (75).

26. The Hebrew verb for "ask" *(šā'al)* appears seven times in 1 Sam 1, though curiously, in spite of Hannah's exclamation in 1:20 ("She named him Samuel, for she said, 'I have asked him of the LORD'"), the "ask" term underlies the name of *Saul* rather than Samuel. See discussion in Birch, "First and Second Books of Samuel," 976.

Hannah's reversal of fortune reaches its height in her passionate song, exulting in the defeat of her "arrogant enemies" and eventual despair of "she who has many children" (2:1-5). Although Hannah's psalm names no names and looks far beyond her personal situation, it's hard not to hear a triumphal dig against Peninnah in the background. In any case, there is no hint of rehabilitation for Peninnah or reconciliation between household rivals.

Bathsheba and Abishag

The bitter household battle for succeeding David's throne comes to a head at the opening of 1 Kings. With Amnon and Absalom already dead, the eldest remaining son Adonijah and younger Solomon jockey to take over their dying father's kingdom. But while this monarchical rivalry primarily engages the leading men of the realm, two women also play key roles: Abishag, David's bed-warming "attendant," and Bathsheba, one of David's wives. The former emerges from a nationwide search for a "very beautiful young virgin," chosen to snuggle with the geriatric, hypothermic king; however, given David's debility, he "does not know her sexually" (1 Kings 1:1-5). At an earlier time (see 2 Sam 11–12), the also "very beautiful" Bathsheba had been personally chosen by a younger, more virile David as his bed partner; only she was no virgin — being another man's wife! — and did know David sexually — because he forced her![27] Moreover, she eventually became David's wife and the mother of Solomon. Now, however, as the years have advanced, Bathsheba finds her place in David's bed supplanted by the nubile Abishag and her position at court, along with Solomon's, threatened by the ambitious Adonijah, David's son by another cowife, Haggith.

After the "handsome" Adonijah boldly proclaims himself the heir apparent king at a grand royal banquet, the prophet Nathan dispatches Bathsheba to David's bedchamber with a clever scheme to secure the throne for Solomon (1 Kings 1:5-14). The opening language of the scene is telling: "So Bathsheba went to the king in his room. The king was very old;

---

27. Although not identified in terms of rape as explicitly as Shechem's violation of Dinah (Gen 34) or Amnon's violation of Tamar (2 Sam 13), the gendered power dynamics of David's "sending for" (2 Sam 11:3-4) and sexually "taking" (12:4, 9) Bathsheba amounts to the same crime. See discussion in Danna Nolan Fewell and David M. Gunn, *Gender, Power, and Promise: The Subject of the Bible's First Story* (Nashville: Abingdon, 1993), 157-60.

Abishag the Shunammite was attending the king" (1:15). As Adele Berlin observes, this information is redundant from the narrator's and readers' points of view. The bedroom scene has already been set for us in 1:1-5 — *but not for Bathsheba*. Now in 1:15 she sees it for herself or, more to the point, she sees *her* — the other woman, Abishag — for herself. If Bathsheba's precarious place in David's heart and kingdom had not sunk in before, it surely hits her now: "one can feel a twinge of jealousy pass through Bathsheba as she silently notes the presence of a younger, fresher woman."[28] Though Abishag and Bathsheba exchange no words (Abishag says nothing throughout the narrative), their rivalry is palpable.

As the scene develops, Bathsheba has plenty to say to David by way of both reminder and complaint. Addressing David as "my lord," she first reminds him of the solemn oath he "swore to your servant by the LORD your God" that *Solomon* would succeed him on the throne (1:17). Bathsheba then complains not only that Adonijah has usurped David's authority and kingdom, but also that "you, my lord the king, *do not know it*" (1:18). What and who (Abishag) David "does not know" can still hurt Bathsheba very much, and it is high time he wakes up and takes action.[29] Although he says nothing about Abishag's fate, David eventually agrees with Bathsheba (and Nathan) and confirms Solomon as his successor (1:28-40).

Installed as king following David's death, Solomon naturally inherits David's royal possessions, including all his servants and attendants, like Abishag. But Adonijah is not through scheming yet, and in a brazen — and ultimately foolish — move, he asks Bathsheba to petition Solomon for Abishag's hand in marriage. Adonijah enlists Bathsheba's aid partly because he thinks Solomon "will not refuse" his mother (2:17), but also perhaps because he assumes Bathsheba will jump at the chance to remove her rival from Solomon's retinue. As it happens, Bathsheba does present Adonijah's "one small request" to Solomon, no doubt knowing all the while, however, that there is nothing *small* about it (2:19-21). To ask for David's last bed partner, likely viewed as a concubine, is tantamount to asking for part of David's kingdom. Solomon interprets the request as nothing less than treason, meriting Adonijah's execution (2:22-25). Nothing more is said about Abishag's status, but she could hardly benefit from any associa-

28. Adele Berlin, *Poetics and Interpretation of Biblical Narrative* (Sheffield: Almond, 1983; Winona Lake: Eisenbrauns, 1994), 28 (see also p. 74).

29. Abishag also remains a threat to Bathsheba, even though David "does not know her" in the sexual sense (1:4).

tion, explicit or tacit, with Adonijah. In any case, Bathsheba's position as queen mother clearly outranks that of any of Solomon's attendants. The young, silent virgin is no match for the shrewd, older wife of David, mother of Solomon, friend of Nathan — and the Lord![30]

Naomi and Ruth

The relationship between mother-in-law (Naomi) and daughters-in-law (Orpah and Ruth) in the book of Ruth begins not in rivalry over men's affections and childbearing capacities, but in solidarity over common widowhood and childlessness. The Judahite Naomi from Bethlehem and Moabites Orpah and Ruth, married to Naomi's sons, all lose their husbands to death in the first five verses in "the country of Moab." Naomi suffers a triple hit in a foreign land — "the woman was left without her two sons and her husband" (Ruth 1:5) — and Orpah and Ruth evidently had borne no children. Unlike the previous stories we have considered, however, neither childless woman is said to be "barren." Any deficiency seems to fall to their deceased husbands, inauspiciously named "Sickness" (Mahlon) and "Spent" (Chilion).[31]

Although coming from different peoples historically in conflict with each other, these bereft women support and nurture one another. Although Orpah eventually "turns back" to Moab as Naomi returns to her homeland in Bethlehem of Judea, she does so at Naomi's insistence for her (Orpah's) own good (1:12-15). Ruth, however, goes the second mile and then some with her mother-in-law, despite Naomi's protestations, sticking beside her and adopting Naomi's God and people as her own (1:16-18). Following the deaths of the three husbands, the overall spirit among the surviving women is mutually sensitive and solicitous.

But that scarcely means that all is well. Upon arriving in Bethlehem with Ruth, Naomi, punning on her name, lets forth a piercing fourfold

---

30. The divine Lord's authorization of Bathsheba's (and Nathan's) scheme to make Solomon the true successor of the Davidic line is evident in 1 Kings 1:32-37; 2:1-4, 23-24, 44-45. Throughout the narrative Bathsheba proves to be remarkably perceptive, rhetorically skilled, and "in the know." See Berlin, *Poetics*, 27-30; F. Scott Spencer, *Dancing Girls, "Loose" Ladies, and Women of "the Cloth": The Women in Jesus' Life* (New York: Continuum, 2004), 33-35.

31. Adele Berlin, "Ruth," in *The HarperCollins Study Bible* (gen. ed. Harold W. Attridge; rev. ed.; New York: HarperCollins, 2006), 382.

lament to her townspeople that also implicates the Lord in no uncertain terms:

> "Call me no longer Naomi [pleasant],
>   call me Mara (*mārā'* [bitter]),
>   for [1] the Almighty has dealt bitterly *(mārar)* with me.
> I went away full,
>   but [2] the LORD has brought me back empty;
> why call me Naomi
>   when [3] the LORD has dealt harshly with me,
>   and [4] the Almighty has brought calamity upon me." (1:20-21)[32]

In her complaint, Naomi asks nothing of the Lord to relieve her distress; she seems thoroughly resigned to her embittered fate.

But another man soon enters the picture — Naomi's "kinsman on her husband's side, a prominent rich man . . . whose name was Boaz" (2:1). However, while Naomi would seem to have in Boaz a prime candidate for protecting and nurturing her, Ruth takes the initiative and goes to work in the fields, with Naomi's permission, in hopes of "finding favor" with some man there; and she just "happens" to glean in Boaz's part of the field and attract Boaz's attention (2:2-9). The conditions seem ripe for the younger woman to steal Naomi's kinsman ("my lord") from her and further add to her misery (we half expect mandrakes to pop up in the field at any moment). But in fact, defying expectations, solidarity continues to prevail over rivalry. Boaz's interest in Ruth is more avuncular than romantic, motivated mostly by Ruth's remarkable faithfulness in caring for Naomi and uniting with Israel's God and people (2:11-12). And for Naomi's part, she couldn't be happier that her daughter-in-law and near kinsman have hit it off. Indeed, Naomi even finds her sorely tested faith in God suddenly renewed: "Blessed be he by the LORD, whose kindness has not forsaken the living or the dead!" (2:20). Ultimately, Naomi goes so far as to doll up Ruth for a private liaison with Boaz, which soon leads to their marriage and the Lord's blessing them with a son. Naomi's scheme for Ruth's weal, rather than woe, comes to fruition: "I need to

---

32. Cf. Danna Nolan Fewell and David M. Gunn, "'A Son Is Born to Naomi!' Literary Allusions and Interpretation in the Book of Ruth," in *Women in the Hebrew Bible: A Reader* (ed. Alice Bach; New York: Routledge, 1999), 234: "Her [Naomi's] worldview is theistic. She lays blame for her calamity at Yahweh's door and her language echoes that of Job. . . . She sees herself alone."

seek some security for you [Ruth], so that it may be well with you" (3:1; cf. Ruth 3–4).

What, then, becomes of Naomi, who, for all of Ruth's good fortune, remains an elderly, childless widow — typically a recipe for ignominy and acrimony in biblical narrative? Might all her interest in Ruth's welfare ultimately backfire and leave her in the lurch, with all the attention focused on the young mother and her son? Does not the blessing of the town elders and people bestowed on Boaz — "May the LORD make the woman who is coming into your house *like Rachel and Leah,* who together [both] built up the house of Israel" (4:11) — for all its positive memory of the combined contribution of Jacob's cowives, also raise the ominous specter of the younger (Rachel is listed first) woman's favored status at the elder's expense? In fact, expectations of household rivalry continue to be subverted through the end of Ruth's narrative. Boaz acknowledges that he "acquires," through standard "redemption" procedures, "*from the hand of Naomi* all that belonged" to her deceased husband and sons, including Ruth (4:9-10). Thus Boaz affirms both Naomi's role in brokering the deal for Ruth and his responsibility to provide for Naomi as well as Ruth. But even more importantly for Naomi, the women of Bethlehem rally together (1) to name Ruth's son (Obed), (2) to give Naomi comaternal rights, as it were, to Ruth's son ("A son has been born *to Naomi*"), and (3) to bless the Lord for "restoring" Naomi's life and granting her an exceptional "daughter-in-law who loves you, who is more to you than seven sons" (4:14-17). Hannah should have been so lucky![33] The book of Ruth stands as a dynamic story of divine and human *redemption* — for Naomi, for Ruth, and, to some extent, for prior stories of women's household rivalry in the Hebrew Bible that fall short of Naomi/Ruth's sustained solidarity.[34]

At least that's one way to read the book of Ruth, certainly the most positive way and the way that I think rings truest with Ruth's overall story. But as Carol Gilligan observes about our typical cultural conditioning: we have considerable "difficulty in hearing a story about women that does not

---

33. Recall that Elkanah thought he should be worth ten sons to Hannah. He wasn't and never could be. But Ruth's value to Naomi was priceless, given Ruth's unwavering loyalty to her mother-in-law, not to mention her ability to give Naomi a son.

34. In addition to the Leah-Rachel story, the book of Ruth explicitly recalls and implicitly further redeems the Tamar narrative from Gen 38 (see Ruth 4:11-12). For a classic literary- and feminist-critical exposition of the book of Ruth as a redemptive "human comedy" out of tragic circumstances, see Phyllis Trible, *God and the Rhetoric of Sexuality* (Philadelphia: Fortress, 1978), 166-99.

pit them in competition."[35] We've seen this pattern borne out in previous OT accounts. And even now with Ruth, some eerie silences from a key singer subtly skew the lovely chorus of women's solidarity. Fewell and Gunn expose five such fade-outs by *Naomi* at strategic segments of the score, suggesting a simmering, rather than dissipating, bitterness about her own fate and toward Ruth — or alternately, an ongoing "bittersweet" appraisal of Naomi's situation.[36] For example, after Ruth's famous declaration of loyalty to Naomi's God and people, Naomi does not reply. In fact, the text stresses: "When Naomi saw that she [Ruth] was determined to go with her, *she said no more to her*" (1:18). Not exactly a warm, embracing response of gratitude. Would Naomi have preferred this alien Moabite go back home with sister Orpah, *as Naomi had strongly urged* (1:15)? At the story's end, while the *women of the village* extol Ruth's value to Naomi ("your daughter-in-law . . . loves you [and] is more to you than seven sons") and pronounce Naomi's surrogate motherhood ("a son has been born to Naomi"), Naomi herself utters nary a word (4:13-17). Is this all good news or more of a mixed bag for Naomi? Is the nagging threat of a Moabite interloper, with all that bad past blood between Israel and Moab, fully resolved? Is Naomi really safe and secure now with this "mixed" little one at her breast? Fewell and Gunn tease out the abiding ambiguities and insecurities:

> The message of the women . . . interprets Ruth to be a surrogate, which brings into focus . . . from the Rachel and Leah story dimensions of jealousy and resentment that come when other women bear children for the barren. We are reminded also of Sarah and Hagar. . . . Is [Naomi] mother or only nurse? . . . [T]he narrative exposes the precariousness — and the irony — of her position. She owes her restoration to . . . Ruth the Moabite woman . . . whose radical action challenges the male-centered values that permeate both the story and Naomi's worldview. . . . Oh, how we hate to be saved by Samaritans![37]

While I don't believe Naomi's awkward silences drown out the dominant redemptive-cooperative strains of the story (the fragility of arguments from silence are well known), they do mark puzzling pauses that give us pause about declaring perfect peace among potential household rivals.

---

35. Carol Gilligan, *Joining the Resistance* (Cambridge: Polity, 2011), 147.

36. Fewell and Gunn, "'A Son Is Born,'" 233-39. "Naomi's silence is bittersweet" (238).

37. Fewell and Gunn, "'A Son Is Born,'" 238-39.

Elizabeth and Mary

Compared with Matthew's nativity narrative, Luke's stands out for presenting the miraculous births of two sons, John and Jesus, born six months apart to two women, Elizabeth and Mary, not from the same household but still related in some sense as kinswomen (*syngeneis* [Luke 1:36]).[38] One way or another, all four canonical Gospels negotiate the precise relationship — including potential rivalry — between the dynamic prophets John and Jesus and their respective followers.[39] But only Luke grounds this relationship in their closely paralleled births to related mothers.

Elizabeth is introduced first as a descendant of Aaron and wife of a Judean priest named Zechariah; together the couple are lauded as "righteous before God, living blamelessly according to all the commandments and regulations of the Lord" (1:6). But finally — and forebodingly, in light of previous scriptural stories — Elizabeth appears as elderly and "barren" (*steira* [1:7]). By contrast, her niece or cousin Mary is a young "virgin" (*parthenos*) engaged to a nondescript Galilean man named Joseph from the line of David (1:26-27).

Notably, however, poignant expressions of bitterness and/or sorrow we have come to expect from barren women in the Bible are muted with Elizabeth. Not that she blithely accepts her condition without a thought. We might assume that she partners with Zechariah in continuing to pray for children (1:13), and once she conceives a child with Zechariah, following the angel's temple annunciation, she announces: "This is what the Lord has done for me when he looked favorably on me and took away the disgrace I have endured among my people" (1:25). Elizabeth does not sugarcoat the public "disgrace" (*oneidos*) she has long suffered. But overall she chooses to dwell on "what the Lord has done" for her now in redressing her shame, and at no point does she blame the Lord or Zechariah or anyone else for her extended sterility.

Meanwhile, during Elizabeth's sixth month of pregnancy with John, the same angel (Gabriel) who appeared to Zechariah comes to Mary, announcing that she, too, will wondrously conceive and bear a special son named Jesus. The similarities between the two announced sons reflect a

---

38. I dealt extensively with Mary's maternal, prophetic, and theological roles in chapter 3. Here my concern is strictly with Mary's kinship relationship with Elizabeth, which I touched on briefly above.

39. See F. Scott Spencer, *What Did Jesus Do? Gospel Profiles of Jesus' Personal Conduct* (Harrisburg, Pa.: Trinity, 2003), 53-61.

pattern of "climactic parallelism."[40] Though one birth (John's) will be great, the other (Jesus') will be greater; put another way, Mary and her son are destined to "one-up" Elizabeth and her child. Whereas Elizabeth has conceived a son in her old, barren state who is "filled with the Holy Spirit" from her womb and destined to serve as "the prophet of the Most High" after the fashion of Elijah (1:15, 76), Mary will conceive a son in her young, *virginal state* through the generative power of the Holy Spirit who "will be called *the Son of the Most High*" and sit on the throne of David (1:30-33). With ancient mothers as jealously ambitious for their sons' success as modern soccer moms (recall Mrs. Zebedee's pitch for her boys to sit at Jesus' right and left hands [Matt 20:20-23]), the stage seems set for the eruption of inner-family rivalries for favor and status.

But the type-plot aborts largely due to Elizabeth's prescience and magnanimity. When the newly pregnant Mary heads south "with haste" to visit Elizabeth, the older woman joyously welcomes the younger girl into her home, spurred by the leaping enthusiasm of the child in her womb upon hearing Mary's greeting. Elizabeth then, "filled with the Holy Spirit," gives voice to her and her fetus's joy, blessing Mary and the son she carries and commending Mary's exceptional faith in "what was spoken to her by the Lord" (1:39-45). In turn, Mary bursts forth in ebullient song, confirming Elizabeth's proclamation of her "blessed among women" state — but in a spirit of deep humility and gratitude, rather than haughtiness and arrogance. In no sense does Mary lord her extraordinary honor as "mother of the Lord" (cf. 1:43) over Elizabeth. Indeed, Mary marvels at God's regard for the "lowliness of his slave-girl," as she conceives of herself, and takes God's dealings with her as paradigmatic of a larger purpose of "lifting the lowly" and helping the poor while, conversely, demoting the powerful and "scattering the proud" (cf. 1:46-55). Although in many respects modeling her song after Hannah's in 1 Samuel 2, Mary's version includes no sweet revenge toward Elizabeth, as Hannah's likely did toward the arrogant irritant, Peninnah (see above). Of course, Elizabeth had given Mary no cause for malice; in every respect — age, attitude, fertility — Elizabeth is the anti-Peninnah.

Luke's narrative consistently resists the potential for household rivalry between Elizabeth and Mary in the interest of their solidarity and mutual support in fulfilling God's overarching purpose for them and their sons. Moreover, as Brigitte Kahl discerns, Luke 1 in fact weaves a new "feminist-

---

40. See F. Scott Spencer, *The Gospel of Luke and Acts of the Apostles* (Nashville: Abingdon, 2008), 110-12.

egalitarian" pattern out of well-known biblical materials from Genesis and Samuel, including some we have examined above: "The age-old rivalry between one woman and another woman, between firstborn and younger son, which is inherent in the rules of patriarchy, finally turns into sisterhood and brotherhood: Hagar and Sarah, Leah and Rachel, Hannah and Peninnah as well as Cain and Abel, Ishmael and Isaac, Esau and Jacob finally become reconciled in Elizabeth and Mary, John and Jesus."[41]

The only hint, and it's nothing more than that, of possible underlying tension comes in Mary's apparent absence when Elizabeth gives birth to John and celebrates the Lord's "great mercy" toward her with "her neighbors and relatives *(perioikoi kai syngeneis)*" (1:57-58). Just before the birthday party, Luke dispatches Mary back home to Galilee, after noting, however, that she stayed *three months* with Elizabeth (1:56). Mary exits the scene while Elizabeth takes center stage. Subsequently, when Mary gives birth to Jesus in Bethlehem, shepherds and angels share the joyous experience — but not relatives Elizabeth, Zechariah, and John (2:8-20). Of course, narrative absences are as tricky to negotiate as narrative silences, like those discussed above with Naomi. In Luke 1, the presence of only the birth mother at the delivery scene likely serves to spotlight her special moment, not to diminish the other woman. After Mary's visit to Elizabeth's home in 1:39-56, the two women never meet again in Luke's story. Then again, after the infancy accounts, both women largely drop from view (Elizabeth entirely), with the focus shifting to sons John and Jesus.

Martha and Mary

By introducing his Gospel with a portrait of congenial bonds between kinswomen where we might otherwise expect rivalry, Luke seems to tip his presentation of female household relations more toward what we found in the book of Ruth than in Genesis or Samuel-Kings. But, as sketched above, Luke also frankly admits problems of household *division* among women and men in the chapters immediately following the Martha/Mary episode in 10:38-42. Also, we may remember from our previous discussion of Mary's "destiny" and "anxiety" in 2:22-52 that, soon after the births of John and Jesus, Luke introduces the prospect of familial strife and tension,

41. Brigitte Kahl, "Toward a Materialist-Feminist Reading," in *Searching the Scriptures: A Feminist Introduction* (ed. Elisabeth Schüssler Fiorenza; New York: Crossroad, 1993), 237.

though not necessarily between female relatives. After blessing the parents at infant Jesus' dedication in the temple, the prophet Simeon abruptly warns Mary that "this child is destined for the *falling and the rising* of many in Israel, and to be a sign that will be *opposed* . . . and a sword will *pierce* your own soul too" (2:34-35); then the story of the twelve-year-old Jesus staying behind in Jerusalem and amazing the temple scholars, far from swelling his parents' pride, fuels their anger and angst ("Child, why have you treated us like this? Look, your father and I have been searching for you in great anxiety" [2:48]).[42] We must also not forget that Jesus' first sermon in his hometown synagogue so sets his kinfolk and neighbors on edge that they try to hurl him off the edge of a cliff (4:29)![43]

So Luke sends somewhat mixed messages about kinship values and domestic dynamics, as does the biblical household rivalry type-scene in general, as we have seen. So where does the Martha/Mary incident fit in all this? From the start, we must acknowledge a notable *divergence* from *all* the previous examples, namely, that Martha and Mary's relationship has nothing to do with their marital or maternal identities. No husbands or children are in the picture: the women are only presented as *sisters* (*adelphē* [10:39-40]) in *Martha's* house, according to some texts ("into her [Martha's] home" [*eis oikian autēs*] [10:38]).[44] Whatever the best reading, Martha appears as the primary host of Jesus ("Martha welcomed him" [10:38]), which likely signifies her role as elder sister and household head. In any case, Martha and Mary are single siblings sharing the same domicile, not mothers, cowives, concubines, mistress/maids, or in-laws, as in the foregoing type-scenes. The closest affinity would be with Leah and Rachel, who were sisters as well as cowives, but their rivalry still revolved around their fertility and favoritism vis-à-vis husband Jacob.

42. Though we also recall the surprising counterpoint that, following his dramatic assertion of independence from his parents in the temple, the adolescent Jesus still returns to Nazareth with Mary and Joseph and remains "subject" to them (2:51) until he launches his public ministry.

43. See Spencer, *What Did Jesus Do?* 36-38.

44. Although the vast majority of manuscripts include "into her house," the pair of early papyri that omit the phrase may be more original since it seems more likely a scribe would add than subtract this elaborative note to the bare statement, "Martha welcomed him." In any case, as Roger L. Omanson remarks, "the variant readings of 'into her house/home' surely represent the implicit meaning of 'she received/welcomed him,' and translators may decide to make this explicit" (*A Textual Guide to the Greek New Testament: An Adaptation of Bruce M. Metzger's* Textual Commentary *for the Needs of Translators* [Stuttgart: Deutsche Bibelgesellschaft, 2006,] 129).

While this critical disjuncture with biblical precedent may seem to disqualify the Martha and Mary episode altogether from the household rivals type-scene, we should recall Luke's overall limited interest in women's roles as wives and mothers.[45] Even in the birth stories, Elizabeth's and Mary's roles have as much to do with their attentiveness to God's word and Spirit-inspired prophecy as with their childbearing and caring duties (though, as we saw in chapter 3, their maternal capabilities should not be discounted). And they thoroughly overshadow their husbands: Zechariah spends most of the story mute, and Joseph is barely in the picture at all; Mary doesn't even need him for the usual fertilizing function. During the Galilean phase of his ministry, Jesus encounters three married or formerly married women with no accompanying husband (Simon's mother-in-law [4:38-39]; the widow at Nain [7:11-17]; Joanna [8:3;[46] cf. 24:10]), three individual woman with unknown marital histories (Mary Magdalene, Susanna, hemorrhaging woman [8:2-3, 43-48]), and only one married couple whom he deals with together (he allows the "father [Jairus] and mother [unnamed]" to be present when he raises up their deceased daughter [8:51]).[47] Across the balance of Luke's Gospel, no other married women or mothers appear, except Lot's wife, remembered for her misplaced loyalty and salty demise (17:32),[48] and the

45. In her major study of women in Luke-Acts, Turid Karlsen Seim (*The Double Message: Patterns of Gender in Luke-Acts* [Nashville: Abingdon, 1994]) "show[s] repeatedly how marriage and childbirth, which was normally women's primary possibility in life and their legitimation, is dismissed as irrelevant in the community of Jesus as Luke describes it" (185). See further Seim's essays: "Children of the Resurrection: Perspectives on Angelic Asceticism in Luke-Acts," in *Asceticism and the New Testament* (ed. Leif E. Vaage and Vincent L. Wimbush; New York: Routledge, 1999), 115-25, and "The Virgin Mother: Mary and Ascetic Discipleship in Luke," in *A Feminist Companion to Luke* (ed. Amy-Jill Levine and Marianne Blickenstaff; London: Sheffield Academic, 2002), 89-105.

46. Though Joanna's husband does not seem to accompany her with Jesus, at least he is named (Chuza). See the thorough discussion of Joanna in chapter 4.

47. Still, the father Jairus is the more prominent parent involved in his daughter's case (Luke 8:40-42), similar to that of the father who brings his convulsive son to Jesus in 9:37-43; in this latter example, as in the parable of the lost son (15:11-32), no mother appears. We might consider also the *absences* (omissions?) in Luke of Matthew/Mark's story of the desperate Canaanite/Syrophoenician mother (Matt 15:21-28/Mark 7:24-30) and Matthew's incident of Mrs. Zebedee's petitioning Jesus on behalf of her two sons (Matt 20:20-21). Bottom line: outside of the opening birth narratives, mothers are rare in Luke's Gospel.

48. In this same discourse, Jesus also associates "marrying and being given in marriage" and other typical aspects of this-worldly life with the clueless days of Noah preceding the flood (Luke 17:26-27); later Jesus characterizes life in the new resurrection age as "like angels" who "neither marry nor are given in marriage" (20:34-36).

"daughters of Jerusalem" whom Jesus laments would be better off — indeed "blessed," given the coming catastrophes — if they had been barren (tell that to Sarah, Rachel, Hannah, and Elizabeth!) and never borne children (tell that to Jesus' own "blessed among women" mother!) (23:27-29).

Apart from the apocalyptic doomsday scenario, this relativistic attitude toward traditional female family roles fits Jesus' avowed higher commitments to "fictive" spiritual kin: first, in response to his biological mother and half brothers' desire to see him — "My mother and my brothers are those who hear the word of God and do it" (8:21); and second, in response to an anonymous woman's exclamation of the "blessed" nature of his mother's womb/breasts that bore/nursed him — "Blessed rather are those who hear the word of God and obey it!" (so much again for Mary as "blessed among women") (11:28).[49]

In short, the household that matters most in Luke is the *household of God* where *God's word* has ultimate authority mediated through *Jesus the Lord* or household master *(kyrios)*. Accordingly, women's primary relationship of devotion and obedience is to God and his Son Jesus rather than to husband or children. In terms of Jesus' fertility parable of the sower, faithful disciples are called to receive the "seed" of the "word of God" implanted by Jesus and to "bear fruit with patient endurance" (8:11-15).[50] In Pauline terms that suggestively echo the Martha/Mary episode, it is better for women (and men) "to be free from [domestic/marital] anxieties *(amerimnous)*," to be "anxious *(merimna)* [only] about the affairs of the Lord *(kyriou)*" in the priority interest of "unhindered devotion to the Lord *(kyriō)*" (1 Cor 7:32-35).[51] As with Jesus' parting lamentation to the "daughters of Jerusalem" regarding inevitable maternal ago-

---

49. Notice, too, in comparison with Matthew's tamer account of the family cost of discipleship in terms of loving Jesus more than father, mother, son, or daughter (Matt 10:37), Luke uses stronger "hate" language and specifies a wider cast of negligible family members, including "wife and children": "Whoever comes to me and does not hate father and mother, wife and children, brothers and sisters, yes, and even life itself, cannot be my disciple" (Luke 14:26). See Dale B. Martin, *Sex and the Single Savior: Gender and Sexuality in Biblical Interpretation* (Louisville: Westminster John Knox, 2006), 106 (cf. 106-9).

50. That Jesus' foundational teaching about discipleship through the sower parable in 8:4-15 applies to both men and women is made clear by the framing texts featuring both male and female followers in 8:1-3 and 8:19-21.

51. Notice the similar terminology: "But the Lord *(kyrios)* answered her, 'Martha, Martha, you are worried *(merimnas)* and distracted by many things'" (Luke 10:41). On the connection with 1 Cor 7:32-35, see Michael D. Goulder, *Luke: A New Paradigm*, vol. 2: *Part II (cont.). Commentary: Luke 9:51–24.53* (Sheffield: Sheffield Academic, 1989), 493-94.

nies in the coming days of tribulation (Luke 23:28-29), Paul's advice about mitigating family worries and encouraging exclusive consecration to the Lord becomes especially urgent "in view of the impending crisis" (1 Cor 7:26).

Although Luke has largely spiritualized kinship relations, the potential for household rivalry among biological kin, like that depicted in the biblical type-scenes, persists around the dominant figure of Jesus as Lord and his word (seed). In the triangular household scene with Martha, Mary, and Jesus, Mary occupies a seemingly favored position in relation to Jesus, sitting at his feet and taking in his "his word" *(ton logon autou)* — a situation that frustrates the neglected elder sister Martha, as she perceives it. Accordingly, like Sarah, Rachel, and Bathsheba, she complains to the "lord" in the house; and since Jesus also represents the divine Lord in Luke, she also decries her condition in a kind of prayerful lament to the Lord, like Leah (implicitly), Hannah, and Naomi.

The thrust of Martha's complaint follows a line taken by other biblical women who blame the Lord in some sense for their misery: "Lord *(Kyrie)*, do you not care!" (10:40). This charge assumes that Jesus is somehow responsible for Martha's consternation and could do something to rectify it, if he just would. But what Martha specifically demands of Jesus seems at first blush quite distinct from the desires of other embittered household rivals. For example, corresponding to Rachel's demand of Jacob — "Give me children or I shall die" — would be something like Martha's imploring Jesus, "Give me your teaching, Lord; let me bear your word like (or instead of) my sister Mary." But in fact, Martha does not want what Mary has at this moment; she does not want to take Mary's place at Jesus' feet. Rather, Martha wants Jesus to "tell her [Mary] to help me [Martha]" with the latter's "many tasks." Martha is not so much jealous of Mary's relationship with Jesus as angry that "my sister has left me to do all the work by myself" (10:40) — and that Jesus has tolerated, if not encouraged, Mary's indolence. Martha wants to put Mary in her proper place — that is, *with Martha*. Martha does not want her irritating, irresponsible sister sent away, like Sarah expels Hagar, or cropped from the family album, like Bathsheba wants Abishag out of the picture. Instead, she wants her sister to join her, like Ruth clung to Naomi, as partners in household service. Martha wants sisterly solidarity — *but on her own terms*.

Moreover, although Martha obviously values her servant duty over her sister's student posture in this case, it's not because Martha's devotion to Jesus is any less fervent than Mary's. Martha "welcomes" (*apodechomai*

[10:38; cf. 19:6; Acts 17:7]) Jesus, as we have seen, from the beginning of the scene, and her "many tasks" (NRSV) — better rendered as "much service/ministry" (*pollē diakonia* [Luke 10:40]) — are all performed *for* Jesus out of her deep love and care *for* him. Martha has become overwhelmed and "distracted" by her demanding work, but *not* distracted *from* her devotion to Jesus.[52] If anything, her frustration is exacerbated by how much she wants to do *for* Jesus.

How then does Lord Jesus respond to Martha's complaint? He does not ignore her, as Jacob does Leah; nor does he cave in to her demands, as Abraham complies with Sarah's wishes and David with Bathsheba's; nor does he discount or misread Martha's concerns, as Elkanah and Eli fail to understand Hannah. Rather, Jesus takes Martha seriously and addresses her directly with an admixture of love and discipline. First, he matches her formal, single vocative "Lord" with a personal, double address — "Martha, Martha" — conveying both a ring of intimacy and compassion and a sting of authority and correction: "I love you, Martha, you know that. But come on now, do you hear yourself?"

Second, Jesus, specifically identified now by the narrator as "the Lord," pinpoints Martha's shortcoming: "You are worried *(merimnas)* and troubled *(thorybazē)* about many things *(polla)*" (cf. 10:41). He chides her attitude, not her action. The problem is not Martha's commitment to service/ministry *(diakonia)*. How could it be since the Lukan Jesus regularly embodies and endorses "diaconal" work? For example, as we have already stressed in this book, at the Last Supper with his disciples Jesus reinforces his own identity, appropriate for "the greatest among you," as "one who serves" *(ho diakonōn)* "at the table" (22:24-27). But while Martha's "much service" of hospitality — including such things as greeting, anointing, housecleaning, food preparation, and table service[53] — is commendable, her fussing and fuming over it are not. "Worrying" *(merimnōn)* about even good things of life and ministry is precisely what "chokes" Jesus' word/seed

---

52. Here Goulder (*Luke,* 493-94) overpresses the parallel between Luke 10:38-42 and 1 Cor 7:32-35. While these provide suggestive intertexts, I do not see Luke's Martha as an exact mirror image of Paul's "married" woman pulled away from her devotion to the Lord by domestic preoccupations. Her domesticity, though excessively irksome to her, still exhibits, rather than inhibits, her spirituality.

53. Contrary to popular opinion, there is no reference in Luke's text to a "kitchen" or even "meal" preparation as such. While feeding Jesus was no doubt a major part of Martha's "welcoming" and "much service," it would have been combined with many other common gestures of hospitality.

and stifles its fruitfulness (8:14; cf. 12:22-26) — and puts Martha at odds with her contented, noncombative, and attentive sister.

Third, Jesus defends Mary's choice as "the good part" *(tēn agathēn merida)* — not necessarily the "better" part — which will not be denied her, and he reminds Martha, according to one early reading, that "few things are needed, or rather one" *(oligō de estin chreia hē henos)* (cf. 10:42). Gordon Fee opts for the originality of this clumsy, hazy version (which is it: few or one?) over the shorter, crisper "one thing is needed" *(henos de estin chreia)* because it represents the patently more difficult reading. Though grammatically awkward, however, Jesus' statement is pastorally astute, affirming Martha's multiple acts of service — though trying to reduce them, for Martha's sake, from "many" to "few" — even as he pushes her to appreciate Mary's single-minded ("one") devotion to his word. As Fee concludes, "the text is not so much a 'put down' of Martha, as it is a gentle rebuke for her anxiety."[54]

We are not told how Martha reacts to Jesus' response and thus do not have a clear resolution of the household rivalry voiced by Martha and supported by Jesus to the extent that he does not accede to Martha's wishes. On the one hand, we are left with no idyllic picture of female solidarity, as with Naomi/Ruth and Elizabeth/Mary. Martha does not prep sister Mary for her seminar at Jesus' feet, as Naomi did with Ruth for her threshing-floor rendezvous with Boaz; and Martha is scarcely bursting with joy over sister Mary's attention to Jesus' word, as was Elizabeth over the virgin Mary's faithful reception of "what was spoken to her by the Lord" (1:45; cf. 1:38). But on the other hand, we are not left with the sense of irrevocable separation and bitterness as in the Sarah/Hagar, Hannah/Peninnah, and Bathsheba/Abishag dramas. Jesus' response leaves the door (or floor) wide open for Martha to join Mary at his feet, receiving Jesus' embedded word/ seed. Mary offers no counterobjection; she's not trying to hog Jesus for herself. Moreover, the wider context of Jesus' teaching in Luke demands that Mary not remain passively or quietly at Jesus' feet but rather bring forth active fruit generated by Jesus' word — fruit that will mirror her elder sister's faithful acts of *diakonia.*

54. Gordon D. Fee, "'One Thing Is Needful'? Luke 10:42," in *New Testament Textual Criticism: Its Significance for Exegesis; Essays in Honour of Bruce M. Metzger* (ed. Eldon Jay Epp and Gordon D. Fee; Oxford: Clarendon, 1981), 61-75 (citation is from 75). Cf. Kathleen E. Corley, *Private Women, Public Meals: Social Conflict in the Synoptic Tradition* (Peabody, Mass.: Hendrickson, 1993), 138-40; Barbara E. Reid, *Choosing the Better Part? Women in the Gospel of Luke* (Collegeville, Minn.: Liturgical Press, 1996), 148-49.

In short, we are left with potential harmony and solidarity between sisters Martha and Mary in their distinctive relationships with their Lord Jesus. But nothing is guaranteed, given the counterpointing potential for Jesus to bring division rather than peace within households (12:51) and the persisting conflict in some biblical household rivals type-scenes. For Luke the ultimate, determinant bond for God's household coheres around the full, faithful reception of Jesus' word — both hearing and doing what Jesus says, both sitting attentively and serving actively.

Individuality and Mutuality

My reading of the Martha/Mary scene attempts to mediate the household rivalry by appreciating both the individual integrity and the mutual solidarity of the sisters' choices and actions. In the Lukan snippet, each sister is doing a "good" thing — serving or listening — which Lord Jesus "will not take away from her"; but also, in the larger Lukan schema, each sister — indeed, every disciple, female and male, not to mention Jesus himself — must engage in both "good" works: serving and listening; hosting and heeding; ministering *(diakonia)* in deed and word, at table and pulpit, *to one another.* Such an individual/mutual dialectic is a marvelous community ideal, but a delicate balance to achieve. Paul gets at it with his famous body of Christ image, where each connected "member" exercises his or her functional "gift" for the "common good" of the entire organism (1 Cor 12:4-26; cf. Rom 12:3-8; Eph 4:7-16). However, this is not quite Luke's picture. Whereas Paul emphasizes discretely gifted persons — including a separate, distinctive gift of *service/ministry* (*diakonia* [Rom 12:7]) — working in close concert with one another in Christ's body, Luke stresses more a mutual, multitasking workforce in God's household, donning the towel and apron one minute, sifting or sharing God's word the next, or doing both at the same time.

We are all called to be Marthas and Marys in the one family of God led by Lord Jesus. But does such mutuality not ultimately efface Martha and Mary as valuable, embodied, individual persons — as women — in their own rights? Negotiating this "separate-but-equal," personal-yet-communal, individual/mutual tension has been key in the church's history of interpreting the Martha/Mary episode and in wider feminist thought about women's capabilities and functions.

Reception History: Types and Allegories

Out of all proportion to its size, Luke's little story of Martha and Mary has generated lively debate throughout Christian history. As Giles Constable observes:

> Every generation, almost since the beginning of Christianity, has tried to fit the story of Mary and Martha to its needs and to find in it a meaning suited to the Christian life of its time. Over the years its significance for the lives both of withdrawal and worldly activity and for this life and the next have changed, and the parts of Mary and Martha and the significance of Christ's words to Martha have been interpreted in different ways. The very variety and ambiguity of these interpretations is evidence for the richness of the text and the ingenuity of the interpreters.[55]

Much of this rich reception history wrestles with whether the sisters, as models of active works (Martha) and contemplative faith (Mary), represent divergent or compatible types of spirituality. While such models were naturally applied to women, Constable stresses the prevailing tendency that "there was almost no awareness of Mary and Martha distinctively as women, and no hesitation in applying their roles to men."[56] That's good and bad news for women: good, to the extent that they are viewed as significant *types* of particular human beings and doings, worthy of men's attention and emulation; bad, however, to the extent that they become generic, nongendered *allegories* or mere ciphers of human conduct void of identity as women.

Church fathers in third-century Alexandria began to drive a wedge between Martha's and Mary's patterns of piety. Clement cast the sisters as antipodes of law (Martha) and gospel (Mary). Drawing on categories of Greek philosophy, Origen associated Martha with *practical* deeds and Mary with *theoretical* ideals; he regarded Mary's spiritual contemplation as the higher virtue but still recognized the value of Martha's material actions.[57] Reflecting on Jewish-Christian relations, Origen matched Mary

---

55. Giles Constable, "The Interpretation of Mary and Martha," in his *Three Studies in Medieval Religious and Social Thought* (Cambridge: Cambridge University Press, 1995), 141. This lengthy study (1-141) provides the most extensive and sophisticated treatment of the reception history of the Martha/Mary incident. I rely on it heavily in this section.

56. Constable, "Interpretation," 107.

57. Constable, "Interpretation," 16-17; Blake R. Heffner, "Meister Eckhart and a Millennium with Mary and Martha," *Lutheran Quarterly* 5 (1991): 172-73.

with the *church* and Martha with the *synagogue:* Mary with Gentile believers devoted to "one necessary" spiritual obligation of love, and Martha with Jewish believers still burdened by "many" legal distractions unnecessary for salvation.[58]

In the sixteenth century, Martin Luther pressed further the legalistic-Martha/faithful-Mary dichotomy in the service of his Protestant agenda. Citing Luke 10:42, he commends Mary's superior approach to Jesus as one who "should not seek after works and merits but rather hang on His lips and believe His words." Lecturing on Galatians, he uses Luke's story of Martha and Mary to illustrate that "a man becomes a Christian not by working but by listening."[59] While sometimes granting a valid place, albeit a subordinate one, for Martha's endeavors, Luther was also capable of harsher judgment: "Martha, your work must be punished and counted as nought. . . . I will have no work but the work of Mary; that is the faith you have in the word."[60]

Other patristic, medieval, and Reformation thinkers, however, offered more charitable opinions of Martha's service, viewing it as separate but equal to Mary's devotion. In the early fifth century, John Chrysostom resisted the allegorical approach of the Alexandrian school and treated the Lukan Martha and Mary not as countertypes of spirituality but as followers of Jesus at a particular moment. Timing is critical: in Chrysostom's view, there was a time to labor and a time to listen for all disciples. Mary had the "better" sense of the moment on *this* occasion. As Blake Heffner interprets Chrysostom, "When the Lord comes to one's house declaring the in-breaking of the kingdom, then it is time to drop everything and be attentive."[61]

Augustine of Hippo also viewed Martha and Mary as mutually attractive and supportive figures: "both were pleasing to the Lord, both amiable, both disciples . . . both innocent, both laudable — two lives in the same house and just one fountain of life." The active Martha more helps than hinders her contemplative sister: "Martha has to set sail in order that Mary can remain quietly in port."[62] Similarly, Francis of Assisi, known for his de-

---

58. Constable, "Interpretation," 15-16; Fee, "'One Thing Is Needful'?" 66.

59. Cited in Constable, "Interpretation," 127, from Luther's *Sermons on the Gospel of St. John* 6-8 and *Lectures on Galatians* 3.2.

60. Cited in Elisabeth Moltmann-Wendel, *The Women around Jesus* (trans. John Bowden; New York: Crossroad, 1997), 17-18.

61. Heffner, "Meister Eckhart," 173.

62. Cited in Heffner, "Meister Eckhart," 173-74, from Augustine's Sermon 104; cf. Constable, "Interpretation," 18-19.

vout blend of Christian practice and prayer, endorsed Martha and Mary's household as a prototype for his hermitages. Comprised of three or four brothers, each Franciscan hermitage should display a balanced mix of "mothers" and "sons": the "mothers" should assume the active life of Martha and afford the "sons" protected time for contemplation. However, such a rule was not absolute: "sons," taking on the Mary part, "should sometimes assume the role of the mothers, as from time to time it may seem good to them to exchange roles."[63]

In his commentary on Luke 10:38-42, John Calvin shows none of Luther's squeamishness about the merits of good works. Alluding to Martha's example, Calvin comments: "But we know that men were created to busy themselves with labour and that no sacrifice is more pleasing to God than when each one attends to his calling and studies to live well for the common good." And reprising Chrysostom's point about timing, Calvin stresses that interpreters should not freeze Luke's single frame into a universal morality tale. One snapshot does not tell the sisters' whole story: "Luke says that Mary took her station at Jesus' feet. Does this mean that she was doing this the whole of her life? Rather the Lord commanded that the time of a man who wishes to advance in Christ's school should be so divided up that he shall not be an attentive yet unpractising hearer but shall make use of what he has learnt. There is a time for hearing and a time for doing. Hence the monks are foolish to seize on this passage, as if Christ were comparing the speculative life with the active."[64]

Two less familiar, artistic bits of evidence further forge Martha and Mary together. The earliest known image of Martha and Mary, according to Constable — the eighth-century Ruthwell cross — "shows the two sisters face to face, with their arms stretched out towards each other and with no clear differentiation between them. This representation has been associated with the monastic life, which embraced both action and contemplation."[65] And impishly treating the sisters — and their OT counterparts

---

63. Cited in Heffner, "Meister Eckhart," 176; cf. Constable, "Interpretation," 108-9.

64. Citation from John Calvin, *Calvin's Commentaries*, vol. 2: *A Harmony of the Gospels: Matthew, Mark, and Luke* (trans. T. H. L. Parker; ed. David W. Torrance and Thomas F. Torrance; Edinburgh: Saint Andrews, 1972; reprinted, Grand Rapids: Eerdmans, 1979), 89; cf. discussion of Calvin's treatment of Luke's Martha/Mary story in Frances Taylor Gench, *Back to the Well: Women's Encounters with Jesus in the Gospels* (Louisville: Westminster John Knox, 2004), 75-76.

65. Constable, "Interpretation," 25-26.

Leah and Rachel — as equal objects of mockery, twelfth-century satirist Walter of Châtillon produced the doggerel:

> Now Martha and Lia [Leah] are busier than they should be.
> Rachel and Mary exert themselves less than they should;
> Neither chooses the better part because
> They falter equally unproductively on the way.[66]

This association of sisters Martha/Mary with Leah/Rachel captures our attention in light of our comparative analysis of the biblical household rivalry type-scenes. But in this case the parallels are wholly dismissive and undiscerning, tarring all the parties as "equally unproductive" or incapacitated: regardless of how they try, too little or too much, women just can't get it right. Fortunately, most other assessments of Martha and Mary have been less crassly misogynistic. But the tendency to nonindividuated, representational typecasting and allegorizing — whether wedging or blending the two figures — remains strong in the history of interpretation, with the notable exceptions of Chrysostom's and Calvin's keen sense of the historical moment in which Luke's Martha and Mary responded differently and individually to Jesus, implying nothing about how they did or should respond at other occasions. But even here and in other congenial readings, Martha and Mary appear chiefly as models for *men's* balanced discipleship of action and contemplation, whether for Franciscan monks or "a [Calvinist] man who wishes to advance in Christ's school." Not that women are entirely excluded from Christian service and devotion, but Martha and Mary seem much less women's sisters than men's. And Martha and Mary seem less their own embodied, capable women-selves than iconic ideals for men's "advancement" (Calvin), not unlike Woman Wisdom in Proverbs. We should no doubt affirm feminine-biblical models wherever we find them, and encouraging men to "serve" and "listen to" God and other people (including women!) is all to the good, but the "better part" is to appreciate women like Martha and Mary as the robust, capable women *they* are, "apart and together."[67]

In some respects, maintaining Martha's and Mary's distinctive historical and literary identities is best served by maintaining their *rivalry.* This

---

66. Cited in Constable, "Interpretation," 51.

67. Drawn from the headings of two of Constable's three main sections in his extensive "Interpretation of Mary and Martha" study: "The Sisters Together" (3-43) and "The Sisters Apart" (93-142).

way they remain alive to fight for themselves, their rights and choices. If we rush too quickly to stress their solidarity and complementarity, we run the risk of blurring their individuality and creating a fuzzy composite picture that does full justice to neither woman. Of course, in playing the rivalry game based on Luke's story, Mary most always comes out the winner, with poor petulant Martha sent back to the "kitchen" to bide her time and bite her tongue. Such has been the general drift of interpretation right up to popular sermons in our own day.[68]

Periodically, as we have seen in the examples above, Martha could garner equal billing with her famous sister. But that was usually a stretch for Martha, always the striving one. With Jesus' explicit commendation, Mary's status was never in doubt. The problem worsened with Mary of Bethany's popular conflation — precipitated by Pope Gregory the Great's homily on September 21, 591 — with Mary Magdalene and the anointing woman in Luke 7.[69] It's hard enough to compete with one Mary, much less a combined icon second only to the Virgin Mary as the most blessed of Christian women. Nevertheless, against the odds, Martha has from time to time not merely complemented Mary (Magdalene), but even *surpassed* her, particularly in the Middle Ages, remarkably predating Martha's resurgence in contemporary feminist scholarship by a millennium.

Reception History: Martha's Medieval Renaissance

In the late-eleventh-century *Miracles of Robert of La Chaise-Dieu,* Marbod of Rennes lauded Robert as a "new saint [who] turned the old order

68. Invariably "mature" women students (over thirty) in my seminary courses, who have heard plenty of sermons from male preachers on Luke's Martha/Mary story, roll their eyes and groan when I introduce it in class. They are weary of and much "troubled" by the typical denigration of Martha's good service and legitimate complaint about Mary's cushy position.

69. As Katherine Ludwig Jansen ("Maria Magdalena: *Apostolorum Apostola,*" in *Women Preachers and Prophets through Two Millennia of Christianity* [ed. Beverly Mayne Kienzke and Pamela J. Walker; Berkeley: University of California Press, 1998], 60) puts it, in this sermon Pope Gregory I "established for Western Christendom a new Magdalene, indeed a figure who would have been almost entirely unrecognizable to her colleagues in the primitive church." See further on the composite Mary (Magdalene) figure developed in Christian history, Susan Haskins, *Mary Magdalene: Myth and Metaphor* (New York: Riverhead, 1993), 93-94, 133-34; Jane Schaberg, *The Resurrection of Mary Magdalene: Legends, Apocrypha, and the Christian Testament* (New York: Continuum, 2004), 73-120.

around for us" by giving priority to menial service over mystical experience.[70] After devoting himself to the mystical life with its extraordinary visions of divine glory, "by degrees" Robert "came down to active labour and human affairs, and finally to the work of a stonemason." Flouting "established custom and the faith of ancient history," Robert, according to Marbod, "placed Martha before Mary and blasphemed, if not in voice but (which is worse) in deed, [because he was] contrary to the judgment of Christ, Who said that Mary's was the best part." In Marbod's judgment, however, Robert's "blasphemy" was not just forgivable, but commendable. Weary of scholastic debates about the relative merits of contemplative and active pursuits, Marbod extolled Robert's bold, Martha-like choice: "Contemplatives are greatly moved to action not only rightly but also necessarily, and they do not lose any prior merit." Constable regards this account of the spiritual pilgrimage of Robert of La Chaise-Dieu as the "turning-point not only in the interpretation of Mary and Martha but also in the history of medieval spirituality."[71]

In letters written around the turn of the thirteenth century, Pope Innocent III affirmed the model of the "ambidextrous prelate," equally adept at Mary's mysticism and Martha's pragmatism.[72] But he also betrayed a marked preference for Martha and her biblical foresister, Leah. Writing to Peter of Castelnau in 1204, Innocent advised that anyone devoted to contemplation must also pay "the debt of love" "by assuming the burdens of action," as Leah (and Martha) did, that "brings both advantage and profit to herself and others." While Mary's choice is more tranquil, "the active life [of Martha] can be considered more useful because it profits itself and others and bears tribulations and afflictions by which the virtues are increased." In 1199 Innocent instructed his legate, Rainerius, to adopt a course similar to that of Robert of La Chaise-Dieu. While Rainerius desired a meditative life at Jesus' feet, Innocent exhorted: "You should rather out of obedience come down from the contemplation of Mary to the ac-

---

70. For a discussion of this little-known work and the citations I use, see Constable, "Interpretation," 40-42, 90-91.

71. Constable, "Interpretation," 41. Further, "It was a comparatively small, but very important, step from this even-handed treatment of the two lives and the two sisters, of whom neither was superior, to an assertion of Martha's superiority, which appeared to contradict Christ's commendation of Mary in the Gospel" (87).

72. The model of the "ambidextrous prelate," equally adept at both active and contemplative pursuits, was derived from William of St. Thierry, Bernard of Clairvaux, and Robert Pullen. See Constable, "Interpretation," 99.

tion of Martha so that by your preaching you may make Rachel's sterility fecund in Lia [Leah], preach upon the housetops, as the Gospel orders, what you learned in the silence of solitude and the cloister, and make a profit out of the talents you have received."[73] Score one again for Leah as Martha's productive biblical prototype.

Reflecting on Luke 10:38-42 in the early part of the fourteenth century, Dominican monk Meister Eckhart bucked common opinion among the religious as he "displaced Mary and set Martha on the throne"[74] and "turn[ed] the literal sense of Luke's Bethany story inside-out."[75] In Eckhart's reading, the active Martha emerges as the more mature sister, in spiritual attainment as well as in age, anxious about the progress of the more naïve Mary. Specifically, Martha worries about young Mary's motivation for listening to Jesus: "We harbor the suspicion that dear Mary was sitting there more for enjoyment than for spiritual profit. Therefore Martha said, 'Lord, tell her to get up,' because she feared that [Mary] might remain stuck in this pleasant feeling and would progress no further."[76] Martha knows by experience that faithful communion with Christ prompts loving ministry. Thus, as Constable summarizes Eckhart's view: "Mary was in the process of becoming what Martha already was. Mary was only at the beginning of the mystic fulfillment which involved work, asceticism, and apostolic activity as well as contemplation, and Martha was closer to God."[77] Jesus' affirmation of Mary's choice comes not so much as a rebuke to Martha as an assurance that Mary will eventually heed Jesus' instruction and live up to Martha's model of service. For Eckhart, this goal came to fruition after Jesus' ascension, when Mary (Magdalene) — with Martha — received the Holy Spirit and embarked on a missionary journey across the Mediterranean Sea. "'Mary sat at the feet of the Lord and listened to his words,' and learned, for she had just been put in school and was learning to live. But afterwards, when she had learned and Christ had ascended to heaven and she received the Holy Spirit, then she really for the first time

---

73. The opinions of Pope Innocent III in this paragraph are cited from Constable, "Interpretation," 97-99.

74. Moltmann-Wendel, *The Women around Jesus*, 28.

75. Heffner, "Meister Eckhart," 179; see further on Eckhart's maverick interpretation of the Martha/Mary story (especially Sermon 86), Bernard McGinn, *The Mystical Thought of Meister Eckhart: The Man from Whom God Hid Nothing* (New York: Herder and Herder/Crossroad, 2001), 157-61; Constable, "Interpretation," 116-17; Gench, *Back to the Well*, 75.

76. Cited in Heffner, "Meister Eckhart," 179, from Eckhart's Sermon 86.

77. Constable, "Interpretation," 116.

began to serve. Then she crossed the sea, preached, taught, and became the servant and washerwoman of the disciples. Thus do saints become saints; not until then do they really begin to practice virtue."[78]

Such legends concerning Mary Magdalene and Martha's European exploits were popular in medieval Christianity, exemplified in the twelfth-century Cistercian hagiography *The Life of Saint Mary Magdalene and of Her Sister Saint Martha (VBMM)*.[79] The prologue introduces the lives of the two heroines: "The contemplative life of that sweet lover of Christ, dearly loved by him and worthy to be named with reverence, the blessed Mary Magdalene; the active life of her glorious sister, the servant of Christ, Martha" (*VBMM*, Prologue 1-5). While this work maintains the traditional distinction between Mary's contemplation and Martha's action and gives greater attention to Mary's career, it also consistently admires Martha's industry, including some extraordinary deeds beyond hospitality.

Before recounting the sisters' travels to Marseilles and environs, *VBMM* discusses their roots in Judea and Galilee and in the Gospel tradition. While the NT suggests nothing about Martha and Mary's socioeconomic status beyond possessing a home and enough resources to host a dinner party, this work greatly expands their portfolio: "[T]hey were nobly born and of noble society, they possessed . . . many lands and slaves and much money" (*VBMM* 2.34-37). In addition to the house in Bethany of Judea, the family (two sisters and Lazarus) held estates in Magdala of Galilee and Bethany beyond the Jordan — and, most notably, "owned the greater part of the city of Jerusalem!" (2.37-44). As the eldest, Martha operated as CEO — in successful fashion, because she remained single and possessed a "manly spirit" — as well as abounded in hospitality. Not the most favorable assessment of *women's* leadership, but a tribute to *Martha* all the same.

> Martha, as the first-born, administer[ed] all their belongings and all their lands, a trust which she did not insolently abuse, but, bearing in her woman's breast a manly spirit, performed it liberally. Since she desired never to marry, her good name flourished. To her own she was sweet and loving; to the poor, gentle and friendly; to all, in short, merciful and liberal. And, to speak briefly, the woman was respected and venerated by all, for she was nobly born, blessed with many gifts, celebrated

---

78. Cited in Heffner, "Meister Eckhart," 180, from Eckhart's Sermon 86.

79. See the excellent introduction and translation by David Mycoff, *The Life of Saint Mary Magdalene and of Her Sister Saint Martha: A Medieval Biography* (Kalamazoo, Mich.: Cistercian, 1989). All citations are from this work, abbreviated as *VBMM* (from its Latin title).

for beauty, glorious in chastity, hospitable, generous, and gracious to all. Such was Martha. (2.45-55)

Commentary on the Gospel reports provides little new information about Martha's role, except that she hosted Jesus in Magdala, rather than Bethany, and "prepared all that belongs to hospitality and feasting, giving to him her heart as well as her goods." Moreover, in the incident corresponding to Luke 10:38-42, Martha entertains not only Jesus and her sister, but also "the twelve apostles, and the seventy-two disciples, and a multitude of noble women" (*VBMM* 10.398-403). No wonder she is troubled with much serving! Still, she is not alone. Though Mary "feasted . . . at the table of contemplation," Martha is assisted in serving the dinner table by "the excellent Marcella, the chief caretaker of her house," and also by Joanna and Susanna. Jesus and the disciples "returned often" to Martha and Mary's home in Magdala and came to depend on their support: "The sisters ministered to all his needs obligingly, with a free spirit, out of their own means. If, as sometimes happened, household affairs required that they stay behind at home while the Lord was preaching far off, they sent whatever supplies they believed the Savior and his followers need to have replenished" (10.410-37).

Following Jesus' ascension, Martha, Mary, and Lazarus became prominent contributors to the Jerusalem church, and following the pattern described in Acts 2:44-45 and 4:32-47, they sold all their vast holdings and laid the proceeds at the apostle Peter's feet (*VBMM* 34.1944-52). However, in the wake of Peter's imprisonment, James's beheading, and a surging, "savage storm of persecution" (36.2112), Martha's family fled west across the sea. Lazarus became bishop of Cyprus, while the sisters' voyage, accompanied by Archbishop Maximinus, one of the original seventy-two disciples, took them to Marseilles in the province of Gaul. From there "they went out and preached everywhere, and the Lord worked with them, confirming their words with the signs that followed after" (37.2158-61).

Mary spent most of her time in ecstatic, angelic communion with the risen Christ: "Drawn by the sweetness of her beloved she became drunk on the cup of heavenly desire, composing herself and raising herself up so that, dissolved at last in the heat of a most chaste love, she drank in interior joy" (38.2224-28).[80] But on occasion she also "left the joys of contempla-

---

80. *VBMM* 39.2300-2314 describes further feats concerning Mary's popping back and forth between heaven and earth every day and eating angel-catered fare of the "highest

tion and preached to the unbelievers or confirmed the believers in the faith," drawing on her poignant experiences of penitence, conversion, and unctuous devotion to Jesus (38.2233-57),[81] and "performed miracles with inexpressible ease to establish the truth of her words and to provoke faith in her listeners" (39.2284-86).

But Martha's mighty deeds and influence with the people, described at length in chapters 40–43, outshone her sister's. Two feats stand out. First, she subdued the fierce dragon that had been terrorizing the inhabitants of Vienne, taming the wild beast with the sign of the cross and a noose of her girdle, as the crowd then proceeded to hack the creature to pieces (*VBMM* 40).[82] Martha then took up residence in the dragon's lair on the edge of the river Rhône and "built a house of prayer for herself" in which she lived an ascetic life and "lost [herself] completely in holy prayer and night-long vigil" (Mary wasn't the only contemplative in the family). But Martha's hospitality also persisted, as "she always shared her table with the needy," as well as her gifts of proclamation and miracle working (41:2383-2467). Her second memorable act occurred one day while preaching at the gates of Avignon near the banks of the Rhône. Desperate to hear Saint Martha, a young man on the other side of the river tried to swim across, only to drown en route. A search party dredged him up the next day, and "the nobles of the city, of both sexes, begged and pleaded on their knees" for Martha to restore his life. On condition of the nobles' conversion to Christianity, Martha indeed raised the young man from the dead in Christ's name (*VBMM* 42).

This popular medieval image of Martha's life-giving and dragon-taming power "reached a climax," according to Moltmann-Wendel, "in the

---

heaven." Though somewhat skeptical of this story, the *VBMM* author grants, "if this is understood in a mystical sense, it is not completely unbelievable" (39.2308-2309). However, the story's further description of Mary's flight (following Jesus' ascension) to the Arabian desert, where she hides naked in a cave until a priest comes along from whom she begs a garment, the author regards as purely "false and a fabrication" (39.2315-2325). In any case, the *VBMM* writer exercises critical judgment and is aware of tendencies to embellish hagiographical legends.

81. This obviously reflects a conflation of the Mary in Luke 10 with the anointing women in Luke 7:36-50 and Mark 14:3-9//John 12:1-8.

82. This tradition is vividly supported in medieval art. See Moltmann-Wendel, *The Women around Jesus*, 39-48, including the introductory summary: "Martha defeating the dragon now no longer recalls the housewife in Luke who is reprimanded by Jesus. Martha does not just exude tranquility and superiority: she is proud, confident of victory, self-assured" (39).

feminist culture of the Renaissance. Here are signs of a new humanism: nature is integrated, and new value is attached to women." However, Moltmann-Wendel goes on to lament that soon "the Reformation and the Counter Reformation ended almost everywhere the emancipation of Martha."[83] Instead of binding the dragon with her girdle, Martha became strapped again in her own stays and apron strings. Still, as the wheel of history and tradition rolls on — and sometimes back on itself — Martha is enjoying in recent feminist biblical interpretation another renaissance, a fresh release to speak her mind and act her part as a model of faith and practice.[84]

The medieval Martha more than holds her own as a vigorous, multi-talented, distinctive individual woman. As the dragon-tamer, she herself cannot be tamed into some generic type or self-effacing allegory. Her fire will not be quenched or controlled. And for the most part, even as Martha outshines her sister Mary, who continues to dazzle in her own right, Martha's ministry remains compatible with and complementary to Mary's, as Martha's contemplative stint in her "house of prayer" showcases. Both sisters in fact seem adept at a full range of "services" — spiritual, miraculous, didactic, evangelistic, domestic, and economic. The economic component featured in *VBMM*, concentrating on Martha and Mary's frequent hosting and funding of Jesus and the apostles, nicely connects with our investigation of Joanna's similar functions in the previous chapter.

Overall, then, the tensions between women's individuality and mutuality seem nicely balanced — with, however, a couple of nagging caveats. First, the tendency to subsume, and thereby consume, Martha's character under male interests persists in Marbod's encomium of Robert of La Chaise-Dieu, in Pope Innocent's charges to Peter of Castelnau and Rainerius, and in the Cistercian *VBMM*'s attribution of Martha's managerial acumen to a "manly spirit." Second, the highly hagiographical thrust of the Martha/Mary legends blunts their connectedness to ordinary women. Saints are, by definition, exceptional in every way, and thus beyond the reach of everyday people. Martha the dragon-tamer, like Buffy

---

83. Moltmann-Wendel, *The Women around Jesus*, 47.

84. See, e.g., Gench, *Back to the Well*, 56-83, and four studies from *A Feminist Companion to Luke* (ed. Levine and Blickenstaff): Veronica Koperski, "Women and Discipleship in Luke 10:38-42 and Acts 6:1-7: The Literary Context of Luke-Acts" (161-96); Loveday C. Alexander, "Sisters in Adversity: Retelling Martha's Story" (197-213); Warren Carter, "Getting Martha Out of the Kitchen: Luke 10:38-42 Again" (214-31); Pamela Thimmes, "The Language of Community: A Cautionary Tale (Luke 10:38-42)" (232-45).

the vampire-slayer, may inspire women older (Martha) and younger (Buffy) to greater achievements, with or without girdle and miniskirt, and provide nice female counterparts to Saint George[85] and Van Helsing. But they also may do little more than offer a bit of escapist release from the work-a-day drudgery and subordination of most "real" women.[86]

Feminist Theory: Freedom and Responsibility

The tension between women's individual identity, or freedom to choose and chart their own lives, and women's mutual responsibility to support one another and to work with men for the good of the entire community (and wider environment) pulses through feminist thought and has implicitly informed our investigation of the biblical household rivalry typescene. We cannot fully unpack here the complex debates in feminist theory, but in concluding this chapter, we briefly consider two approaches to the individuality/mutuality issue of relevance to the Martha/Mary sibling rivalry case in Luke.

First, we return to Martha Nussbaum's "Capabilities Approach,"[87] introduced in chapters 1 and 3 and taken up again in chapter 8. Here we concentrate on her distinction between *capabilities* and *functions*. At root the Capabilities Approach "takes *each person as an end,* asking not just about the total or average well-being but about the opportunities available to

---

85. However, Moltmann-Wendel (*The Women around Jesus,* 45) also notes the "striking" distinction between the dragon-defeats of the masculine George and feminine Martha, especially in terms of their use of violence: "In the masculine version, a man, booted and spurred, thrusts his lance into the dragon's mouth with all his might. In some accounts, the lance breaks. The dragon is fatally wounded. In the feminine version the heroine conquers and tames the dragon with vulnerable bare feet and in a flowing robe, using holy water and a sprinkler or a cross. It is the people who kill the monster. In the masculine version force comes up against counterforce. Martha encounters the dragon without killing it. Martha overcomes the threat without force."

86. See the fascinating and incisive feminist critique of the popular *Buffy* (and *Xena*) television series and other contemporary media portrayals of "warrior women" in Susan J. Douglas, *Enlightened Sexism: The Seductive Message That Feminism's Work Is Done* (New York: Times Books/Henry Holt, 2010), 76-100.

87. The capitalized use of "Capabilities Approach" or "Human Development Approach" is Nussbaum's most recent preferred designation. See her *Creating Capabilities: The Human Development Approach* (Cambridge: Harvard University Press, Belknap Press, 2011), 18.

each person. It is *focused on choice or freedom,* holding that the crucial good societies should be promoting for their people is a set of opportunities, or substantial freedoms, which people then may or may not exercise in action: the choice is theirs."[88] In Nussbaum's vision, the approach is feminist in its particular concern for respecting the dignity of each *woman* as a capable person against prevailing historical and cultural patterns of restricting women's freedom. Moreover, she staunchly supports a feminist-*individualist* model that promotes and protects *each* woman's life *choices.* "Capability" thus translates into "capacity or opportunity to choose" — or *not* to choose, as the case may be. Here the distinctive element of *functioning* comes in as "an active realization of one or more capabilities. . . . Functionings are beings and doings that are the outgrowths or realizations of capabilities. . . . The notion of *freedom to choose* is thus built into the notion of capability."[89] In short, women's *options* for a flourishing life must be as fully open as men's and mutually supported by social structures, but what each woman actually *opts* to do is up to her.

Tempering Nussbaum's predominant individual-choice theory, however, is her keen awareness, sharpened by her global study of women in traditional systems in India, that women too often choose *against* their capabilities because of ignorance and internalized social values of helplessness and subordination. Hence their negative choices are not *free* choices at all. In such situations, women's individual capacities must first be consciously created and nurtured through support groups, educational initiatives, and institutional reforms — in other words, liberating networks of *mutual* exchange.[90]

---

88. Nussbaum, *Creating Capabilities,* 18 (emphasis in original).

89. Nussbaum, *Creating Capabilities,* 24-25 (emphasis in original).

90. E.g., Nussbaum ("Human Capabilities, Female Human Beings," in *Women, Culture, and Development: A Study of Human Capabilities* [ed. Martha Nussbaum and Jonathan Glover; Oxford: Oxford University Press, 1995], 91) cites (1) the survey of Indian women's health by Amartya Sen (*Commodities and Capabilities* [Amsterdam: North-Holland, 1985]), which shows a marked disparity between the women's self-perceptions of their "good" physical conditions and that of health professionals who detected serious deficiencies; and (2) the study of rural Bangladeshi women's educational status by Martha Chen (*A Quiet Revolution: Women in Transition in Rural Bangladesh* [Cambridge: Schenkman, 1983]), which reports how teachers seeking to train these women first had to overcome their ingrained obliviousness to the need for literacy and other educational attainments. See also Nussbaum, *Women and Human Development: The Capabilities Approach* (Cambridge: Cambridge University Press, 2000), 41-59; Nussbaum, *Sex and Social Justice* (Oxford: Oxford University Press, 1999), 11-14, 29-34. See also the largely positive presentation of Nussbaum's po-

So what does Nussbaum's Capabilities Approach contribute to our analysis of Martha and Mary's situation? Luke's account in fact hinges on different functional *choices* each sister has made during Jesus' visit. Mary has "chosen" *(exelexato)* to attend to Jesus' words (Luke 10:42); Martha has chosen to minister to Jesus' hospitality needs *and* to challenge Mary's choice. As we have seen, Jesus affirms each sister's individual "part" and, by extension, women's general capabilities for diaconal *(diakonia)* helping and logical *(logos)* hearing. Of course, women's helping/serving capability and functioning scarcely needed Jesus' encouragement in his day, *except* when some woman, like Mary, dared to neglect her traditional duty and make a different choice. This is precisely what irks Martha and prompts her urging Jesus to get Mary back in line. Martha thus betrays her culturally limited range of choice and capability, punctuated by the fact that she presses Lord Jesus — the present male household authority — to get Mary in line, rather than negotiating directly with Mary. Jesus, then, engages in a bit of expanded capability-protecting and consciousness-raising. He explicitly safeguards Mary's free opportunity to listen to his word — "which will not be taken away from her" (Luke 10:42) — and implicitly invites Martha to join in the seminar while still affirming her service choice. Though still reflecting a kyriarchal system with Jesus as undisputed *kyrios,* within that arrangement, Luke's Martha/Mary episode supports women's individual freedom of opportunity and their mutual capability of functions.

Second, we consider the suggestive relevance to the Martha/Mary scene of feminist political philosopher Iris Marion Young's seminal essay, "Throwing Like a Girl"[91] — "one of the most widely read and frequently anthologized papers of Second Wave feminist theory."[92] This phenomenological study of women's patterns of bodily movement (motility) and sense of physical space (spatiality) focuses more on personal freedom than

---

sition (with some critique of its applicability to contemporary American women somewhat less encumbered by entrenched patriarchy) in Kimberly A. Yuracko, *Perfectionism and Contemporary Feminist Values* (Bloomington: Indiana University Press, 2003), 41-46.

91. Iris Marion Young, "Throwing Like a Girl: A Phenomenology of Feminine Body Comportment, Motility, and Spatiality," *Human Studies* 3 (1980): 137-56; reprinted in Young, *"Throwing Like a Girl" and Other Essays in Feminist Philosophy and Social Theory* (Bloomington: Indiana University Press, 1990), and *On Female Body Experience: "Throwing Like a Girl" and Other Essays* (Oxford: Oxford University Press, 2005), 27-45. Page references are to the original study.

92. Sandra Lee Bartky, "Iris Young and the Gendering of Phenomenology," in *Dancing with Iris: The Philosophy of Iris Marion Young* (Oxford: Oxford University Press, 2009), 47.

shared responsibility, though the latter features prominently in Young's later writings.[93] Drawing on Maurice Merleau-Ponty's theoretical framework "of the relation of the lived body to its world,"[94] Young delineates various typical aspects of women's embodied relations to a patriarchal world, particularly "the kind of movement . . . in which the body aims at the accomplishment of a definite purpose or task."[95] Though allowing for dynamic exceptions, Young observes a common social pressure toward women's "inhibited intentionality" of spatial negotiation, amounting to a type of disability.[96] "Women in sexist society are physically handicapped. Insofar as we learn to live out our existence in accordance with the definition that patriarchal culture assigns to us, we are physically inhibited, confined, positioned, and objectified. As lived bodies we are not open and unambiguous transcendences which move out to master a world that belongs to us, a world constituted by our own intentions and projections."[97] Evidence of such constrictions emerges in all sorts of women's socialized-internalized choreographies, including more modest and huddled modes of sitting than men's (not to mention women's general pressure to sit quietly rather than move freely), tighter walking strides and arm-swinging, and, of course, the classic "throwing like a girl" with less torso torque, arm extension, and forward force than male hurlers.

Young is not happy about this limiting state of affairs or resigned to its permanence (women can regraph their social coordinates), but she candidly acknowledges its pervasive and persisting influence.[98] And she admits its high potential for insecurity and *frustration:*

93. See her last writing, published posthumously: Iris Marion Young, *Responsibility for Justice* (Oxford: Oxford University Press, 2011), and the reissue of her 1990 award-winning *Justice and the Politics of Difference* (new foreword by Danielle S. Allen; Princeton: Princeton University Press, 2011).

94. Young, "Throwing Like a Girl," 141, drawing on Maurice Merleau-Ponty, *Phenomenology of Perception* (trans. Colin Smith; New York: Humanities, 1962).

95. Young, "Throwing Like a Girl," 140.

96. Young is careful to note that women's limited motility that she describes does not result from innate physical capacities but from pressures and situations imposed by society. Moreover, she admits that her examples derive primarily from observing contemporary American women, though she suggests that the basic model of women's more inhibited sense of space and movement would apply cross-culturally, perhaps even more so in traditional than progressive societies. See "Throwing Like a Girl," 140-42, 152-55.

97. Young, "Throwing Like a Girl," 152.

98. Bartky ("Iris Young," 47-51) notes that Young later became more explicit about resisting any fatalistic and victimizing conclusions some might draw from "Throwing Like a

All the . . . factors operate to produce in many women a greater or lesser feeling of incapacity, frustration, and self-consciousness. We have more of a tendency than men to greatly underestimate our bodily capacity. We decide beforehand — usually mistakenly — that the task is beyond us, and thus give it less than our full effort. At such a half-hearted level, of course, we cannot perform the tasks, become frustrated, and fulfill our own prophecy. In entering a task we frequently are self-conscious about appearing awkward, and at the same time do not wish to appear too strong. Both worries contribute to our awkwardness and frustration.[99]

This embeddedness in a "system of frustrations correlative to its hesitancies" creates a potentially paralyzing can-do/cannot tension: "When the woman enters a task with inhibited intentionality, she projects the possibilities of that task — thus projects an 'I *can*' — but projects them merely as the possibilities of 'someone,' and not truly *her* possibilities — and thus projects an '*I* cannot.'"[100]

This stress on women's frustrated performance of bodily tasks within confined household space[101] aptly describes Martha's situation in Luke's story, with the added complication of sister Mary's contrasting spatial orientation. Martha moves to welcome Jesus into her domestic domain, which he then dominates as Lord, a hierarchy both sisters readily accept. Jesus' presence further dictates Martha's movements, as she bustles about her "many tasks" of hospitable service. But soon this situation begins to close in on Martha, cramping her freedom with a creeping sense of "I cannot" do this work without some help, which Mary seems determined not to provide in her stationary position at Jesus' feet. While quiescent sitting may be an appropriate "woman's place" in some settings, here it clashes with household service duties. Martha seems helpless to motivate and re-

---

Girl." Women can and must learn to "throw" and use their bodies in all sorts of new and liberating ways. But it remains critical for women and girls to face squarely what society foists upon them, and pressures to contain and control female bodies remain alarmingly strong to the present day.

99. Young, "Throwing Like a Girl," 144.

100. Young, "Throwing Like a Girl," 147 (emphasis in original).

101. Though critical of his sexist, psychoanalytic interpretations, Young builds on Erik Erikson's experimental observations that "females tend to emphasize what he calls 'inner space,' or enclosed space, while males tend to emphasize what he calls 'outer space,' or a spatial orientation which is open and outwardly directed" (Young, "Throwing Like a Girl," 149; cf. Erikson, "Inner and Outer Space: Reflections on Womanhood," *Daedelus* 3 [1964]: 582-606).

position Mary — hence her plea for Jesus' authoritative intervention. In this scenario of women's restricting and conflicting bodily postures and locations, Martha's frustration erupts.

What does Jesus do? First of all, we must notice what Jesus does *not* do in this case: he does *not* disrupt the present choreography either by redirecting Mary's energy, as Martha wishes, or by helping out Martha himself. This latter option is very much on the table, as the Lukan Jesus repeatedly functions as host as well as guest, servant as well as Lord. But on this occasion, perhaps because he is the only man in the picture,[102] Jesus does not blend his teaching and serving vocations. He does not disrupt the teacher-student arrangement with Mary.

What Jesus does do, however, is challenge Martha's angst and frustration, which on one level seems rather insensitive of him, especially since his visit precipitates the "need" for hospitable service. How *is* Martha supposed to cater the meal and fulfill a host of other hostess responsibilities all by herself? A fair question — particularly in a culture where women and girls routinely shared domestic duties. While Jesus is not especially interested in this issue at this point, he does not exacerbate the problem: he does not rudely blurt back, "What concern is that to you and to me?" (as he does to his mother at the Cana wedding in John 2:4); and he pounds no tables, insisting, "Where is my dinner, Woman?" In fact, just as he makes no move to help serve, he also shows no interest in being served. Dinner can wait. This is a profoundly teachable moment, and he short-circuits bitter rivalry, mitigates mounting anxiety, and *opens space* for women's participation with him in discipleship: in Mary's case, by affirming her listening/sitting choice; and in Martha's, by gently chiding her insecurity and frustration and implicitly welcoming her (as she had welcomed him) to join his and Mary's study session. There's plenty of feet and elbow room for all to sit down — and, we might imagine, even sprawl out — in God's household at Jesus' feet.

---

102. Since Jesus is still traveling with his twelve disciples and other followers ("Now as *they* went on their way . . . [Luke 10:38]), we might assume a larger gathering in Martha's home (as *VBMM* does), which would have only heightened her hosting frustrations. But Luke quickly crops the scene to focus on Jesus and the two sisters ("*he* entered a certain village, where a woman named Martha welcomed *him* into her home" [10:38]).

6. A Hungry Widow, Spicy Queen, and Salty Wife: "Foreign" Biblical Models of Warning and Judgment (Luke 4:25-26; 11:31; 17:32)

Combining two well-known features of Luke's work — (1) the pervasive appropriation of biblical language, thought, and typology continuing the OT story of Israel, and (2) the prevalent appearance of female characters, more than any other NT writing — might lead us to surmise that Luke frequently alludes to *OT women* as models and/or foils. Our previous chapter, in which we correlated Luke's story of Martha and Mary with several OT household scenes featuring women rivals, would seem to confirm this hunch, though we cannot be certain that Luke had these particular intertexts in mind at this point. However, Luke's biblically stylized birth narratives readily recall stories of Sarah, Miriam, and Hannah, including explicit name associations with Mary (Mariam/Miriam) and Anna (Hannah); and Elizabeth, Mary, and Anna are further linked with venerable OT genealogical lines of Aaron, David, and Asher, respectively (Luke 1:5, 27; 2:36).

But, in fact, after Luke 1–2 the presence of OT or OT-like women precipitously diminishes. Unlike Matthew's provocative inclusion of four "righteous" foremothers in Jesus' family tree (Matt 1:3, 5-6),[1] the Lukan genealogy, spliced between Jesus' baptism and temptation, lists *no* women on the long ancestral track back to "son of Adam, son of God" (Luke 3:38). Female prophets in the Miriam/Hannah mold disappear in the balance of Luke's Gospel, giving way to the dominant preacher-sons, John and Jesus. The Pentecostal scene in Acts reprises the Joel promise of Spirit-inspired

---

1. See F. Scott Spencer, "Those Riotous — yet Righteous — Foremothers of Jesus: Exploring Matthew's Comic Genealogy," in *Dancing Girls, "Loose" Ladies, and Women of "the Cloth": The Women in Jesus' Life* (New York: Continuum, 2004), 24-46.

prophetesses (Acts 2:17-18), which the rest of the narrative, however, never delivers, giving only the briefest nod (and no name or voice!) to Philip's four daughters "who had the gift of prophecy" (21:9).[2]

Two Gospel cases identify anonymous women as daughter-descendants of Israel's biblical heritage — one a "daughter of Abraham" (Luke 13:16), the other "daughters of Jerusalem" (23:28). But these are conventional markers of all Israelite women with primary stress on patriarchal (Abraham) and monarchical (Jerusalem, city of David) foundations. In the extended reviews of OT history by Stephen and Paul in Acts (7:2-50; 13:16-41), the only woman mentioned is Pharaoh's daughter who adopted baby Moses (7:21). Otherwise in the long Moses section at the heart of Stephen's speech, we hear nothing of Moses' mother, sister Miriam, wife Zipporah, or the brave midwives Shiphrah and Puah. Paul focuses on the legacies of Abraham, Samuel, Saul, and David, with no concern for the women in their lives. Particularly telling is the acknowledgment of "the prophet Samuel" with no word about his prophetic mother Hannah (13:20).

In short, for all his attention to OT Scripture and to women characters, Luke seems to care little about merging these interests. But sprinkled across the Gospel are references to three particular, albeit anonymous,[3] OT women, drawn from the patriarchal (Genesis) and monarchical (1 Kings) periods of Israel's history: the widow at Zarephath (Luke 4:25-26/1 Kings 17:8-24), the queen of the South (Luke 11:31/1 Kings 10:1-13), and the wife of Lot (Luke 17:32/Gen 19:24-26). This triad of OT women is worthy of consideration, not because Luke devotes much space to them, but because of their affiliated social identities and theological functions in Luke's story. For all their differences, they (1) share a *foreign* identity from Israel's per-

---

2. See Spencer, "Out of Mind, Out of Voice: Slave-Girls and Prophetic Daughters in Luke-Acts," in *Dancing Girls*, 144-65.

3. On the tendency in biblical narratives to treat anonymous female characters as flat stereotypes (mothers, wives, widows, and such) rather than as distinctive individuals and to subordinate them to named male figures, see Linda S. Shearing, "A Wealth of Women: Looking Behind, Within, and Beyond Solomon's Story," in *The Age of Solomon: Scholarship at the Turn of the Millennium* (ed. Lowell K. Handy; Leiden: Brill, 1997), 441-42, and Adele Reinhartz, "Anonymous Women and the Collapse of the Monarchy: A Study of Narrative Technique," in *A Feminist Companion to Samuel and Kings* (ed. Athalya Brenner; Sheffield: Sheffield Academic, 1994), 43-67. Both of these studies focus on unnamed women in 1 Kings, which include two of the three OT women Luke references: the widow at Zarephath and the queen of the South/Sheba. One aim of my study is to bring these women further out of the shadow of anonymity.

spective; in other words, they are all Gentiles from "alien" border locations: Sidonian Zarephath to the north, Sheba/Arabia (?) to the south, and the lower Dead Sea/"Plains" city of Sodom; and they (2) serve a *forensic* function in Luke's narrative world; that is, they all feature as object lessons in Jesus' prosecutorial message of warning and judgment for various audiences: Jesus' xenophobic kinfolk (Luke 4:16-30), "this evil generation" (11:29-32), and sign-seeking Pharisees and Jesus' disciples (17:20-37). These two elements coalesce in a symbolic biblical universe where "foreign" or "strange" women often represent perilous border figures threatening the stability of "natural," "native" groups. Surveying the particular threats that such peculiar border women pose and the warning labels they carry provides a framework for understanding Luke's — and the Lukan Jesus' — prophetic critique through the examples of the Sidonian widow, the southern queen, and the Sodom-based wife of Lot.

Dangerous "Foreign" Liaisons in Feminist, Hellenistic, and Deuteronomic Perspectives

Feminist Corrective Lenses

The earliest waves of American feminist activism, whether traced to the suffrage movement of the early twentieth century (building on nineteenth-century women's efforts in social reform, particularly the abolition of slavery) or to the equal rights movement of the 1960s-1970s, for all their promotion of women's interests, tended to define those interests in parochial terms relevant to the predominantly *white, married, educated, privileged* women who led these movements. Many pioneering feminists operated under what Audre Lorde identifies as a myopic "pretense to homogeneity," ignoring significant historical, social, and political differences and particular interests *among women*, not least the starkly varying experiences of poor, underprivileged black women (many single, abandoned, divorced, or widowed) compared to white feminists, who more likely functioned like overlords and patronizers (in other words, like men) than sisters and partners.[4]

---

4. Audre Lorde, *Sister Outsider: Essays and Speeches* (Berkeley, Calif.: Crossing, 1984), 116: "By and large within the women's movement today, white women focus upon their oppression as women and ignore differences of race, sexual preference, class and age. There is a pretense to a homogeneity of experience covered by the word *sisterhood* that does not in fact

In a tragic twist of irony, early feminist advocacy for emancipation and civil rights continued to leave black females in the dust of a "pseudo-maternalism," as Patricia Hill Collins puts it.[5]

Fortunately, however, one of the great virtues of feminism on the whole — though not often recognized by knee-jerk opponents — is its rich variety, its vitality, and, especially, its willingness sooner or later (I would argue *sooner* than most other ideologies) to self-correct in the interest of greater inclusivity. Committed to a hermeneutics of suspicion, it can suspect itself of blinkered perspectives and move to expand them.[6] And thus the latter years of the twentieth century witnessed a sea change in feminist awareness of race and class discrimination alongside gender inequities. As leading African-American feminist (womanist) cultural critic bell hooks observes: "No intervention changed the face of American feminism more than the demand that feminist thinkers acknowledge the reality of race and racism."[7] More fully,

> [W]hen black women and other women of color raised the issue of racial biases as a factor shaping feminist thought there was an initial resistance to the notion that much of what privileged class women had identified as true to female experience might be flawed, but over time feminist theory changed. . . . By the late '80s most feminist scholarship reflected an awareness of race and class differences. Women scholars who were truly committed to feminist movement and feminist solidarity were eager to produce theory that would address the realities of most women.[8]

---

exist." See discussion of Lorde's point in Susan Brooks Thistlethwaite, *Sex, Race, and God: Christian Feminism in Black and White* (New York: Crossroad, 1989), 18-24.

5. Patricia Hill Collins, *Black Feminist Thought: Knowledge, Consciousness, and the Politics of Empowerment* (2nd ed.; New York: Routledge, 2000), 234: "Some strands of White Western feminism have been tireless in raising women's issues in defense of women who remain suppressed and therefore unable to speak for themselves. This is important work and often leads to valuable coalitions among First and Third World women. Yet the kinds of coalitions among groups such as these can become problematic. Because the groups remain so unequal in power, this inequality can foster a pseudo-maternalism among White women reminiscent of how U.S. middle-class social workers approached working-class, immigrant women in prior eras."

6. See my discussion of a feminist hermeneutic of suspicion in chapter 2.

7. bell hooks, *Feminism Is for Everybody: Passionate Politics* (Cambridge: South End, 2000), 55.

8. hooks, *Feminism Is for Everybody*, 21-22; on the problem of feminist approaches to racial issues, see further Thistlethwaite, *Sex, Race, and God;* and regarding neglected class is-

From this initial spring of womanist critique, supercharged by the revolution in global communications in the decades bracketing the turn of the millennium, cascaded a flood of distinctive multicultural feminist perspectives from African, Asian, and Latina worlds, challenging the hegemony of white Western feminism. Such perspectives have been especially enriched by postcolonial theory and experience.[9] If that's not enough to demonstrate the inclusive-holistic orientation of feminism(s),[10] feminist thinkers — not least feminist theologians and biblical scholars — have readily responded to ecological challenges and incorporated them into their academic and activist work. Feminist resistance to kyriarchal-androcentric norms naturally extends to destabilizing technological-anthropocentric hierarchies.[11]

In short, concern for the "other," the "foreign," the "strange" from various angles has proven integral to feminist study and spurs our interest in the three doubly "other" women cited in Luke — that is, from the "other" testament, still too often neglected or subordinated in NT scholarship, and from the "other" (Gentile) side of the principal Jewish ethnic tracks in Luke's narrative world. However, the precarious complexity of this latter dimension must be acknowledged from the start for two reasons. First, though ethnic Jews/Israelites represent the protagonist "chosen" people throughout the Bible, they are *rarely dominant* in any sociopolitical con-

---

sues, such as those related to blue- and pink-collar working women, see Dorothy Sue Cobble, *The Other Women's Movement: Workplace Justice and Social Rights in Modern America* (Princeton: Princeton University Press, 2004), and Elizabeth V. Spelman, *Inessential Woman: Problem of Exclusion in Feminist Thought* (Boston: Beacon Press, 1988).

9. In biblical-theological studies, see Musa W. Dube, *Postcolonial Feminist Interpretation of the Bible* (St. Louis: Chalice, 2000); Kwok Pui-lan, *Postcolonial Imagination and Feminist Theology* (Louisville: Westminster John Knox, 2005).

10. While more recent feminism has stressed women's solidarity and inclusion across lines of class, race, age, and geography, there has also been a strong countermovement toward "intersectionality" or a fragmenting into separate identity and interest groups. On this divisive phenomenon and the need to maintain a connectional, "inclusive feminism" in order to achieve common social and political goals, see Naomi Zack, *Inclusive Feminism: A Third Wave Theory of Women's Commonality* (Lanham, Md.: Rowman and Littlefield, 2005), 1-22.

11. See David G. Horrell, Cherryl Hunt, and Christopher Southgate, *Greening Paul: Rereading the Apostle in a Time of Ecological Crisis* (Waco, Tex.: Baylor University Press, 2010), 11-47. Among prominent pioneering feminist theologians who expanded their work in ecological (ecofeminist) directions, see Rosemary Radford Ruether, *Gaia and God: An Ecofeminist Theology of Earth Healing* (New York: HarperCollins, 1992), and Sallie McFague, *The Body of God: An Ecological Theology* (Minneapolis: Fortress, 1993).

text and in fact are frequently exploited and exiled by "foreign" imperial powers. Of course, Luke's Jewish Jesus and Luke's original audience, composed most probably of Hellenistic Diaspora Jews and sympathetic Gentiles (like Theophilus perhaps [Luke 1:3]),[12] lived and worked under the strong arm of Roman rule. Second, in the history of NT interpretation, Luke's writings have been appropriated chiefly by *Gentile* Christian readers as legitimating, apologetic documents for the church's supposed early turn away from recalcitrant Jews toward receptive Gentiles — like them! Hence, to note another tragic twist of irony, "others" from Zarephath, the South, Sodom, or wherever in Luke's Gospel too quickly become Christian interpreters' compatriots; textual aliens become readers' allies — and vice versa — which will quickly lead us down the slippery slope of anti-Judaism if we're not careful. As Elijah bypassed many widows in Israel to go to the welcoming widow of Sidon, so Jesus must flee his angry hometown and kinfolk to find acceptance among outsiders (Luke 4:24-30). Bad Jews, good Gentiles — *except it's not remotely as simple, or as insidious, as that!*

Hellenistic-Jewish Heroines

To obtain a more balanced, informed framework for understanding the cross-dynamics of ethnic and gender relations in Luke's world, we turn to roughly contemporaneous Hellenistic-Jewish narratives, which share a broad literary milieu with Luke's writings.[13] A major concern of this corpus — namely, group identity and boundary definition in the Jewish Diaspora — is often negotiated through the experiences of representative female figures in their precarious dealings with male authorities. As Amy-Jill Levine summarizes: "Like any product of a community facing the threats occasioned by diaspora and colonialism, the ancient [Hellenistic Jewish] texts indicate the mechanisms by which such groups achieve self-identity. Specifically, they address ethnic pride, personal piety, and class structure.

---

12. On Luke's primary audience, see Philip F. Esler, *Community and Gospel in Luke-Acts: The Social and Political Motivations of Lucan Theology* (Cambridge: Cambridge University Press, 1987), 24-45.

13. This is not to say, however, as some have claimed, that Luke should be classified generically as Hellenistic-Jewish *historical fiction* or *romance* or *novel*, which itself is a subset of a wide range of Hellenistic-Jewish literature, including historiographical and philosophical works. For a helpful assessment of Luke's broad literary milieu, see David E. Aune, *The New Testament in Its Literary Environment* (Philadelphia: Westminster, 1987), 116-57.

And they locate their discussions, subtly but inexorably, on the bodies of women."[14] Further, women represent "means by which the Jews, suddenly finding themselves part of an alien empire, worked through their disorientation and the threat to cultural cohesion." Not surprisingly, then, in this unstable environment, women struggled for survival in "muddying . . . borders, both of body and society . . . as well as a confusion between public and private, privileged and marginalized."[15]

In most cases, the ethnic-gender polarity is played out by *Jewish women* dealing with *Gentile men* in a *sexually charged situation*, where the ravishing Jewish women somehow maintain their sexual purity — and their people's religious-national identity — against Gentile penetration and domination. The roles are thus reversed from our focal Lukan examples, featuring Gentile women, and are much more romantically oriented, though the prospects of some underlying sexual tension in Luke's references will be considered below. The pious, wise, and wealthy widow Judith, the eponymous Jewess, delivers her besieged people — cut off from food and water by the surrounding Assyrian army — by crossing over to the enemy camp. Feigning moral support for Assyria's cause and sexual desire for the all-"wise" General Holofernes (Jth 9:8), Judith cunningly returns to her people from Holofernes' bedchamber with his head in a food sack, all the while preserving her dietary and sexual purity. She thus secures Judah's faith and identity against foreign domination and even prompts the Ammonite leader Achior to be circumcised and to join the house of Israel (14:10).

Lovely Queen Esther similarly rescues her imperiled people from Persian annihilation, though in the Greek additions she lacks Judith's steely bravery (fainting dead away at the king's power and anger [Esther 15:1-6 LXX]) and strict purity (she must do her queenly duty); but while servicing the king at required moments, she loathes every second of it, pleading to the Lord: "You have knowledge of all things, and you know that I hate the splendor of the wicked and abhor the bed of the uncircumcised and of any alien" (14:15). Illicit sexual pressure also impinges on the beautiful Susanna, this time in the Babylonian Diaspora and at the slimy hands — and salacious eyes — of two dirty old *Jewish* elders; though trapped in her garden, harassed and "hemmed in on every side" (Sus 22) and threatened

14. Amy-Jill Levine, "'Hemmed In on Every Side': Jews and Women in the Book of Susanna," in *Reading from This Place*, vol. 1: *Social Location and Biblical Interpretation in the United States* (ed. Fernando F. Segovia and Mary Ann Tolbert; Minneapolis: Fortress, 1995), 179.

15. Levine, "'Hemmed In,'" 180.

with false charges of adultery, Susanna refuses to give in. Unlike Judith and Esther, Susanna can only do so much and requires the intervention of the wise young man Daniel. In this story *he* ultimately protects the integrity of *his* people in a foreign land, embodied in the righteous, yet vulnerable, woman Susanna.

Although these stories feature the purity and loyalty of Jewish women within foreign lands, certain elements blur the ethnic borderlines. As already indicated, the LXX Esther does intermarry and have intercourse with Artaxerxes, however reluctantly. Judith's name, for all its representation of the quintessential "Jewish/Judean woman," also reprises Esau's (Edom's) marriage to "Judith daughter of Beeri *the Hittite*" who, along with another Hittite daughter, "made life bitter for Isaac and Rebekah" (Gen 26:34-35).[16] And Judith specifically aligns herself with "my ancestor Simeon" (Jth 9:2-4), who brutally and deceptively avenged the rape of sister Dinah by Shechem the Hamorite, despite Shechem's supposed "tender love" for Dinah (Gen 34:3, 8). Simeon's (and Levi's) vicious reprisals draw mixed reviews in the Genesis account, as father Jacob laments the "odious" reputation that tars his family among their foreign neighbors (34:29-30). Finally, in Susanna's case, Theodotion's text attributes the lying, lecherous actions of the two Jewish elders "who were supposed to govern the people" to "wickedness [that] came forth *from Babylon*" (Sus 5), and through the voice of Daniel renationalizes one of the elders as "you offspring of *Canaan and not of Judah*" (56) (the Old Greek [LXX] version states, "Why was your progeny corrupted *like Sidon* and not like Judah?").[17] In sum, Jewish-Gentile, male-female intercourse in the Diaspora remains an unstable, volatile mixture.

Aseneth the Egyptian "City of Refuge"

While these Diaspora tales that focalize Israel's precarious identity through Jewish heroines usefully inform Luke's Hellenistic milieu, a narra-

---

16. Amy-Jill Levine, "Sacrifice and Salvation: Otherness and Domestication in the Book of Judith," in *Women in the Hebrew Bible: A Reader* (ed. Alice Bach; New York: Routledge, 1999), 368.

17. The Old Greek [LXX] version of Sus 56 reads, "Why was your progeny corrupted *like Sidon* and not like Judah?" But the Canaan link still applies by way of Gen 10:15, which identifies the original Canaan as the father of Sidon. See the discussion in Levine, "'Hemmed In,'" 189.

tive that features a *Gentile* woman engaged in Jewish liaisons offers a more direct comparison with Luke's treatment of the Sidonian widow, Southern queen, and Sodom-rooted wife of Lot. Here the Hellenistic-Jewish romance of *Joseph and Aseneth* potentially fits the bill.[18] This historical novel offers a juicy midrash fleshing out the circumstances surrounding Joseph's marriage to Aseneth, daughter of the Egyptian priest Pentephres, cursorily mentioned in Genesis 41:45, 50 (there she is Asenath, daughter of Potiphera) without comment. But the union of a leading Israelite patriarch with a pagan Egyptian woman begs for commentary in the Hellenistic Diaspora.

The Aseneth story commences with the heroine's appearance in her father's home as an eighteen-year-old virgin, "very tall and handsome and beautiful to look at beyond all virgins of the earth" (*Joseph and Aseneth* 1:4).[19] However, more important than her sexual-virginal status — which, of course, is very important — is her *moral-ethnic* distinction. Though Egyptian by nationality, she has more in common with Israel's matriarchs: "And this (girl) had nothing similar to the virgins of the Egyptians, but she was in every respect similar to the daughters of the Hebrews; and she was tall as Sarah and handsome as Rebecca and beautiful as Rachel" (1:5). Desired by every noble young man in the realm, including Pharaoh's number one son, she snootily snubs all her suitors. And when the illustrious Jewish agricultural minister Joseph comes calling — though not for her hand — she especially snubs him. Joseph may not be thinking about marriage, but that doesn't stop Aseneth's father from trying to arrange it. The esteemed Joseph is Pentephres' top choice for his daughter. But Aseneth will have none of it. Notice her red-hot moral-ethnic indignation.

18. Scholarly debate continues regarding whether *Joseph and Aseneth* derives from a Jewish or Christian provenance, though the general consensus holds that it stems from Egyptian Judaism around the first century. Supporting this view, see John J. Collins, "*Joseph and Aseneth*: Jewish or Christian?" *Journal for the Study of the Pseudepigrapha* 14 (2005): 97-112; Randall Chestnutt, "Joseph and Aseneth," in *The Anchor Bible Dictionary* (hereafter *ABD*) (New York: Doubleday, 1992), 3:969-71; Chestnutt, "The Social Setting and Purpose of *Joseph and Aseneth*," *Journal for the Study of the Pseudepigrapha* 2 (1988): 21-48; Susan Docherty, "*Joseph and Aseneth*: Rewritten Bible or Narrative Expansion?" *Journal for the Study of Judaism* 35 (2004): 31-33.

19. Citations from C. Burchard, "*Joseph and Aseneth*: A New Translation and Introduction," in *The Old Testament Pseudepigrapha*, vol. 2: *Expansions of the "Old Testament" and Legends, Wisdom and Philosophical Literature, Prayers, Psalms, and Odes, Fragments of Lost Judeo-Hellenistic Works* (ed. James H. Charlesworth; London: Darton, Longman and Todd, 1985), 177-247.

"Why does my lord and my father speak words such as these, to hand me over, like a captive, to a man (who is) an alien, and a fugitive, and (was) sold (as a slave)? Is he not the shepherd's son from the land of Canaan, and he himself was caught in the act (when he was) sleeping with his mistress, and his master threw him into the prison of darkness; and Pharaoh brought him out of prison, because he interpreted his dream just like the older women of the Egyptians interpret (dreams)? No, but I will be married to the king's firstborn son, because he is king of the whole land of Egypt." (4:9-11)

Poor Joseph can't seem to escape that whole nasty business with Potiphar's wife, even though he was completely innocent (cf. Gen 39).[20] Beyond despising his moral laxity, Aseneth demeans Joseph's social status as a "shepherd's son" from Canaan and erstwhile slave in Egypt. Though thinking no man worthy of her, she now settles on Pharaoh's son as the best she can do: at least "he is king of the whole land of Egypt," miles ahead of this alien interloper Joseph. Ironically, however, Pharaoh does not want to give his son to Aseneth, because she is "beneath" him (*Joseph and Aseneth* 1:8). Moral, ethnic, and class distinctions complicate the soap opera at every turn.

Of course, Joseph and Aseneth eventually win each other over, with a good bit of paternal and angelic assistance along the way. First, Pentephres assures his daughter that Joseph is as virginal and parochial as she is — more like "your brother" than a stranger: "Greet your brother, because he, too, is a virgin like you today and *hates every strange woman,* as you, too, *every strange man*" (8:1). Joseph himself confirms such personal convictions directly to Aseneth in rather condescending fashion: "It is not fitting for a man who worships God [like him] . . . to kiss *a strange woman* [like her!] who will bless with her mouth dead and dumb idols and eat from their table bread of strangulation. . . . Likewise, for a woman who worships God it is not fitting to kiss a *strange man,* because this is an abomination before the Lord God" (8:5).[21]

So how in the world, then, will these two "strangers" ever get together? By one of them converting wholly to the other's faith and way of life, of

---

20. On the popularity and development of the Genesis tale of Mrs. Potiphar's pursuit of Joseph, see James L. Kugel, *In Potiphar's House: The Interpretive Life of Biblical Texts* (New York: HarperCollins, 1990), 21-65.

21. On the key role that kissing plays in the story as an identity marker and kinship sign, see Michael Penn, "Identity Transformation and Authorial Identification in *Joseph and Aseneth,*" *Journal for the Study of the Pseudepigrapha* 13 (2002): 171-83.

course — which is precisely what Aseneth does. Following her fervent discipline of prayer and confession of sin, a high-ranking heavenly messenger — "commander of the whole host of the Most High" (14:8)[22] — appears to Aseneth and pronounces her "formed anew and made alive again" and fit for consuming the "blessed bread of life" and marrying the righteous Joseph (15:5-6). In the venerable tradition of Joseph's father Jacob/Israel, she even receives a name change:

> And your name shall no longer be called Aseneth, but your name shall be City of Refuge, because in you many nations will take refuge with the Lord God, the Most High, and under your wings many peoples trusting in the Lord God will be sheltered, and behind your walls will be guarded those who attach themselves to the Most High God in the name of Repentance. For Repentance is in the heavens, an exceedingly beautiful and good daughter of the Most High. And she herself entreats the Most High God for you at all times and for all who repent in the name of the Most High God, because he is (the) father of Repentance. (15:7)

Aseneth actually receives a double new moniker — *Polis-Kataphygēs Metanoia*, City-of-Refuge Repentance — with strong ethnic-political and forensic-ethical implications.[23] As the ideal proselyte-convert, Aseneth now represents the haven in the desert, the Zion in the Diaspora, as it were, under whose wings the nations *(ethnē)* may flock for protection and behind whose walls they may be safeguarded. This wings/walls imagery of refuge bears striking resemblance to the Lukan Jesus' outreach to his own Jerusalem-anchored people, but with an even more striking tragic counterpoint: whereas Jesus, as God's Messiah, longs to gather Jerusalem's children under his/her (he speaks as a mother hen) saving wings, they "were not willing!" (Luke 13:34-35); and consequently, rather than finding refuge in the holy city and temple, they will find its walls crumbling down around them, "not one stone . . . left upon another" (21:5-6; cf. 19:41-44;

---

22. Burchard ("Joseph and Aseneth," 225 note k) explains that this title designates the archangel Michael.

23. On the ethnic-political implications of Aseneth's identification as City of Refuge, see Ronald Charles, "A Postcolonial Reading of *Joseph and Aseneth*," *Journal for the Study of the Pseudepigrapha* 18 (2009): 279-83. On Aseneth as the "earthly counterpart" to Repentance, "daughter of the Most High" (15:8), see Ross Shepard Kraemer, *Her Share of the Blessings: Women's Religions among Pagans, Jews, and Christians in the Greco-Roman World* (Oxford: Oxford University Press, 1992), 112-13. Note also Aseneth's extended prayer-psalm of confession of sin in 21:10-21.

23:27-31).[24] The only way to escape this tragic, disastrous fate is through *repentance (metanoia)* — a renewed turning to Israel's God backed by faithful actions (3:3, 7-14; 5:29-32; 13:1-5; 15:1-32; 17:3; 24:47)[25] — as Aseneth the pagan Egyptian exemplifies in her context. But in Luke's world, the model response of certain Gentile elites doesn't just confirm and complement Jewish faith; it also confronts and complicates it: as Jesus remarks to the Roman centurion in Capernaum, "I tell you, not even in Israel have I found such faith" (7:9; cf. 23:47; Acts 10:1-48).

While climaxing at the high points of Aseneth's exemplary conversion and union with the virtuous Joseph, the tale does not simply leave us with a "happily ever after" denouement. The final chapters (*Joseph and Aseneth* 22–29) develop Aseneth's persisting role as contested territory. Pharaoh's son does not concede his loss of Aseneth to Joseph graciously, but rather hatches a plot, with the aid of four of Joseph's half brothers (those born to maidservants Bilhah and Zilpah), to capture Aseneth. After some intrigue, the scheme is ultimately foiled by the firebrand brothers, Simeon and Levi, recalling again, as in Judith, their vengeful discomfiting of the Shechemites in Genesis 34 — only this time the magnanimous Aseneth stays their militant hands from killing their traitorous brothers (*Joseph and Aseneth* 28:9-17). In any case, Diaspora relations within Jewish families and among Gentile authorities remain fraught with tension. While grace breaks through, the Diaspora is no idyllic garden paradise.[26]

"Strange" Women in Deuteronomic History

Our brief survey of ethnic and gender relations in Hellenistic Jewish novels recalled and glossed certain narratives from Genesis — particularly those surrounding Dinah and Shechem, Potiphar's wife and Joseph, and Aseneth and Joseph. Thereby we made some initial probes into the social

---

24. On this cluster of texts and theme of Israel's tragic rejection of the Messiah in Luke, see David L. Tiede, *Prophecy and History in Luke-Acts* (Philadelphia: Fortress, 1980), 65-96, and Robert C. Tannehill, "Israel in Luke-Acts: A Tragic Story," in his *The Shape of Luke's Story: Essays on Luke-Acts* (Eugene, Oreg.: Cascade, 2005), 112-13.

25. On the central Lukan theme of repentance, see Guy D. Nave Jr., *The Role and Function of Repentance in Luke-Acts* (Atlanta: Society of Biblical Literature, 2002).

26. Suggestively, both *Joseph and Aseneth* 2:11-12 and Sus 15-27 situate their virtuous heroines in enclosed, fortified garden settings. Of course, in Susanna's case, the garden security was breached by the two elders who assaulted her.

and literary world of the patriarchs, which the wife of Lot also inhabits. To gain some sense of the monarchical biblical environment surrounding Luke's other two foreign OT women — the widow at Zarephath and the queen of the South — we must sketch some of the ethnic-gender contours reflected in the Deuteronomic History (Joshua–Kings), especially related to liaisons with "strange" women.

Gail Streete has conveniently categorized "foreign" women in the Deuteronomic narratives as (1) *defensive*, like Jael; (2) *dangerous*, like Jezebel; or (3) *domesticated*, like Ruth.[27] Though somewhat overdrawn, as labels tend to be, they serve a useful heuristic function.

Jael emerges in the book of Judges at the end of the Israelites' battle with the forces of King Jabin of Canaan, led by Commander Sisera. She is identified simply as "the wife of Heber the Kenite" (Judg 4:17) — and thus probably herself a Kenite — part of a nomadic border group in Canaan ambiguously associated with the Israelites: sometimes as tolerated allies (so Saul in 1 Sam 15:6); at other times, as exploited aliens (so David in 1 Sam 27:10; 30:29). As Jione Havea summarizes, "The Kenites thus appear on the biblical radar as one of the figures for the dispossessed other. Traces of the Kenites, nonetheless, remain in the story of Abraham's descendants, so [they] also become figures of the repressed who could not be erased, similar to the way that sympathy for Cain cannot be exorcised from the biblical narrative."[28] In Jael, doubly marginalized since her husband Heber had even "separated from the other Kenites" (Judg 4:11), we meet an independent woman who supports Israel's cause, though for uncertain reasons. His army thoroughly whipped by Israel's troops, Sisera flees on foot to Jael's tent, since "there was peace between King Jabin of Hazor and the clan of Heber the Kenite" (4:17).[29] And Jael seems more than ready to receive him,

27. Gail Corrington Streete, *The Strange Woman: Power and Sex in the Bible* (Louisville: Westminster John Knox, 1997), 57-72.

28. Jione Havea, "Kenites," in *The New Interpreter's Dictionary of the Bible* (hereafter *NIDB*), vol. 3 (gen. ed. Katherine Doob Sakenfeld; Nashville: Abingdon, 2008), 478. Etymologically, the Kenites appear related to Cain and his itinerant descendants of metalworkers (Gen 4:17-22); their land is promised to Abraham's descendants in Gen 15:18-19. Judg 1:16 and 4:11 also trace the Kenites' origins back to Moses' father-in-law Hobab (known as Jethro/Reuel in Exodus).

29. Danna Nolan Fewell and David M. Gunn, *Gender, Power, and Promise: The Subject of the Bible's First Story* (Nashville: Abingdon, 1993), 124, suggest that Heber the Kenite (or "Joiner the Smith") located near Jabin the Canaanite because the latter offered a profitable market for Heber's iron chariot business. General Sisera logically seeks asylum, then, in the home of a presumed war ally. Among the many ironies in the story, however, is that Heber's

even coming out and inviting (enticing?) him to "turn aside to me" (4:18). But in fact, though seeming quite hospitable and desirable, Jael provides anything but succor and satisfaction for the beleaguered general: she's no Aseneth-like "city of refuge"! Tucking Sisera cozily into bed with a warm cup of milk (food seems to find its way into these women's stories one way or another), Jael agrees to play sentry at the tent flap, lying to any search party about his presence inside. But the threat Sisera really should worry about is his hostess, who, once he drifts off to sleep, promptly nails him to the ground with a tent peg rammed through his skull (4:17-24; 5:24-27)!

Thus Israel is defended and the enemy defeated by the violent "hand of a woman" (4:9), reminiscent of Judith, except that Jael is manifestly no Jewess. Moreover, Jael's motives are never disclosed in the narrative. Perhaps as a "woman caught in the middle" between the defeated Canaanites of Hazor her husband had befriended and their Israelite conquerors, she simply acts to secure her survival.[30] Be that as it may, while the results of her action clearly defend Israel's interests, she remains a borderline, undomesticated figure. She receives a nice poetic blessing from Deborah (5:24-27), but no divine promise of fecundity like the protective Hebrew midwives Shiphrah and Puah (Exod 1:15-21); and she is not incorporated into the Israelite community like the Canaanite prostitute Rahab (Josh 6:22-25). While these other women use remarkable courage and cunning to defend Israel, they never resort to violence or any bedroom intrigue, like Jael.[31] Perhaps, in an odd way, Jael's closest biblical counterpart is her Midianite (Kenite?) foresister Zipporah, Moses' wife, who wielded a mean flint rock and bloodily hacked off their son's foreskin to protect Moses from *the Lord's* lethal nocturnal attack (Exod 4:24-26). A strange scene by any account — but then so is Jael's shocking assassination of Sisera. To-

---

residence will prove no more protective for Sisera than his iron war machine, whose destruction is the reason Sisera seeks refuge.

30. So suggest Fewell and Gunn, *Gender, Power, and Promise,* 124. The narrative, however, never discloses Jael's motives. For other options, see Jacqueline E. Lapsley, "Jael," in *NIDB,* 3:174.

31. Even though Rahab is a prostitute, she does not appear to use her sexual wiles protecting the Israelite spies and supporting their people (Josh 2). On erotic elements in the Jael story, see Susan Niditch, "Eroticism and Death in the Episode of Jael," in *Women and the Hebrew Bible* (ed. Bach), 305-15; Streete, *The Strange Woman,* 57-62. Fewell and Gunn (*Gender, Power, and Promise,* 124-26), however, view Jael's behavior as more maternal-domestic than sexual-erotic, but no less disturbing and destabilizing as she "'mothers' Sisera to death" (125).

gether these stories of "strange" defendant women resist formulaic sameness and retain the sense of boundary instability we've seen thus far.

Jezebel enters the Deuteronomic History as the wife of King Ahab of Israel, "daughter of King Ethbaal of the Sidonians" (1 Kings 16:31), and antagonist of the prophet Elijah the Tishbite. She thus intersects Luke's first two foreign OT women: like the widow at Zarephath, she has roots in Sidon and dealings with Elijah; like the queen of the South, she enjoys royal rank and interacts with an Israelite king. She also differs from these women in key respects, which will be discussed in the relevant sections below. But for now, we are interested in her basic biblical profile as a threatening alien woman, indeed, "as the quintessential foreign woman of power . . . the quintessential Other, to be feared and blamed."[32] As Phyllis Trible aptly assesses her notoriety: "No woman (or man) in the Hebrew Scriptures endures a more hostile press than Jezebel."[33]

So what does Jezebel do to merit such opprobrium? She vigorously violates the heart of Israel's covenantal law at the twin cruxes of *idolatry* and *injustice:* on the one hand, prompting her husband and his people to worship Sidonian gods, guided by a formidable corps of 850 prophets of Baal/Asherah "who eat at Jezebel's table" (yes, it's feeding time again) and buttressed by a murderous campaign against YHWH's prophets (1 Kings 16:31-34; 18:19); and on the other hand, goading her husband to confiscate the ancestral land of a local Israelite (Naboth) after deceptively orchestrating the latter's execution (21:1-16). So Jezebel places other gods before YHWH, erects their images for public devotion, and murders and steals from Israel's faithful citizens — in other words, smashes the two tables of the Decalogue in pieces. Of course, this is nothing Israel's own leaders haven't done through the years, with and without provocation from foreign wives. And Jezebel does *not*, as far as we are told, ever *commit adultery* against husband Ahab or use her sexual wiles; for all her social and political acumen, she is never described, as most of the other women we've investigated, as physically attractive. Through the centuries she has in fact been vilified as the arch-sexual vampire (cf. Rev 2:20), but quite unfairly from the textual evidence that limits her "whoredoms" to the metaphorical, religious variety (2 Kings 9:22). Jezebel gets what she wants by sheer royal muscle and shrewd political maneuvers. She's no underling Philistine woman of Timnah or

---

32. Fewell and Gunn, *Gender, Power, and Promise*, 167.

33. Phyllis Trible, "Exegesis for Storytellers and Other Strangers," *Journal of Biblical Literature* 114 (1995): 4.

Delilah of Sorek resorting to nagging and pillow talk to achieve her anti-Israelite aims (see the Samson stories in Judg 14:1-19; 16:1-22).

But, her marital faithfulness notwithstanding, Jezebel suffers the harshest judgment and goriest end of any biblical woman, foreign or domestic. Thrown off her palace balcony by disloyal eunuchs, she is crushed by horses and crunched by dogs beyond recognition. The culinary theme takes a bloody turn: while pursuer Jehu "went in and ate and drank," Jezebel's flesh and blood became banquet fare for ravaging curs (2 Kings 9:30-37). Thus the tables are viciously turned on the wayward foreign queen who set the table for her lackey prophets of Baal and Asherah.

So much for alien Jezebel — suitably and thoroughly disposed of. But she will not be dismissed that easily. Careful, critical reading of the Kings narrative exposes a more complicated juxtaposition of Elijah and Jezebel as haunting "mirror images" of each other as much as polar opposites and bitter rivals. From their starkly estranged standpoints in terms of ethnicity, gender, religion, and class, they nonetheless form an "odd couple" of matched, codependent characters, as Trible sees them: "Elijah and Jezebel, beloved and hated. In life and death they are not divided. Using power to get what they want, both the YHWH worshiper and the Baal worshiper promote their gods, scheme, and murder. . . . In a pro-Jezebel setting Elijah would be censured for murdering prophets, for imposing his theology on the kingdom, for inciting kings to do his bidding, and for stirring up trouble in the land."[34] Moreover, in her own strange way, Jezebel aligns not only with Elijah, but with a sweeping

> genealogy of schemers, connivers, and murderers who populate the story of Israel. The list includes *males and females, foreigners and natives:* Abraham, Rebekah, Jacob, Rachel, Jael, Abigail, Joab, David, and on to Esther and Judith. The company Jezebel keeps is large and complex. Judgments about them vary, usually based on the principle of whether they promote the purposes of Israel and its god. As a group, these characters surround Jezebel like kindred spirits. She *the stranger* joins her own, though they receive her not. Yet their machinations, especially when approved, allow to her values and perspectives that run counter to the harsh indictment heaped up on her.[35]

34. Trible, "Exegesis for Storytellers," 17-18; also see Trible, "The Odd Couple: Elijah and Jezebel," in *Out of the Garden: Women Writers on the Bible* (ed. Christina Büchmann and Celina Spiegel; New York: Fawcett Columbine, 1994), 166-79.

35. Trible, "Exegesis for Storytellers," 10 (emphasis added).

We are thus cautioned to evaluate warnings and judgments surrounding foreign OT women in Luke critically and dialectically, to take them with a grain of salt (especially regarding Lot's wife!). All may not be as cut and dried as it seems.

Of course, we do not have to resort to deconstructive reading strategies to find positive models of foreign women in the OT who become integrated or "domesticated," as Streete puts it, into Israel's community. These are repentant, devoted female converts, like Aseneth in the Hellenistic pseudepigrapha. In the Hebrew Bible, Ruth the Moabite woman, descended from Lot's incestuous daughters (Gen 19:30-38) and notorious, Baal-inspired seducers of Israel's wilderness generation (Num 25:1-5), emerges as the most salient example of a "redeemed" and "redeeming" proselyte, wholly embracing Israel's deity and people as her own (Ruth 1:16-17; cf. 3:9-13; 4:1-15) and extolled in rabbinic tradition as "the paradigmatic convert to Judaism."[36] Proving more valuable "than seven sons," perhaps the highest honor the Bible could afford a woman (4:15), she bears a son in the line that will produce the Lord's great anointed son David, following in the train of Canaanite foremothers Tamar and Rahab, who faithfully perpetuated Judah's messianic-covenant people, as Matthew will highlight in Jesus' genealogy (Matt 1:4-5; cf. Ruth 4:12). On the surface, little ambiguity appears to cloud these foreign women's stories, as they so completely and decisively leave their own corrupt people and cleave to God's chosen race. Sneaky sexuality comes into play again, at least with Tamar and Ruth, but toward ultimately "righteous" and "worthy" aims (Gen 38:26; Ruth 3:10-11).[37] All's well that ends well.

But one does not have to engage in too much hermeneutical suspicion to be wary of perfect endings in biblical narratives. The sprawling and painfully realistic Hebrew Bible, in particular, resists fairy-tale endings at every turn. Tamar's securing of Judah's family line is followed by Judah's (and the larger clan of Jacob's) near starvation during a time of famine; Joseph's rise to power in grain-rich Egypt saves his family while also relocating them in the Diaspora. All is well there for a time, until a pharaoh arises "who knew not Joseph," and then genocide threatens (Exod 1). Eventually back in the Promised Land, Rahab helps to ensure Israel's victory over the mighty Canaanite stronghold of Jericho — a victory quickly soured, however, by

---

36. Katheryn Pfisterer Darr, *Far More Precious Than Jewels: Perspectives on Biblical Women* (Louisville: Westminster John Knox, 1991), 71-72.

37. See Spencer, "Those Riotous — yet Righteous — Foremothers of Jesus."

defeat at the piddling town of Ai, due to an Israelite's inability to resist a little Canaanite booty (Josh 2; 6–8). And generally, the anarchic book of Judges (see the epitaph in 21:25), with its horrific "texts of terror" toward women (chapters 11; 19–20),[38] taints the memory of the preceding "conquests" of Joshua almost beyond recognition. The idyllic little romance of Ruth, nestled in between Judges and 1 Samuel in the LXX and OT, provides much needed light between the dark endings of Judges and beginnings of monarchy under hapless Saul, but it's hardly enough to dispel the deep shadows surrounding it, which is maybe why the Hebrew Bible, placing Ruth much later among the Writings, doesn't even try. Moreover, wherever it's placed in the canon, Ruth's narrative portrait seems to bear a few smudges of its own that complicate a utopian reading. In chapter 5 we intimated that Naomi may not be as happy with her "clingy" daughter-in-law as readers have been; on the matter of Ruth's supposed model conversion, Amy-Jill Levine counters: "Ruth's Gentile background remains a stigma: her Moabite ancestry associates her with an aggressive form of seduction and with the taint of idolatry. For her loyalty she is commended, but her Gentile associations prevent her from being fully incorporated into the covenant community. Ruth remains 'Ruth the Moabite.'"[39] So Ruth's "redeeming" value may be less than commonly assumed.

So, alas, foreign female "converts," for all their positive contributions, scarcely eliminate all threats of oppressive domination from without or moral decay or ethnic discrimination from within the biblical people of Israel. These women remain, to use a tired but still telling axiom, "the exception that proves the rule." Warning, judgment, and danger ever crouch at the door in Israel's dealings with "other" peoples, especially when women are involved.

Mapping the Framework

Tracking Deuteronomic perspectives on "strange" women should obviously extend into the narratives surrounding King Solomon — (in)famous for his myriad, multicultural harem — and, in turn, into Solomonic wis-

---

38. Phyllis Trible, *Texts of Terror: Literary-Feminist Readings of Biblical Narratives* (Philadelphia: Fortress, 1984), 64-116.

39. Amy-Jill Levine, "Ruth," in *Women's Bible Commentary* (ed. Carol A. Newsom and Sharon H. Ringe; 2nd ed.; Louisville: Westminster, 1998), 84-85.

dom traditions, with their moralistic advice to Jewish sons about the mysterious ways of women, foreign and otherwise. We will reserve this Solomonic probing for the section below on the queen of the South, where it is most directly pertinent. But for now, we have canvassed enough background material concerning ethnic-gender dynamics in Israel's history to sketch a preliminary framework for analyzing Luke's three forensic references to foreign OT women. Consider the following summary points, worth bearing in mind for purposes of comparison and contrast as we hone in on Luke's special presentation.

1. Women in general and foreign women in particular represent contested border zones in ancient patriarchal Jewish societies. Hence, though they may be conquered, converted, or otherwise tamed, foreign women are never innocent in and of themselves. Their presence is automatically threatening, one way or another, to the established, male-dominated order.

2. Scripts of ethnic-gender border conflict are commonly written on women's *bodies,* especially at key openings or checkpoints controlling staple processes of *food* and *sex.* Again, dealings with foreign women at table and in the bedroom are always fraught with tension and never innocent affairs. Simply put, women's bodies are not their own, but rather an integral part of the "body politic."[40]

3. Inextricably tied to foreign women's obvious ethnic and gender identities are also elements of *class,* involving social, economic, and political status. Powerful women like Judith, Aseneth, and Jezebel naturally pose powerful threats, but less socially prominent figures, like Shiphrah/Puah, Jael, and Ruth, can also suddenly take the stage for command performances through various strategies of cunning and subterfuge.

4. Dangerous situations surrounding foreign women lead to a range of forensic judgments and resolutions, ranging from retribution (Jezebel) to repentance (Aseneth) to redemption (Ruth). But such decisions seldom settle matters once and for all. They remain more fluid than final, more set on shifting sand than in hardened stone, as life on

---

40. Cf. Fewell and Gunn, *Gender, Power, and Promise:* "Politics are written on women's bodies" (163); "Jezebel's body . . . is apostate religion which will be consumed before YHWH's avenging agent and left with its symbols of power — head, hands, and feet — lying lifeless and disjointed. Her body is the body politic" (171).

Diaspora borders remains unstable; despite pressures toward homogenization and acculturation, ethnic, gender, and class distinctions refuse to go down without a fight.

5. Finally, along with acknowledging the dogged determination of "others" to maintain their differences, the canonical and apocryphal narratives featuring Gentile women interacting with Jewish men also deconstruct sharp polarities through mind-bending, "mirror imaging" techniques. Opposites attract as well as repel: sometimes attracting all the way, like the equally "strange" and virginal Joseph and Aseneth, into one-flesh marital union; at other times attracting but never admitting the match, indeed, abhorring the thought of any commonality, like the equally zealous and religious Elijah and Jezebel. In any case, we are duly warned about peremptory and permanent affixing of warning labels.

Excursus: The Missing Syrophoenician/Canaanite Mother

Though poised to plunge into Luke's narrative-theological deployment of three foreign OT women, we pause a bit longer to consider a curious omission. Since Luke places on the lips of Jesus these references to Gentile biblical women — one of whom has Syrian (Zarephath widow) and another Canaanite (Lot's wife) roots — it's hard to see why Luke would not follow his Synoptic cohorts in presenting Jesus' "borderline" dealings with a Syrophoenician (Mark 7:24-30)/Canaanite (Matt 15:21-28) woman. Yes, it's a notoriously difficult, even embarrassing, episode in Jesus' career, but that tends to certify its place in the historical tradition.[41] Like it or not, this story won't go away easily, just like the dogged female protagonist in the story; and again like her, it *begs* to be treated (Mark 7:26). Of course, Luke would have been free to redact and interpret this incident to serve his own purposes, as Mark and Matthew do. So to ignore it altogether remains an odd editorial excision. Not including the Canaanite and other foreign foremothers in Jesus' family tree is a natural oversight (Matthew is the oddball here, since Jewish genealogies normally did not include women,

---

41. See the helpful survey and analysis of recent approaches to this story in Kwok Pui-lan, "Overlapping Communities and Multicultural Hermeneutics," in *A Feminist Companion to Reading the Bible: Approaches, Methods, and Strategies* (ed. Athalya Brenner and Carole Fontaine; Sheffield: Sheffield Academic, 1997), 203-15.

and Matthew features only a select quartet), but not including this more contemporary "Canaanite" mother is harder to discern.[42]

Further complicating the matter, explanations for any narrative lacunae inevitably derive from speculative arguments from silence. Crafting a persuasive theological biography *(bios)* of Jesus within a limited space, say, the standard length of a papyrus roll,[43] entails a host of complex compositional decisions, not least regarding a bunch of good stuff that doesn't quite work and winds up on the cutting-room floor. Hence, just because Luke left out the Syrophoenician/Canaanite woman story does not necessarily mean that he found it obstructive to his aims. A Gospel writer simply could not include the full repertoire of episodes from Jesus' life (cf. John 21:25).

But just as we cannot guarantee that Luke excluded the story in question on hard ideological grounds, we cannot deny that he might have. Silence can be very telling or tell nothing at all. A feminist hermeneutic of suspicion, honed from habitual squelching of women's voices throughout history, is especially attuned to pick up subliminal messages in otherwise silent voids. And in Luke's stifling of the Syrophoenician woman's voice and experience, Elisabeth Schüssler Fiorenza detects a definite purpose. In her view, the original tradition credited this alien border woman with catalyzing "one of the most crucial transitions" in the mission of Jesus and the early church, namely, expanding its scope beyond Israel's ethnic-nationalistic margins to the Gentile world.[44] Whereas Jesus was adamant that the children of Israel "be fed first, for it is not fair to take the children's food and throw it to the dogs," this persistent woman, in her canine postures of bowing and begging, *changed Jesus' mind* with her persuasive countermessage ("for saying *this word* [*logos*]"): "Sir, even the dogs under the table eat the children's crumbs" (Mark 7:24-29). This watershed moment, however, Luke simply cannot abide, not only because it makes Jesus look slow on the uptake, but also because it undercuts Luke's conviction

---

42. Some scholars also note another Lukan redactional oddity concerning a woman's story, this time involving the shift of Mark's/Matthew's anointing woman episode from the passion narrative to early in Jesus' ministry (Luke 7:36-50). However, Luke's version varies sufficiently that it may represent a different woman altogether. At any rate, even if it reflects the same story, at least Luke does not eliminate this one.

43. A plausible suggestion accounting for Luke's two volumes — each filling the space of a typical ancient scroll.

44. Elisabeth Schüssler Fiorenza, *But She Said: Feminist Practices of Biblical Interpretation* (Boston: Beacon Press, 1992), 97.

that *God* is ultimately responsible for bringing light to the Gentiles through "the male apostle *Peter* and the Gentile missionary *Paul* as the central figures of early Christian mission and church."[45] In sum: "This Lukan historical model has no room for a story about an educated Greek woman, who as a religious and ethnic outsider argues with Jesus for the Gentiles' share in the power of well-being. In short, Luke cannot incorporate a story about a woman who wins the theological argument against erecting narrow ethnic and religious exclusive boundaries."[46]

Without a doubt, the development of the Gentile mission constitutes one of the main organizing theological aims driving Luke's two-volume work. And in all likelihood, such an agenda shapes to some degree Luke's inclusion of particular Gentile OT women and exclusion of Mark's/Matthew's Syrophoenician/Canaanite mother. But Schüssler Fiorenza's specific thesis concerning Luke's motivation for disenfranchising the foreign female progenitor of the Gentile mission remains shaky at various points. First, it is too confidently advanced. Once more, we must admit that arguments from silence, while often suggestive, are never definitive. Though Luke indeed makes "no room" for the pleading Gentile mother in his Gospel, he does not highlight the fact *that* there was no room for her in Jesus' life or hint in so many words *why* this might have been the case. Moreover, the assertion that Luke "*cannot* incorporate" this woman into his narrative constitutes a parade example of the intentional fallacy; of course, Luke *can* introduce her — he's not bound by some coercive spirit, divine or demonic — in all manner of ways, including negatively, if he objects to her character and/or actions. He simply chooses not to feature this woman for reasons that remain buried in Luke's psyche.

Second, though Luke does constrict women's direct rhetoric and argumentation in his two volumes, as we have repeatedly noted, he is not opposed *in principle* to women's prophetic influence (Acts 2:17-18; 21:8-9) and has no particular axe to grind against elite, "educated Greek women."[47] In

---

45. Schüssler Fiorenza, *But She Said,* 97.
46. Schüssler Fiorenza, *But She Said,* 97-98.
47. On the Syrophoenician woman's educated-elite status endorsed by Schüssler Fiorenza in Mark's story, see Gerd Theissen, *The Gospels in Context: Social and Political History in the Synoptic Tradition* (Edinburgh: T. & T. Clark, 1992), 61-80; Sharon H. Ringe, "A Gentile Woman's Story, Revisited: Rereading Mark 7:24-31a," in *A Feminist Companion to Mark* (ed. Amy-Jill Levine and Marianne Blickenstaff; Sheffield: Sheffield Academic, 2001), 83-100; and Frances Taylor Gench, *Back to the Well: Women's Encounters with Jesus in the Gospels* (Louisville: Westminster John Knox, 2004), 18-20. I remain dubious, however, that

fact, Luke singles out many "Greek women of high standing" in Thessalonica and Damaris in Athens as model believers, albeit briefly and without allowing them to voice their own convictions (Acts 17:12, 34).[48]

Third, on the matter of who spearheaded the Gentile mission, Luke certainly gives pride of place to "*God* [who] first looked favorably on the Gentiles, to take from among them a people for his name" and who "made a choice among you, that [*Peter*] should be the one through whom the Gentiles would hear the message of the good news and become believers" (Acts 15:14, 7). Equally patent are the seminal roles of *Jesus* in preparing God's way for the Gentiles (Luke 4:25-27) and of *Paul* in propelling it forward (Acts 9:15; 22:21; 26:17-18). So Luke enshrines his male missionary hall of fame with seemingly no more access for women than in the exclusive apostolic club of twelve *men* (Acts 1:21-22). Still, Luke's densely populated narrative, taken as a whole, tends to deconstruct its own stereotypes, not least regarding pioneers of the Gentile mission. For interspersed among the "big four" Jewish missionaries (God, Jesus, Peter, and Paul) are rather surprising contributors to cross-cultural outreach: the Hellenistic-Jewish table-waiter-turned evangelist Philip (6:5; 8:26-40) and even Roman centurions, like Cornelius, on the male side (Luke 7:1-10; 23:47; Acts 10:1-48); and the Galilean village girl Mary and Greek God-fearing purple merchant Lydia (Acts 16:11-15, 40),[49] on the female side. Cornelius and Mary offer particularly notable cases. The former plays as much, if not more, of a key role as Peter in confirming God's saving embrace of uncircumcised Gentiles (Cornelius's vision from God *precedes* Peter's [10:1-8, 17-23, 30-33]). And Mary's prescient Magnificat first adumbrates the universal scope of the messianic mission. Her sweeping proclamation that God's "mercy is for those who fear God *(phoboumenois auton)* / from generation to generation" (Luke 1:50) strikingly echoes Peter's opening announcement to Cornelius, "I truly understand that God shows no partiality, but in every nation anyone who fears him *(phoboumenos auton)* and does what is right

---

Mark provides sufficient evidence to determine the Syrophoenician mother's social status (see *Dancing Girls*, 62-63). But whatever her level, high or low, it seems unlikely Luke would omit her story on such grounds.

48. We might also include the well-to-do purple merchant and homeowner Lydia from Thyatira in this circle, though we don't know how educated or "high-standing" she was in the community (Acts 16:14-16, 40). Also, we should be reminded of Joanna's apparent aristocratic status associated with Herod's court, though she was not of Greek origin.

49. Lydia leads her entire household to Christian baptism and becomes head and host of the young congregation established in Philippi (Acts 16:15, 40).

is acceptable to him" (Acts 10:34-35). But the young Mary beats the seasoned apostle Peter to this inspired insight by four decades or so of story time and a volume and a half of discourse time. God moves *within* as well as *toward* the margins of society.[50]

Finally, speculation about Luke's motives for omitting Jesus' encounter with the Syrophoenician woman must entertain other potentially problematic aspects of her character, apart from ethnicity, vocality, gender, and class. For example, Luke might have been bothered more by her *familial status* and/or *aggressive demeanor,* though again certainty escapes us. Family-wise, excepting the specialized cases of Mary and Elizabeth in the opening chapters, Luke shows scant interest in *mothers'* concerns. Although two of the referenced foreign OT women — Lot's wife and the widow at Zarephath — appear as mothers in their original biblical contexts (Gen 19:14-16; 1 Kings 17:12, 17-24), Luke does not portray them as such. The few maternal characters Luke does feature outside of Mary and Elizabeth are not exactly poster figures for the joys and values of motherhood. The widow at Nain and "daughters of Jerusalem" weep for recently deceased or mortally threatened children (Luke 7:11-13; 23:28-30); the importance of Jesus' own mother is relativized by his primary spiritual kinship with all women who heed God's word (8:19-21; 11:27-28); and the cursory introductions of the "mother of James" (24:10) and the mother of John Mark (Acts 12:12) serve only to differentiate these two additional women named Mary, not to highlight their maternal identities. As for desperate parents who implore Jesus to heal their sick children, Luke focuses on *fathers* like Jairus, pleading for his daughter's restoration (the mother is mentioned once as an afterthought [8:51]), or an anonymous suppliant for his epileptic son (9:37-43). And as numerous commentators have noticed, the mother in the tense family drama surrounding the prodigal son is con-

---

50. Cf. the incisive analysis of Justo L. González, *Santa Biblia: The Bible through Hispanic Eyes* (Nashville: Abingdon, 1996), first, with reference to Jesus' "lost" parables in Luke 15: "In short, Jesus is not speaking to the margin, but to the center. He is not merely speaking of God's love for the margin, but he is speaking of those who think they belong at the center, telling them that unless they too go out and seek the lost sheep and the lost coin, and welcome the younger brother, they are not true servants of God" (45); and second, with reference to Peter's encounter with Cornelius in Acts 10–11: "This entire story is usually called the conversion of Cornelius. But when one reads it carefully, it is the conversion of Peter just as much as of Cornelius. . . . Peter is converted from a follower of an exclusivistic Way, limited to those of his own heritage and traditions, to a proclaimer of a Way that is open to all persons, including the unclean Romans" (50).

spicuous by her absence (15:11-32). Once more, we should not make too much of Luke's silences and slights concerning mothers (imagine what Freud might say!). But if Luke did deliberately bar the Syrophoenican woman from his account, her *motherhood* could disqualify her as much as anything else.

Or maybe, irrespective of her being a Gentile or a mother, the problem was her persistent hounding of Jesus until she got what she wanted. One must treat Jesus more respectfully and not push him too hard, particularly if one is a woman. But that logic hardly works with the pushy hemorrhaging woman, who presses through the crowd to touch Jesus' garment and trigger his flow of healing power without his permission (8:43-48), or with the feisty widow of Jesus' parable, who badgers the callous judge until he grants her justice (18:1-8). But neither of these women has anything to do with the Gentile mission, so maybe the *ethnicity* of the Syrophoenician woman was a problematic factor for Luke after all, *combined with* her audacious persistence. The parallel case of a Gentile seeking Jesus' aid for an ill household member — namely, a centurion's healing petition for his beloved infirm slave — diverges from the Syrophoenician episode not only in terms of the Roman officer's (and servant's) male gender, but more critically in the remarkably *humble deference* he shows toward Jesus' authority: "I am not worthy to have you come under my roof," he conveys to Jesus through brokers; "therefore I did not presume to come to you. But only speak the word, and let my servant be healed" (7:6-7). To be sure, this demonstrates a type of bold faith (7:9), but of an altogether different variety than that shown by the intrusive Syrophoenician mother who intercedes directly with Jesus.

Ultimately we cannot know what may or may not have motivated Luke's bypassing the tradition of Jesus' encounter with the Syrophoenician/ Canaanite woman. But this brief discussion supports the value of this tradition as a suggestive intertext to compare with Jesus' three references to foreign OT women in Luke. Moreover, apart from Luke's literary and theological relationship to it, the Gentile woman story in Matthew/Mark shares many elements with the canonical and apocryphal border narratives discussed above:

1. Women's bodies (daughter's demon possession) and body language (mother's bowing/begging) as markers of ethnic-religious boundary disputes.
2. Focus on food and table fellowship.

3. Possibility of conflicting social, economic, and political dynamics, *if* we grant either the Syrophoenician woman's elite status or Jesus' "conquest" mode.[51]

4. Response of repentance or conversion, though with the twist that the Hellenistic woman provokes the Jewish male (Jesus) to change his mind about socioreligious relations.

5. Blurring and breakdown of polarities, as the foreign female outsider and native male insider engage in give-and-take negotiation, each in turn defending one's own turf and deferring to one another's stances.

Hungry Widow of Zarephath (Luke 4:25-26)

Jesus alludes to a foreign OT woman in his first Sabbath sermon to his hometown synagogue in Nazareth (Luke 4:16-30). By substantially expanding Mark's version and shifting it to the beginning of Jesus' public ministry, Luke signals its programmatic significance for Jesus' mission. The *main text* Jesus cites combines Isaiah 61:1-2 and 58:6 announcing the prophet's Spirit-anointed vocation to "bring good news to the poor," evidenced in mighty acts of liberation (Luke 4:17-19). Jesus also provides a *supplemental midrash* on the Isaiah reading, featuring Elijah's feeding the hungry widow at Zarephath along with Elisha's healing the leprous commander Naaman of Syria (4:25-27; 1 Kings 17:8-16/2 Kings 5:1-14). Following these references, the story shockingly turns sour with the audience's moblike attempt to fling Jesus off the cliff at the town's edge — a fate he narrowly (and mysteriously) escapes (Luke 4:28-30).

Expounding Scripture can be hazardous to one's health in Luke, and patently, the brief allusion to Elijah's aiding the widow at Zarephath is more provocative than it first appears. Much more is involved than a nice

---

51. For a critical postcolonial reading of Matthew's account of the Canaanite woman as an intrusive, imperial "conquest" of a foreign enemy by the Jewish Jesus, see Dube, *Postcolonial Feminist Interpretation*, 147-55. As I remain cautious about profiling the Syrophoenican/Canaanite woman's socioeconomic status (see n. 47 above), I am even more skeptical about viewing her as a target of Jesus' colonizing agenda. For one thing, the woman approaches Jesus, and he initially appears more indifferent toward her than interested in exploiting her. Moreover, in Mark's version, Jesus purposefully enters Phoenician territory to be alone and unobtrusive (Mark 7:24). Cf. F. Scott Spencer, "Feminist Criticism," in *Hearing the New Testament: Strategies for Interpretation* (ed. Joel B. Green; 2nd ed.; Grand Rapids: Eerdmans, 2010), 303-4, 317-18.

charity story about helping a poor widow; in this context, the story some-how poses a clear and present *danger* to the Nazareth congregation. Such threatening potential fits the framework for understanding foreign biblical women sketched above. We now aim to tune in more precisely to the warn-ing bells the Zarephath widow sets off in Luke's account.

We begin with the responsive tones sounded by Jesus and the crowd to the Isaiah lection. After Jesus rolls up the prophetic scroll, all eyes rivet upon him, awaiting his commentary; and befitting the high dramatic mo-ment, Jesus drops a bombshell: "Today this scripture has been fulfilled in your hearing" (4:21). Though a terse and tantalizing pronouncement, its implication is clear enough: a climactic (eschatological) era of salvation — a banner Year of Jubilee (4:19) — has somehow dawned, according to Jesus or, better, *in* Jesus; in other words, Jesus seems to claim that *he* is the Spirit-anointed prophet profiled by Isaiah, ready to get on with his liberating mission "today." That's a lot for the hometown folks to swallow, to put it mildly, and their initial response as Luke narrates it allows for predictable ambivalence and ambiguity. The verb *emartyroun* may mean "All spoke well of him," as the NRSV has it, or it may connote a more neutral "All were bearing witness to him," that is, they heard and took in what he was saying. But doesn't the addendum that all "were amazed *(ethaumazon)* at the gracious words" (4:22) seal their positive verdict? Not necessarily. "Amazement" in Luke's narrative can cut two ways — toward either *ap-proving wonder:* "Wow, that's glorious! Oh happy day!" or *apprehensive shock:* "Whoa, that's horrendous! How dare he say that!"[52] Jesus' words in-deed herald a "gracious" reality. But can he deliver the goods? This is "Jo-seph's son," remember, one of us Nazareth villagers (4:22).[53] Again, the range of possible responses varies: "Wow, we never dreamed Joseph's boy was destined for this! He's going to put us on the map!" Or, more likely, given the prevailing ethos of kinship solidarity and suspicion of upward

---

52. The verb for "amazed" in 4:22, *thaumazō*, and its close synonym, *existēmi*, appear fre-quently in Luke's two volumes in a variety of contexts. A good example of the open ambiguity of both "amazement" terms occurs in the Pentecost crowd's bewilderment over early believ-ers' sudden multilingual abilities: "Amazed *(existanto)* and astonished *(ethaumazon)*, they asked, 'Are not all these who are speaking Galileans?' . . . All were amazed *(existanto)* and per-plexed, saying to one another, 'What does this mean?' But others sneered" (Acts 2:7-13).

53. Jesus' filial status is presented as a rhetorical question, implying a positive response: "Isn't this Joseph's son? Of course it is!" Yet readers of Luke's story up to this point know the matter of Joseph's parentage is not so settled. Joseph "was thought" to be Jesus' father (3:23), but we know the true story of God's paternity.

mobility: "Whoa, who does this guy think he is, acting all high and mighty? He's just an ordinary son of an ordinary Joe, for goodness' sake, just like the rest of us."

If Jesus senses this oscillating tension in the air, he does nothing to ease it. In fact, he ratchets up the pressure with two proverbial provocations. First, he presumes the audience's underlying taunt, "Doctor cure yourself!" gigging him to perform miracles on the spot, as he had reputedly done in Capernaum, and thus vindicate his claims to prophetic power (4:23). Second, he presumes the congregation's compliance with the spiritually callous norm: "No prophet is accepted in the prophet's hometown" (4:24). So Jesus effectively tars his homefolk as dubious power-grubbers and prophet-snubbers. Not the best strategy for winning them over.

It's at this hot spot in the story that Jesus brings in the Elijah/Elisha material. Never a bad idea, it would seem, to go back to Scripture in a synagogue service. And the evocation of Elijah/Elisha follows quite logically, reinforcing Jesus' emphasis on miracle-working prophets of Israel who challenge God's rebellious leaders and people. Moreover, expectations of Elijah's return as the Spirit-sent harbinger of Israel's eschatological restoration continued to percolate into Jesus' day.[54] So there's potential for Jesus now to take a more hopeful tack. But curiously, among the welter of wondrous Elijah/Elisha stories from 1 Kings 17–2 Kings 9 Jesus might adduce, he selects the two that feature their ministries to *non*-Israelites who *accept* (eventually) the prophets' work (Luke 4:25-27). So Jesus' focus abruptly pivots from *his own people* who characteristically *reject* God's prophets to Gentiles who receive them.

But while such a shift may appear to deflect attention away from Jesus' indictment of Nazareth, it may also drive the wedge deeper and precipitate the audience's violent reaction. Though he does not connect the dots as such, it's hard not to take Jesus' highlighting of Elijah/Elisha's outreach to the Sidonian widow/Syrian leper as a final slap against his hometown and native land, especially with his accent that the ancient prophets bypassed the "many widows" and "many lepers" *within Israel* (Luke 4:25, 27). Hence, Jesus hints at a cause-and-effect nexus: *because* the Nazareth community has followed its Israelite ancestors in spurning God's prophet, the prophet will spurn them and seek out receptive Gentiles instead. The Lukan Paul will make such a move painfully explicit in another synagogue: "It was

54. Cf. Mal 4:5-6; Sir 48:10; 4Q521 2 iii 1-2; Mark 9:11-13; 15:34-35; Luke 1:17; 9:7-9; Mishnah *Eduyyot* 8:7.

necessary that the word of God should be spoken first to you. Since you reject it and judge yourselves to be unworthy of eternal life, we are now turning to the Gentiles" (Acts 13:46). Of course, *unlike* Paul's Jewish audience, which turned belligerent *before* Paul's Gentile reference, Jesus' congregation has remained fairly calm so far amid their "amazement" and confusion. It's Jesus who incites them with his "foreign" OT stories; he pushes them over the edge emotionally, sparking their attempt to push him over the edge physically (Luke 4:28-29). He thus engages in self-fulfilling prophecy: his provocative, scriptural scenario of prophetic rejection catalyzes a local lynch mob.

So we appear left with a stark division between blameworthy Jewish rejecters and exemplary Gentile receptors of God's purposes in Luke, bolstered by Jesus' appeal to Elijah's mission to the widow at Zarephath. But recall from our heuristic framework the wariness we developed for strict polarities along moral, ethnic, and/or gender lines, that is, unequivocally good or bad Jews/Gentiles, males/females. So we press for more nuanced understandings of Jesus' prophetic judgments on his hometown via the analogy with Elijah's dealings with the Sidonian widow, focusing on issues of *setting*, related to time and place, and *status*, related to the widow's social class and moral character.

Setting: Time and Place

1. Famine and Fellowship Jesus sets the OT scene during "the time of Elijah" when the sky "was shut" *(ekleisthē)* for three and a half years, yielding no rain and causing a "severe famine *(limos megas)* over all the land" (Luke 4:25). The drought and famine derive from 1 Kings, but Luke extends the crisis six months beyond the third year (cf. 1 Kings 18:1) and stretches its boundaries to encompass, along with the northwestern border territory of Sidon, "all *(pasan)* the [promised] land," presumably including the southern kingdom of Judah, whereas the OT pinpoints that "the famine was severe *in Samaria* [northern kingdom]" (1 Kings 18:2).[55] This mapping suits Luke's wider geographical context of Israel's experience, further evidenced

---

55. See Larrimore C. Crockett, "Luke 4:25-27 and Jewish-Gentile Relations in Luke-Acts," *Journal of Biblical Literature* 88 (1969): 177-78. Whereas 1 Kings suggests a three-year drought and does not use the image of "shutting the heavens," Luke's applying this image to a three-and-a-half-year crisis matches the allusions in Sir 48:3; James 5:17; Rev 11:6.

in two additional famine references: one, recalled by Stephen, that spread "throughout Egypt and Canaan" in the patriarch Joseph's era (Acts 7:11); and the other, the more contemporary "severe famine *(limon megalēn)* over all the world" forecast through the prophet Agabus (11:28). All three cases negotiate border relations between Israelites/Jews and Gentiles in the interest of *feeding* or famine *relief*.

- Elijah is sent by God to the destitute Gentile widow at Zarephath, who is down to her and her son's last morsel; soon, however, they are miraculously and abundantly fed until the drought ceases.
- Joseph, first exiled and then exalted in Egypt as Pharaoh's right-hand officer, receives his relocated clan from Canaan and sustains them with food during the multiyear famine.
- Agabus's prediction of empire-wide famine during Claudius's reign prompts the mixed Jewish-Gentile congregation in Syrian Antioch (up the eastern Mediterranean coast from Zarephath) to dispatch famine relief to the poor Jewish mother church in Jerusalem (Acts 11:27-30).

Luke's use of the famine-feeding motif from the histories of ancient Israel and the early church thus advocates, as Larrimore Crockett comments, "that God's intention in the new age is to save both Jews and gentiles and bring them into a productive mutual relationship."[56] So, despite first impressions, Jesus may *not* be rejecting his own people in Nazareth in favor of foreigners. He may *not* be promoting taking food from the children of Israel and giving it to Gentile dogs. Conversely, perhaps he *is* suggesting God's long-standing — and continuing — interest in the dogs' well-being and in the "productive mutual relationship" between Jews and Gentiles in God's household, where both people feed each other. Such reciprocity is most evident in Acts where the mixed Jewish-Gentile Antiochene congregation feeds the Jewish Jerusalem church and Cornelius hosts Peter (Acts 10–11). The crux of the latter episode has as much or more to do with the scrupulous Peter's *acceptance of Gentile hospitality and spirituality* as with the God-fearing Cornelius's acceptance of the Jewish-Christian gospel (Acts 10:17-48; 11:11-18).

This often neglected point prompts us to reconsider the social dynamics behind Elijah's encounter with the Sidonian widow referenced by Jesus.

---

56. Crockett, "Luke 4:25-27," 181 (cf. 178-81).

We discover what the OT plainly indicates and the biblically savvy Jesus and fellow Nazarenes surely knew, namely, that Elijah "was sent" in the first place by God *to be fed by a Gentile woman:* "Then the word of the Lord came to him, saying, 'Go now to Zarephath, which belongs to Sidon, and live there; for I have commanded *a widow there to feed you*'" (1 Kings 17:8-9).[57] Accordingly, upon arrival Elijah asks the woman for some bread and water, though her cupboard is all but bare. Nudged by Elijah's promise, quite preposterous under the circumstances, of an endless supply of grain and oil, the widow proceeds to feed the prophet *first* from her meager larder and *only then* discovers its miraculous replenishment for her, her son, and the prophet's future needs (17:10-16). The story chiefly extols YHWH's power to nourish and nurture. But such power extends to and *works through* both Israelites and foreigners — in this case even giving priority to the Gentile woman. The desperate dog first feeds the suppliant child.

On the whole, this episode showcases a *mutual fellowship meal* between Israelite and Gentile in God's banquet house, a strong sign of pilgrims coming "from east and west, from north and south [to] eat in the kingdom of God," where typical place settings of "first" and "last" are reshuffled (Luke 13:29-30). Therefore, applied to the Nazareth synagogue scene in Luke, Jesus aims not to exclude his kinfolk from God's restorative mission, but to expand their view of kinship to include borderline women and Gentiles, like the widow at Zarephath. Of course, such inclusiveness can still be perceived as highly threatening. It may start with a poor, innocent, benevolent Gentile widow — but can a horde of marauding aliens be far behind? Or then again, might the dominoes fall the other way? Might not a lone Spirit-anointed prophet and faithful receptive woman trigger a glorious reconciling revolution?

2. Land and Lordship   This more positive, inclusive take on Jesus' appeal to the OT foreign widow finds further support in the geography of the case. Elijah is dispatched to a particular address: "Zarephath in Sidon" (Luke 4:26). In Elijah's day, Zarephath was a port town located roughly equidistant between Sidon and Tyre on a twenty-mile stretch of the northeastern Mediterranean coastline. Sidon and Tyre were more powerful cen-

---

57. Notice the mandate for Elijah to "live" or "dwell" *(yāšab)* in Sidonian Zarephath, implying a long-term residence and relationship with the widow that does ensue in the narrative. However, the Greek version (LXX) of 1 Kings 17:8-9 drops the live/dwell element.

ters in the territory of Phoenicia and could each designate the wider region and its people. Hence Zarephath could be considered part of Sidon or part of Tyre, and its citizens Sidonians, Tyrians, or Phoenicians. Zarephath was known for its rich commerce in grain, oil, and purple dye derived from shellfish.[58] These resources figure ironically in the widow's situation: her supply of grain and oil are all but depleted when Elijah arrives, and we can bet that purple-hued cosmetics or clothing is way beyond her means.

From the Deuteronomic perspective of 1 Kings, however, such misfortune serves the widow and her land right. This is Baal country, indeed, the very land of Queen Jezebel who, during this period via marriage with Ahab, has brought her Baal-loving, YHWH-offending policies and prophets into Israel. But look at Baal now: not much of a storm-rain-fertility god during this famine! YHWH, the God of Israel, truly controls the cosmos, regulating rain and harvest, *even on Baal's — and Jezebel's — home turf!* Good for YHWH, but what is gained for YHWH's suffering people back home in Israel by scoring this victory in Sidon? There are in fact many widows *there* in desperate need. So why go to one across the border in Zarephath? It's nice to do some "foreign missions" work now and again, but doesn't charity begin at home?

But where exactly is home for God's people? What are the boundary lines of the Promised Land? In a fascinating study, Magnus Ottosson maps the maximum borders of Israel during the glory days of King David.[59] The infamous census patrol tracked the people "through all the tribes of Israel, from Dan to Beer-sheba," north to south, and to the trans-Jordanian region of Gilead to the east (2 Sam 24:2, 6). The upper tip at Dan is located due north of the Sea of Galilee and on the same latitude as Tyre and Sidon. But rather than cordoning off this Phoenician coastal strip from David's kingdom, the census *includes* it: "from Dan they went around to *Sidon*, and

58. On Zarephath (Sarepta in Greek), see James B. Pritchard, "Sarepta in History and Tradition," in *Understanding the Sacred Text: Essays in Honor of Morton S. Enslin on the Hebrew Bible and Christian Beginnings* (ed. John Reumann; Valley Forge, Pa.: Judson, 1972), 99-114; Dale W. Manor, "Zarephath," in *NIBD*, 5:956-57; Ray L. Roth, "Zarephath," in *ABD*, vol. 6 (New York: Doubleday, 1992), 1041; Choon-Leong Seow, "The First and Second Books of Kings: Introduction, Commentary, and Reflections," in *The New Interpreter's Bible*, vol. 3 (ed. Leander E. Keck et al.; Nashville: Abingdon, 1999), 128. The great wealth of Tyre and Sidon is detailed in Ezekiel 27–28.

59. Magnus Ottosson, "The Prophet Elijah's Visit to Zarephath," in *In the Shelter of Elyon: Essays on Ancient Palestinian Life and Literature in Honor of G. W. Ahlström* (ed. W. Boyd Barrick and John R. Spencer; Sheffield: JSOT, 1984), 185-98.

came to the fortress of *Tyre* and to all the cities of the Hivites and Canaanites" (24:6-7). Positioned between Sidon and Tyre, Zarephath would have been included as well. In the only other OT reference to Zarephath besides 1 Kings 17, the prophet Obadiah envisions a final restoration of Israel along similar lines of David's census:

> They shall possess the land of Ephraim and the land of Samaria,
>   and Benjamin shall possess Gilead.
> The exiles of the Israelites who are in Halah
>   shall possess *Phoenicia as far as Zarephath;*
> and the exiles of Jerusalem who are in Sepharad
>   shall possess the towns of the *Negeb* [the area of Beersheba].
> (Obad 19-20)

So the ideal geographical parameters of God's people may be mapped counterclockwise from Gilead (east) to Dan (north) to Sidon-Zarephath-Tyre (northwest) to Beersheba-Negeb (south). And hardly by accident, this is precisely the route Elijah follows on his feeding and rainmaking mission in 1 Kings 17–19.

- After forecasting the drought to King Ahab, Elijah is sent to hide in the Wadi Cherith in *Gilead,* where he receives food from predatory, nonkosher ravens, of all creatures, and drinks from the creek until it dries up (17:1-7).[60]
- God then dispatches Elijah "to live" in Sidonian *Zarephath* and, first, to be fed by, and then to feed, a destitute widow there. As it happens, he also winds up restoring life to the widow's only son (17:8-24).
- After his dramatic knockout victory over the prophets of Baal at Mount Carmel (down the coast from Phoenicia), Elijah predicts the resumption of rain, races southeast ahead of the downpour to the royal town of Jezreel, and then quickly flees from an irate Jezebel south to *Beersheba* and the wilderness beyond (18:41–19:4).

Gilead → Zarephath → Beersheba: Elijah rides the circuit of *Israel's* outer borders, which are often contested — especially the northwest, Phoenicia-influenced territory — but are still considered, ideally at least, *part of Israel.* Thus, as Ottosson claims, Elijah's trek to Baal-dominated Zarephath

---

60. On the uncleanness of "every raven of any kind" and other related "detestable" fowl, see Lev 11:13-19; Deut 14:11-18; Seow, "First and Second Books of Kings," 127.

"is an ideological confirmation of Yahweh's authority within the Promised Land . . . demonstrat[ing] Yahweh's power in what was traditionally his own territory. Political realities aside, *Zarephath was Israelite and the Sidonian god had no place there*."[61]

So what does this make the widow at Zarephath? Is she really a foreigner after all? Ottosson notes that the OT narrative never explicitly identifies her as a Sidonian and that "later tradition (Gemara) makes her an Israelite woman."[62] Still, she cannot fully escape her threatening alien potential from a YHWH-istic perspective in this Baal-riddled region that produced Princess Jezebel, now queen of Israel. She is best viewed, then, as an ambiguous, marginal, borderline figure — distinguished from "many widows in Israel," as Jesus states, by ethnic-geographic location, but not segregated in an incompatible "far country" beyond the pale of God's grace and God's community. In fact, as patron and client, host and guest, of God's prophet, she appears right at home with God's people at God's table.

Having considered the OT angle on Sidonian geography, we must also track the Lukan view. Only one additional reference emerges in the Gospel, but it is a revealing one. We soon find in a key summary text of Jesus' ministry that, after calling his twelve disciples, a sign of restoring all Israel, he "stood on a level *(pedinou)* place, with a great crowd of his disciples and *a great multitude* of people from all Judea, Jerusalem, *and the coast of Tyre and Sidon*. They had come to hear him and to be healed of their diseases" (Luke 6:17-18). As it happens, Jesus does not bolt Elijah-style from recalcitrant Nazareth *to* Sidonian Zarephath; rather Sidon comes *to him* — in droves! — *along with* a throng from more central Jewish territory. The OT widow of Zarephath thus adumbrates an inclusive restoration of many "foreign" border peoples *with Israel* in God's messianic kingdom. Jesus is indeed *leveling* the ground of fellowship among Jews and Gentiles, rather than reinforcing walls and fences separating them.[63] This extended reconciliation project becomes more aggressive in Acts, as early missionaries move up the Philistine-Phoenician-Syrian coast of the Mediterranean — from Gaza to Azotus to Caesarea to Ptolemais to Tyre to Antioch (Acts 8:26, 39; 10:1–11:30; 15:3; 21:1-16) — but all the while, as we have seen, maintaining solidarity with Jewish roots in Jerusalem.

61. Ottosson, "The Prophet Elijah's Visit," 193 (emphasis added).

62. Ottosson, "The Prophet Elijah's Visit," 191.

63. See Petr Pokorný, *Theologie der lukanischen Schriften* (Göttingen: Vandenhoeck & Ruprecht, 1998), 182-85; F. Scott Spencer, *The Gospel of Luke and Acts of the Apostles* (Nashville: Abingdon, 2008), 142-44.

Status: Class and Character

1. Down and In In presenting a widow caught in the throes of a terrible famine, the Lukan Jesus evokes a stock figure of destitution in the ancient world. Adding other aspects of the widow at Zarephath's situation from 1 Kings 17, particularly her maternal responsibility and material poverty, we can scarcely imagine a lowlier person on the social ladder. She epitomizes "the poor" in desperate need of the good news that Isaiah and Jesus proclaim. Apart from her ethnic distinction, she represents the kind of "lowly" person the Nazareth community could relate to, as evidenced in Mary's Magnificat (Luke 1:48, 52) and sacrifice of a pair of turtledoves or pigeons (2:22-24), the offering of the poor in lieu of a costlier sheep (Lev 12:1-8).

In both her OT and Lukan contexts, the widow at Zarephath's underclass status is underscored in juxtaposition with upper-class counterparts. In 1 Kings, she contrasts with the Phoenician princess Jezebel,[64] as we have seen, but also with the wealthy Shunammite woman, who feeds and lodges the prophet Elisha in a loft apartment and benefits from his resuscitating her dead son and support during another famine season (2 Kings 4:8-36; 8:1-6).[65] The Zarephath widow herself also appears to rise in status *after* the miraculous bounty of grain and oil; more like the Shunammite woman, the Sidonian widow is now known as "mistress of the house," which is large enough to include an "upper chamber" where Elijah resides and revives the widow's comatose son (1 Kings 17:17-24).[66]

Luke directly pairs the widow at Zarephath with the leper from Syria, but though sharing Gentile identity and the need for Israelite prophets' curative powers, they *differ* markedly in socioeconomic status (and gender), as the named military commander Naaman occupies a lucrative and lofty position in his land (2 Kings 5:1-14). As for other widows in Luke, the

---

64. K. A. D. Smelik, "The Literary Function of 1 Kings 17,8-24," in *Pentateuchal and Deuteronomistic Studies: Papers Read at the XIIIth IOSOT Congress Leuven 1989* (ed. C. Brekelmans and J. Lust; Leuven: Leuven University Press, 1990), 239-43.

65. Cf. Jopie Siebert-Hommes, "The Widow of Zarephath and the Great Woman of Shunem: A Comparative Analysis of Two Stories," in *On Reading Prophetic Texts: Gender-Specific and Related Studies in Memory of Fokkelien van Dijk-Hemmes* (ed. Bob Becking and Meindert Dijkstra; Leiden: Brill, 1996), 231-50.

66. Claudia V. Camp, "1 and 2 Kings," in *Women's Bible Commentary* (ed. Newsom and Ringe), 112. 1 Kings 17:8-16 and 17:17-24 may derive from two independent widow traditions that the Deuteronomic editor has stitched together.

prophet Anna sets the stage: though her full portfolio remains undisclosed, her honored place in the temple and intertextual link with the prosperous and pious Judith, who also lived as a pious widow to a ripe old age, suggest something of a privileged and perhaps well-to-do status (Luke 2:36-38).[67] The first widow that appears following the Nazareth episode recalls the Zarephath character at the point of Jesus' Elijah-style raising of her "only son" from the dead and restoring him back to her (7:11-17). In this case we can probably infer a more common, underprivileged widowhood in contrast with the preceding higher-class figure, a male Roman centurion, helped by Jesus (7:1-10). In fact, the diptych of Jesus' ministry in Luke 7:1-17 mirrors the widow at Zarephath/Naaman model, with the *exceptions*, however, that this is a *Jewish* woman from *Nain in Galilee* (a nearby village southeast of Nazareth), not a foreign town, and nothing is said of Jesus' *feeding* or otherwise providing materially for her, though raising her son may have restored her primary means of economic support. We note once more that, while generally following Elijah's prophetic pattern, Jesus himself does *not* dash across the border: he finds a widow to aid and eventually a multitude to feed (9:10-17) among his own people in Galilee.[68]

Overall, apart from Jebezel, the company the lowly widow at Zarephath keeps in the Kings and Luke narratives involves *positive* associations with others both like and unlike her on the social spectrum — including higher-class males (Syrian general, Roman centurion) and Jewish women (Shunammite, Anna, widow at Nain). Thus Jesus' appeal to her story appears more inclusive than exclusive, more embracing than replacing — cutting across class, gender, and ethnic lines rather than cutting out certain folk, his Nazareth kinfolk in particular, mired for the moment in xenophobic prejudice. The Lord's messianic banquet table is long and wide and

---

67. This represents a change of view on Anna's social status from F. Scott Spencer, "Neglected Widows in Acts 6:1-7," *Catholic Biblical Quarterly* 56 (1994): 721-23, which I owe to Barbara Reid, "The Power of the Widows and How to Suppress It (Acts 6.1-7)," in *A Feminist Companion to Acts* (ed. Amy-Jill Levine and Marianne Blickenstaff; London: T. & T. Clark, 2004), 74-76. See more on Lukan widows in chapter 7.

68. The mass feeding scene is set in a "deserted place" near Bethsaida where Jesus had "privately withdrawn" (Luke 9:10-12). Bethsaida was situated at the northern tip of the Sea of Galilee in borderline territory, though John 1:43-44 seems to place it fully within Jewish Galilee. In any case, even with the sense of Jesus' more isolated, border location, there is no hint in Luke, as in Mark's second feeding story, of outreach on this occasion to Gentiles in the Decapolis region (see Mark 7:31–8:10).

stocked full: there is room and food enough for all, even during trying times of social division and material deprivation.

2. Faith and Works   But this gracious outreach is no cheap universalism whitewashing moral and religious distinctions. Conviction and character, faith and works, matter — which brings us back to the Jezebel connection. We hinted earlier at Jezebel's ambiguous portrait, how she ironically mirrors as well as opposes Elijah. But still, from YHWH's sovereign perspective, she typifies alien Baal-worshiping, throne-usurping, land-grabbing peril to covenant values and community. She remains irredeemably outside God's realm, carrion for rapacious dogs, grossly unfit for the Lord's Table (2 Kings 9:30-37). How does her compatriot from Zarephath fare in comparison? The fact that she feeds and is fed by Elijah represents a polar culinary opposite to Jezebel. The widow's literary association with predatory, unclean creatures in the preceding story in 1 Kings 17 reinforces the counterpoint. As the ravens — who usually are pecking at other creatures' carcasses and banned from kosher kitchens — defy their natural instincts by catering to Elijah at the Wadi Cherith (1 Kings 17:1-7), so the Sidonian widow, a subject of the idolatrous King Ethbaal, Jezebel's aptly named father (16:31), hosts and dines with Elijah in her homeland. Clearly, Israel's God and prophets accommodate opportunities for open commensality with strangers.[69]

But why does the Sidonian widow have a reservation at the Lord's Table while Jezebel is blacklisted? Certainly the widow's lack of power to murder YHWH's prophets and market Baal religion in Israel has something to do with it. But surely she also does something more active to merit Elijah's gracious treatment and mitigate her threatening identity. Acts of faith, obedience, repentance, and conversion to Israel's God seem in order, à la Rahab, Ruth, Aseneth, and the foreign widow's "partner" in Jesus' sermon, Naaman, with his bold confession: "Now I know that there is no God in all the earth except in Israel; please accept a present from your servant" (2 Kings 5:15). But the widow never quite rises to such soaring rhetoric, while Naaman, for his part, is not the purest convert one might hope for.

In Luke 4 Jesus details nothing about the widow's and Naaman's motives or actions, focusing simply on their common roles as beneficiaries of prophetic ministry. One distinction, however, which Jesus makes, suggests the widow's *passivity* in contrast to Naaman's initiative. Elijah "was sent" *to*

---

69. See Seow, "First and Second Books of Kings," 129-30.

her place in Zarephath (Luke 4:26); she didn't take a step outside her home, whereas Naaman "was cleansed," according to Elisha's instructions, *in Israel's Jordan River* as the OT explains (2 Kings 5:10-14). Naaman had made a grand journey *to Elisha's home* and was rather hoping for a grander reception and treatment than dipping in the measly, muddy Jordan, barely a trickle compared to the mighty "Abana and Pharpar, the rivers of Damascus" in Syria (5:12).[70] Naaman must overcome his considerable ethnic prejudice, not to mention his desire to pay handsomely for medical services rendered. He would like to maintain some control and dignity in this whole humiliating leprosy affair. But Elisha will have none of it (5:15-16). The healing God of Israel is in charge here, and all Naaman must do is wash in the Jordan seven times, which really means this is not about anything Naaman does at all, except obey the prophet's command. His cure results from YHWH's grace and power, period,[71] extended even to foreign officers. So it is, too, with the alien widow's feeding and her son's resuscitating. Unlike Naaman, however, she seems more inclined to accept the Lord's prophet and his ministrations without ado, less encumbered by pride and prejudice.

But she's still a potentially threatening foreign woman — and a well-fed one now after Elijah's visit! Is she still aligned with Baal and her country with its pagan king and daughter Jezebel? With the widow's economic conditions improved, she might be more dangerous than ever — unless we see clear signs of repentance and conversion. A bold "Your people shall be my people, / and your God my God" would be nice (Ruth 1:15), if not Naaman's eventual "no other God but Israel's" confession. And we might expect that Jesus would highlight such proselyte responsiveness by both the Sidonian widow and the Syrian general, given his concern with the border-crossing outreach of God's saving ministry in his first sermon. But in fact, from the start at Nazareth and throughout his ministry, Luke's Jesus shows scant interest in converting Gentiles to Israel's faith or recruiting them to his movement.

Notice his two main interactions with needy foreigners. First, concerning the Roman centurion in Capernaum who beseeches Jesus to heal his sick slave, Jesus marvels at his extraordinary faith found "not even in

---

70. In this case Elisha does not step out of his home; in fact, he doesn't even greet Naaman personally but rather dispatches a messenger outside to instruct the leprous foreign official to dunk himself in the Jordan (2 Kings 5:9-10).

71. Naaman is right about one thing: the unimpressive Jordan has no therapeutic powers in itself.

Israel," but does nothing to instigate such faith and issues no summons for the officer to follow him. In fact, he never meets the man or speaks with him directly (mirroring Elisha's dealings with Naaman); the centurion was already known for sympathizing with Israel's God before Jesus arrived (Luke 7:4-5). Second, dealing with the Gerasene demoniac who confronts him "opposite Galilee," Jesus liberates the man from the vicious "Legion" horde that possesses him, but not because of any faith or desire on the demoniac's part; in fact, the spirits who control him plead that Jesus "not torment" them. After his exorcism, the man begs to accompany his deliverer, but Jesus "sends him away," back to his Gentile hometown, to testify there to God's power. The demoniac has certainly been transformed by Jesus' action, but there is no indication of his becoming a proselyte as such to Jesus' Jewish faith, practice, and mission (8:26-39).

How, then, does Luke's underplaying of foreigners' conversions square with the OT's portrayal of the widow at Zarephath? A major feature of her story involves serving her last biscuit to Elijah in response to his request and promise that the Lord would bless her with an unlimited supply of grain and oil. Though such a gesture seems to reflect remarkable faith in action, the larger narrative complicates the nature of that faith. Following Elijah's first petition for "a morsel of bread," the widow responds rather tartly, distancing herself from Elijah's deity ("As the LORD *your* God lives") and decrying her desperate situation to which Elijah seems oblivious: "I am now gathering a couple of sticks, so that I may go home and prepare [my last little cake] for myself and my son, that we may eat it, and die" (1 Kings 17:11-12).[72] She cannot be terribly happy with any god (or prophet) right now, be it Baal, who has failed miserably in his rainmaking duties, or YHWH, who has engineered the drought. Whatever game the gods are playing, she's caught in the middle and about to be squashed to death. She has little to lose now by complying with Elijah's absurd demand, and as it happens, his promise of sustenance comes true! She and her son will survive (for the moment), but significantly, the replenishing meal jar and oil jug do *not* prompt a single word of gratitude or devotion to YHWH from her.[73]

72. On the self-distancing effect of the widow's calling YHWH "*your* God" — that is, Elijah's God, *not* hers — see Seow, "First and Second Books of Kings," 125; Camp ("1 and 2 Kings," 112) interprets the widow's initial reference to YHWH as swearing (in almost mocking tone) an "oath of resignation." Elijah's deity YHWH may live, but she's about to die! Cf. Fewell and Gunn, *Gender, Power, and Promise*, 178.

73. While appreciating the direness of the widow's situation and "what must have appeared to be a heartless insistence on Elijah's part" that she feed him first from her last grain

As the narrative continues and her circumstances improve, the widow continues to host Elijah, but misfortune strikes again, sparking sharp words of lament. Her son suddenly dies, and she would like to know what Elijah *has against her* by "bring[ing] my sin to remembrance" and punishing her for it by killing her son! Yes, she now addresses Elijah as "man of God" and acknowledges her sinfulness, though not with any specificity (17:17-18). But in the face of her current tragedy, she remains more petulant than penitent — an attitude Elijah understands and shares! How dare YHWH treat this hospitable widow this way! Stretching himself across the deceased boy, he demands that God restore the child's life. When God finally does just that, Elijah reunites the boy with his mother (17:19-23). Now at last, after this second miracle, the widow at Zarephath musters a worthy confessional statement: "Now I know that you are a man of God, and that the word of the LORD in your mouth is truth" (17:24). It starts out like Naaman's testimony ("Now I know") and shares its positive tone, but *not* its exclusive content. Her word is more of a vote of confidence in Elijah's integrity than in YHWH's superiority; she offers no "no other God but YHWH" Shema acclamation. Of course, a final check of Naaman's story reveals a telling loophole in his confession as well. For the sake of political expedience, he asks that "the LORD pardon [him] on one count," namely, when he continues to accompany his master-monarch in worshiping the Syrian storm god Rimmon (2 Kings 5:18). Not exactly a small "count." So much for YHWH as Naaman's "One God, the Lord alone." But more revealing is that Elisha does not care that much, dispatching the healed Naaman back home "in peace" (5:19).

One can't expect too much of foreigners, it seems, and that's all right. It's good enough if they at least give a little, even as they take a lot. Diplomacy is a delicate matter, allowing for compromise and negotiation. The threat of foreign "others" like the widow at Zarephath (and Naaman) cannot be entirely neutralized, but "they" cannot rest at complete ease with "us" either. Tension, caution, and ambiguity persist. The God of Jesus and Israel can and will graciously feed, heal, and revive the nations *and* maybe capriciously starve, afflict, and kill them (and us!) from time to time, regardless of their response. YHWH's sovereign judgment remains firm — and frustrating.

---

supply, Matthew J. M. Coomber ("Exegetical Notes on 1 Kings 17:8-16: The Widow of Zarephath," *Expository Times* 118 [2007]: 390) underplays the widow's sarcasm and frustration and overplays her "generous nature" and "leap of faith, placing her life, and that of her son, on the trust of the Israelite God."

Spicy Queen of the South (Luke 11:31)

Whereas Jesus' reference to the widow at Zarephath occurs in the well-defined Galilean setting of the Nazareth synagogue at the strategic commencement of his public ministry, his appeal to "the queen of the South" comes at an undisclosed location somewhere along a meandering journey to Jerusalem extending from Luke 9:51 to Luke 19:28. The audience now is a generalized throng, "increasing" in numbers and representative of "this [entire] generation" of Jews (11:29). Jesus reminds his burgeoning audience of the familiar story of a foreign queen's encounter with the wise King Solomon, clearly referring to the queen of Sheba's (as she is more commonly known) visit to Solomon's court in 1 Kings 10:1-13 (cf. 2 Chron 9:1-12), a few chapters prior to Elijah's meeting with the Sidonian widow. While such a tale seems a "happy" (1 Kings 10:8) and salutary affair for Israel, Jesus cites it in the interest of warning and judgment. Again, the threat level rises when a foreign woman enters the picture. But like the Zarephath widow, this female stranger, as Jesus presents her, threatens not to undermine his people's faith and security, but rather to expose their own apostasy and vulnerability by contrast. "This generation" is in fact an "*evil* generation," and the exemplary "queen of the South will rise *at the judgment . . . and condemn them*" (Luke 11:31).

To understand the details and dynamics of this forensic-foreign case, we turn again to the wider Lukan cotext and OT intertext. Though not embedded in a single, sustained episode, the reference to the Southern queen does slot in a loosely connected series of conflict-and-challenge crowd scenes in Luke 11:14-54.[74]

1. **Accusing Jesus of Alliance with Beelzebul (11:14-26)**
   "Some" *(tines)* in the crowd foolishly denounce Jesus' exorcisms as somehow inspired by "Beelzebul, the ruler of the demons," and demand "a sign from heaven" as further proof of his divine power.
2. **Blessing All Who Hear God's Word (11:27-28)**
   When "a woman in the crowd" extols the mother who suckled Jesus, he responds by blessing all those, regardless of biological kinship or gender, "who hear *(akouontes)* the word of God and obey it."

---

74. Note the mention of the "crowds" *(ochlos)* in 11:14, 27, and 29 and continuing in 12:1, 13. Jesus finally turns back to addressing his disciples more intimately in 12:22. Jesus associates the crowd with "this [evil] generation" in 11:29, 30, 31, 32, 50, 51.

3. **Desiring Signs of God's Rule (11:29-32)**
   Jesus decries the crowd's penchant for dramatic signs as itself a sign of their evil orientation and counters by presenting the *judgmental sign* of the "men *(andres)* of Nineveh's" repentant response to Jonah's witness, *paired with* the queen of the South's rapt attention *(akousai)* to Solomon's wisdom.

4. **Judging Light and Darkness (11:33-36)**
   Jesus continues to expound his judgment theme via a common light/darkness dualistic trope, but with the provocative proviso: "Consider whether the light in you is not darkness" (11:35).

5. **Denouncing Hypocrisy and Rejection of God's Wisdom (11:37-54)**
   When a Pharisee host becomes "amazed" that Jesus fails to wash up before dinner, Jesus launches into a tirade against the hypocrisy of Pharisees in general and other legal scholars, who in "this generation" follow Israel's tragic history of rejecting prophetic emissaries of "the Wisdom of God" (11:49-50).

In the center of this larger unit, the foreign-female monarch of the South defies ethnic-gender stereotypes and stands out, in contrast to and condemnation of many Israelites of "this evil generation," as a blessed hearer *(akouō)* of God's word (11:27-28, 31)[75] and receptor of God's Wisdom *(Sophia* [11:31, 49]). Likewise, she also holds center stage with Solomon in the narrower unit of 11:30-32, flanked by Jonah and the male Ninevites.

Jonah/Ninevites (11:30)

For just as Jonah became a sign to the people of Nineveh *(tois Nineuitais)*, so the Son of Man will be to this generation.

Solomon/Queen of South (11:31)

The queen of the South will rise at the judgment with the people of this generation and condemn them, because she came from the ends of the earth to listen to the wisdom of Solomon, and see, something greater than Solomon is here!

---

75. Associating the Southern queen in 11:31 with "the community of faith [that] functions irrespective of gender" in 11:27-28, see Amy-Jill Levine, "Luke 11:31: Queen of the South," in *Women in Scripture: A Dictionary of Named and Unnamed Women in the Hebrew Bible, the Apocryphal/Deuterocanonical Books, and the New Testament* (gen. ed. Carol Meyers; Grand Rapids: Eerdmans, 2001), 445.

Jonah/Ninevites (11:32)

The people/males of Nineveh *(andres Nineuitai)* will rise up at the judgment with this generation and condemn it, because they repented at the proclamation of Jonah, and see, something greater than Jonah is here!

Jesus' opening statement in 11:29 to the sign-seeking crowds that "no sign will be given . . . except the sign of Jonah" leads us to expect the primacy of Jonah's example in what follows. But Luke's exclusive focus on the Ninevites' response to Jonah's preaching — with no mention of Jonah's three-day-and-night ordeal foreshadowing the Son of Man's death-and-resurrection (Matt 12:40) — sandwiched around the queen's meeting with Solomon (which she initiates!), intimates that *her story* is equal to, if not greater than, Jonah's story in importance. This generation must not miss the sign of her impending "rise in judgment" against it.

The framework in Luke 11:29-32 of male-female, Jew-Gentile juxtapositions in prophetic-monarchical contexts recalls similar arrangements in Jesus' Nazareth speech. But the particular situations of the Sidonian widow and Southern queen are also distinctive at various points, not least pertaining to their geographical and social locations. We now turn to profile the queen more fully in dimensions of time/space and class/character.

Setting: Time and Space

1. Good Times and End Times   If the extended famine ravaging the land during the days of the widow at Zarephath typified the worst of times, the early reign of Solomon when the queen of Sheba visited him marked the best of times in Israel and the surrounding area. The queen marvels at Solomon's panoply of wisdom and wealth, displayed most impressively in the magnificent temple to YHWH he has erected (1 Kings 10:1-8). Moreover, in the midst of his great power and opulence, Solomon has not neglected the needs of poor, marginal women, as evidenced in the famous case of the two prostitute-mothers (3:16-28).

While Luke's Jesus clearly recalls this "great" and glorious Solomonic age of old (Luke 11:31; 12:27; cf. Acts 7:47), temporally he also looks ahead to the coming eschatological age of divine judgment *(krisis)* that will critically assess behavior in the "here" and now ("something greater than Solomon is *here* [*hōde*]"). Remarkably, in Jesus' view, on the basis of her model *past* conduct (discussed below), the queen of the South will come to life at the final, *future* resurrection "with the men *(andrōn)* of this [*present*] generation and condemn them" (Luke 11:31). She, not Solomon, will play the part of faithful judge. Again we stress that the queen's threatening role to men is and will be an *apt and just* one, which they deserve.

2. Realm of the South and Ends of the Earth   The surprising punch of the queen's forensic authority is enhanced not only by her gender, but also by her ethnic-geographic status. This is a righteous "Southern" female judge of "evil" men in Israel. The "South" *(notos)* charts the general direction from Israel of Seba or Sheba, the country of the Sabeans in the Arabian Peninsula, east of the Red Sea. Though Kings and Chronicles designate Sheba as the queen's realm, Josephus, followed by many later legends, situates her in the region of Egypt and Ethiopia — still *south* of Israel, but more African than Arabian.[76] The OT generally portrays Sheba as a prosperous commercial center trading in aromatic spices and precious metals with similar mercantile hubs like Tyre to the north and Tarshish to the west. But unlike Tyre in particular, notorious for its Baal worship and exploitative greed and hubris, Sheba, though doing business with Tyre, largely escapes the latter's biblical reputation for idolatry, injustice, and corruption of Israel.[77] Likewise, it never becomes a marauding imperial juggernaut, like eighth-century Nineveh/Assyria.

Sheba's commercial pairing with Tarshish in Ezekiel 27:22-23, 38:13, and Psalm 72:10 is noteworthy for our purposes, in view of the latter city as Jonah's ill-fated destination — where he tried to *flee to* instead of going to Nineveh, as the Lord directed (Jon 1:3) — and of both places as outposts at the "ends of the earth" in the biblical world conveying gifts and tribute *to* Israel's just and compassionate Solomonic king, as the queen of Sheba does.

> Give the king your justice, O God,
>   and your righteousness to a king's son.
> May he judge your people with righteousness,
>   and your poor with justice. . . .

---

76. Josephus, *Antiquities* 8.159, 164-165. See Edward Ullendorff, "The Queen of Sheba," *Bulletin of the John Rylands Library* 45 (1963): 491-93; Cain Hope Felder, *Troubling Biblical Waters: Race, Class, and Family* (Maryknoll, N.Y.: Orbis, 1989), 22-36.

77. See Ezek 27:22-23 (in the context of a prophetic tirade in Ezek 26–28 against Sheba's trade partner Tyre); Job 6:19; Ps 72:10-15; Isa 60:6; Jer 6:20; Ernst Axel Knauf, "Sabeans," in *NIBD*, 5:11.

> May he have dominion from sea to sea,
>   and from the River to the *ends of the earth*. . . .
> May the kings of *Tarshish* and of the isles
>   render him tribute,
> may the kings of *Sheba and Seba* bring gifts.
> May all kings fall down before him,
>   all nations give him service.
> For he delivers the needy when they call,
>   the poor and those who have no helper. . . .
> Long may he live!
>   May gold of *Sheba* be given to him. (Ps 72:1-15)

Luke picks up the "ends of the earth" cartography as the "South" pole from which the queen comes to hear Solomon's wisdom, though not, in this account, to lavish him with gifts (see more below). She thus fits Jesus' inclusive-ingathering vision of many Gentiles streaming to God's messianic banquet from all four corners of the earth, including the "south" (*notos* [Luke 13:29]) — a vision reinforced by the image of Woman Wisdom's drawing many guests to her sumptuous feast in her cosmic "seven-pillar" mansion, as wide as all creation (Prov 9:1-6; cf. 8:22-36).[78] The queen of the South will join "Abraham and Isaac and Jacob and all the prophets [including Solomon, as Wisdom's chief OT emissary] in the kingdom of God." But the Lord's Table retains its sharp edge, too, and the banquet hall its "narrow" entrance, as those who do not embrace God's way will be "thrown out" (Luke 13:22-30).

The journey of the remote Sheba queen to Jerusalem prepares the way for similar treks of her descendants in Acts. "Arabs" are mentioned last (farthest away?) in the long list of Diaspora pilgrims at Pentecost (Acts 2:11). Presumably these are Arabian Jews or proselytes from the extreme south of the known world.[79] If we follow Josephus's identification of Sheba with Egypt/Ethiopia, then the story of the Ethiopian eunuch's encounter with Philip also offers an interesting parallel (8:26-40). This exotic figure, who happens to be the chief financial officer of *the queen* (Candace) of

---

78. Cf. William P. Brown, *The Seven Pillars of Creation: The Bible, Science, and the Ecology of Wonder* (Oxford: Oxford University Press, 2010), 166-67.

79. The catalogue of "every nation under heaven" in Acts 2:9-11 represents a circle or box around Jerusalem running roughly counterclockwise in a four-corner track from northeast to northwest to southwest to southeast (Arabia). See F. Scott Spencer, *Journeying through Acts: A Literary-Cultural Reading* (Peabody, Mass.: Hendrickson, 2004), 44.

Ethiopia, makes a long pilgrimage "to worship" in Jerusalem. Though clearly a God-fearing Gentile, he was likely barred, as a eunuch, from becoming a full convert to Judaism (cf. Deut 23:1).[80] On his return trip, however, he meets Philip the evangelist and is baptized in an isolated stretch of the road to Gaza — but still within Palestine. He then heads home "rejoicing" into the sunset; we learn nothing of his subsequent life in Ethiopia.

Overall, then, in Luke's scheme, Jews and Gentiles from the earth's southern limits come *to* God's Messiah and people *in* the land of Israel. The early church's mission, commanded by the risen Christ, to bear witness from Jerusalem and Judea *out to* the "ends of the earth" (Acts 1:8) never gains much momentum southward in Acts. There is no concerted missionary campaign to Arabia or Africa; but at least the Arabian pilgrims at Pentecost, the queen-serving Ethiopian eunuch, and a few Cyrenians and Alexandrians here and there (2:10; 11:20; 13:1; 18:24) hint, along with Sheba's monarch of old, that Israel's Creator Deity is as much God of the South as of any other area.

Status: Class and Character

1. Wealth and Power   As an independent monarch with no apparent male consort, the queen of the South represents the highest authority in her land. Her long trek to Solomon's court from the world's outer limits attests to her considerable wealth, although Luke's Jesus says nothing of the massive lode of gold and spices she lavished on Israel's king (cf. 1 Kings 10:10). Elsewhere Luke happily features the beneficence of wealthy women, as we saw with Joanna and Mary Magdalene (Luke 8:2-3), but that is not his concern here. Soon after mentioning the queen's visit, Jesus warns against the dangers of misusing and trusting in wealth, observing that God sustains his creation, not least the lilies of the field, on a level even the great Solomon cannot match (12:27-28). The focus falls on the foreign queen's engagement with the Israelite king's *wisdom* — not wealth — despite the "happy confluence of wisdom and wealth"[81] in Solomonic historical and wisdom traditions (cf. 1 Kings 3:10-14; 4:20-34; Prov 3:13-18). In fact, the Lukan Jesus' personal

---

80. See F. Scott Spencer, *The Portrait of Philip in Acts: A Study of Roles and Relations* (Sheffield: Sheffield Academic, 1989), 150-51, 160-72; Edward Ullendorff, "Candace (Acts VIII, 27) and the Queen of Sheba," *New Testament Studies* (1955/56): 53-56.

81. Claudia V. Camp, *Wise, Strange, and Holy: The Strange Woman and the Making of the Bible* (Sheffield: Sheffield Academic, 2000), 179.

pattern of "growing in wisdom" from humble social origins (Luke 2:40, 52) and serving as Woman Wisdom's prophetic emissary (7:35; 11:49; 21:15) on a shoestring seriously challenges the Deuteronomic wealthy-wise model.

2. Wisdom and Judgment   The wisdom emphasis accents the moral-religious stature of the queen of the South over her material-political status. But beyond a general sense of her positive character, how might we fill out her wisdom profile? Luke simply reports that "she came from the ends of the earth to listen to the wisdom of Solomon" (Luke 11:31). She thus gets props for her *initiative:* she came on her own, not because she was summoned by Solomon or one of his officials or even a hoopoe bird, as in later legends (see below); her *diligence:* she came a long, hard way; and her *attentiveness:* she came to hear divinely revealed word/wisdom — a prime directive for disciples in Luke's world (8:11-20; 9:33-35, 44; 10:39-42). But is anything more implied about her character — anything *spicier* in her "coming," or *smarter* about her own capacity for wisdom, or *saintlier* about her devotion to Israel's God and, by symbolic extension, to God's Messiah Jesus?

Like her nominally related royal counterpart, Queen Bath-Sheba ("daughter of Sheba"), Solomon's mother, the queen of Sheba has been implicated in all sorts of spicy, "hair"-raising scenarios of sexual dalliance, including bearing Solomon a son.[82] This is not particularly surprising, given Solomon's sexual obsession with foreign women in the biblical tradition, both negatively, in the Deuteronomic Historian's tabloid portrait of

---

82. In the Qur'an, Solomon dispatches one of his exotic bird-servants, the hoopoe, with a letter summoning the queen of Sheba to come to Solomon's court and pay him due homage. Eventually she arrives in Jerusalem and is stumped by Solomon's riddles (she does not quiz him in this version); for example, she mistakenly identifies the glistening floor of his glass pavilion as a pool of water, prompting her to raise her skirt and bare her legs (Sura 27:15-45). The Aramaic *Targum Sheni Esther* (ca. 500 C.E.) elaborates that this immodest gesture revealed the hairiness of the queen's ankles and legs — a disgusting, even demonic, condition in Solomon's view in contrast to her otherwise remarkable beauty. Other traditions attest to Solomon's provision of a depilatory treatment for the queen, preparing her for sexual relations with the king. The medieval Ethiopian epic *Kebra Nagast* ("Glory of Kings") cleans up the story considerably (no hoopoe or hairy legs) in honoring the queen of Sheba. She does bear a son by Solomon back in her native land, but he proves more loyal to his mother than his father. On this lively tradition history, see Ullendorff, "The Queen of Sheba," 486-504; Shearing, "A Wealth of Women," 450-55; Carole Fontaine, *Smooth Words: Women, Proverbs, and Performance in Biblical Wisdom* (London: T. & T. Clark, 2004), 206-41; Alice Ogden Bellis, "The Queen of Sheba: A Gender-Sensitive Reading," *Journal of Religious Thought* 51 (1994/95): 17-28.

his thousand foreign wives and concubines who "turned away his heart" from God (1 Kings 11:1-8),[83] and more positively, in the Solomonic poet's graphic depictions of the mutual passions between the king and his "black and beautiful" bride-lover (Song 1:5).[84] But the primary *scriptural* evidence for the queen of Sheba's threatening romantic involvement with Solomon is sketchy at best. Her OT story appears at the climax of Solomon's exemplary early reign in 1 Kings 3–10, just before things go sour with the foreign harem. Put another way, the Sheba queen "returned to her own [south] land" (10:13) just before things "went south" morally and spiritually with Solomon. Moreover, at the time of the queen's visit, Solomon was already joined in an apparently good and proper marriage to *one* foreign woman, Pharaoh's daughter, who had not yet corrupted his heart (cf. 1 Kings 3:1; 9:24).[85] In the encounter itself, some "erotic subtext" and "seductive strangeness"[86] pulse in innuendos surrounding the queen's "coming" to Solomon, her virtual swooning over his prowess, her suggestive notation of how "happy are your wives!" — though the Hebrew text less anachronistically reads, "Happy are your *men-[servants]*"[87] — and Solomon's

83. In the wider Solomonic tradition, the book of Proverbs warns young wise men of the debilitating dangers of seductive "strange/foreign" women; see Prov 2:16-19; 5:1-23; 7:4-27; 9:13-18.

84. On medieval identification of the king's lover in Song of Solomon with the queen of Sheba, see Marina Warner, "In and Out of the Fold: Wisdom, Danger, and Glamour in the Tale of the Queen of Sheba," in *Out of the Garden* (ed. Büchmann and Spiegel), 154; Carole R. Fontaine, "1 Kgs 10:1-13; 2 Chr 9:1-12: Queen of Sheba," in *Women in Scripture* (ed. Meyers), 270-71; Shearing, "A Wealth of Women," 446.

85. The largely positive, or at least neutral, treatment of Pharaoh's daughter in 1 Kings 3:1; 7:8; 9:16, 24; 11:1 (only the last reference implicates her with the later harem that corrupts Solomon's loyalty to YHWH) may be linked with the key role another Egyptian princess played in protecting baby Moses and in Joseph's happy and nonthreatening marriage with the prominent Egyptian Aseneth. Moreover, 1 Kings 9:24 indicates that Pharaoh's daughter had relocated to the house Solomon had built for her, thus removing her somewhat from Solomon's presence. The version in 2 Chronicles excises Solomon's idolatrous alliances with his thousand foreign women and strengthens his separation from Pharaoh's daughter by stressing *his decision* that she move to another residence and "not live in the house of King David of Israel, for the places to which the ark of the LORD has come are holy" (2 Chron 8:11). On all this, see Shearing, "A Wealth of Women," 430-31, 443-45.

86. Camp, "1 and 2 Kings," 108.

87. The NRSV in 1 Kings 10:8 follows the Greek (LXX) and Syriac versions in reading "Happy are your women/wives *(gynaikes)*." But the Hebrew (MT), "Happy are your *men* [*'anāšêk*]; happy are your servants," fits better since up to this point in the narrative Solomon has only *one* wife (Pharaoh's daughter). The huge, corrupting harem is introduced in the next chapter (11:1-8).

granting "her every desire" before she leaves (10:1, 5, 8, 13). But while the atmosphere is no doubt sexually charged, there is no evidence of consummation. The queen brokers a lucrative business deal for Solomon with "all the kings of Arabia and the governors of the land," but without any fringe sexual benefits (10:15).

As for Luke's appeal to the queen of the South, there is no trace of erotic undertones beyond the mention that she "came" to Solomon, which obviously does not require any sexual nuance (*erchomai* is the vanilla term for all sorts of comings and goings).[88] The foreign queen's coming *from* a distant land *to* the renowned king stresses her determined quest for wisdom (see more below); her *diligent initiative,* noted above, distinguishes her from both the widow at Zarephath and citizens of Nineveh, who *receive* the itinerant prophets Elijah and Jonah, respectively. Moreover, any possibility of sexual tension in Luke's reference to the Southern queen is further neutralized by Jesus' mixed role as both type and antitype of King Solomon. He well fits, indeed surpasses ("greater"), Solomon's vocation as wise ruler, but not his accumulation of wealth and women, which ultimately clouds Solomon's wisdom. Jesus' single, celibate lifestyle encourages similar freedom and discipline from his followers. If a married woman joins Jesus' movement, she must, like Joanna — and the queen of the South (whose marital history remains a mystery) — be willing to hit the road and use her resources independently of any male relatives or rulers.

If the queen of the South is less spicy than many interpreters have imagined, she is *more sapiential,* an astute sage in her own right. Yes, she serves a clear narrative function in the OT to exalt Solomon's superior wisdom, but she does so as a worthy, credible judge of wisdom: as a world-class wise woman, she knows a wise man when she meets one. Unlike the two prostitutes who provide a banner case from *their maternal experience* for Solomon to display his wisdom at the beginning of 1 Kings 3–10, the queen of Sheba peppers the king with a bank of challenging, "hard questions" (riddles) from *her mental expertise* at the end of this unit

---

88. Luke generally shows little interest in sexual matters. Neither of Luke's two volumes features any "romantic" plots typical of ancient or modern "romance" literature. The deeply emotional scene in Luke 7:36-50 represents something of an exception as a "sinful" woman displays her passionate love for Jesus (she anoints his feet with perfume, wipes them with her hair, and repeatedly kisses them). However, though erotically charged, this woman's actions are by no means regarded by Jesus as improper or immoral (he in fact commends her lavish hospitality). For a thorough discussion of this episode, see my chapter "Passions and Passion: The 'Loose' Lady, Woman Wisdom, and the Lukan Jesus," in *Dancing Girls,* 108-43.

(10:1).[89] More importantly, she stands in a position to *evaluate* the breadth and depth of his answers: she "*observes* all the wisdom of Solomon" and deems it as stunning as his magnificent palace, munificent table (food, yet again), myriad attendants, and manifold offerings to the Lord (10:3-5). She is left breathless, not because she is some silly woman easily swept off her feet, but because she has made her point, given her expert report, and there's nothing more to say (10:6-9).[90] Solomon has received an A+ wisdom grade from no less than the royal sage of Sheba.

While the OT gives ample evidence of the queen's erudition, the Jewish historian and Luke's contemporary Josephus "smartens up" the story even more, as Edward Ullendorff asserts.[91] As previously noted, Josephus identifies Solomon's visitor as "queen of Egypt and Ethiopia" (*Antiquities* 8.165), not Sheba, as in 1 Kings 10/2 Chronicles 9. The Egypt connection grounds her in a venerable realm internationally renowned for prowess in

---

89. The Kings narrative stresses the queen's direct, challenging speech *to* the king: "she came to test him with hard questions. . . . she told him all that was on her mind. . . . she said to the king" (10:1-6). The Chronicles version, however, reports that the queen "discussed *with* him [the king] all that was on her mind" (2 Chron 9:1), perhaps, as H. G. M. Williamson suggests, "softening . . . a text in which the Queen of Sheba might have appeared as the dominant partner" (*1 and 2 Chronicles* [Grand Rapids: Eerdmans, 1982], 234); cf. Shearing, "A Wealth of Women," 445 n. 52.

90. For other perspectives supporting the queen of Sheba's mental astuteness in 1 Kings 10, see Susanne Gillmayr-Bucher, "'She Came to Test Him with Hard Questions': Foreign Women and Their View on Israel," *Biblical Interpretation* 15 (2007): 135-42, 148. In the narrative's multifaceted presentation of "such a dazzling and simultaneously challenging woman" (142), we see "the queen of Sheba is portrayed as a critic, who has been convinced" by her probing questions to Solomon and analyses of his responses, which, however, are not reported. In fact, "while the queen of Sheba is shown [and heard] in great detail the voice of Solomon is not heard" (139) at all. She might be "breathless" from observing and evaluating Solomon's wisdom and wealth, but he is voiceless!

Fewell and Gunn (*Gender, Power, and Promise,* 176-77) take a more critical stance, but one equally admiring of the queen "as a woman of great intellect [and] remarkable independence." They see her as indulging Solomon's "compulsive need to show off" and using him for her purpose, which is "certainly not sex with this bore" but perhaps a haul of Solomon's gifts and/or a trade agreement. In any case, she becomes breathless in the sense of "winded," exhausted by playing up to this insatiable narcissist. On the way home, she may well have gasped for breath amid "gusts of laughter or incredulous snickers" as she regaled her attendants with tales of Solomon's preening.

91. Ullendorff, "The Queen of Sheba," 491. On Josephus's treatment of the queen of Sheba, see Louis H. Feldman, "Josephus' View of Solomon," in *The Age of Solomon* (ed. Handy), 348-74; Feldman, "Josephus' Portrait of Solomon," *Hebrew Union College Annual* 66 (1995): 103-67; Shearing, "A Wealth of Women," 447-49.

wisdom and philosophy (overshadowing the less prestigious, remote spice center of Sheba) and befits Josephus's introduction of the queen as "thoroughly trained in wisdom" and deeply "desirous" *(epithymia)* of testing Solomon's putative "virtue and understanding" for herself, "and not merely by hearsay."[92] Expanding on the biblical account, Josephus describes the queen's coming first and foremost to sift Solomon's "wisdom by propounding questions and asking him to solve their difficult meaning" (8.165-66). In turn, Solomon "was studious to please her in all ways, in particular by mentally grasping with ease the ingenious problems she set before him and solving them more quickly than anyone could have expected" (8.167). On the whole, Josephus depicts a high-level intellectual exchange between two wise world leaders. Solomon comes out on top, of course, as the consummate philosopher-king, but his greatness emerges not so much at the queen's expense as in respectful engagement with her expertise.[93]

As in the biblical report, Josephus further describes the queen's gift giving and amazement over Solomon's lavish prosperity and construction projects, but the focus stays squarely on wisdom matters. Concerning Solomon's estate, for example, the queen especially admires "the arrangement of the buildings, for in this she saw the great wisdom of the king" (8.168-69). And her final tally of gold deposited in Solomon's coffers comes to 20 talents, no mean amount, but considerably less than the Bible's 120 (8.174; cf. 1 Kings 10:10). Feldman suggests that the reduced contribution would be more in keeping with a royal *gift* than required *tribute* and thus evidences how "Josephus seeks to keep the Queen and Solomon on the same plane" — politically, materially, and philosophically.[94]

How does Luke's brief reference to the queen of the South stack up with the OT and Josephus's highlighting of *her* wise acumen? The prospect

---

92. Citations of Josephus in this section are from the translation by H. St. J. Thackery and Ralph Marcus in *Jewish Antiquities Books V–VIII* (Loeb Classical Library; Cambridge: Harvard University Press, 1938).

93. Contra Athalya Brenner, "Are We Amused? Small and Big Differences in Josephus' Re-Presentations of Biblical Female Figures in the *Jewish Antiquities* 1–8," in *Are We Amused? Humour about Women in the Biblical Worlds* (ed. Athalya Brenner; London: T. & T. Clark, 2003), 100: "Josephus may expand a biblical description simply by exaggeration. Note what a fool the queen of Sheba makes of herself by blabbering Solomon's praises (*Ant.* 8.164-75)." While it is true that the queen lauds Solomon in effusive terms, this need not be seen as a mark of ditzy foolishness on her part; her praise may serve strategic rhetorical ends, stroking the king's gigantic ego and putting him in a receptive mood for her business dealings (cf. Fewell and Gunn, *Gender, Power, and Promise*, 176-77).

94. Feldman, "Josephus' Portrait of Solomon," 147.

of her "rising at the judgment with the men of this generation" may imply that she has some important opinions to offer, but the emphasis falls more on the basic forensic model she represents at *the judgment* — where God is the supreme judge — than on any *particular judgments* she might render. And what she preeminently models is not her own generative wisdom but her diligence in journeying to "listen to the wisdom of Solomon." Of course, this is how wise youth develop, by first seeking out and heeding the words of established sages (e.g., Prov 2:1-8; Sir 51:13-14). So the queen's attentive quest for wisdom in Luke is an admirable move and apt warning to this rebellious generation who refuses to listen. Nonetheless, she does not attain the full stature of a wisdom prophet and teacher: here she poses no questions, hard or easy, and makes no definitive judgments. The ironic pattern holds: though wisdom is personified as a prophetic woman, by and large Lukan women hear rather than speak, receive wisdom rather than proclaim it. The male Solomon is the prototypical Wisdom model[95] and Jesus her supreme eschatological emissary (Luke 11:49). The precocious, wisdom-filled twelve-year-old Jesus supplants both Solomon and the queen of the South early on by taking his place among the temple teachers, "listening to them and asking them questions" and sparking wonder "at his understanding and his answers" (2:46-47; cf. 2:40, 52).[96] If "something greater than Solomon is here," then the greatness of the queen of the South is diminished all the more.

This complication of the queen's wisdom profile is not unique to Luke, however, especially when we bring her foreign status back into the picture. The ever lurking threat in Proverbs of the foolish, "loose" Woman Stranger/Alien set in flagrant opposition to the prudent, "pure" Lady Wisdom makes the notion of a *wise foreign* woman a virtual contradiction in

95. See, however, Claudia Camp's fascinating exploration of Solomon as a *woman* "that emphasizes the relationship of Wisdom, personified here in Solomon, and woman, the form of wisdom's personification in the tradition's definitive text, the book of Proverbs, which is, completing the circle, ascribed to Solomon. . . . I would not be so bold as to call Solomon 'woman' were it not for the pervasive strangeness of both women and wisdom throughout this narrative, and ambiguity in . . . a sense of crossed boundaries: Solomon is the quintessential wise man and also the embodiment of Israel's most fundamental estrangement" (*Wise, Strange, and Holy*, 144-45; cf. 144-86).

96. Perhaps in this episode we might cast Mary (with Joseph) in a queen-of-the-South-like role, as she searches for Jesus, finds him in the temple after a three-day trek, becomes amazed at his wisdom, and questions him. Of course, as we have seen, Mary's query is more accusative than inquisitive, and she "does not understand" Jesus' response. Overall, however, Luke portrays Mary as thoughtful and perceptive, though he never labels her "wise" as such.

terms.[97] Though stranger/alien language in Proverbs need not be strictly limited to *ethnic* foreignness, such status predominates in the portrayal in 1 Kings of Solomon's wisdom-sapping relations with a bevy of idolatrous Gentile women. While we have noted that the Sheba queen bolsters rather than undermines Solomon's wisdom and returns home just before he musters his multinational harem, she remains literarily, and perhaps religiously, a little too close for comfort to these other dangerous foreign women in Solomon's life. Ultimately the issue hangs on the Southern queen's attitude toward Israel's God. If she wholly embraces Solomon's YHWH-istic faith for herself, like Ruth or Aseneth, then there's no problem — threat averted. Joseph seals Aseneth's conversion to the Most High God with a threefold kiss imparting to her a "spirit of life . . . spirit of wisdom, and . . . spirit of truth" (*Joseph and Aseneth* 19:11). There we have a proper foreign wise woman, whose strangeness has been largely neutralized.[98]

But what about the queen of Sheba? To what extent does her wisdom rely on Israel's Lord, the fountain of all true wisdom? How does she speak of and relate to Solomon's God? The biblical evidence in this case remains ambiguous. 1 Kings 10:1 connects the "fame of Solomon" that the queen heard about with the "name of the LORD," but it is not clear whether the queen herself, or only the narrator, makes the fame-name linkage. After she tests the king's wisdom and tours his house and the "house of the LORD" (or at least notes the magnanimous sacrifices he offers there), the queen unabashedly extols his wisdom and "the LORD your God, who has delighted in you and set you on the throne of Israel! Because the LORD loved Israel forever, he has made you king to execute justice and righteousness" (10:9-10). Hence the Southern queen patently acknowledges YHWH's value *for Solomon* ("the LORD *your God*")[99] and his people, but she never changes her mind, beyond confirming to an unexpected degree what she already believed ("not even half had been told me" [10:6-7]); she never touts YHWH's superiority above all gods, as Naaman will; she never renounces her own deities; and she gives massive quantities of precious

97. Cf. Camp, *Wise, Strange, and Holy*, 177: "If her combined wisdom and strangeness ambiguate the character of the Queen of Sheba, further complications appear when characters of the king and queen are triangulated with Woman Wisdom of Proverbs."

98. See Ross S. Kraemer, "Aseneth and Wisdom," in *Wisdom and Psalms: A Feminist Companion to the Bible* (ed. Athalya Brenner and Carole Fontaine; 2nd ser.; Sheffield: Sheffield Academic, 1998), 218-39.

99. Similar to the widow at Zarephath's initial distancing divine reference (noted above), in conversation with Elijah, as "the LORD your God" (1 Kings 17:12).

spices and stones *to King Solomon* (note double emphasis on "she gave the king" at the beginning and end of 10:10), not to Solomon's Lord, her primary concern being to cement an economic rather than a religious alliance. While respecting Solomon's faith, the queen of Sheba shows no signs of converting to it. Thus, from a Deuteronomic perspective, she is still worth keeping an eye on.

Readings closer to Luke's time appear even less inclined to "baptize" the queen of Sheba into covenantal Jewish religion. While boosting her political status and cosmopolitan wisdom credentials in the interest of promoting Solomon's even greater stature as philosopher-king, Josephus, playing to a critical Greco-Roman audience, tends to "detheologize" the encounter with Solomon, as Feldman observes.[100] In contrast to the Bible's implied motivation that the queen "wished to find out whether the source of Solomon's wisdom was divine inspiration," Josephus's account accentuates the rigor of intellectual debate such that "very significantly, everything consequently depends upon Solomon's *human wisdom* rather than divine inspiration."[101] Philosophy rather than theology drives this meeting, with economics running a close second in Josephus's extended report of the final exchange of "many fine gifts" between the two monarchs (*Antiquities* 8.174-75).

In the *Testament of Solomon,* a radical revision of Solomon's biblical portrait from a Hellenistic Jewish-Christian perspective (first to third century C.E.), "Sheeba, Queen of the South," as she is called, arrives among a stream of other world leaders to observe and contribute funds to Solomon's crowning temple project. But distinguished from "all the kings," this queen comes as "a *witch* [or sorceress, *goēs*] . . . with much arrogance," even as she "bow[s] down before [Solomon]" (19.2-3).[102] She shows no interest in true wisdom or Israel's God;[103] thus, as Todd Klutz comments, "the honour she pays Solomon in *T. Sol.* 19.3 (cf. 21.1-4) has a far more ambivalent, or even potentially negative, effect than does the interchange depicted

---

100. Feldman, "Josephus' Portrait of Solomon," 142 (cf. 140-43).

101. Feldman, "Josephus' View of Solomon," 360 (emphasis added).

102. Citations from D. C. Duling, "Testament of Solomon: A New Translation and Introduction," in *The Old Testament Pseudepigrapha,* vol. 1: *Apocalyptic Literature and Testaments* (ed. James H. Charlesworth; Garden City, N.Y.: Doubleday, 1983), 935-87.

103. Though Duling ("Testament of Solomon," 982) notes that a sixteenth-century manuscript (P) provides a more orthodox addendum, in which the queen of the South "bowed down before me to the earth, and because she had heard of my wisdom, she glorified the God of Israel."

in 1 Kgs 10.1-10, 13."[104] The presentation of this "witchy woman" becomes even more curious later in the narrative when Solomon proudly reports Sheeba's entry into the restricted "inner part of the temple." So a foreign witch traipses into the Holy of Holies — where only the Jewish high priest was permitted once a year! — and Solomon preens over her admiration of the altar, Bronze Sea, and all the other marvelous furnishings adorning this sanctum (*Testament of Solomon* 21:1-4). Curious indeed! And hardly flattering of Solomon's judgment, much less the queen's.[105] But matters get even more bizarre in this unit's closing statement, noting Sheeba's observation that "all were busy working in the temple [. . .][106] of pay amounting to one gold talent apart from the demons" (21:4). Apart from the demons? Demons employed in Jerusalem temple service? However strange that may seem to us, it's not so odd for this testament, which extensively details Solomon's control over the whole demonic realm, including Beelzeboul, the Prince of Demons, whom Solomon forces to "cut blocks of Theban marble" for the temple (6:9; cf. 3:1-6; 6:1-11)! So yes, Solomon commandeers the forces of darkness as a slave labor gang for constructing the Lord's temple; allowing the diabolical Sheeba to witness this power arrangement perhaps also puts her in her rightful, subjugated place. In any event, controlling demons and witches does not entail converting them to righteous faith and character.

We may note with interest that the reference to the queen of the South in Luke's narrative comes on the heels of a heated debate about Jesus' alleged alliance in his exorcising exploits with "Beelzebul, the ruler of the demons." In no uncertain terms, Jesus establishes that casting out evil spirits means conquering them, not collaborating with them, and that he accomplishes this liberating work by "the finger of God" in the service of "the kingdom of God," not the demonic realm (Luke 11:14-23). But unlike the *Testament of Solomon*, Luke's interest in Beelzebul and company does not carry over to his portrait of the foreign queen who visits Solomon. In Luke

---

104. Todd E. Klutz, *Rewriting the Testament of Solomon: Tradition, Conflict, and Identity in a Late Antique Pseudepigraphon* (London: T. & T. Clark, 2005), 69.

105. Klutz (*Rewriting*, 68-73) views this temple scene as part of a marked anti-Solomonic and anti-Judaic strain in chapters 19–26 of *Testament of Solomon*.

106. Duling ("Testament of Solomon," 983) notes this lacuna in the text, which complicates the meaning of the statement somewhat. He leaves as an open question: "Did the non-demonic workers get paid one talent?" That seems to be the point of the passage, but we can't be sure.

11:31, the spotlight trains on the queen's favorable response to Solomon's wisdom, not on her occult background or his magic powers over demons.

But how far does her favorable response go? Significantly, whereas the OT, Josephus, and *Testament of Solomon,* to varying degrees, pull up short of the queen's religious conversion and ultimately dispatch her back home somewhat richer and wiser but otherwise unchanged, Luke pushes her story to the culmination of the eschatological age. By prophesying the queen's "rise at the judgment with the men of this generation," Jesus guarantees her honored place in the restored kingdom of God, at the grand final feast with the children of Abraham (cf. 13:28-29). More than that, her presence, if not her words, as one who faithfully attended to God's wisdom mediated through Solomon, will function to judge those who have closed their ears and minds to God's "greater" word incarnated in Jesus. Luke does not stress the queen's *repentance* before Solomon, as with the Ninevites' response to Jonah (11:32), nor her devotion to the Lord God per se. As noted above, repentance *(metanoia)* constitutes a major theological theme in Luke, as in *Joseph and Aseneth.* Hence a touch of ambiguity shades the queen's response: she doesn't quite attain the status of a model convert. But she will, nonetheless, enjoy eating at the Lord's Table in her resurrected body, as she feasted with Solomon long ago, and exemplifying an open attitude toward divine wisdom to the embarrassment of those less receptive.

Salty Wife of Lot (Luke 17:32)

Jesus' last reference to a foreign OT woman comes during the final leg of his journey to Jerusalem (cf. 17:11). As he nears his fateful visit to the Holy City, warnings and judgments ramp up surrounding the climactic establishment of God's rule on earth. It's full steam ahead now, no "turning back" *(epistrephō,* 17:31), as the wife of Lot did during the holocaust of Sodom long ago, thus sealing her own salt-entombed fate (17:32). While biblical characterizations of the widow at Zarephath and queen of the South exhibit various dynamic tensions and ambiguities, both figures, as we have seen, still tilt more toward a positive, heroic assessment. But Lot's wife seems petrified in a permanent negative, villainous state. How can she possibly break out of her salty shell? How can she be viewed as anything but a dangerous threat to God's ways and God's people?

For a start, we might compare Lot's anonymous spouse with Ahab's named wife and notorious villainess, Jezebel, whose own despicability and perfidy, we might recall, are not as clear-cut as often thought. But focusing on Jezebel's bad side, we find a powerful woman who engineers prophet-killings and property-takeovers. By contrast, Lot's wife has no political power. She can do nothing to avert or avenge her city's destruction; all she does is look back while fleeing, thereby becoming a victim herself of Sodom's annihilation. But perhaps Luke would not have us "remember" any of that tragic stuff. So what is the fuller context and deeper meaning of Luke's interest in Lot's wife? As with our previous two examples, we begin with sketching Luke's immediate literary setting and then branch out in more detail to larger issues of time/place and class/ character in both OT and Lukan frameworks.

The call to "remember Lot's wife," who aborted her flight from Sodom by "turning back," appears toward the end of Jesus' discourse on the coming of God's kingdom and "the days of the Son of Man" (17:20-37), addressed first, briefly, to the Pharisees (17:20-21) and then, more fully, to the disciples (17:22-37). Both audiences, the more "outsider" Pharisee critics and the "insider" disciple associates, incur Jesus' challenge and correction, thus blurring stereotypical boundaries. As Joel Green comments on Luke's characterization pattern: "The move back and forth between Pharisees (along with legal experts) and disciples has been normal fare in chs. 15–17, highlighting the permeable quality of the perimeter separating the two. The Pharisees continue to be instructed by Jesus, for they may yet respond to his message; the disciples continue in their susceptibility to the miscalculations concerning the purpose of God otherwise characteristic of the Pharisees."[107] If neat good/bad, hero/villain categories prove so porous and "permeable" among two main character groups, then perhaps, too, the character of Lot's wife is not as set in stone as it appears.

The Pharisees, for their part, have a *perception* problem. They keep looking around and ahead for God's kingdom that is already near and now, already "among" *(entos)* them, evidenced not only in Jesus' mighty acts of liberation (11:16, 20, 29), but also in mysterious ways pervading beyond observable phenomena "here" or "there" (17:20-21; cf. 13:18-20). The disciples, on the other hand, have a nagging *perseverance* problem that clouds their vision and action. They know full well that Jesus has come as God's royal agent, the Son of Man, inaugurating God's final kingdom — a reality vindicated in the early church by witnesses to the resurrection of Jesus. But another, competing reality also persists — that of corrosive evil

---

107. Joel B. Green, *The Gospel of Luke* (Grand Rapids: Eerdmans, 1997), 631.

and suffering. However "already here" the kingdom of God may be, it is patently "not yet" realized in full. And that tension, Jesus discloses, will become near unbearable at times for his followers. In the short run, he reiterates his shocking imminent destiny as the Son of Man who "must endure much suffering and be rejected by this generation" (17:25; cf. 9:21-22, 31): the cross will precede the empty tomb and never fade from memory. In fact, the postresurrection church must regularly symbolize his broken body and shed blood "in remembrance" of him (22:19-22). But this retrospective look must be balanced by a prospective hope "until the kingdom of God comes" again at the Son of Man's consummating return (22:16-18; cf. 21:25-28; 22:69-70).

But how long must God's people wait in the difficult interim between the Son of Man's resurrection and reappearance? In the longer run, in the perilous "coming days," Jesus admits that things will get so bad for his disciples that they will pine for "just one of the days of bliss" the Son of Man might afford (17:21).[108] Moreover, in their wishful, desperate thinking, they might succumb to foolhardy, premature pursuits of the reemergent Son of Man "here" or "there." Jesus warns that no mystery will cloud the Son of Man's final banner "day," which will explode with lightning flashes spanning the horizon that no one can miss (17:23-24).

But there's another interim problem: when the disciples are not hyped up with futile Messiah chases, they tend to drift into numbing complacency, business as usual, a static antidote to the manic "Look there, look here!" approach. Frustrated longing for "the days of the Son of Man" leads to languishing in "the days of Noah and Lot," clueless about and totally unprepared for God's reign (17:26-29). So while not entertaining false, rash hopes of the Son of Man's return, the disciples must not abandon faithful, alert readiness for his pending parousia (cf. 12:35-48). They must keep pressing on, amid hard times, toward the eschatological goal, not bogging down in this present evil age or harking back to what was or might have been — like the "wife of Lot" during the ominous "days of Lot" in the odious city of Sodom (17:31-33). We now turn to examine more closely the warning inscription on her salt mausoleum, as it were, in light of the critical "days" and place she inhabited.

---

108. See John T. Carroll, *Response to the End of History: Eschatology and Situation in Luke-Acts* (Atlanta: Scholars, 1988), 92 n. 211: "I am inclined to see in the phrase 'one of the days' an indirect reference also to the depth of testing and extent of waiting experienced by believers: the 'days will come' when they will be so hard-pressed and anxious for redemption, that they will be eager for just one of the days of bliss.'"

Setting: Time and Place

1. Days of Lot and Noah   Luke makes much of the ancient "days" surrounding Noah and Lot as typical of the futile period of human life suddenly interrupted by the future and final "day" of the Son of Man's coming in salvation and judgment, where some will be "taken" and others "left" (17:34-35).[109] But what attitudes and actions precisely dominate these unprepared days? The bare mention of Noah's and Lot's eras immediately conjures up images of rampant violence, corruption, immorality, and "only evil continually" (Gen 6:5) — in other words, the kind of total depravity meriting divine annihilation by flood and fire (cf. Wis 10:6-8; 2 Pet 2:6-8; Jude 7). But remarkably, Jesus says nothing about such wickedness; instead of their *evil practices,* Jesus decries their *everyday preoccupations.* In staccato fashion, he delineates their routine habits of eating/drinking, marrying/giving in marriage, in Noah's age, and eating/drinking, buying/selling, planting/building, in Lot's time (Luke 17:25-29). And Jesus insinuates nothing about debauchery in the eating/drinking, or about licentiousness in the marrying/giving in marriage, or about fraud in the buying/selling. His warning is against overrootedness in earthly business as usual, inhibiting one's readiness to move on a dime in response to God's inbreaking kingdom. Jesus wants his followers to travel swift and light, as he does, ever alert to follow wherever he, as God's viceroy, leads.

Notice that Jesus' profile of Lot's days particularly stresses material-economic obsession with food, goods, and crops. Notably absent, compared to Noah's days, is any reference to marital-sexual activity, aberrant or otherwise, which we typically associate with ancient Sodomite behavior from Genesis 19:4-11 and modern connotations of "sodomite" practices. But Jesus chiefly warns against Sodom's desire to gather and secure personal belongings, even in the face of disaster, such as that which will attend the days of the Son of Man's appearing (Luke 17:31-33).[110] The problem is

109. It is difficult to know the particular focus of Jesus' dualistic scenarios in Luke 17:34-35: Will one be "taken" or "left behind" for salvation or for judgment? Either way, Jesus effectively makes his point of persevering readiness for the Son of Man's coming, without advancing some elaborate, end-times "rapture" agenda.

110. The "sins" of Sodom seem closer here to that enumerated in Ezek 16:49-50 — "This was the guilt of your sister Sodom: she and her daughters had pride, excess of food, and prosperous ease, but did not aid the poor and needy. They were haughty, and did abominable things before me." See also Jer 23:14; Sir 16:8; 3 Macc 2:5; Wis 19:14 for varied assessments of Sodom's wickedness, focused on arrogance, to complement denunciations of the city's

similar to diehards today, who stay behind or try to go back home during hurricanes and wildfires, ignoring evacuation orders, often to their peril. Attempting to save their stuff, they lose their lives (cf. 17:33). Such was the tragic fate of Lot's wife: looking back on — and longing to reconnect with — her besieged family and friends, house and furnishings, food and clothing, she forfeits everything. Her womanly devotion to daily realities does her in. For now, we simply register this Lukan point; we will assess its implications for the moral character of Lot's wife below.

2. Ways of Sodom and Gomorrah   The symbolic significance of the Sodom locale warrants further consideration. If Zarephath and "the South" (Sheba) needed to be brought out of the shadows of obscurity, Sodom (and its twin Gomorrah) needs clarifying in the face of over-familiarity as Sin City, the Las Vegas or New Orleans of its day in the minds of certain firebrand preachers. Of course, the reputation of the city carries over to its citizens, like Lot and his wife, by way of either resistance or compliance. As Jesus characterizes Sodom in Luke 17 as more of a busy mercantile than bawdy malevolent center, so Genesis and Luke elsewhere qualify its bad rap as one big red-light district or long skid row. To be sure, when we first learn about Sodom as Lot's chosen place of settlement separate from his uncle Abram, the Genesis narrative makes clear that "the people of Sodom were wicked, great sinners against the LORD" (Gen 13:13). But it also gives no indication that Lot knew of such a reputation or, if he did, that he selected Sodom *because* it was a great party town and vice center. Rather, Lot based his decision on the real estate appraisal that the area "was well watered everywhere like the garden of the LORD, like the land of Egypt" (13:10). When a coalition of kings raided Sodom and captured its citizens and provisions, Abram came to the rescue and "brought back all the goods, and also brought back his nephew Lot with his goods, and the women and the people" (14:16). Nothing is said about Sodom's prompting either conquest (due to wickedness) or restoration (because of repentance): both just happen as a matter of course; at least for the moment, Sodom is worth saving.

Soon, of course, an "outcry" or "cry for help" comes to God "against

---

immorality in 2 Pet 2:6-8 and Jude 7. Cf. James L. Kugel, *Traditions of the Bible: A Guide to the Bible as It Was at the Start of the Common Era* (Cambridge: Harvard University Press, 1998), 328-50; Kugel, *In the Valley of the Shadow: On the Foundations of Religious Belief* (New York: Free Press, 2011), 150.

Sodom" for its oppressive practices (18:20-21). Though we are not told where this plea comes *from,* the most apt source would be from victims of injustice *within* Sodom, which sets the stage for Abraham's bargaining with God about how many righteous — that is, unjustly treated — Sodomites it would take for God to spare the city (18:22-33).[111] Ultimately, however, it seems that most oppressed folk also found others to oppress (equal opportunity oppression), and so, without even ten wholly innocent people, Sodom merited fiery destruction. But that "outcry for help" still haunts the incident (19:13), not to mention the rescue afforded Lot and his family. Is this because they were the only truly righteous "aliens" (19:9) in this wicked town, or is it more a nepotistic favor to Abraham? The story stays silent on the subject. Is Lot's wife innocent right up to her backsliding moment, which she pays for dearly, or are other dynamics at work? A certain ambiguity hovers about the character of both Lot and his wife, not to mention his daughters (see more below).[112]

Shifting to Luke's assessment of Sodom, one key reference preceding Jesus' kingdom discourse in chapter 17 occurs at the end of his commission to the seventy disciples. Anticipating some rejection (as well as reception), Jesus advises his emissaries not to linger in hostile places, but rather, on the way out of town, to (1) shake the dust off their feet in protest; (2) pronounce a sentence of judgment, "Yet know this: the kingdom of God has come near"; and (3) leave any further avenging to God "on that day" of reckoning when "it will be more tolerable for Sodom than for that town" (Luke 10:11-12). Note the parallel with Luke 17 surrounding the immanence of God's kingdom and that here again the "sin" of Sodom has less to do with its criminal record than its lack of readiness for God's realm and hos-

---

111. See David M. Gunn, "Narrative Criticism," in *To Each Its Own Meaning: An Introduction to Biblical Criticisms and Their Applications* (ed. Steven L. McKenzie and Stephen R. Haynes; rev. ed.; Louisville: Westminster, 1999), 222: "Implied by the term 'cry for help' [in Gen 18:20-21] are many who are oppressed. Are they all at the same time and equally oppressors deserving destruction? Neither the narrator nor God makes any attempt to clarify the matter. The term 'cry for help' remains, disturbing the notion of total depravity." And also Robert Alter, *Genesis: Translation and Commentary* (New York: Norton, 1996), 80: "The Hebrew noun [for 'outcry' in Gen 18:20-21], or the verb from which it is derived, *tsa'aq* or *za'aq,* is often associated in the Prophets and Psalms with the shrieks of torment of the oppressed."

112. The two surviving daughters of Lot are not our focus here. But their incestuous plan in the cave near Zoar "so that we may preserve offspring through our father," though not explicitly condemned in Gen 19:30-38 and perhaps justified as desperate action for desperate times, certainly qualifies as morally ambiguous (at least). What is not ambiguous, however, is Lot's earlier inexcusable offer of his virgin daughters for gang rape (19:8).

pitality toward God's agents. Hospitality constitutes a major theme in Luke's writings[113] and in Genesis 19, where Lot stands out as a protective host to two angelic visitors in the face of a most inhospitable mob desiring to molest them (Gen 19:4-5). At the end of the day, Lot winds up shaking the dust from his feet, as it were, and abandoning the city with the angels and his wife and two daughters. But once more, the moral matter is not as simple as that. Lot's initially admirable hospitality toward God's messengers is shockingly sullied by offering his own virgin daughters for gang abuse in place of the visitors — a horrible proposal that might well have been transacted had the angels not "reached out their hands" and wrenched Lot inside the house (19:8-10). Moreover, Lot scarcely leaves the doomed city with alacrity: in response to his "lingering," the angels again resort to seizing him "by the hand" and whisking him and his family away (19:16). Is Lot's lingering any better than his wife's looking? Is it not perhaps worse, especially conjoined with his willingness to stay and sacrifice his daughters' bodies? The story bristles with moral uncertainty, which we now consider further with particular focus on Lot's wife.

Status: Class and Character

1. Family and Fortune   The Bible never explicitly identifies the ethnic origin of Lot's wife, but since Lot is apparently a young single man when he leaves Haran with his uncle Abram and wife Sarai (Lot has no accompanying wife or other family) and then goes his own way from Canaan to the region of the "cities of the Plain," finally settling in Sodom, the narrative implies that he meets and marries a local woman from that area (Gen 12:5; 13:10-11). Targumic tradition specifies that Lot's wife was indeed "from the daughters of Sodomites" and looked back on the smoldering city to certify "the end of her father's house."[114] So we have a mixed union: "resident alien" (19:9) Lot takes a native woman of Sodom as his wife. Although Genesis does not legislate against miscegenation, complications surround-

---

113. See Brendan J. Byrne, *The Hospitality of God: A Reading of Luke's Gospel* (Collegeville, Minn.: Liturgical Press, 2000); John Koenig, *New Testament Hospitality: Partnership with Strangers as Promise and Mission* (Philadelphia: Fortress, 1985), 85-123.

114. *Targum Pseudo-Jonathan* Gen 19:26; *Targum Neofiti* Gen 19:26; citations from *Targum Pseudo-Jonathan, Genesis* (trans. Michael Maher; Collegeville, Minn.: Liturgical Press, 1992), and *Targum Neofiti 1, Genesis* (trans. Martin McNamara; Collegeville, Minn.: Liturgical Press, 1992).

ing Abraham's fathering a child by the Egyptian slave-girl Hagar (16:4-16; 21:8-21) and Esau's marrying a pair of Hittite women (26:34) do not bode well for Lot's marital experience. The threat of a "foreign" wife in a "foreign" land always crouches at the door, especially, one might think, in "sinful" Sodom, although in Lot's case he alone miserably fails to protect the family threshold by his willingness to throw his daughters to a rapacious mob. Lot's wife has nothing do with this proposal — in fact, we might imagine her vociferous protest.

We do not know the precise social status of Lot's wife's family of origin. She has no royal standing that we know of, like the later Jezebel and queen of Sheba, but may still have been a woman of substance in a prosperous region well stocked with "goods and provisions" (cf. 14:12, 16). When she joins Lot's household, she seems to live quite comfortably in an urban dwelling under sturdy roof beams (19:8), in contrast to the nomadic, tent habitat of Lot's uncle Abraham (cf. 18:1-10).[115] With sufficient resources, a living husband, and multiple children and perhaps grandchildren,[116] the wife of Lot seems socially miles away from the widow at Zarephath, beset by famine and the death of her only son — *until* the end of the story! *Then,* some ironic-tragic parallels emerge: as the Sidonian widow suffers near-starvation and the devastating loss of her son during a protracted season of drought, when God shut off the rains from heaven, so the Sodomite wife suffers the loss of family members during a blazing sulfuric deluge that God "rains" down on her city (19:24), paralyzing her into a salt lick for wandering cattle, but no longer providing any spice or food for her loved ones.[117]

---

115. See the translation and discussion of Lot's "roof-beamed" residence in Alter, *Genesis*, 86.

116. The mention of plural "sons-in-law, sons, daughters, or anyone you have in the city" in Gen 19:12 suggests a larger kinship clan than the two virgin daughters engaged to prospective sons-in-law in Sodom (cf. 19:14). Perhaps some grandchildren had been provided for Lot and his wife through either their sons or other daughters who had already married.

117. The "salt lick" image derives from early rabbinic tradition in *Pirqe Rabbi Eliezer* 325, described by Louis Ginzberg, *The Legends of the Jews*, vol. 1: *Bible Times and Characters from the Creation to Jacob* (trans. Henrietta Szold; Philadelphia: Jewish Publication Society of America, 1909), 255: "When the angels had brought forth Lot and his family and set them without the city, he bade them run for their lives, and not look behind, lest they behold the Shekinah, which had descended to work the destruction of the cities. The wife of Lot could not control herself. Her mother love made her look behind to see if her married daughters were following. She beheld the Shekinah, and she became a pillar of salt. This pillar exists unto this day. The cattle lick it all day long, and in the evening it seems to have disappeared,

Though she may be viewed, like the widow at Zarephath, as a victim of horrendous circumstances beyond her control, she receives no miraculous, last-minute sustaining provision or restoration.

But that's not quite the whole truth, is it? God's angelic fire-bombers initiate a rescue operation for Lot's clan — "sons-in-law, sons, daughters, or anyone you have in the city" (19:12). The fact that all of them except Lot, Lot's wife, and two daughters opt to stay behind is not God's fault. In the case of Lot's wife, who does flee, doesn't her defiance of the angelic order not to "look back or stop anywhere in the Plain . . . or else you will be consumed" (19:17) justify her fate? The character issue again moves front and center, and again it is not so neatly adjudicated.

2. Crime and Punishment First, we might wonder whether Lot's wife even knew about the no-looking-back command. Grammatically, the angels direct their warning only to Lot ("Flee for *your* life; do not look back . . . or else *you* will be consumed!")[118] Did he bother to share this vital piece of information with his wife? Lot has not exactly proven himself to be a responsible family protector. Witness how younger, "third wave" feminist writers and activists Jennifer Baumgardner and Amy Richards size up the jarring juxtaposition of Lot and his wife in rather salty language, querying "why the hell Lot's wife was turned into a pillar of salt when her husband was busy offering up their virgin daughters to the marauders. (And why the hell she didn't have a name.)"[119] Why indeed.

But, secondly, even if Lot's wife were aware of the prohibition and consequences, does her punishment truly fit the crime? Or more to the point, what exactly is so criminal about taking one last look at one's obliterated hometown, family, and friends? Isn't the response more tragic than illicit? Can we really blame her for looking back? That all depends on moral-psychological assessments of her basic character and motivation, which the Bible never offers beyond the bare fact of her peering back in disobedience to the angels' mandate (which, again, she may not even have known about). But that has not stopped interpreters, ancient and modern, from fishing for some fuller dossier of the woman's attitude and behavior.

---

but when morning comes it stands there as large as before." Note also the stress on Lot's wife's primary "mother love" concern for family left behind.

118. Both pronouns are masculine singular.

119. Jennifer Baumgardner and Amy Richards, *Manifesta: Young Women, Feminism, and the Future* (rev. ed.; New York: Farrar, Straus and Giroux, 2010), 13.

Surely something more sinister than a back-glance accounts for the "pillarying" of Lot's wife.[120]

The Wisdom of Solomon sharply contrasts the "righteous man" Lot with the "ungodly" citizens of Sodom who forsook "wisdom" and embraced "folly" — including Lot's wife whose salt-block end "stand[s] as a monument to an *unbelieving soul (apistousēs psychēs)*" (Wis 10:6-8). Associating Lot's wife with foolishness and faithlessness fits the wisdom tradition's wary perspective toward foreign women. In this view, so-called righteous Lot is doubtless better off without such a spouse holding him back. But what exactly did she *not believe* (the angels' warning? the Lord's sovereignty?), or how was she *unfaithful* (sexually? religiously?)? The author never specifies, any more than he details Lot's supposed "righteousness," which would have been hard to prove from the Genesis narrative.

In his *Jewish Antiquities,* Josephus glosses the Genesis account with the added information that Lot's wife "was continually turning round towards the city, curious to observe its fate, notwithstanding God's prohibition of such action" (1.203).[121] Whereas a quick, furtive peek over the shoulder might have been forgiven, repeated turning back toward Sodom reveals the true, evil object of her heart's desire, meriting divine retribution. And her *curiosity,* apart from being too reminiscent of Eve's (mis)behavior and trivializing her action as rubbernecking on others' disaster, suggests doubting the veracity of God's judgment. As Josephus seems to see it, the angels had left nothing to be curious about; the matter was cut and dried: wicked Sodom must be wiped out, and any who do not resolutely set their faces away from that doomed place will be engulfed in its destruction. Nothing to negotiate: all that remains, especially for a woman, is to obey orders and follow one's husband without question or equivocation. No one ever accused Josephus of feminist leanings[122] (though he did give the exceptional queen of Sheba her due; of course, she apparently had no husband to worry about).

---

120. I borrow the apt wordplay on "pillorying" from Fewell and Gunn, *Gender, Power, and Promise,* 64, and Gunn, "Narrative Criticism," 221.

121. Citation from translation by H. St. J. Thackeray in *Josephus Jewish Antiquities Books I–IV* (Loeb Classical Library; London: Heinemann, 1930). See discussion in Michael Avioz, "Josephus's Portrayal of Lot," *Journal for the Study of the Pseudepigrapha* 16 (2006): 9-10; Brenner, "Are We Amused?" 98.

122. See Betsy Halpern-Amaru, "Portraits of Biblical Women in Josephus' *Antiquities*," *Journal of Jewish Studies* 39 (1988): 143-70; Cheryl Anne Brown, *No Longer Be Silent: First Century Jewish Portraits of Biblical Women* (Louisville: Westminster John Knox, 1992); Brenner, "Are We Amused?" 90-106.

Targumic and later Jewish midrashic commentaries take a more imaginative tack in explicating the sin of Lot's wife and connecting it to her final fate. Before leaving town and looking back, "she had *sinned through salt by publicizing* (the presence) of the afflicted ones" (*Targum Pseudo-Jonathan* Gen 19:26). The scenario takes us back to Lot's hospitality toward the visiting angels. Whereas the Bible indicates, quite unusually, that "*he* [*Lot*] made them a feast and baked unleavened bread" — which in fact hardly amounted to banquet fare[123] — midrashic tradition presents the more apt situation that Lot commanded his wife to cook for his guests.[124] In particular, Lot insists that his wife spice up their normally bland menu with *salt.* However, pitiful hostess that she is, she has none in the pantry and must borrow some from her neighbors. Of course, in the process of her salt-finding mission, she "publicizes the presence" of her visitors, which soon brings the rabble of townsmen to her door seeking fresh sexual meat. So the nasty near-assault of the angels and her daughters is all her fault, and her salty demise is poetic justice.[125] Serves her right for not being a good cook and for being a bad gossip. According to *Targum Neofiti,* she will remain in her salt-block state "until the time the dead are brought to life." But we are given no reason to expect that she will rise to *good, paradisal* life or rise in judgment (like the queen of the South in Luke) against wicked Sodomites or anyone else. She stands as the monumental object, rather than arbiter, of judgment.

However strained these embellishments of the biblical narrative might appear, they confirm that the sparse and harsh treatment of Lot's wife in

---

123. Alter (*Genesis,* 85) regards Lot's offering as a "scanty-looking 'feast'" in which "the only item mentioned is lowly unleavened bread *(matsot)* of everyday fare, not even the loaves from fine flour that Sarah prepares [for divine visitors in Gen 18:6]."

124. Cf. Abraham's ordering Sarah in the previous chapter to prepare cakes for the three "men" (divine messengers) who suddenly appeared. Abraham also dispatches a servant to prepare some choice veal (Gen 18:1-8). Overall, Abraham and Sarah lay out a bigger spread and prove much better hosts to their special visitors than Lot and his wife. On this culinary contrast, see Alter, *Genesis,* 85.

125. *Genesis Rabbah* 50:4; 51:5 state: "Because Lot's wife sinned in connection with salt, she became a pillar of salt" (Ginzberg, *Legends of the Jews,* 241 n. 174; see discussion on pp. 253-55). *Targum Pseudo-Jonathan* Gen 19:26 reads: ". . . because she [Lot's wife] had sinned through salt by publicizing (the presence) of the afflicted ones, behold she was made into a pillar of salt." Further on these traditions, see Elie Wiesel, "Lot's Wife," in *The Future of Prophetic Christianity: Essays in Honor of Robert McAfee Brown* (ed. Denise Lardner Carmody and John Tully Carmody; Maryknoll, N.Y.: Orbis, 1993), 76-87; Rebecca Goldstein, "Looking Back at Lot's Wife," in *Out of the Garden* (ed. Büchmann and Spiegel), 10-12.

Genesis cries out for some explanation. But must an explanation bury Lot's wife deeper in guilt and shame, whether associated with infidelity, curiosity, or inhospitality? Compelled by a sketchy story to use our interpretive imaginations, must we use them to pour more salt into the poor woman's wounds? Somewhat surprisingly perhaps, the church father Irenaeus thoroughly rehabilitates the salty image of Lot's wife as a *type of the church's enduring strength in an unstable world.*

> And while these things were taking place, [Lot's] wife remained in [the territory of] Sodom, no longer corruptible flesh, *but a pillar of salt which endures for ever;* and those natural processes which appertain to the human race, indicating the Church also, which is the salt of the earth, has been left behind within the confines of the earth, and subject to human sufferings; and while entire members are often taken away from it, *the pillar of salt still endures, thus typifying the foundation of the faith* which maketh strong, and sends forward, children to their Father.[126]

As remarkable as her physical transformation into a column of salt, here Lot's wife is spiritually transformed into a *pillar of the church*, a "foundation of the faith," quite the opposite of an "unbelieving soul."

While we might applaud the result of Irenaeus's allegorical reading, it's hard for us modern and postmodern interpreters to get there from Genesis or Luke. Negative associations with Lot's wife are not so neatly neutralized. The most we can hope for is complication, not redemption; ambiguity, not absolution. And contemporary feminist readers tend to ground their complicating readings in some aspect of Lot's wife's close connectedness with the maternal, material, social, quotidian world she has been forced to flee but cannot abandon, even at the cost of her life. She does not long for the wild nightlife or wicked pleasures of Sodom, whatever those might have been. Certainly the evil we know about — gang rape by a male mob — she abhors as much as God does, and apparently more than Lot! We can easily imagine that she longs for and laments the loss of any children left behind in the burning city, other family and friends, her home and furnishings, her daily routines of shopping, cooking, and sharing food (with or without salt), sewing, sweeping, gossiping about neighbors and strangers alike, and so on — just living life, in other words. Is that so awful or hard to appreci-

---

126. Irenaeus, *Adversus haereses* 4.31.3; translation from *The Ante-Nicene Fathers*, vol. 1: *The Apostolic Fathers with Justin Martyr and Irenaeus* (ed. Alexander Roberts, James Donaldson, and A. Cleveland Coxe; Grand Rapids: Eerdmans, 1979), 505.

ate?[127] Where narrative falls short and allegory goes too far, poetry may step in to strike just the right note. Hear the mournful strains of Anna Akhmatova:

And the just man trailed God's shining agent,
over a black mountain, in his giant track,
while a restless voice kept harrying his woman:
"It's not too late, you can still look back
at the red towers of your native Sodom,
the square where once you sang, the spinning-shed,
at the empty windows set in the tall house
where sons and daughters blessed your marriage-bed."
A single glance: a sudden dart of pain
stitching her eyes before she made a sound. . . .
Her body flaked into transparent salt,
and her swift legs rooted to the ground.
Who will grieve for this woman? Does she not seem
too insignificant for our concern?
Yet in my heart I never will deny her,
who suffered death because she chose to turn.[128]

Or the candid reflections of Gene Fendt:

Sodom must not have been perfect in evil.
Not, at least, to Lot's wife, who could remember
days washed in sunshine, setting the clothes
to dry on prickly pear and eucalyptus,
talking to her neighbor with the sweet
clean smell rising around them.
Quotidian work, oblivious of evil,
too ordinary to be of note
to God, or Abraham, or Lot.

---

127. Cf. Tzipora Ne'eman, "Mothers and Sons: In Defense of Lot's Wife," *Jewish Quarterly* 28 (2000): 200: "After she fled Sodom and looked back at the destruction, was she grieving for her children and grandchildren left behind in the conflagration instead of grieving a lost, unacceptable lifestyle, as traditionally indicated? Is it not likely that she was shedding bitter tears of salt for her children? Is it possible that she disobeyed the command not to turn and look back out of her feelings as a mother?"

128. Anna Akhmatova, *Poems of Akhmatova: Izbrannye Stikhi* (trans. Stanley Kunitz and Max Hayward; New York: Little, Brown, 1973).

> Knowing that, she lacked the one virtue
> needed for decisiveness in life:
> Don't look back. The thought of what you lose
> would turn anyone to stone.[129]

Lot's wife looks back where she belongs, where she feels at home: to "the square where [she] once sang, the spinning-shed / . . . the empty windows set in the tall house / where sons and daughters blessed [her] marriage-bed" (Akhmatova); where she engaged in "quotidian work, oblivious of evil" (Fendt).[130] In this innocent, mundane mode, the vital stuff of *lo cotidiano*,[131] what threat could she possibly pose to anyone? Isn't the threat all against her and to her everyday way of life?

On a descriptive level, the Lukan Jesus agrees with this perspective: in Luke 17, as we have seen, what we must "remember" about Lot's wife is her deep attachment to embodied life, to everyday pursuits of eating/drinking, buying/selling, planting/building that she cannot bear to lose. But on an evaluative level, Jesus regards such attachments as lethal impediments to productive discipleship and keen alertness to God's rule. He audaciously summons any would-be disciples to "deny themselves and take up their cross daily and follow [him]" — that is, leave their *daily lives* behind to attend fully to his urgent kingdom business. And he does not brook any excuses, even for seemingly worthy family duties, like burying dead fathers or bidding farewell to those at home (Luke 9:57-61). One must shake the dust even from one's hometown and get going. "No one who puts a hand to the plow and *looks back* is fit *(euthetos)* for the kingdom of God" (9:62): such is the kingdom motto, and such is precisely what Lot's backward-looking wife must be remembered as violating as a disqualified, unfit dis-

---

129. Gene Fendt, "Lot's Wife," *Theology Today* 50 (1993): 116.

130. Citing part of Akhmatova's poem on "Lot's Wife" and another poem of the same title by Kristine Batey, both of which accentuate her deep humanity, Gunn ("Narrative Criticism," 221-24) argues that, among all the characters in the Sodom tragedy, Lot's wife provides the true redemptive "seasoning" (224).

131. Latina Christian feminist interpreters utilize *lo cotidiano* or the "daily lived experience" of ordinary women as a principal guide for biblical-theological reflection and action in the world. See Ada María Isasi-Díaz, "Communication as Communion: Elements in a Hermeneutic of *Lo Cotidiano*," in *Engaging the Bible in a Gendered World: An Introduction to Feminist Biblical Interpretation in Honor of Katharine Doob Sakenfeld* (ed. Linda Day and Carolyn Pressler; Louisville: Westminster John Knox, 2006), 27-36, and Barbara E. Reid, *Taking Up the Cross: New Testament Interpretations through Latina and Feminist Eyes* (Minneapolis: Fortress, 2007), 7-8.

ciple. Moreover, one must "hate" encumbering family members, all possessions, "and even life itself" to become a faithful disciple of Jesus (14:26-27, 33). Such is the high cost of following God's kingdom way (cf. 14:25-33) — a price Lot's wife was not willing to pay. Consequently, she paid for it with her salt-encrusted life; and far from being a good type of the church's salt-of-the-earth mission, à la Irenaeus, she represents the bad kind of salt, the stale, tasteless kind, "fit" *(eutheton)* for nothing, not even the dung heap. Such is the antidisciple with ears blocked against hearing God's word and eyes locked on the transitory realms of this world (14:34-35).

Despite the many unanswered, tantalizing questions that swirl around the all-too-thin sketch of Lot's wife in Genesis, Luke appears to grant her little room to move from her frozen state. He nails her negative character to the wall as a warning sign for all to see and "remember": DO NOT LOOK BACK! DO NOT TRY TO SECURE YOUR LIFE IN THIS WORLD! Message delivered and received — but perhaps still qualified somewhat in the very next chapter. For there, toward the end of Luke 18, while reaffirming his disciples' priority of leaving their families, homes, and livelihood to follow Jesus — unlike the rich ruler who cannot completely tear himself away from his wealth or Lot's wife who clings to her roots — Jesus reassures his followers that their losses will not be discounted; indeed, these who have relinquished everything "for the sake of the kingdom of God . . . will . . . *get back very much more (pollaplasiona) in this time (kairō toutō),* and in the age to come eternal life" (18:29-30). In other words, the day-to-day needs of this world are not entirely deferred to the one to come (cf. the Lord's Prayer: "Give us *each day* our *daily bread*" [11:3]).

Consider, too, an earlier segment that opens Luke 18 and immediately follows the call to remember Lot's wife. In this text, Jesus relates a parable about a widow mired "in a certain city" where she suffers at the hands of both an exploitative "opponent" and a callous judge who refuses to "grant her justice." But rather than fleeing this abusive situation and never looking back, she stays and fights for her rights (18:2-5). On some level — to be examined carefully in our next chapter — the widow typifies the faithful activist whom the Son of Man hopes to find "on earth" when he comes to restore God's kingdom (18:8). Eschatological preparedness involves more than a high-alert readiness to escape judgment, leave this doomed world behind, and welcome the restorative coming Son of Man. It also entails a proactive commitment to promote justice, to change this damaged world for the better, and to help construct God's kingdom "on earth," which the coming Son of Man will complete. If we thus join the bereft home- and land-focused wife of Lot in common cause with the tenacious widow of Jesus' parable who fights for her family and property, perhaps she can be remembered positively to some degree as the "salt of the earth." Though Luke scarcely regards her as a pillar of the church, as Irenaeus does, maybe he would allow at least a pinch of her experience to season his Gospel for good.

Conclusion: Look Out and Move On

Without flattening the rich, distinctive portraits of the three OT "foreign" (Gentile) women Luke features into a composite group character, I briefly summarize their roles within the framework of ethnic-gender dynamics in Israel's history sketched in the first section and suggest a broad theme of judgment linking these women in Luke under the banner "Look Out and Move On."

1. The locations of the three OT foreign women represent contested border zones in Luke's narrative and social world:
   a. Jesus cites the *Zarephath widow* as a target of prophetic outreach beyond his parochial hometown of Nazareth and his native land of Israel.
   b. The *Southern queen* crosses into Israel's borders, indeed, into its Jerusalem center (which will, sadly, prove hostile to Jesus' mission), from the exotic and eccentric — and thus unstable — "ends of the earth" to engage God's (Solomon's) wisdom.
   c. *Lot's wife* is permanently paralyzed in liminal territory between the incinerated Sodom behind her and the way to salvation ahead. In Luke 10:11-16, Jesus links Sodom in tragic irony with Chorazin, Bethsaida, and Capernaum, cities closer to home in Jesus' Galilee that reject God's rule; *and* he also surprisingly *contrasts* these recalcitrant places (albeit in a backhanded way) with wicked *Tyre and Sidon*, which, of all places, retain the capacity to repent and accept God's reign: "For if the deeds of power done in you had been done in Tyre and Sidon, they would have repented long ago, sitting in sackcloth and ashes. But at the judgment it will be more tolerable for Tyre and Sidon than for you" (10:13-14, following the Sodom reference in 10:12). Of course, with these redemptive possibilities for Tyre and Sidon in the face of God's "deeds of power," we come full circle to the Sidonian widow from Zarephath.

2. Scripts of ethnic-gender border conflict are written on the *bodies* of Luke's OT foreign women, to some extent at key checkpoints related to *food* and *sex:*

   a. The *Zarephath widow* has the strongest food connection, representing the hungry persons God feeds through Jesus (cf. 1:53; 6:20-21; 9:10-17).

   b. While the *Southern queen* has only the most allusive associations with food and sex via her OT story (bringing literal spices and using saucy language), Luke features her personal, embodied movement — she doesn't send delegates in her place — in a long, arduous trek to Solomon's court. Moreover, in Jesus' Jewish thought, the notion of her "rising in judgment" against this evil generation entails her *bodily* resurrection (cf. 20:17-40).

   c. The salty element of *Lot's wife* has an obvious culinary flavor, accentuated in later legends. But Luke's reference, which doesn't explicitly identify her salty state, stresses the need to "remember" her monumental bodily, back-looking position as a woeful type of unawareness of God's present kingdom and unpreparedness for God's future judgment.

3. Varied elements of *class,* involving social, economic, and political status, emerge in Luke's trio of OT foreign women, typical of Luke's wide-ranging interests across the social spectrum:

   a. The *widow at Zarephath* mainly fits the profile of the poor, destitute figure in desperate need of God's "good news" (gospel) Jesus came to bring (cf. 4:18; 6:20; 7:22), although her 1 Kings story hints at her escalating standard of living over the course of Elijah's visit.

   b. The *queen of the South* situates on the opposite pole socially as well as geographically: she is Solomon's virtual equal in monarchic and monetary power. This is one "powerful" person Luke does not wish to topple from her throne and a "rich" woman who is not "sent away empty" (cf. 1:52-53).

   c. *Lot's wife* perhaps slots somewhere in the middle of scale, no queen of the realm certainly, but well-off enough, it seems, to have a house and possessions worth longing for and trying (futilely) to secure (cf. 17:31-33).

4. Luke's OT foreign women participate in a range of forensic responses and resolutions, with varying degrees of ambiguity:

   a. Here the *widow at Zarephath* fits more in the middle range of the three figures. Jesus stresses more that Elijah "was sent" to help her than that she welcomed his aid. God's border-crossing outreach, through prophets Elijah and Jesus, is the keynote. Implicitly, of course, the widow must receive God's provision, and in the OT she belatedly acknowledges the truth of Israel's God (1 Kings 17:24); but she scarcely qualifies as a repentant convert, and Luke shows little interest in making her, or any other Gentile, one before Jesus' resurrection.

b. The *queen of the South* demonstrates the most positive, active response to Israel's God by seeking out and affirming God's wisdom epitomized in David's son Solomon and, by Lukan extension, in David's climactic messianic son Jesus. Again, she falls short of what we might call "proselyte" or "disciple" status in the present age, but in the age to come she will "rise" as a bona fide agent of God's judgment. The only people she threatens are those "evil" ones who defiantly position themselves outside God's will.

c. *Lot's wife* demonstrates the most negative, self-destructive response to God's judgment in her struggle to make a clean break with ungodly Sodom and her consequent petrifying into a pillar of salt. Her lack of resolute repentance leads to divine retribution. But even here, as we "remember Lot's wife," it's hard not to reflect upon, and to some degree sympathize with, her deep sense of loss and longing that prompted her looking back.

5. Finally, these OT stories of Gentile women associated with Jewish men mitigate sharp polarities and thereby reinforce Luke's overall resistance to stark stereotyping. Ethnic-gendered opposites attract to varying degrees:

a. Upon careful examination of her OT story, the *widow at Zarephath* is not simply a passive, pathetic recipient of God's care through Elijah. She feeds Elijah first *before* her meager oil and grain multiply. And in the matter of her son's death, she challenges Elijah's benevolence, which in turn prompts him to challenge God and raise the boy to new life. She's no prophet in her own right, like the widow Anna, but she's no Pollyanna either.

b. The *queen of the South* is no sage on the level of Solomon, but she knows where to find his wisdom, makes the long trip to see him, and listens attentively when she arrives. And there's no swooning or fawning over Solomon in the Lukan Jesus' brief reference. Moreover, in one sense Jesus gives her a higher status "greater than Solomon" in his projection of her "rising up" as eschatological judge.

c. As we "remember *Lot's wife*" and her fateful backward look, we can hardly fail to remember Lot as well, and not with great admiration. He may not look back after the divine messengers have dragged him out of town. But he was hardly inclined to leave of his own accord, and his family values leave much to be desired in his shameful willingness to sacrifice his daughters to a rapacious mob. To be sure, Luke's Jesus doesn't always value the nuclear family all that much, with his jolting exhortation to "hate . . . wife and children" (Luke 14:26) — but this sacrificial spirit also extends to *oneself* (bearing one's own cross [14:27]), which disqualifies Lot. Somehow a salty wife and mother petrified in her longing for home and family seems preferable to a flaky husband and father who lingers in Sodom and then bargains with the angels about his destination (Gen 19:15-23)!

We have endeavored to appreciate the distinctive characters of the three OT Gentile women cited by Luke's Jesus. They are not identical, but rather self-asserting, proactive figures in their own right, for good and ill. But apart from their common gender and foreign ethnicity vis-à-vis Jewish society, they also share a broad *forensic* purpose in Luke's account. In short, we might label Luke's message through these women as "Look Out and Move On!" "Look out" both in the sense of (1) *beware* the consequences of opposing God's purposes in Christ and in the sense of (2) look *beyond* one's parochial milieu for the global scope of God's just and gracious rule. And by all means, don't look *back!* Keep moving on, pressing forward in the journey with God and God's Messiah across temporal, spatial, and social boundaries. A pilgrim mentality prevails in Luke's narrative, through not only the negative example of Lot's wife, but also the positive wisdom trek of the Southern queen. Together, all three OT women's cases stretch Luke's symbolic universe north (Zarephath) and south (Sheba, Sodom), from Dan to Beersheba and beyond, adding leaves in the Lord's Table to accommodate all Northerners and Southerners, female and male, Gentile and Jew, at the great messianic banquet (cf. Luke 13:28-29; 14:15-24), and threatening exclusion to those who insist on more exclusive club dining.

7. The Savvy Widow's Might: Fighting for Justice in an Unjust World (Luke 18:1-8)

Jesus' parable of the widow and the unjust judge (Luke 18:2-5) in its immediate Lukan setting (18:1-8) represents a *locus classicus* for constructive feminist-theological biblical interpretation. Here a female victim of injustice — the ever-vulnerable widow *(chēra)* — at the hands of an exploitative male oppressor *(antidikos)* and in the face of an unresponsive male judge *(kritēs)* rises above her victim position to secure justice through persistent speech and action. From a theological view, while the precise theological links to the parable remain debatable, Luke leaves no doubt that Jesus' story reinforces the practice of importunate prayer and the faithful commitment of God to "grant justice" on earth to those who "cry to him day and night" (18:1, 6-8). So score one on the positive side of the feminist biblical-theological ledger! For a change, it seems, we can simply proclaim and celebrate a text without all the hermeneutical hassle of suspicion and reclamation.

In a pathbreaking collection of feminist essays on Jesus' parables featuring women, editor Mary Ann Beavis introduces the chapter featuring three readings of the tale of the widow and the unjust judge from a "hermeneutics of proclamation" perspective by noting that this story was the most requested assignment by the writers she solicited, befitting "the manifest appeal of the parable for feminist Christian women."[1] One of the selected writers, Barbara Scheele, affirms such esteem for the coveted parable in the following statements:

---

1. The chapter is by Mary W. Matthews, Carter Shelley, and Barbara Scheele, "Proclaiming the Parable of the Persistent Widow (Lk. 18:2-5)," in *The Lost Coin: Parables of Women, Work, and Wisdom* (ed. Mary Ann Beavis; London: Sheffield Academic, 2002), 46-70. Beavis's "Editorial Introduction" is on p. 46.

The widow in Lk. 18.1-8 is reminiscent of Elizabeth Cady Stanton, Susan B. Anthony, and the other women and men who fought so tirelessly for women's suffrage. . . . And they never stopped fighting for what was right.

The widow is an archetype of the woman who puts her understanding of biblical justice into action. She then proceeds to demand right action from the one responsible until it is done.

For practitioners of feminist liberation theology, the widow is a role model. . . . Like feminist scripture students, she sits with Torah and compares the justice it promises with the justice administered in her time, and publishes her findings.

I think of the widow as my matron saint. She taught me to bank the anger for the right moments, to find back alleys and side doors, and not to work harder but smarter.[2]

Amen and amen!

But alas, as we might suspect, all is not entirely sanguine in the FBI[3] files on our parable. At the end of her sermonic study, Scheele briefly acknowledges Barbara Reid's cautionary critical reading.[4] Reid issues her feminist warning in multiple, carefully argued treatments of Luke 18:1-8.[5] She has no quibble with Jesus' parable itself in 18:2-5, in which she sees the widow as a model of *God's* relentless pursuit of justice. But the Lukan frame, in Reid's judgment, does not do the story justice, as it aims to "tame" the powerful widow activist into a docile woman of prayer — of no threat to anyone — and to "trivialize" her courtroom victory as a moralistic little sitcom, complete with slapstick antics. Although her feminist approach offers an astute, fresh perspective, Reid's judgments about Luke's

---

2. Scheele's contribution to the chapter "Proclaiming the Parable of the Persistent Widow" is entitled "Will She Find Faith on Earth?" in *The Lost Coin* (ed. Beavis), 62-70. The citations are taken from 62, 64, 66, and 67, respectively.

3. As used earlier, FBI stands here for Feminist Biblical Interpretation.

4. Scheele, "Will She Find Faith?" 70.

5. Barbara E. Reid, *Choosing the Better Part? Women in the Gospel of Luke* (Collegeville, Minn.: Liturgical Press, 1996), 190-94; Reid, "A Godly Widow Persistently Pursuing Justice," *Biblical Research* 45 (2000): 25-33; Reid, "Beyond Petty Pursuits and Wearisome Widows: Three Lukan Parables," *Interpretation* 56 (2002): 284-94; Reid, "The Power of the Widows and How to Suppress It," in *A Feminist Companion to the Acts of the Apostles* (ed. Amy-Jill Levine and Marianne Blickenstaff; London: T. & T. Clark, 2004), 77-79.

editorial recasting and de-radicalizing of Jesus' parable are common fare in critical scholarship. Many have wondered what exactly the spiritual emphasis on prayer (18:1, 7-8a) and the eschatological call for faith at the Son of Man's coming (18:8b) have to do with the widow's legal drama. What kind of redactional contortions (and distortions) does Luke put our widow through to make his theological points? Or put in the strongest terms, does Luke wind up at the end of the day being a more formidable — and successful — devaluator of the widow than the adversary and unjust judge in the parable?

I don't think so, at least not entirely, and a major burden of this chapter will be to defend Luke's "feminist" reputation in this case, to explicate the aptness of Luke's theological frame around the parable of the widow's quest for justice and his ultimate showcasing of the widow as a savvy, capable woman of purpose and persistence. But given the reasonable objections of critics like Reid and the undeniable ambiguities of Luke's narrative, I will have to make my case with a perspicacity and importunity worthy of the widow herself.

I begin by seeking to discern as much as possible about the widow's *plight* in Jesus' story and the desperate, yet determined, *fight* she mounts for justice. After this immersion in the details of her case, we will then be poised to understand better its connections to Luke's immediate and wider teaching about *prayer* and *faith*.

Plight and Fight

Arguably the most vivid and memorable part of Jesus' parable is the pugilistic image of the last two words in Greek *(hypōpiazē me)*, placed on the lips of the unjust judge: "lest she [the widow] give me a black eye" (18:5). The NRSV obscures this picture in its rendering: "so that she may not *wear me out* by continually coming." On both semantic and syntactical grounds, the better reading would run: "lest by her continual coming she *gives me a black eye* [or *blow to the face*]."[6] This is Jesus' punch line in more ways than

---

6. In the present context, *hypōpiazō* is defined "to blacken an eye, give a black eye, strike in the face," in Walter Bauer, Frederick William Danker, W. F. Arndt, and F. W. Gingrich, *A Greek-English Lexicon of the New Testament and Other Early Christian Literature* (hereafter BDAG) (3rd ed.; Chicago: University of Chicago Press, 2000), 1043. In the only other NT reference, the boxing imagery continues but is applied metaphorically to Paul's rigorous self-discipline: "So I do not run aimlessly, nor do I box as though beating the air; but I punish [or

one: he leaves emblazoned in the minds of his hearers this projection of the judge's fear — this judge who prides himself on fearing neither God nor people (18:2, 4) — that, in her constant flailing away at him, this little old widow lady is apt to land a punch that will make him the laughingstock of the community. A shiner is hard to hide and takes weeks to fade!

So we have ourselves a boxing story — no *Raging Bull* or *Rocky* or even *Million Dollar Baby* (to get the woman's angle), to be sure, but a striking tale nonetheless. This scenario does not tell the whole story of Jesus' parable by any means; for example, we're in a courtroom gallery, as it were, for a legal trial, not in a ringside seat for a prizefight. But the boxing image is worth bearing in mind and provides a loose structure for our analysis of the widow's situation (plight) and success (fight) below.

In This Corner . . .

So who are the contestants? Before a bout, it's customary to provide a "tale of the tape," tracking the measure of each boxer, while the oddsmakers weigh in on the fighters' chances. At the contest itself, each fighter is introduced before the first round's bell: "In this corner, from la-de-dah-ville, weighing in at such-and-such pounds . . ."

Unfortunately, from the start the boxing model breaks down in Jesus' parable, as it provides precious few details regarding the participants. Three figures appear: the two main contestants front and center, an unjust *(adikias)* judge and a supplicant widow, and a third party behind the scenes or, perhaps, a silent presence in the picture — the antijust *(antidikos)* legal adversary of the widow. So it seems to be two against one — two justice-spurning men (judge and opponent), possibly

---

beat, *hypōpiazō*] my body and enslave it, so that after proclaiming to others I myself should not be disqualified" (1 Cor 9:26-27). Sifting through the usage of *hypōpiazō* in ancient Greek literature, Wendy J. Cotter ("The Parable of the Feisty Widow and the Threatened Judge [Luke 18.1-8]," *New Testament Studies* 51 [2005]: 338-42) confirms "that the verb must be translated *literally* every time if the metaphor is to work" (339 [emphasis in original]). In other words, even in a figurative context, the punch of the image should not be pulled or its force blunted. Cf. Luke Timothy Johnson, *The Gospel of Luke* (Collegeville, Minn.: Liturgical Press, 1991), 270: "In this case, the literal rendering of *hypōpiazō* ['give a black eye'] maintains the delicious ambiguity of the original. She [the widow] may in fact give him a sock in the eye!" Contra the more purely or "fully metaphorical" reading in the sense of "disgrace" or "besmirch" or "put to shame" by J. Duncan M. Derrett, "Law in the New Testament: The Parable of the Unjust Judge," *New Testament Studies* 18 (1972): 189-91.

in active collusion, against one oppressed widow. Hardly a fair fight: the widow is clearly the odds-on loser! Beyond these basic moral and gender markers, however, we know little else about these characters — no names, no ages, no physical descriptions (my "little old lady" reference above was pure conjectural cliché), no extensive social and economic profiles, no family histories, no dossiers. Introduced in typically generic Lukan fashion as "a certain *(tis)* judge in a certain *(tini)* city" and "a widow in that city" (18:2-3, my translation),[7] these are stock characters in a stereotypical situation one might expect to find anywhere in the ancient eastern Mediterranean world. So we must be careful about overreading. But we can indulge in some disciplined imagination, with the aid of comparative biblical, historical, and sociological materials, to help us unpack the widow's predicament.

Consider first, at some length, the *widow* herself, followed by briefer discussions of her legal *opponent* and *judge.* Though Jesus and/or Luke may focus somewhat more closely on the judge — as suggested by Jesus' opening interpretive comment, "Listen to what the unjust judge says" (18:6) — our feminist approach will keep the spotlight trained on the widow's identity and activity.

1. Savvy Widow Along with orphans, resident aliens, and the poor, widows typify the "quartet of the vulnerable . . . the bottom ones, the low ones, the lowly"[8] and most pitiable members of biblical society in the precarious position, on the one hand, of needing external social, legal, economic, and emotional support systems[9] and, on the other hand, of being susceptible to crushing exploitation by magistrates and other power brokers that should be helping them. Of course, distinct from orphans, aliens, and the poor,

---

7. Other parables in Luke featuring "a certain *(tis)*" representative character include the following: Good Samaritan (10:30), friend at midnight (11:5), rich fool (12:16), great banquet (14:16), lost sheep and coin (15:4, 8), unjust steward (16:1), and rich man and Lazarus (16:19-20).

8. Nicholas Wolterstorff, *Justice: Rights and Wrongs* (Princeton: Princeton University Press, 2008), 75-79.

9. See Helena Znaniecka Lopata, *Women as Widows: Support Systems* (New York: Elsevier, 1979); Lopata, "Widowhood: World Perspectives on Support Systems" and "Widowhood and Social Change," in *Widows 1: The Middle East, Asia, and the Pacific* (ed. Lopata; Durham, N.C.: Duke University Press, 1987), 1-23, 217-19; Paula S. Hiebert, "'Whence Shall Help Come to Me?' The Biblical Widow," in *Gender and Difference in Ancient Israel* (ed. Peggy L. Day; Minneapolis: Fortress, 1989), 125-41; F. Scott Spencer, "Neglected Widows in Acts 6:1-7," *Catholic Biblical Quarterly* 56 (1994): 715-33.

widows have a gender-specific identity that highlights their perilous station in "no-man's-land" within a patriarchal structure. In any case, the Torah's advocacy for all these unfortunates is as clear as it can be, along with its candid awareness of authorities' selfish proclivities.

> You shall not wrong or oppress a resident alien, for you were aliens in the land of Egypt. You shall not abuse any widow or orphan. . . . You shall not pervert the justice due to your poor in your lawsuits. . . . You shall take no bribe, for a bribe blinds the officials, and subverts the cause of those who are in the right. You shall not oppress a resident alien . . . for you were aliens in the land of Egypt. (Exod 22:21-22; 23:6-9)

> You shall not withhold the wages of poor and needy laborers, whether other Israelites or aliens who reside in your land in one of your towns. . . . You shall not deprive a resident alien or an orphan of justice; you shall not take a widow's garment in pledge. Remember that you were a slave in Egypt and the LORD your God redeemed you from there; therefore I command you to do this. (Deut 24:14, 17-18)

Motivation for treating marginal persons with justice and mercy derives chiefly from Israel's bitter history of enslavement in Egypt, where God's people long suffered as destitute aliens, with many literally being worked to death, leaving numerous widows and orphans in their wake. Moreover, on a deep symbolic-religious level, collective Israel became imaged as an orphaned (or kidnapped) firstborn son and widowed wife, separated from *father-husband God* (Exod 4:22-23; Hos 11:1; Isa 54:4-6; Lam 1:1). But at the heart of the foundational exodus narrative beats the consummate good news that God powerfully reclaimed (redeemed) his bereft son/wife for a covenantal life of freedom and faithfulness to God and one another. Given the tight individual-communal nexus in Israelite society, it is not surprising that Israel's God maintains a special interest in protecting and providing for widows and orphans. God himself stands as the ultimate support system — "Father of orphans and protector of widows / is God in his holy habitation" (Ps 68:5; cf. Deut 10:17-18) — but one designed to work *through* Israel's judges and leaders (Isa 1:16-17). Those officials who abuse widows and orphans will have to answer to God (Exod 22:22-24), and if they persist in their unjust exploits, God will eventually give the nation back over to a widowed/orphaned status of lonely, lamentable exile until it learns its lesson:

How lonely sits the city
that once was full of people!
How like a widow she has become,
she that was great among the nations . . .
because the LORD has made her suffer
for the multitude of her transgressions. (Lam 1:1, 5; cf. Jer 7:1-15;
22:3-5; Exod 22:23-24; Zech 7:8-14)

Right treatment of widows is serious moral and theological business.

Such strong injunctions and protests in the Law and Prophets against callous neglect and abuse of widows evidences biblical widows' ongoing struggles for survival, exposing as more "myth" than "reality," as cross-cultural researcher Helena Lopata observes, that "families in traditional societies [in fact] take care of any member with problems, and this is especially true of their care of widows."[10] For all the ideals bolstering familial and societal support for widows, various practical complications come into play, mostly concerning a widow's dependence upon the household patriarch (paterfamilias) and other male relatives to do right by her. The fact that her case often winds up in court testifies to men's resistance to do their duty. Levirate law makes wonderful provision for a childless widow, but it's only as good as the willingness of the deceased husband's surviving brother(s) to welcome his widowed sister-in-law into his family, or the willingness of a living paterfamilias to "give" the widow to another son. Deuteronomy's public procedure, before "the elders at the gate," for redressing a brother-in-law *(levir)* who "refuses to perpetuate his brother's name in Israel [and] perform the duty of a husband's brother" on behalf of his widow intimates that such a situation arose all too commonly in ancient Israel (Deut 25:7-10). Judah's recalcitrance to give a third son to Tamar provides a narrative case in point, fueled no doubt by suspicion that Tamar was somehow to blame for *killing* her two husbands (Gen 38:1-11), a common stigma also attached to widows in traditional Hindu Indian culture.[11]

---

10. Helena Znaniecka Lopata, *Current Widowhood: Myths and Realities* (Thousand Oaks, Calif.: Sage, 1996), 21.

11. Lopata, *Current Widowhood*, 22-23, depending on G. D. Patil, "Hindu Widows: A Study of Deprivation" (Ph.D. diss., Karnatak University, India, 1990). The death of a Hindu woman's husband might be regarded as a curse resulting from the widow's sins in present or previous lives. Whatever cultural codes inform it, the biblical Tamar story makes it clear that the Lord put to death her two husbands, brothers Er and Onan, for their wickedness — a fact, however, her father-in-law Judah was slow to admit (Gen 38:7-11). In the case of the un-

More fundamental, however, to widows' survival than superstitions surrounding their putative man-devouring machinations were hard-nosed economic-legal issues involving distribution of property, inheritance, and gifts. Assumptions that women in general and widows in particular had no legitimate financial assets of their own and no means of supporting themselves in the biblical world overrun the evidence. In Israel's wilderness period, the five daughters of Zelophehad — Mahlah, Noah, Hoglah, Milcah, and Tirzah (naming confers significant identity) — successfully persuaded Moses to grant each of them a portion of her deceased father's inheritance (Num 27:1-11). Of course, their case was bolstered by having no brothers to superintend their father's estate; later their claims were qualified by upholding traditional arrangements that, if and when these daughters married, their assets would *transfer* to their husbands' accounts or, if marrying outside their father's tribal clan (discouraged, but permissible), to the new patriarchal clan (Num 36:1-13). So we never get very far from women's economic dependence on male kin, but at least discussion of women's rights to family property and possessions remained a live issue.

But again it seems that, more often than not, widows' claims to ownership and security remained especially ripe for *litigation* in the face of male relatives (sons, fathers-in-law, uncles-in-law, and brothers-in-laws) disinclined to share their resources with widows in the family and, in some cases, maliciously bent on taking widows to the cleaners to pad their own accounts. The Deuteronomic prohibition against "[taking] a widow's garment in pledge" — that is, taking the last shirt off her back as collateral for a loan she will never be able to repay (Deut 24:17) — shows how oppressive this system could be for poor widows. But such a system not only squeezed widows down to their last mantle or meal (widow at Zarephath) or mite (cf. Luke 21:1-4); wealthier widows, too, particularly since they had more to grab, became common plaintiffs and defendants in lawsuits against rapacious relatives and scribal-legal opportunists.

Papyri from the Cave of Letters on the western edge of the Dead Sea provide a fascinating glimpse into the family legal affairs of a two-time Jewish widow named Babatha in the early decades of the second century

---

fortunate seven-time widow Sarah in the book of Tobit, despite a maid's accusation that Sarah had killed all her previous husbands, in fact the wicked demon Asmodeus had been the murderer out of pure malice. Praying for divine mercy in her "disgrace," Sarah is freed from Asmodeus's clutches and given in holy marriage to Tobit's son Tobias (Tob 3:7-17).

up to the time of the Bar Kokhba revolt (132-135 C.E.). As Ross Shepard Kraemer comments, these Babatha archives "offer the most detailed portrait yet of an actual Jewish woman from Greco-Roman antiquity."[12] A brief sketch of Babatha's personal history may be reconstructed from these documents.[13]

- *Born:* around 100 C.E. in Ma'oza (near modern-day Petra), in the Roman province of Arabia in the southern Dead Sea region, to well-to-do parents, Simeon and Miriam (we do not know if Babatha had any siblings). Ownership of a productive date palm orchard passes to Miriam at Simeon's death and eventually to Babatha.
- *Marriage, Motherhood, and Widowhood #1:* married, in her adolescent years, an older man named Jesus; bore a son also named Jesus. Husband Jesus dies while son Jesus is still young; son is appointed male guardian *(epitropoi)* for legal purposes, while still remaining under Babatha's care.
- *Marriage, Stepmotherhood, and Widowhood #2:* married an older man named Judah, who brought another wife (Miriam) and daughter (Shelamzion) into this "blended," polygynous family. Some years into the marriage, Babatha loans her second husband 300 denarii, which turns out to be the same amount included in stepdaughter Shelamzion's cash dowry six weeks later in her marriage contract to one Judah Cimber (*Papyrus Yadin Collection* [hereafter *P. Yadin*] 17-18). When

12. Ross S. Kraemer, "Women's Judaism(s) at the Beginning of Christianity," in *Women and Christian Origins* (ed. Ross Shepard Kraemer and Mary Rose D'Angelo; Oxford: Oxford University Press, 1999), 53.

13. For summaries and discussion of Babatha's life and records, see Kraemer, "Women's Judaism(s)," 54-62; Kraemer, "Typical and Atypical Jewish Family Dynamics: The Cases of Babatha and Berenice," in *Early Christian Families in Context: An Interdisciplinary Dialogue* (ed. David L. Balch and Carolyn Osiek; Grand Rapids: Eerdmans, 2003), 130-56; Richard A. Freund, *Secrets of the Cave of Letters: Rediscovering a Dead Sea Mystery* (New York: Prometheus, 2004), 189-207; Freund, *Digging through the Bible: Understanding Biblical People, Places, and Controversies through Archaeology* (Lanham, Md.: Rowman and Littlefield, 2009), 184, 208-14; Jacobine G. Oudshoorn, *The Relationship between Roman and Local Law in the Babatha and Salome Komaise Archives: General Analysis and Three Case Studies on Law of Succession, Guardianship, and Marriage* (Leiden: Brill, 2007), 5-42; Lynn H. Cohick, *Women in the World of the Earliest Christians: Illuminating Ways of Life* (Grand Rapids: Baker, 2009), 117-28. For texts and translations of the documents, see Naphtali Lewis, Yigael Yadin, and Jonas C. Greenfield, eds., *The Documents from the Bar Kokhba Period in the Cave of Letters* (Jerusalem: Israel Exploration Society, 1989); Ross Shepard Kraemer, ed., *Women's Religions in the Greco-Roman World: A Sourcebook* (Oxford: Oxford University Press, 2004), 143-52.

paterfamilias Judah dies, he then leaves cowives/widows (Miriam and Babatha), Judah's brother (Jesus) and sons, and various guardians to bicker and battle over his estate.

The cast of characters becomes hard to unravel, not least because of multiple repeated names and the tangled family melodrama that unfolds. A simple chart of Babatha's relatives may prove useful.

Parents:	Simeon and Miriam	
Husbands:	#1: Jesus	#2: Judah
Cowife:		Miriam
Children:	Jesus (natural son)	Shelamzion (stepdaughter who marries Judah Cimber)
In-Laws:		Jesus (Judah's brother)
Guardians:	Various — for both Babatha and children	

Despite what may appear to us as an atypical soap opera plot, serial widowhood was fairly common in the Greco-Roman world, given the customary age disparity between teenage bride and older groom in first marriages and mortality averages in the forty-year range.[14] With repeated experiences of widowhood naturally came a host of potential legal complications, like those embroiling the widow in Jesus' parable, though we have no idea how many husbands she had lost. But to give us some sense of what she might be contesting in court (Luke gives only the barest of details), we briefly cite some of the contracts and disputes revealed in Babatha's papers.

- *Dispute over Child (Son's) Support.* Within four months of losing her first husband Jesus, Babatha goes to the Roman provincial court on behalf of her now "orphaned" (fatherless) son who is not being adequately supported, despite the substantial "trust funds and properties" established in his name.[15] She contends against a male relative who, "though he had sufficient funds, neither paid family debts, nor contributed to the orphan's maintenance" (*P. Yadin* 13), and against her son's two appointed guardians for "not having given my orphan son

---

14. Cf. Kraemer, "Typical and Atypical Jewish Family Dynamics," 140-41.
15. Lewis, Yadin, and Greenfield, *Documents*, 47.

generous maintenance money commensurate with the income from the interest on his money and the rest of his property, and commensurate in particular with a style of life which befits him" (*P. Yadin* 15).[16] Since Roman law required women to be accompanied by male counsel in court, Babatha was represented by her own guardian, in this case Judah — who became her second husband![17]

- *Provision for Widow's Support.* In Babatha's marriage contract (prenuptial agreement) with second husband Judah, he stipulates to her: "And if I go to my eternal home before you, male children which you will have by me will inherit your *ketubba* money,[18] beyond their share with their brothers . . . and you will dwell in my house and be provided for from my house and from my estate until the time that my heirs wish to give you your *ketubba* money" (*P. Yadin* 10.12-16). It does not appear that Babatha had any children, male or female, by Judah before his death ("home-going") or that he had any sons by his first marriage to Miriam; but that does not deter disputes over Babatha's claims to the estate.

- *Dispute over Cowidows' Support.* Major conflict ensued between Babatha and cowife/widow Miriam over rights to their deceased husband's assets. One document attests to Babatha's summoning Miriam to appear with her in court before magistrate Hasterius Nepos, demanding that Miriam explain "why you seized everything in the house of Judah . . . my and your late husband . . . and, equally important, to attend before the said Nepos until judgment." Miriam counterargues that she had "summoned [warned] [Babatha] not to go near the possessions of my and your late husband," to which, in Miriam's view of their late husband's wishes, Babatha had "no claim" (*P. Yadin* 26). It's hard enough to contend with male adversaries in a patriarchal system,

16. See the discussion in Ann Ellis Hanson, "The Widow Babatha and the Poor Orphan Boy," in *Law in the Documents of the Judean Desert* (ed. Ranon Katzoff and David Schaps; Leiden: Brill, 2005), 85-103; Tiziana J. Chiusi, "Babatha vs. the Guardians of Her Son: A Struggle for Guardianship — Legal and Practical Aspects of P. Yadin 12-15, 27," in *Law in the Documents of the Judean Desert* (ed. Katzoff and Schaps), 105-32; and Oudshoorn, *The Relationship,* 354-77.

17. Babatha's need for a guardian in legal matters was further necessitated by her being illiterate (see *P. Yadin* 15); but her lack of education did not mean she was uninformed or uninvolved with her guardian in her case.

18. *Ketubba* or *ketubah* refers to women's contracted rights and monies stipulated in the prenuptial agreement, ensuring her support in the case of divorce or widowhood.

but when push comes to shove, women can also fight each other for scarce resources.

• *Disputes over Stepnephews' Support.* After Judah's death, the orphan sons of his (deceased) brother Jesus also get into the estate-grabbing act, represented by their guardians, Besas and a woman (somewhat unusually) named Julia Crispina. Babatha also becomes embroiled in this legal mess, as these boys' guardians challenged her claim to three profitable date orchards she managed from Judah's holdings. She had in fact recently sold a year's worth of crops and pocketed the proceeds for her livelihood, but only "in lieu of the dowry and debts [owed to her]" after Judah passed away (*P. Yadin* 20–25). Obviously, legal support for widows like Babatha had to be vigorously *defended* against predatory family usurpers, male and (sometimes) female.

So what might all this suggest about the widow's plight in the Lukan Jesus' parable? Admitting again what we don't know — her full marital history (widowed once or more than once?), maternal experience (any children and, if so, how many and what sex?), or social status — we may still plausibly infer from biblical, papyrological, and Lukan evidence two main interrelated focal areas of conflict — *financial* and *familial* — impinging upon our widow's support and security.

As we have seen, whether struggling to retain the cloaks on their backs or the date orchards on their property, widows of various means in the ancient world were routinely ensnared in *financial* disputes. And we hardly need to be reminded of Luke's pervasive interest in economic justice for all people, not least for widows. The parable in Luke 18:2-5 is flanked, on the front end, by a trio of satirical "rich man" parables in 12:13-21, 16:1-13, and 16:19-31, and on the back side by a pair of more promising, yet still challenging, "rich man" narratives in 18:18-30 (rich ruler) and 19:1-11 (wealthy tax collector). Moreover, Jesus soon makes his climactic entry into Jerusalem, where he first proceeds to clean house in the temple and decry, in Isaiah-Jeremiah tones, the temple's failed functioning as a "house of prayer" (Isa 56:7) and deplorable degrading as a "den of robbers" (Jer 7:11) (Luke 19:45-46). The Jeremiah reference is particularly telling in view of the prophet's original denunciation of the temple system as complicit in "oppress[ing] the alien, the orphan, and *the widow*" (Jer 7:6). That is, temple officials had participated in robbing widows of their rightful support. The Lukan Jesus eventually makes this widow connection explicit by excoriating hypocritical scribes who *"devour widows' houses* and for the sake of appearance say long prayers" (Luke 20:47). Obviously these widows had enough estate resources to attract the attention of financial vultures; unconscionably, however, the very scribe-lawyers enlisted to protect widows' legal rights colluded with other opportunists to subvert them. The tragic consequences might lead to total impoverishment, as in the ensuing case, noticed by Jesus, where a poor widow contributes her last two small copper coins — "all she had to live on" — to the temple treasury (21:1-4). A showcase of this woman's consuming, sacrificial devotion to God also stands as a sham of fair and just social-economic security for widows.[19]

So, in all likelihood, the widow in our parable is seeking just settlement of some dispute over her legitimate assets of property, possessions, monies (from dowry or *ketubba* contracts), entitlements, and/or other inherited gifts. The size of her claim and the severity of her potential loss are not specified.[20] All we know is that she demands *justice,* especially *economic justice,* in our suggested scenario. And while she goes to a public court, as a last resort, to secure this justice, she would *not* be suing the state or local government for public assistance, since no such welfare program was operative in that day. Indeed, the judicial system would doubtless only cost her further in fees, bribes, and sundry other extortions for whatever justice it *might* provide her. That's why people sought to settle disputes out of court, if at all possible. As Jesus earlier warned: last-ditch pleas before public magistrates, failing all prior outside attempts to settle with your legal opponent *(antidikos),* may well take your last penny (12:57-59)![21]

2. Adversary-Opponent   Absent government-subsidized social security, the widow's only lawful claims would have been against contentious and derelict *family* members and their guardian and/or scribal representatives.

---

19. See Addison G. Wright, "The Widow's Mites: Praise or Lament? — a Matter of Context," *Catholic Biblical Quarterly* 44 (1982): 256-65; Spencer, "Neglected Widows," 726-28.

20. Jeremias (*The Parables of Jesus* [3rd ed.; London: SCM, 1963], 153) suggests: "Since the widow brings her case to a single judge, and not before a tribunal, it would appear to be a money-matter: a debt, a pledge, or a portion of an inheritance, is being withheld from her." While his judgment about the financial issue seems reasonable, the evidence that such cases were only handled by single magistrates is limited. For helpful clarification and discussion of comparative judicial evidence involving multiple judges, see William R. Herzog II, *Parables as Subversive Speech: Jesus as Pedagogue of the Oppressed* (Louisville: Westminster John Knox, 1994), 223-25.

21. For a discussion of Luke 12:57-59 as an informing cotext to the parable of the widow and unjust judge, supported by external evidence of corruption in the Roman judicial system, see Cotter, "Parable," 332, 336-38.

It is within these kinship-legal roles that we should probably place the widow's *adversary-opponent (antidikos)* in Jesus' parable. We presume an antagonistic male figure — father, brother, son, uncle, nephew (by blood or step-relations), or corresponding in-laws — given typical patrilineal arrangements and the masculine gender of *antidikos,* but Babatha's legal bouts with cowidow Miriam and her stepnephews' guardian Julia Crispina pose intriguing alternatives. In any event, Babatha's employment of various (male) guardian-scribes of her own has no parallel in Jesus' juridical tale. This widow speaks and acts for herself, which puts her at a further disadvantage since women's self-assertive appearances in open court were generally viewed as irregular and immodest, regardless of their comportment.[22]

3. Unjust Judge   The only character left to account for in the parable is the *judge,* and he can be quickly profiled in relation to the widow as only exacerbating her hardship. As one who neither fears God nor respects people, he is predisposed to show her no sympathy and to care not one whit about God's Torah-anchored support for widow's interests. He appears to be a local Roman magistrate dealing with a Jewish widow. While judges in local Jewish religious courts could be equally callous and corrupt, they would be less inclined than a stereotypical pagan to admit, even privately, as the parable's judge does "to himself" (Luke 18:4), their blatant disrespect for God and all people.[23] Plus, not fearing the one God *(ton theon),* rather than a pantheon of gods, seems more suited to a pagan judge's snubbing of the God of his Jewish supplicants, like the widow, as if to say: "This is my courtroom, as this land is my [i.e., Rome's] territory. Your God will do you

---

22. Cf. Appian's scorn of a senator's daughter named Hortensia who dares to challenge in court the law requiring women to pay taxes supporting the war their husbands were fighting for Rome: "While Hortensia thus spoke the triumvirs were angry that women should dare to hold a public meeting when the men were silent; that they should demand from magistrates the reasons for their acts, and themselves not so much as furnish money while the men were serving in the army. They order the lictors to drive them away from the tribunal" (Appian, *Civil Wars* 4.5-34); cited by Cotter ("Parable," 334) from Appian, *The Civil Wars* (trans. Horace White; Loeb Classical Library; London: Heinemann, 1913).

23. The stereotype of an irreverent, irreligious pagan would resonate among many in Jesus' Jewish and Luke's early Christian audience. However, deep religious devotion — though not monotheistic — was in fact prevalent in Greco-Roman society. See the stimulating study by Luke Timothy Johnson, *Among the Gentiles: Greco-Roman Religion and Christianity* (New Haven: Yale University Press, 2009). Throughout this work, Johnson demonstrates the "pervasive, public, political, pious, practical, and polytheistic" nature of Greco-Roman religion (see summary, 32-39).

no good here, and his laws do not apply. You must please me!"[24] With that attitude, the case easily — and greasily — becomes open to the highest bidder. Who will most lubricate the wheels of justice with the best bribes: the widow? her opponent? both? The prospect that this unjust *(adikos)* judge is already in cahoots with the widow's antijust *(antidikos)* adversary only further stacks the legal cards against her.[25] So the bottom line for our widow's plight is rock bottom. As if her financial-familial crisis hasn't caused enough harm and aggravation in itself, she's up against a thoroughly unhelpful judicial system. Her back is against the wall, or to return to the boxing arena, she is on the ropes and about to go down for the count — with the referee-judge poised to raise her opponent's hand in victory.[26]

4. A Glance Back at Lot's Wife   In concluding this section on the widow's plight, we may fruitfully compare her desperate situation to that of Lot's wife, whom Jesus exhorts his audience to "remember" (17:32) just five verses before he launches into our focal parable. Though not commonly associated by interpreters, these women's plights share some intriguing affinities beyond their close proximity in Luke's narrative. To be sure, the OT figure is a living husband's wife, not a widow. But of course, she herself dies — her salty demise is what we "remember" most about her — leaving husband Lot as a widower and their daughters as both widowed (after Sodom's destruction) and motherless, in a desperate struggle for survival. Moreover, as we observed in the previous chapter, the actions of Lot's wife that precipitated her death were motivated by her terrible anguish over devastating *financial* and *familial* loss in her home city in the wake of a harsh *verdict of judgment* against her and her people. Such a scenario might well evoke deep empathy from the widow in Jesus' parable. But these women's cases also diverge at significant points: from a biblical perspective, Lot's wife and her city merit *God's just judgment,* whereas the parable's widow contends against an *unjust judge;* also, Lot's wife gets stuck in

---

24. In hypothesizing the case of a plaintiff Jewish woman before a Roman magistrate in Jesus' parable, I imagine a situation similar to that reflected in the Babatha documents, except that the latter register no complaint against an unjust or indifferent Roman judge. For an alternative view of the setting of Jesus' parable as a local Jewish court before a "Torah judge," see Herzog, *Parables as Subversive Speech,* 220-25.

25. On the problem of graft, corruption, and collusion in ancient judicial systems, see Herzog, *Parables as Subversive Speech,* 226-28.

26. The judge functions as both arbiter of the widow's case and ally of her adversary. It's hard to fight against a judge who effectively represents your legal opponent!

her situation, regretfully looking back and refusing to press forward, whereas the widow gets what she needs, relentlessly pushing back and fighting for justice. To this fight we now turn.

Winning on Points

Given the odds stacked against her and her seemingly helpless position, the widow's victory — and the judge's concession to her — proves to be a shocking outcome to the match. Of course, the force of Jesus' parables often turns on startling reversals and surprise endings.[27] In the present case, the widow's unexpected success comes not through landing a lucky knockout punch, but through relentlessly answering the bell round after round and peppering away with any strikes she can muster and strategies she can mount. It's not that she threatens the judge's physical condition in any critical way; she would hardly be capable of violently overpowering him.[28] It's more that she "keeps bothering [him] . . . by continually coming" (Luke 18:5). The idiom for "bothering" or "annoying" *(parechein kopon)* — precisely the same one used in the earlier companion parable about persistent prayer, featuring a friend's midnight badgering of his slumbering neighbor to wake up and help him (11:7) — literally means

27. See John Dominic Crossan, *In Parables: The Challenge of the Historical Jesus* (New York: Harper and Row, 1973), 37-78; David B. Gowler, *What Are They Saying about the Parables?* (New York: Paulist, 2000), 28-30; Klyne R. Snodgrass, *Stories with Intent: A Comprehensive Guide to the Parables of Jesus* (Grand Rapids: Eerdmans, 2008), 19-20.

28. Though Jesus presents a literal picture of a boxing widow, its patent absurdity blunts any endorsement of brute violence as a means of obtaining justice. The judge hardly fears for his physical life here, but he does seek to undermine the widow's vigorous demand for justice by branding her as vicious, when he in fact is fueling a brutal, systemic oppression of her and other weak victims. Luise Schottroff (*Lydia's Impatient Sisters: A Feminist Social History of Early Christianity* [Louisville: Westminster John Knox, 1995]), who takes *hypopiazō* in its literal, pugilistic sense, captures well the judge's insidious attitude toward the widow: "The judge's 'sarcasm' is the sexist sarcasm about a woman who does not behave as a woman is supposed to; he surmises that she is now capable of anything, even violence. . . . The sarcasm of the judge . . . is an expression of sexism and a cynical reversal of that reality in which the people seeking justice, rather than the judges, are beaten up by the servants of order" (104; see further, 112-18). Cf. Joel B. Green, *The Gospel of Luke* (Grand Rapids: Eerdmans, 1997), 641 n. 95: "Importantly, Jesus does not portray this widow as acting in a violent way, only in a way that departs from her culturally scripted role. The notion of violence derives from the judge, who may interpret her persistence as an act of violence against the system." On the violence issue, see more below.

"to cause toil or trouble."[29] The widow creates irksome work for the judge "continually," it seems to him, literally "to the end *(eis telos)*." She just won't go down; she refuses to lose; she goes the distance and, by dint of her perturbing pummeling to the final bell, she wins the fight on points. Two particular points related to the widow's indomitable achievement merit further investigation: (1) her *aggressive agency* and (2) her *shrewd strategy*. Or, in other words: (1) her active *will* to pursue justice and (2) her able *wits* to win her case.

1. The Widow's Aggressive Agency   As stressed in our earlier investigation of Mary's "right to choose" and shape her maternal vocation, the importance of women's *agency* again comes to the fore in Jesus' parable of the widow and the unjust judge, though in a different way. In ancient and traditional societies, the critical issue for widows, as we have seen, commonly turns on their delicate vulnerability and desperate need for support systems. Simply put, they need to be cared for by the family, the state, the religious community, a charitable organization, or some combination of these social "systems." Assuming widows' virtual helplessness, little attention is paid to whether or how they might help themselves. Unfortunately, however well-meaning such an approach might be in motivating societal provision for widows, it does not tell the whole story and ultimately demeans capable widows and women generally in patronizing fashion.

Amartya Sen — Nobel laureate economist, philosopher, and leader in the international Human Development and Capabilities movement with Martha Nussbaum and others — makes a vital distinction between *well-being* and *agency* in policies promoting human development overall and that of women in particular. Briefly, *well-being* focuses on needy persons as *objects* of aid and welfare programs; *agency* maintains the position of the needy, however destitute, as *subjects* engaged in their own surviving and thriving. The distinction is one of balance for Sen: both approaches are required to maximize development. But given the heavy tilt toward welfare objectives in early global development projects, Sen advances the corrective

29. Reid ("Beyond Petty Pursuits," 292 n. 25) defines *parechein moi kopon* literally as "to present me with trouble." Johnson (*The Gospel of Luke*, 270) renders the phrase "gives me so much trouble" but adds: "One is tempted to render this, 'giving me such a beating,' for *kopos* has that literal meaning" (this would coordinate with the boxing scenario). Green (*The Gospel of Luke*, 640 n. 92) remarks: "The NRSV rendering . . . as 'bothering me' is weak, suggesting neither the duress the judge was under nor the level the widow's shocking behavior had reached in the judge's view."

of "an agent-oriented approach to the women's agenda," which promotes, among other things, women's literacy, educated participation in politics, access to employment outside the home, independent incomes, abilities to start their own businesses, and rights to their own property. In short, "no longer the passive recipients of welfare-enhancing help, women are increasingly seen, by men as well as women, as active agents of change: the dynamic promoters of social transformations that can alter the lives of *both* women and men."[30] Of course, Sen is not simply shifting from condescending patronage to another form of self-justifying patriarchy, as if to say, "You go, girls! Pull yourselves up by your own bootstraps (if you can). Good luck in making your way in a man's world!" Women, especially widows perhaps, must be given adequate *opportunities/capabilities* within which to make their ways, chart their lives, and secure their futures. It is agency *and* well-being, self-determination *plus* support, freedom *as means to* development.

Martha Nussbaum agrees largely with Sen's approach,[31] and reinforces it with a strong accent on guaranteeing and developing women's capability for basic human *dignity* and *respect,* which she closely ties to creating sufficient social space for *"active striving."*[32] Although the notion of dignity admits "vagueness," defying precise calibration, Nussbaum maintains that it remains "absolutely critical. In a wide range of areas, moreover, a focus on dignity will dictate policy choices that protect and support *agency,* rather than choices that infantilize people and treat them as passive recipients of benefit."[33] With respect to widows, the last thing they need — the ultimate indignity after losing husbands (one or more), bearing children (in most cases), and living full, if not always fulfilling, lives — is to be "infantilized," reduced (further) to pathetic states of utter dependency. They need to be able to take charge of their lives, maybe for the first time in their histories. Again, they need help to do this by way of opened opportunities within society. Nussbaum readily acknowledges that human dignity can be lethally

30. Amartya Sen, *Development as Freedom* (New York: Anchor, 1999), 189 (emphasis in original; see 189-203).

31. Nussbaum does raise some technical distinctions between her and Sen's understandings of well-being and agency, which need not detain us here. See the discussion in Nussbaum, *Creating Capabilities: The Human Development Approach* (Cambridge: Harvard University Press, Belknap Press, 2011), 197-201.

32. Nussbaum, *Creating Capabilities,* 29-32. In relation to her catalogue of ten central human capabilities (which I discuss in chapters 3 and 8), Nussbaum speaks of "the centrality of notions of dignity and respect in generating the entire capabilities list" (26).

33. Nussbaum, *Creating Capabilities,* 30 (emphasis added).

choked by various "social, political, familial and economic conditions [that] may prevent people from choosing to function in accordance with a developed internal capability." Hence, structures must emerge ensuring that all persons receive what they deserve, namely, "equal respect from laws and institutions" that safeguards space for agents to develop their capabilities and direct their courses toward meaningful, flourishing lives.[34]

Tragically, in the case of our parable's widow, precisely what she *cannot* count on is *respect* from the legal system — the judge prides himself on *not respecting* anyone! — or *support* from traditional "social, political, familial and economic" sources. One could hardly blame her, then, for giving up, throwing in the towel, or at best throwing herself entirely on God's mercy, whatever good that might avail her in the harsh terrain of no-man's-land. *And yet, stunningly,* passive capitulation to the oppressive forces stacked against her is *not* the choice she concedes (which essentially would entail having no choice at all). Rather, in the face of an unjust system, she opts for action, for aggressive agency, for *active striving*, as much as she can muster. She represents herself in court, accompanied by no legal assistant or guardian, and she addresses the judge with no customary, deferential terms such as "my Lord" or "your Excellency."[35] She comes right to the point, laying her demand on the line, without a trace of sycophantic equivocation and punctuated by a shaking fist: "Grant me justice — or else!" If she's going down, she's going down swinging! And as it happens, she doesn't go down for the count. She finally gets the justice she seeks and lives to fight another day. We dare not romanticize her victory — for in this environment she will need to *keep* striving and fighting — but we should not discount it either.

Moreover, we should not ignore our parable heroine's affinity with other biblical widows who take matters of survival and justice into their own proactive hands. While the assumption of widows' neediness — along with God's assignment of community care for vulnerable widows — predominates in the Jewish scriptures, some widows are far from helpless when the social system does not meet Torah standards. Twice-widowed, childless Tamar finally makes resistant father-in-law Judah do "right" by her (Gen 38:26); Ruth and Naomi work diligently and opportunistically to

---

34. Nussbaum, *Creating Capabilities*, 30-31. Cf. Nussbaum, *Women and Human Development: The Capabilities Approach* (Cambridge: Cambridge University Press, 2000), 1-33 (discussing the development of widows' capabilities in contemporary India).

35. See examples from legal papyri in Cotter, "Parable," 335-36.

secure their futures in Boaz's Bethlehem clan (Ruth 2–3); and the widow Judith delivers not only herself, but also her entire people, from foreign oppression with a mighty double-strike of her Lord-guided, sword-wielding hand to the neck of General Holofernes (Jth 13:1-10, 15). All these widows function as determined *agents* ensuring their own well-being, with or without God's help. To be sure, they work within the patriarchal structure rather than dismantling it and, one way or another, use their sexual wiles as well as their mental wits to accomplish their aims. But it's *their* bodies, minds, and energies *they* employ for *their* purposes. The sexual/scandalous element may lurk in the background of Luke's widow parable (see below), but it is hardly prominent. In any case, this widow still wins the day, like Tamar and company, with her forceful "hand," savvy mind, and indefatigable spirit.

In comparison with her widowed "sisters" in Luke's narrative, she certainly demonstrates the most initiative and persistence, though Anna's protracted faithfulness in prayer (Luke 2:36-38) and the poor widow's voluntary and, in some respects, valorous contribution of her last coins to God's service (21:1-4) should not be overlooked. Plus, in the previous chapter we noted various elements of the widow at Zarephath's more active engagement with the prophet Elijah than is commonly assumed. Apart from correlating with other widow figures, comparing other female protagonists in Lukan parables also reveals their initiative, diligence, and agency: the baker woman "takes" the yeast and thoroughly "mixes it in" ("hides in" [*engkryptō*]) a huge batch of dough "*until (heōs)* all of it is leavened" (cf. 13:21); and the sweeper woman keeps scouring the house "carefully *until (heōs)* she finds" her lost coin (15:8).[36] This active striving *until* the job is done nicely matches our widow's tenacious pursuit of justice.

However, celebrating the widow's aggressive agency, as important as that is, still doesn't explain fully why her "continual coming" with intent to give the judge "a black eye" succeeds in this particular case. Why doesn't this unscrupulous judge just cite her for contempt, have her hauled out of court and thrown into prison, forget about her, and make his tee time? Why does she win against all odds, not least the judge's utter lack of respect for her and the cause of justice? Here we must examine the social and political dynamics of the widow's *shrewd strategy.*

---

36. See our treatment of the sweeper woman parable in chapter 2 and the discussion of all three Lukan parables featuring women in Reid, "Beyond Petty Pursuits and Wearisome Widows."

2. **The Widow's Shrewd Strategy**   Consider two features of the widow's winning approach: her *nagging* and her *shaming* of the judge. Both are complicated and problematic, not least because they reflect the internal perspective of the *judge himself* (Luke 18:4b-5), who is hardly the most reliable character. To be sure, narrator Jesus confirms the widow's persistent pleading (she "kept coming to him and saying, 'Grant me justice'" [18:3]), and commentator Jesus implores his audience, "Listen to what the unjust judge says [to himself]" (18:6). Listen, yes — but given the "unjust" source — listen closely, carefully, critically.

"Persisting," "persevering," "pressing through," "hanging in there" sound so much better than "nagging," but there is little difference in basic meaning, and "nagging" more specifically connotes *vocal* hammering (or yammering) by a *woman,* as befits our parable: *"she* kept coming . . . and *saying. . . ."* By any definition, the widow in the story is a nag: she finally gets what she wants by nagging a male authority figure, who in turn gives her what she wants *because* (*dia ge,* 18:5) he can't take her nagging any more. Needless to say, despite her success, the widow's means of achieving her aims leave some nagging concerns from a feminist-biblical standpoint.

The Bible's most notorious nagger is the Philistine Delilah, who ultimately emasculates "Judge" Samson with her lethal mix of sexual wiles and perpetual wheedling: "Finally, after she had nagged him with her words day after day, and pestered him, he was tired to death. So he told her his whole secret" (Judg 16:16-17). Delilah thus serves as the top narrative model for the proverbial "loose woman" who entraps impressionable young men "with much seductive speech" (Prov 7:21; cf. 7:6-23; 5:1-6; 9:13-18), and for the "contentious wife" whose constant carping comments are like water torture, "a continual dripping on a rainy day" (27:15-16; cf. 19:13b; 21:9; 25:24). Such are the negative images of the importunate woman, compounded by insidious — and altogether erroneous — presumptions that women already rule their world by their incessant nagging (so what do they really have to complain about?); and that their nefarious goal in life is to undermine men's authority and twist them around their little fingers.[37]

If we're not careful, then (I speak chiefly to my fellow male interpreters here), we can find ourselves almost sympathizing with the poor beleaguered judge in Jesus' parable, his unjustness notwithstanding, and wish-

---

37. See Carter Shelly, "A Widow without Wiles," part of "Proclaiming the Parable of the Persistent Widow," in *The Lost Coin* (ed. Beavis), 56-61.

ing that this hen-pecking widow would just go away or would never have come in the first place, her neediness notwithstanding. We might even gloss over the Lukan Jesus' "unjust" evaluation — which is not in the parable proper — and appreciate the judge's avowed lack of God-fearing and people-respecting as marks of judicial impartiality and integrity, a reasoned refusal to be swayed by prejudicial social and religious conventions. Such dispassion, the argument runs, is the price of fairness.[38]

But apart from the (no small) problem of discounting the Lukan Jesus' clear indictment of the judge's corrupt character, the biblical view of justice and fairness, while generally supportive of inclusive impartiality (cf. Acts 10:34-35), is also quite comfortable with particular advocacy for those most vulnerable and disadvantaged. The same Torah that marks out an even playing field for the whole community — "You shall not render an unjust judgment; you shall not be partial to the poor or defer to the great: with justice you shall judge your neighbor" (Lev 19:15; cf. Exod 23:2-8; Deut 1:17) — also stresses the need for special protection of the least powerful and most peripheral in the rough-and-tumble of the judicial game. The liberation ideal of God's "preference for the poor" is not some alien Marxist manifesto foisted on the Bible: across the canon, not least in Luke's Gospel, we find abundant witness to God's prime support and defense of "the least of these" (Matt 25:45) — the resident alien, the widow, the orphan (noted above), "the poor, the crippled, the lame, and the blind" (Luke 14:13, 21; cf. 4:18-21; 7:22).[39] Moreover, in Roman jurisprudence outside the Bible, however much impartiality might be trumpeted as a basic ideal, a maverick magistrate, like the one in Jesus' parable, with no sense of accountability to divine will or human condition, was a stock *unjust* figure. Livy describes one Roman consul who "had been proud and headstrong . . . and

---

38. Cf. Derrett, "Law," 190-91; Charles W. Hedrick, *Parables as Poetic Fictions: The Creative Voice of Jesus* (Peabody, Mass.: Hendrickson, 1994), 194-97; but especially note the fuller Lukan perspective in Frederick W. Danker, *Jesus and the New Age: A Commentary on St. Luke's Gospel* (rev. ed.; Philadelphia: Fortress, 1988), 295: "The judge is not necessarily to be viewed as a crooked or irresponsible magistrate. . . . he might well have pleaded total integrity: not even God could bribe him. . . . the widow must wait her turn and his careful sifting of the case. Yet, from the perspective of the underclass he is delinquent in office, and he is so characterized in v. 6."

39. See Green, *The Gospel of Luke*, 639: "Within . . . the world of Luke, neither fearing God nor having regard for persons signified one's thorough wickedness. . . . The God who liberated Israel from Egypt is the God who directs his people to show special regard toward, *partiality* on behalf of, the oppressed among them — specifically for the alien, the orphans and the widow" (emphasis in original) (cf. Lev 19:9-10; Deut 24:19-22; 2 Chron 19:4-7; James 1:27).

lacked all proper reverence, not only for the laws and for the senate's majesty, but even for the gods. . . . It was therefore sufficiently apparent that, seeking no counsel, either divine or human, he would manage everything with recklessness and headlong haste." In no uncertain terms, Livy impugns these dispositions as "characteristic faults" (*History* 22.3.4-6).[40]

Regarding the proverbial stereotype of the nagging, harpy woman as a figure of power and influence, relentlessly cajoling men and seeking to control their lives, we must get the whole picture. Perspective is all-important here. For, as feminist OT scholars have noted, the strange woman and strident wife are in fact shadow images of God's dynamic creative partner, Woman Wisdom. Simply put, Woman Wisdom is a Major Nag in her own right — crying out on street corners and public squares, making a loud scene, imploring young men to follow her path (Prov 1:20-33; 8:1-36; 9:1-6). But, of course, her path is God's true path, the way of life, wisdom, justice, and righteousness. So how do we see our "nagging" widow in Jesus' parable? As an obnoxious old harridan gumming up the works of an "impartial" judicial system? Or as a courageous, wise woman pressing to the limit her call for justice in a callous court?[41] Clearly the latter portrait is the only option, if we follow Jesus and Luke's perspective. But the other image still crouches too closely on the patriarchal horizon, I'm afraid, to relax our feminist-suspicious vigilance.

Of course, the hardened judge in our parable is no feminist and thinks the widow is an annoying nag in the most opprobrious sense. So why, we ask again, doesn't he just send her away or somehow shut her up, like Paul eventually does with the irksome fortune-telling slave-girl (though he stifles the girl's ranting "spirit" through exorcism [Acts 16:16-18], a power the unjust judge does not possess)? Our judge no doubt wishes that he had "taken care of" the widow much earlier and more decisively, ensuring by any means necessary that she didn't come back to hassle him! But he woefully underestimates her resolve and resilience. A few initial rebuffs and runarounds do not deter her. And as her appearance becomes a routine fixture on the court's docket, it becomes more and more *public.* Tongues

40. For this reference to Livy and similar opinions from Dionysius and Halicarnassus and Josephus, see Danker, *Jesus,* 294-95; Cotter, "Parable," 331-32; Joseph A. Fitzmyer, *The Gospel according to Luke X–XXIV: Introduction, Translation, and Notes* (New York: Doubleday, 1985), 1178. I cite Livy from the translation by B. O. Foster, *Livy: Books XXI–XXII* (Loeb Classical Library; London: Heinemann, 1929), 209.

41. Shelly, "A Widow without Wiles," 56-61; "In Lk. 18.1-8 Jesus gives a resisting reader's slant to the notion of woman as nag" (57).

begin wagging; the tabloids have a field day, with various delicious angles to pursue. Some, as Derrett suggests, might jump to scandalous conclusions, as gossips are prone to do.[42] This widow keeps "coming" to this public official day after day — what's that all about? Despite his protests (methinks too much), he keeps receiving her — something's going on here! Our widow, recall, is of unknown age and physical description: no reason she can't still be young, attractive, desirable, and full of her own "sensual desires" according to the stereotype (1 Tim 5:11), on the make for marital satisfaction and security (cf. 5:11-16).

More than the sexually salacious angle, the recurrent courtroom scene also exhibits an absurdly hilarious side that is just as salivating to base public tastes. Many have viewed Jesus' parable as a "verbal cartoon"[43] or "burlesque,"[44] and it's not hard to see why. Here we have a feisty "little old widow lady" or "bag lady" (again, in the absence of a clear profile, we supply our own images) storming in every day, shaking her fists, shouting at the top of her lungs, and demanding her just rights from this stone-cold judge everyone knows is a jerk, and a boring bastard at that. But she's livening things up with her dramatic little show, and it's starting to wear on our stoic magistrate. He's beginning to crack from the strain, as each day this raving widow gets closer and closer to him, more and more "in his face."[45] And what if, in all her fist-flailing tirades, she happens to land one right under the old guy's eye? Now that would be a funny picture — not to mention the shiner he would sport for several days thereafter — perfect for tabloid covers.

Whatever the audience perceptions of this story — as salacious, hilarious, or a combination of the two — any way you slice it, the judge comes out on the short end of this publicity as thoroughly *shamed*. He becomes a laughingstock, a discredited fool. But so what? Remember, this man doesn't care what God or people think about him. He seems utterly without shame,

42. Derrett, "Law," 190-91.

43. The phrase is from Danker, *Jesus*, 295; but others also see the humorous angle, such as Johnson, *The Gospel of Luke*, 273; Green, *The Gospel of Luke*, 641.

44. Cotter, "Parable," 342.

45. In his 2011 commencement address at Tulane University, Thomas Friedman praised the freedom demonstrations in Egypt and Libya against repressive dictators, fueled in part by social networking. But he also reminded the audience that computers do not produce democratic change: "You have to get out of Facebook and into somebody's face" (which the crowd applauded). See http://www.nola.com/education/index.ssf/2011/05/new_york_times _columnist_thoma.html.

shameless, which in itself is the height of disgrace in an honor-shame society; but again, so what? Public opinion doesn't matter to him, according to his established curmudgeonly reputation. But *"in himself" (en heautō)* (18:4), at the core of his being, his honor still matters very much, at least to certain people in certain situations. And this savvy, pesky widow is pushing hard beyond his comfort zone.

No one, including otherwise disreputable people, can fully surmount society's deeply embedded aversion to shame.[46] In another Lukan parable featuring an unjust/dishonest *(adikos/adikia)* figure, this time a man indicted for mismanaging his lord's property, the unscrupulous fellow protects his future by working a deal and making "friends" with his master's debtors (16:1-13). We learn — again through soliloquy — that the exposed manager, anticipating imminent dismissal from his job, opts for this financial scheme rather than other modes of income, because "I am not strong enough to dig, and I *am ashamed (aischynomai)* to beg" (16:3). Assessments of shame operate on a sliding scale, it seems: they are not absolute. While clearly *not* ashamed to bilk his boss, as he should be (he never defends himself or apologizes in the story),[47] the dishonest manager *is* ashamed to beg for a living. That would be too humiliating a price to pay. Similarly, it appears, the unjust judge, while feeling no compunction about people's general scorn toward him, no doubt has particular cronies and "friends" — maybe even the widow's legal opponent — whose opinion he does value and for whom he must save face, which the widow is socially threatening. As Wendy Cotter puts it, "The unspeakably humiliating situation of a judge walking through the main streets with a black eye, the jeers, jokes, and snide comments, is a terrible prospect, and one to be avoided at all costs."[48] Further honor complications likely also emerge in relation to gender codes: as this case drags on and the widow keeps punching away,

---

46. Extremely mentally ill sociopaths and psychopaths might be defined by their total lack of shame and sense of wrongdoing. But however callous the judge in the parable might be, there is no hint of his being demon-possessed, insane, or otherwise incapable of alternative behavior.

47. Unlike the prodigal son in the immediately preceding parable, who confesses his "sin" of "squandering" family property in no uncertain terms, both in soliloquy and to his father (15:13, 17-21). Of course, the dishonest steward's "squandering" of his master's property (16:1) is skewed somewhat by his master's and Jesus' surprising commendation of his subsequent action (16:8-9). But the shame of the steward's original fraud still holds and is never acknowledged by the steward.

48. Cotter, "Parable," 341.

the judge becomes increasingly subject to bad press about being bested by the "hand of a woman" (cf. Judg 4:8-9; 4:21-22; 5:26; Jth 13:15; 16:5-6). It would be the rare man in the ancient world, however unfeeling he might claim to be, who would not care about the quintessential indignity of being unmanned and outstripped by a woman's hand.

In sum, along with aggressive agency, the parable's widow wins her case through a savvy strategy of manipulating the honor-shame system to her own advantage. Though far from being a meek and weak woman, as her persistent voice and action demonstrate, she uses her conventional "weaker sex" position for her own purposes, finding strength, we might say, in her weakness.[49] She realizes that the crusty judge, for all his bluster about not fearing or respecting anyone, can't afford being shown up by a petulant widow, and she knows it. Constantly getting "in his face" and even threatening to "blacken his face" equate in terms of public shaming to the Deuteronomic ritual, whereby a widow, whose brother-in-law refuses to "perform the duty" of marrying her, will confront him before the city elders, "pull his sandal off his foot, *spit in his face*, and declare, 'This is what is done to the man who does not build up his brother's house.' Throughout Israel his family shall be known as 'the house of him whose sandal was pulled off'" (Deut 25:7-10). Going through life as a foot-stripped, face-spat (by a woman!) man is, to the say the least, not a propitious prospect. In effect, the man and his household are permanently branded as lawbreakers.

If I'm correct that the judge in Jesus' parable better fits a Roman than a Jewish profile, he could not have cared less about Mosaic Law. But Roman law had its own justice standards, at least in theory, and corrupt judges who took bribes and played favorites had to fly below the radar and watch their backs — and faces! Public exposure of extortive practices could bring the courthouse down, whether Roman or Jewish. And that's just what the justice-seeking widow threatens to do. As Herzog puts it, she aims "to blow

---

49. Cf. 1 Cor 1:25-29; 2 Cor 12:9-10; Reid, *Choosing the Better Part?* 192: "[T]hat God is more akin to a victimized widow than a powerful judge is startling. She embodies godly power in the midst of apparent powerlessness. This is a message that achieves its full flowering in the passion, death, and resurrection of Jesus. His seeming helplessness in the face of his executioners is transformed into the very defeat of the powers of sin and death. Followers of Jesus are invited to take up this same stance: to draw on the power of weakness to overcome death-dealing powers." See also the picturesque commentary of Cotter, "Parable," 341: "The judge is elevated on the ladder of success and has far to fall, while the widow is already on the ground, lower than the bottom rung. Moreover, her place at the very bottom gives her the advantage of being able to give that ladder of success a good shake."

the cover off the operation. . . . Although [the judge] is clear about his role
. . . he still has to wear the mantle of justice in public and keep the cover
story alive."[50]

3. **"Nagging" Feminist Concerns**   While I am very happy to affirm the
widow's shrewd strategy to procure justice for herself and to expose an unjust legal system in the process, four further "nagging" feminist concerns
still simmer under the surface of the widow's approach and the judge's response. First, a tinge of *violence* shades the scene, all the more as we play up
the boxing motif.[51] Even if we opt for a purely figurative interpretation of
the widow's blackening the judge's eye/face, staining his honor without actually striking his head, it still trades on violent imagery, as does "blowing
the cover off his operation" (kaboom!). So, however we negotiate that notoriously tricky line between metaphor and reality, is this parable sending
at least some subtle message to oppressed women, so often victims of male
violence, to fight fire with fire, bashing with bashing? It's hard to see Luke's
Jesus even hinting at such reprisal, in light of his resolute turn-the-cheek,
love-your-enemy policy of nonviolence (Luke 6:27-36). Moreover, from a
practical standpoint, encouraging women to punch back and physically
subdue their male attackers is a ludicrous strategy, barring some serious
martial arts training, and is certainly not the point of our widow's action.
Now there is biblical precedent for female warrior-types: Judge Deborah
with the Israelite army under her command, Jael with her lethal mallet and
tent peg, and Judith with her sword (well, she used Holofernes' sword
against him!) and food bag. You go, girls! Xena and Buffy would be very
proud![52] But while, as we have seen, these great OT heroines provide models for the parable widow's aggressive agency, she does not match their
combat strength or strategy: she hires no hit man to do her dirty work (she
has no Barak to dispatch) and, again we stress, she lands no knockout blow
against the judge, as if she could! This is not a parable about "might makes
right" in terms of violence.

Second, we must be careful about how we understand *victimhood* in
Jesus' parable. The widow is obviously a victim of her opponent's unjust
claims against her and of the judge's recalcitrance to grant her justice.

50. Herzog, *Parables as Subversive Speech*, 229-30.

51. In n. 28 above, I began to address the violence issue, drawing on the insights of
Schottroff and Green. Here I offer a fuller response.

52. Cf. Susan J. Douglas, *Enlightened Sexism: The Seductive Message That Feminism's
Work Is Done* (New York: Times Books, 2010), 76-100.

But she by no means succumbs as a helpless victim. Good for her! But not good for the judge, and he's the one who gets the last word in the parable and whom Jesus challenges us to hear. And the disturbing word that lingers in the air is the judge's pathetic plea that *he* is the one ultimately done wrong *by this shameless widow!*[53] "Lest she keep coming, wear *me* out, and give *me* a black eye." Poor baby. Here we have a classic case of blaming the female victim and co-opting her oppressed status.[54] We should not buy this poppycock ploy for a second. I don't think Jesus or Luke do, but they do leave it dangling out there, perhaps because it is so common. But in any case, a feminist hermeneutic of suspicion must clearly expose this common strategy as a last-ditch backlash by a shameful male authority.

Third, closely tied with the potential danger of co-opting the widow's victimhood is that of usurping her *vocality* as well. Again, the problem arises when Luke's Jesus moves from parable to interpretation: "And the Lord *(kyrios) said,* 'Listen to what the unjust judge *(kritēs) says*'" (18:6). Suddenly the widow's persistent pleas for justice seem muffled by a double barrel of authoritative male voices from the Lord Jesus and the unjust judge. Why doesn't Jesus say right from the start, "Listen to what this remarkable widow says in the parable and says to us now"? She's the voice of justice and mercy! This would have been a more positive, and certainly more feminist, approach. Now in fact, "what the unjust judge says" at the end of the parable is all about the widow's strategy and its ultimate effect on him; and then Jesus proceeds, not to repeat the judge's words, but to focus on God's special care for those beleaguered "chosen ones" who — like the widow — inexorably cry out for justice (18:7). So Jesus scarcely forgets about the widow. But he could have accentuated her *voice* over that of the unjust judge more clearly and forcefully. Of course, by this point in Luke's

53. On the shamelessness of the widow's conduct from the dominant culture's perspective, represented by the judge, see Bernard Brandon Scott, *Hear Then the Parable: A Commentary on the Parables of Jesus* (Minneapolis: Fortress, 1989), 182-83, 187; Cotter, "Parable," 332-34, 341; Mary W. Matthews, "'Go Thou and Do Likewise': A Homiletical Commentary," part of "Proclaiming the Parable of the Persistent Widow," in *The Lost Coin* (ed. Beavis), 50: "In the eyes of first-century Galilee, the widow was as shameless as the judge."

54. See Scheele, "Will She Find Faith?" 66-67, and Elisabeth Schüssler Fiorenza, *Sharing Her Word: Feminist Biblical Interpretation in Context* (Boston: Beacon Press, 1998), 155: "The soliloquy of the judge expresses a typical sentiment of those who act violently; the judge blames the wo/man victim for 'battering' him although she only seeks her rights and vindication whereas he acts violently by denying justice to her."

narrative, feminist interpreters have become rightly concerned over the notable *silencing* and domesticating of women since the opening birth accounts. Where have all the women prophets gone? The widow finally gives us someone to latch on to and listen to, but within the safe confines of a fictional parable. Or maybe not so safe at all: Jesus' parables carry a lot of Luke's subversive political freight, and their stock characters, though sometimes caricatures, also reflect *typical* perceptions of *common* folk, the "little tradition."[55] As Elizabeth Dowling avers with respect to our focal story, "Perhaps in the parable we hear a different voice from that in the dominant narrative. Whereas the dominant voice reinforces the public silence of women, this widow's voice reflects the voice of resistance to women's public silence and marginalization."[56]

Finally, we need to address the *humor* component more precisely. As we observed, there's no getting around the cartoonish, slapstick element of the parable, especially the prospect of a huffy widow slugging a haughty judge in the mug. As Luke Timothy Johnson says, "We are meant, I think, to laugh."[57] Yes, but laugh how? Too easily we can laugh *off* a serious scene as a bit of eccentric comic relief, a cute story but so aberrational as to *not* be taken seriously. But that's not the only way humor functions. It plays a key role in societal satire, making fun of the powers that be for the sake of undermining them, challenging them, and ultimately changing them. We laugh to keep from crying. We laugh to mock and make a difference.[58] Jesus' parable of the widow and unjust judge is a cartoon all right, but an edgy *political* cartoon, like many of his parables, lampooning and upending the unjust system stacked against widows, orphans, immigrants, and

---

55. On reading Jesus' parables from the "little tradition" perspective of peasant farmers and village folk in first-century Galilee (as opposed to the dominant "great tradition" of the elite establishment), see William R. Herzog II, "Sowing Discord: The Parable of the Sower (Mark 4:1-9)," *Review and Expositor* (forthcoming 2012), drawing on James C. Scott, "Protest and Profanation: Agrarian Revolt and the Little Tradition," *Theory and Society* 4 (1977): 1-38, 211-46; see also Herzog, *Jesus, Justice, and the Reign of God: A Ministry of Liberation* (Louisville: Westminster John Knox, 2000), 149-55; Herzog, "Onstage and Offstage with Jesus of Nazareth: Public Transcripts, Hidden Transcripts, and Gospel Texts," in *Hidden Transcripts and the Arts of Resistance: Applying the Work of James C. Scott to Jesus and Paul* (ed. Richard A. Horsley; Atlanta: Society of Biblical Literature, 2004), 41-60.

56. Elizabeth V. Dowling, *Taking Away the Pound: Women, Theology, and the Parable of the Pounds in the Gospel of Luke* (London: T. & T. Clark, 2007), 213 (cf. 182-85, 201-6, 212-13).

57. Johnson, *The Gospel of Luke*, 273.

58. Athalya Brenner, introduction to *Are We Amused? Humour about Women in the Biblical Worlds* (ed. Athalya Brenner; London: T. & T. Clark, 2003), 1-5.

the like. We may find productive humor in this boxing vignette, provided it is underscored by a robust feminist laugh track.

Prayer and Faith

Having investigated the literary and socioeconomic dimensions of the widow's plight and fight in the parable proper, we turn to the spiritual and theological connections of the widow's dealings with the judge with the parable's Lukan frame, connections that I take to be true and firm, though not altogether transparent and straightforward. Luke particularly uses the parable to illustrate points about the *spiritual practice of prayer* (18:1, 7a) and the *eschatological persistence of faith* (18:7b-8). More pointedly, Luke elevates *the widow* as the dynamic model of such conduct for Jesus' followers. "This widow" *(tēn chēran tautēn)* (18:5) takes the spotlight in the parable and framing narrative. As Luise Schottroff stresses: "It is not appropriate to make the judge's or God's action the focal point. . . . The text's center of gravity is the behavior of the believers (Luke 18:8), of the elect (v. 7) or the women and men disciples of Jesus addressed in v. 1; they are to behave toward God like this stubborn widow, to pray without ceasing and not to despair (v. 1), to cry to God day and night for their rights (v. 7), and to have faith (v. 8). Their whole existence is to be like that of the widow in relation to the unjust judge."[59]

Jesus' disciples — male as well as female — are to "pray without ceasing" and "have faith to the end" *as the parable's widow exemplifies.* And she models prayerfulness and faithfulness in quite *specific* fashion. In the actions she undertakes and the strategies she employs, as discussed above, the widow embodies particular ways of expressing prayer and exhibiting faith that need to be unpacked. She may start out as a stock character, but her memorable performance puts her own distinctive stamp on the story. *These* are the ways, like *this* widow, we should pray and have faith.

Prayer Warrior: The Spirituality Factor

Nowhere else does Luke introduce a parable of Jesus with such stark clarity concerning what the tale is all about. This one is "about their need to pray

59. Schottroff, *Lydia's Impatient Sisters*, 102.

always and not to lose heart" (18:1). It takes a bit of the fun out of hearing the parable, frankly, like knowing the punch line in advance. But soon, our curiosity is piqued, as the story does *not* in fact feature a figure praying in a suitable setting like temple or synagogue, as the next parable does (18:9-14). Still, a basic connection is not that hard to find, as the widow fervently (without "losing heart") pleads for personal justice — a common enough component of prayer from God's "chosen ones" in crisis situations (18:7).

Even so, a couple of nettling loose links complicate the fit of the parable's widow into Luke's prayer chain: (1) the *theological* problem of associating the callous unjust judge to whom the widow "cries out" for justice with God to whom believers pray; and (2) the *feminist* challenge that using a woman as a model of prayer follows a Lukan tactic of "taming," "toning down," and "trivializing" women's prophetic and political capabilities — cloistering or "corseting" them in the safe confines of the prayer closet, so to speak.[60]

1. Theological Problem: The Unjust Judge as God Figure?   While Jesus' parables, as revealing vignettes about the reign of God on earth, are unmistakably *theological* in "intent"[61] and impact (while ethically charged, they are not moralistic tales), the role of God or a God figure (and Christ or Christ figure) within the stories is complex, if present at all. In only one among the dozens of Jesus' parables does God actually make a cameo appearance as God's self (Luke 12:20), and common allegorical moves to identify God with kings, fathers, masters, managers, and other kyriarchal figures need to be made with great caution and nuance.[62] Jesus' parables, while simply structured, are far from simplistic God lessons for children's Sunday school. In our focal parable, God is clearly not *in* the scene, except as a reference point for the judge's *un*godly orientation (he had "no fear of God" [18:4, 2]). So this judge is not a stand-in for God; indeed, he may be viewed as God's opponent and opposite: this is *not* what God is like. Accordingly, a popular, prayer-centered interpretation plays up the contrast

60. Annette Merz, "How a Woman Who Fought Back and Demanded Her Rights Became an Importunate Widow: The Transformations of a Parable of Jesus," in *Jesus from Judaism to Christianity: Continuum Approaches to the Historical Jesus* (ed. Tom Holmén; London: T. & T. Clark, 2007), 83: "[A]t a secondary stage the parable was forced into the corset of a parable about the hearing of prayer."

61. A major thesis of the massive study of Jesus' parables by Snodgrass, *Stories with Intent.*

62. A major thesis of Luise Schottroff, *The Parables of Jesus* (trans. Linda J. Maloney; Minneapolis: Fortress, 2006).

between the parable's judge and God in a lesser-to-greater, "how much more" fashion: if this godless, care-less judge eventually grants justice to a pleading widow, *how much more* will the merciful, right-full God grant justice to God's "chosen" supplicants! True enough. But even this antithetical good-judge/bad-judge model does not fully capture the theological dynamics of Luke 18:1-8. For one thing, Luke does not incorporate the "how much more" *(posō mallon)* formula here, as elsewhere (11:13; 12:24, 28). The point is *not* that God is just a bigger and better version of the hard-nosed, slow-working judge, analogous to God's function as the ideal heavenly counterpart of flawed, but well-meaning, fathers (11:11-13).[63] God does not need to be badgered into listening to the pleas of oppressed widows, responding only grudgingly to protect God's semblance of honor. Again we insist: God is not this unjust judge, is nothing like this unjust judge, and is actively set against everything this unjust judge stands for.

And yet . . . Luke's Jesus leaves open this awkward, yea absurd, juxtaposition of God and the parable's judge, not as a way of neutralizing the widow's achievement (see below) and not as a means of paralleling or even comparing God and the judge *personally*. But we are meant, I think, to compare *situationally* the courtroom drama of the widow and judge with the worldly experience of God's suffering prayerful people; and we are meant to be honestly bothered by the association. That's what parables do: they brazenly bring together incongruous elements to expand horizons and explore deeper dimensions of truth.

In the present case, I suggest Jesus is addressing a perennial problem of *theodicy*, literally, of *God's justice*, ever percolating in an evil world where injustice too often rules the day. Where is God in all this mess? Why doesn't God act more swiftly and decisively to restore justice to pleading widows, crying Israel, and a groaning creation? How long, O Lord? This is the stuff of the vibrant scriptural tradition of *prayer* commonly known as *lament*.[64] As Gail O'Day profitably mined this tradition to help expound Matthew's version of the Canaanite woman's insistent pressing of Jesus to heal her daughter — in the face of his *atypically uncompassionate* resis-

---

63. The lack of explicit "how much more" reasoning in Luke 18:1-8 represents a *marked distinction* from the otherwise closely parallel 11:1-13.

64. See Nancy C. Lee, *Lyrics of Lament: From Tragedy to Transformation* (Minneapolis: Fortress, 2010), 73-179; Sally A. Brown and Patrick D. Miller, eds., *Lament: Reclaiming Practices in Pulpit, Pew, and Public Square* (Louisville: Westminster John Knox, 2005); Patrick Miller, *They Cried unto the Lord: The Form and Theology of Biblical Prayer* (Minneapolis: Fortress, 1994), 68-86.

tance to comply (he had readily responded to other parental pleas [Matt 9:18; 17:14-20])[65] — so we may reflect on the lament experience to negotiate tensions between Jesus' parable of the widow and teaching about prayer. Widows, of all people, the special objects of God's tender care, should be able to pray for justice and support and receive immediate heavenly attention. No waiting line, no runaround, no "crying out day and night," as if God were asleep and needed widows' extended wailing to rouse him (cf. Ps 44:23-26). But the tragic reality is: too often in this disappointing world, it's not just widows' desperate pleas to family members and judges but also their *petitions to God* that seem to fall on deaf ears. Should we not imagine prayer as a pious Jewish widow's *first response* to her needs? As we've seen, the widow in the parable would only have approached this callous judge as a *last resort,* when all other avenues had hit dead ends — *including prayer.* For whatever reason, the God of justice had not yet come through for her, and she was at the end of her rope (and on the ropes). She is hanging by a thread in a banner case of theodicy, where the unthinkable starts roiling in her heart and mind, namely: What difference is there, really, between God and this unjust judge? She truly seems all alone in this world, forsaken even by God.

So how is Jesus going to get out of this theological trap he's sprung by his own parable? His commentary seems to provide a swift and nifty escape: "And will not God grant justice to his chosen ones who cry to him day and night? Will he delay long in helping them? I tell you, he will quickly grant justice to them" (Luke 18:7-8a). Again, the usual reading follows a blithe "how much more" logic or, flipping it around, "how much less": if an unjust judge on earth forces a poor widow to badger him for days on end, *how much less* will the just God of heaven play such cruel dilatory games. Surely God will jump in *quickly.* Really? In the widow's case, God evidently did not respond quickly; actually God didn't respond at all, unless we assume God's subtle, belated working through the non-God-fearing judge. And if pressed, many other devout, destitute people might confess to wondering what good their prayers have accomplished for them. Such is the candid testimony of "righteous sufferers" in biblical lament psalms (why do the wicked prosper at our expense?), which Luke's Jesus knows well.[66] So a breezy theology of

65. Gail R. O'Day, "Surprised by Faith: Jesus and the Canaanite Woman," in *A Feminist Companion to Matthew* (ed. Amy-Jill Levine and Marianne Blickenstaff; Sheffield: Sheffield Academic, 2001), 114-25.

66. Luke 24:44 attests to Jesus' personal awareness of "everything written . . . in the law

prayer based on a facile contrast between Jesus' parable and interpretation ("Fear not, poor widow; God will quickly save you") doesn't work. Surely the gutsy, savvy widow in the parable wouldn't buy this Pollyanna spirituality for a second, nor would the first widow of Luke, the venerable prophet Anna (*not* Polly Anna), who prayed "night and day" over *seven decades* for Jerusalem's liberation (2:36-38)!

So again, what do we do with Luke 18:7-8a? Perhaps a careful rereading is in order. Consider the following adjustments to and interpretation of the NRSV:

A. **Rhetorical Question:** But will God not by all means *(ou mē)* grant justice *(poiēsē tēn ekdikēsin)* for his chosen ones who keep crying out *(boōntōn)* to him day and night?

B. **Realistic Statement:** And he [God] is patient *(makrothymei)* with them.

C. **Optimistic Punch Line:** I tell you that he [God] will grant justice *(poiēsei ekdikēsin)* for them suddenly *(en tachei)*.

A. **Rhetorical Question:** The use of the emphatic double negative *(ou mē)* with a subjunctive verb assumes a strong positive answer. "Will God *not* grant justice to his chosen supplicants? How could he not? Of course he will! By all means!"[67] The bedrock conviction of God's commitment to justice for God's people is precisely what drives the lament tradition. Lamenters are not fundamentally doubters; they are first and foremost believers, who believe so strongly in God's justice that they can't comprehend why such justice seems throttled in their experience. They lament in *hope,* daring to call God to be faithful to God's nature. I suggest that the strongly rhetorical force of Jesus' query creates space for this lament mentality: "By all means — which seem to be few and far between of late — you will do

---

of Moses, the prophets, *and the psalms.*" And his intense weeping over Jerusalem (19:41-44; cf. 23:27-31) and sweating over his imminent trial and death (22:39-45) suggest more than a passing acquaintance with Jewish lament tradition.

67. See Martin M. Culy, Mikeal C. Parsons, and Joshua J. Stigall, *Luke: A Handbook on the Greek Text* (Waco, Tex.: Baylor University Press, 2010), 560: "So won't God certainly give justice to his chosen ones who cry out to him?" (cf. 564). The construction *ou mē* + subjunctive in question form is rare in the NT. Its usage in Luke 18:8 is similar to John 18:11, expecting a strong affirmative answer: "Am I not to drink the cup that the Father has given me? [Of course, I will!]" (John 18:11). Cf. Stanley E. Porter, *Idioms of the Greek New Testament* (2nd ed.; Sheffield: Sheffield Academic, 1992), 279.

justly, O God. Of course you will. Then please get on with it! What are you waiting for?"

B. Realistic Statement: Here is my starkest divergence from the NRSV ("Will he delay long in helping them?"). Grammatically, in my judgment, the "and" *(kai)* conjunction combined with a tense-and-mood verb shift from *aorist subjunctive (poiēsē)* to *present indicative (makrothymei)* breaks the interrogative flow. So Jesus now makes a declarative statement, focused on the Lord's *patience,* which is the basic meaning of *makrothymia/-eō.* In its present context, this conventional affirmation of God's patient dealings takes on a provocative double edge: (1) stressing that God patiently hears his people's round-the-clock cries; that is, God is a good listener, in no way bothered or offended by persistent pleas, as is the unjust judge, while also (2) suggesting that this patient God will not necessarily *help* his petitioners beyond assuring them that he hears and cares; that is, the statement may well convey: "and the Lord *is slow to help them*"[68] — as the parable's widow and a host of other lamenters would concur. Thus Jesus applies a dose of spiritual reality: God often does not move as swiftly as we would like or expect.

C. Optimistic Punch Line: Biblical lament, while brutally honest about its frustrations with God's delays, is not ultimately depressive or nihilistic. It inexorably presses through to defiant hope that God *will* execute justice; that a just God can do no other, even if God can take God's own sweet time, from our viewpoint, to get there. So concludes Jesus, but not quite as the NRSV renders, that God will do justice *speedily,* which would seem to contradict the "patiently" working God he just identified, not to mention the parable of the widow. Hence, I opt for the translation "suddenly" (see more on *en tachei* below), which still includes the notion of rapid response *when* it happens, but still allows for delay in answering the call. That is, *when* God decides to bring full justice to the world through his royal-judicial agent, the Son of Man, it will burst in like a lightning flash or firestorm and shake the cosmos to its core. This links right up with Jesus' immediately preceding teaching about the dramatic coming of God's rule (17:20-37). Make no mistake: God's just reign will suddenly break in at some point: "*But first* he [the Son of Man] must endure much suffering and be rejected by this generation" (17:25), a fate also awaiting those who follow God's Human Envoy. We are clearly in eschatological territory now sliding into 18:8b, which we will consider further in the next section.

---

68. An option specified for this text in Barclay M. Newman Jr., *A Concise Greek-English Dictionary of the New Testament* (Stuttgart: Deutsche Bibelgesellschaft, 1993), 101.

So to summarize this fresh "lament" take on 18:7-8a: God's distressed people, oppressed by crushing, exploitative forces, bombard heaven with pleas for justice and deliverance; God patiently and sympathetically hears their cries, but for God's inscrutable reasons, often seems too patient, too resistant, in acting to rectify the situation; the longer the wait, the more God's supplicants move in their "optic of suffering"[69] toward honest, impassioned, even fist-shaking lament, without abandoning hope; indeed, hope remains tenacious, against the odds, that God can and will indeed be roused to put things to rights suddenly, climactically, once-for-all; even so, Lord — even after much suffering and long delay — come quickly (cf. Rev 22:20)! Thus the theodicy problem connected with prayer is effectively addressed, though not completely erased.

To reinforce this perspective on prayer and tie it in more closely with the widow's case in Jesus' parable, we compare a key intertext in Sirach 35:14-25, which bears striking similarities to Luke 18:1-8 in terms of vocabulary, structure, and theme.[70]

Do not offer him [the Lord] a bribe, for he will not accept it;
  and do not rely on a dishonest *(adikō)* sacrifice;
for the Lord is the judge *(kritēs)*,
  and with him there is no partiality.
He will not show partiality to the poor;
  but he will listen to the prayer of one who is wronged
  (ēdikēmenou).

---

69. I draw this apt phrase from James A. Metzger, "God as F(r)iend? Reading Luke 11:5-13 & 18:1-8 with a Hermeneutic of Suffering," *Horizons in Biblical Theology* 32 (2010): 53-55. This study (33-57) shows close affinities with my approach, though it draws heavily on process theology and suggests the mutability of God's nature and purpose, even the potential for God's "moral transformation" that frustrated human sufferers can spark within God. While affirming Metzger's endorsement of candid, plaintive, even angry conversation with God, I do not see the point of prayer via the parable of the widow as changing God's mind or character. The issue is principally one of timing (delay), not of God's fundamental commitment to justice, which remains constant. *Challenging* God through passionate lament to be true to God's just nature is different than *changing* God's moral perspective.

70. See the detailed study by Pierre Dumoulin, "La Parabole de la Veuve de Ben Sira 35,11-24 à Luc 18,1-8," in *Treasures of Wisdom: Studies in Ben Sira and the Book of Wisdom* (Festschrift M. Gilbert; ed. N. Calduch-Benages and J. Vermeylen; Leuven: Leuven University Press, 1999), 169-79; note also Kenneth E. Bailey, *Through Peasant Eyes*, in *"Poet and Peasant" and "Through Peasant Eyes": A Literary-Cultural Approach to the Parables in Luke* (Grand Rapids: Eerdmans, 1983), 127-30; Bailey, *Jesus through Middle Eastern Eyes: Cultural Studies in the Gospels* (Downers Grove, Ill.: IVP Academic, 2008), 261-63.

He will not ignore the supplication of the orphan,
or the widow *(chēran)* when she pours out her complaint.
Do not the tears of the widow *(chēras)* run down her cheek
as she cries out against *(kataboēsis)* the one who causes them
to fall?
The one whose service is pleasing to the Lord will be accepted,
and his prayer will reach to the clouds.
The prayer *(proseuchē)* of the humble pierces the clouds,
and it will not rest until it reaches its goal;
it will not desist until the Most High responds
and does justice for the righteous *(dikaiois)*, and executes
(poiēsē) judgment.
Indeed, the Lord will not delay *(ou mē bradynē)*,
and will not be patient with them *(oude mē makrothymēsē
ep' autois)*[71]
until he crushes the loins of the unmerciful
and repays vengeance *(ekdikēsin)* on the nations;
until he destroys the multitude of the insolent,
and breaks the scepters of the unrighteous *(adikōn)*;
until he repays mortals according to their deeds,
and the works of all according to their thoughts;
until he judges the case of his people
and makes them rejoice in his mercy.

This text seems to offer the perfect counterpart to Jesus' parable and commentary. We have the same basic characters and plot — a wronged widow pleading her case before a staunchly impartial judge (cf. Sir 35:15). But there is a marked difference in setting: in Sirach the entire scene plays out in a *heavenly courtroom* where the widow's prayerful cries "reach to the clouds" and to the ears of the divine magistrate ("for the Lord is the judge"); there is no countervailing *earthly courtroom* scene, as in Jesus' parable, before a hardened secular judge. Without this this-worldly judicial complication, the Sirach drama unfolds without a hitch. Yes, there is hurtful earthly opposition to the widow (and the poor, the orphaned, the humble), provoking her stream of tearful cries to God against her persecutors; and yes, she may need to persist ("not rest," "not desist") in her praying "until the Most High responds." But respond God most assuredly will, and

71. Here I adjust the NRSV to conform to the Greek text. The NRSV follows the Hebrew in reading: "and *like a warrior* will not be patient."

not with any pokey pace: "the Lord will not delay *(ou mē bradynē)*, / and will not be patient with them *(oude mē makrothymēsē ep' autois)*" (35:22). Nothing slow or slack about this Lord. He will by no means delay/be patient (notice emphatic double negative *ou mē* in the parallel lines) in dealing with "them," which, in light of what follows, refers primarily to those "unmerciful," "insolent," and "unrighteous" vultures of widows and company (35:22b-23).[72] The Lord will hit the warpath to wreak retributive justice *(ekdikēsin)* on all, including nations, who oppress God's people. The Sirach story moves swiftly and decisively from the widow's plight and prayer to a grand apocalyptic vision of restored global order (35:22-26).

In broad strokes, the Lukan Jesus would concur with this glorious cosmic hope of God's sovereign, righteous reign. But in the midst of a colonized people, replete with disadvantaged widows, orphans, and poor peasants, and himself en route to a Roman cross in ill-fated Jerusalem, this Jesus Son of Man has more genuine empathy for the hard human situation than the aristocratic Jesus son of Sirach.[73] Thus Jesus thickens the plot with this thorny parable and its crusty widow. This widow is way beyond tears now: she's just plain mad, with nothing to lose. Her head is not remotely in Sirach's "clouds," but firmly in the trenches. She's not looking for world peace or cosmic justice; first, she herself must survive: "Grant *me* justice." And she's not trying to overthrow the Roman government, crusade for judicial reform, or even impeach this particular corrupt judge. She just wants her fair shake. She shamelessly threatens to shame this unjust official's "face" — no small consequence, as we have seen — but she calls down no fire from heaven on his head, and he receives no angelic smackdown. Overall, she's given up on speedy trials, quick fixes, magic bullets, and celestial thunderbolts and ultimately wins her case with her irrepressible will and wits. She takes matters into her own capable hands.[74]

Everything about this parable screams *delay* — in direct contrast to

72. Dumoulin, "La Parabole de la Veuve," 175-77.

73. Cf. Metzger, "God as F(r)iend?" 50-51: "Employing an optic of suffering and foregrounding intertexts in which God is portrayed unfavorably, I have argued that in Luke 11:5-13 and 18:1-8 Jesus acknowledges a negative experience of the deity among some of Roman Palestine's 'poor . . . captives . . . blind . . . [and] oppressed' (4:18-19)."

74. Cf. Stephen Curkpatrick, "A Parable Frame-up and Its Audacious Reframing," *New Testament Studies* 48 (2003): 31: "The widow of Luke's parable takes Yahweh's responsibility into her own hands. Like the prophets, she champions the cause of justice. . . . In Luke's parable, the widow does not wait for Yahweh to execute justice. She takes the issue into her own hands."

Sirach's point. And Jesus' commentary confirms this point and extends it to the practice of prayer, flipping Sirach's language on its head: "God *is* patient, slow-acting *(makrothymei)*" toward his "elect" *(eklektōn)* beloved yet besieged people who cry out to him day and night (Luke 18:7).[75] In Israel's wisdom tradition, Jesus is much closer to Job than Ben Sira.[76] No use denying or soft-pedaling it. *Delay* — including *divine* delay — is a lamentable conundrum of daily life for God's people. Yes, the just rule of God is dawning "today" in Jesus' liberating mission (cf. 4:18-21), but *not yet* with consummate brightness. Yes, the "kingdom of God *is* among you" as a sign of the full restoration to come, *but first,* the righteous, innocent Son of Man will be crucified and rejected even by his own kin in an unspeakable *travesty of justice* (17:21-25). The final "Day" of justice is postponed. By Luke's time, well after Jesus' resurrection, the delay problem has been exacerbated. A generation has passed with no culminating parousia, except the cataclysmic "coming" of Rome's armies in 70 C.E., dismantling the temple, destroying the city, and dispersing the inhabitants of Jerusalem. What in the world are God and the Son of Man waiting for? Sirach's hopes for divine vengeance *against* Israel's enemies remain dashed. By any account, this is a *lamentable* situation, lamentable *for an unreceptive Jerusalem,* as the Lukan Jesus poignantly realizes (19:41-44; 21:20-24; 23:27-31), but also, I suggest, lamentable *before an unresponsive God,* who puts off apocalyptic action.

To whatever extent God delayed redemption and allowed foreign demolition of Jerusalem — whether by Babylon in 587 B.C.E. or Rome in 70 C.E. — *because of* Israel's unfaithful leadership (it's their fault, then, not God's), it's hard to see how this would bring any great comfort or understanding to Israel's widows, orphans, and other poor population. They haven't *caused* the problem and have only suffered more because of it. They have a lot to cry about to God day and night. They should still cry in tenacious hope, Jesus insists, that God will one day, some day, suddenly intervene on their behalf. God remains firmly on their side, however the timetable unfolds. But in the meantime, theodicy also remains a struggle, requiring oppressed widows' persistent praying and working as long as it takes, with no illusions of quick and easy solutions.

---

75. Whereas Sirach speaks of the Lord's *not* being patient (dilatory) toward *unjust* persons ("them"), Luke refers positively to God's being patient (dilatory) with God's *chosen* people. See Dumoulin, "La Parabole de la Veuve," 176-77.

76. On Job as a key intertext, see Metzger, "God as F(r)iend?" 36-37, 47-50.

2. Feminist Challenge: Prayer as Weak Women's Work? So why bother with prayer at all at the end of day? Is it just, in Marxist terms, a pathetic opiate of oppressed people, dulling a bit of their pain and all of their nerve to act; or, in feminist terms, a ploy by male authorities to keep pious disadvantaged women weak and docile? "Let them pray all they want and see what that gets them; just keep them from nagging and shaking their fists at me, day after day," the unjust judge might well say. A praying widow who wears out her knees at home, synagogue, or temple is no threat to the judicial system. It's when she gets on her feet and opens her mouth in public that we have a problem. And some feminist scholars think Luke is a big part of that problem by forcing her on her knees; in other words, Luke's prayer-focused frame files down the sharp teeth of the parable and its widow protagonist to harmless nubs. Note the following suspicions from incisive critics:

Barbara Reid:
[I]t is important to recognize Luke's concern to tame this story of an unconventional woman. By adding v. 1, he recasts her in a docile and acceptable role — an example of one who prays incessantly, much like Anna in the temple (2:36-38). There is nothing threatening about a widow who prays all day long. Luke's redaction of this parable and the translations and interpretations of New Testament scholars through the ages have largely tamed and even trivialized a powerful portrait of a godly widow pursuing justice.[77]

Annette Merz:
[Luke's] new interpretation as a parable about prayer . . . involves a massive transposition of the image of the widow. In the parable, she overcomes the judge by her active conduct, which is motivated by the desire for justice. But the framework destroys these associations by its allegorical interpretation of the widow as an image of the chosen ones of God who cry out to him day and night. This portrait of a woman was felt to be scandalous, and it was toned down even before Luke wrote his Gospel. He carried the process further by his interpretation of the widow's behavior as the model of [praying without ceasing] . . . and by making [her] . . . only one of a number of figures who are modeled on the traditional image of the widow [like Anna].[78]

---

77. Reid, "Beyond Petty Pursuits," 293.
78. Merz, "Woman Who Fought Back," 84.

Wendy Cotter:
The [Lukan framing] commentaries try to move the widow back to a conventional role of a meek woman. . . . Thus the parable loses its burlesque of the court system and its particularly challenging revelation to the listener about the power for justice wielded by those who remain independent, refusing to conform to the dominating social codes so convenient to the elite. . . . [T]he feisty widow is recast as his helpless victim and recessed modestly in accord with society's conventions for the virtuous woman.[79]

Barbara Scheele:
It is striking Luke used a woman to deliver [his] message, a woman who does *not* sit around passively praying but takes herself bodily to confront the judge.[80]

I have also argued in this book and other studies that Luke is not altogether comfortable with vocal active women. But I also don't think he's on a rabid campaign to shut them up. He settles for a "mixed message" about women's proclamation and activism, trying to walk a tightrope between radical freedom and respectable behavior and sometimes tripping on it, if not plummeting off, in the process. At times, Luke does appear to employ his major prayer motif in the interest of shushing women prophets. I've been particularly struck by how the dynamic, vocal Mary of Nazareth drops off the ledge after Luke 2, to resurface *only* in Acts 1 with "certain women" "constantly devoting themselves *to prayer*" (Acts 1:14). Of course, the male apostles are also part of this early Christian prayer circle, but their leader, Peter, soon rises from his knees and has a lot to say as the church progresses. Mary, by contrast, is never seen or *heard from* again. Via the prophet Joel, Peter offers at Pentecost a remarkably inclusive vision of Spirit-inspired speech, in which "your sons and *your daughters,*" even "slaves, both men and *women,* . . . shall prophesy" (2:17-18), but we listen in vain for any actual sermons from women in the rest of Acts. Mary the mother of John Mark and Lydia the purple-dealer host and participate in *prayer groups* — and no doubt *lead* congregations in their homes! — but Luke never lets them preach (12:12-17; 16:13-15). The overall Lukan narrative leaves a yawning gap between vision and reality at the point of women's vocality.

79. Cotter, "Parable," 343.
80. Scheele, "Will She Find Faith?" 65.

But viewing prayer in Luke and Acts generally as a weak, tame endeavor and specifically as a means of keeping women in their private, dependent place fails to do justice to this vital spiritual activity. The common cleavage between so-called "contemplative" and "active" pursuits — too commonly based on the Martha and Mary vignette in Luke 10:38-42, in favor of the latter's "better," contemplative choice — doesn't hold, as we saw in chapter 5, not least because Martha's *doing* is also affirmed by Jesus and regarded, in Lukan terms, as wholly complementary with Mary's *hearing* (she's not in fact praying) the word. More to the point, however, prayer in Luke is by no means purely passive, pensive, and apolitical. Mary's Magnificat, as a song of praise, blends together prophecy, prayer, and psalm in a political tour de force (1:46-55).[81] Psalms are not just nice little comfort ditties. We know this about laments, but other types as well — like psalms of deliverance, victory, praise, and thanksgiving, à la Mary's — proclaim profound truth (prophecy) before God (prayer), God's people, and the world (politics).[82]

The widow Anna's sixty-plus years of incessant, 24/7 praying in the temple are scarcely to be viewed in Lukan or any biblical terms as a feeble waste of her life or calculated confinement of a dynamic prophetic woman in isolated space where she cannot threaten society and its prevailing structures. She's praying in the temple, not languishing in prison! Yes, she plays second fiddle to Simeon in Luke's prophetic drama: Simeon gets much more stage time and all the prophetic lines (2:25-35). One would wish to hear Anna's direct speech. But the concluding report that Anna, upon encountering the Christ child, "began to praise God and to speak about the child to all who were looking for the redemption of Jerusalem" (2:38) is not an innocent throwaway tag line. Anna's praise and prophecy are of a piece with her praying — and all focus on "the redemption of Jerusalem," a thoroughly justice-centered, political, eschatological, revolutionary concept, especially when the Holy City is under Herodian-Roman control. The Jerusalem temple structurally represents the citadel where God

---

81. Curkpatrick ("A Parable Frame-Up," 26-29) offers a detailed comparative analysis of the Magnificat as "an interpretative theme" for the parable of the widow and unjust judge in Luke 18:2-5. Unfortunately, however, he argues that Luke's immediate frame in 18:1, 6-7 "eclipses the parallel vision" between Mary's song and Jesus' story. While I grant certain tensions, I see overall continuity between spiritual and political elements of Luke's project grounded in prayer and praxis.

82. See Walter Brueggemann, *Israel's Praise: Doxology against Idolatry and Ideology* (Philadelphia: Fortress, 1988); William P. Brown, *Seeing the Psalms: A Theology of Metaphor* (Louisville: Westminster John Knox, 2002).

dwells and rules the earth, the throne where God sits and dispenses justice. It is a "house of prayer" dedicated to practicing and promoting God's just reign. Prayer spurs righteous action rather than substituting for it. And such action can turn fiery and indignant in the face of injustice, as Jesus' table-flipping tirade shows in his last week, when he demonstratively laments the devolution of the "house of prayer" into an oppressive "den of thieves" (19:45-46). Anna may not have toppled any furniture, but the political-redemptive tenor of Luke's birth narratives[83] strongly suggests that she was struggling day and night in prayer with God's faithfulness and justice, crying out for God's long-awaited — and overdue! — messianic liberation. Her praying works — not (solely) by providing her some inner peace and helping her muddle through a hard life — but chiefly by moving God to send the world-changing, right-making Messiah. Such victorious praying prompts powerful prophetic exclamation.

In terms of the active, this-worldly engagement of ordinary people's (not only prophets') everyday petitionary prayer, we need look no further than the model Lord's Prayer Jesus outlined for himself and all his followers. The focus on God's coming kingdom on earth, provision of daily bread, remission of personal and interpersonal debts, and protection from harmful trials could scarcely be more entwined with social, economic, political, and judicial realities in quotidian life (Luke 11:1-4).[84] While not a lament per se, it certainly acknowledges that circumstances of hunger, debt slavery, and exploitative trial-cases are antithetical to God's just rule and urgently need to be changed (the petition-verbs are boldly imperative). And the prayer assumes no quick panacea. It exemplifies a persisting practice "whenever you pray," reinforced by the ensuing parable featuring a friend who gets the bread he needs by brazenly and repeatedly beseeching his neighbor at an inconvenient hour (11:5-8). Finally — also connected with the related parable — the Lord's Prayer does not substitute for human action; indeed, it positively demands it: "for we ourselves forgive everyone indebted to us" (11:4). That is to say, *we ourselves* must *enact* this prayer as much as intone it. This prayer quintessentially reflects the char-

---

83. See Richard A. Horsely, *The Liberation of Christmas: The Infancy Narratives in Social Context* (New York: Crossroad, 1989), 1-38, 61-123; Marcus J. Borg and John Dominic Crossan, *The First Christmas: What the Gospels Really Teach about Jesus' Birth* (New York: HarperOne, 2007), 55-78.

84. See John Dominic Crossan, *The Greatest Prayer: Rediscovering the Message of the Lord's Prayer* (New York: HarperOne, 2010); Leonardo Boff, *The Lord's Prayer: The Prayer of Integral Liberation* (trans. Theodore Morrow; Maryknoll, N.Y.: Orbis, 1983).

acter of God's just reign that *we ourselves* must initiate in God's name with God's strength. So, in the dynamic spirit of the prayer, we move to release the captive and indebted and share our daily bread with one another, as the neighbor in the parable does.

As many have observed, Jesus' bread parable and teaching about prayer in Luke 11:1-13 offer more than a casual parallel with the widow parable and narrative in 18:1-8. What is often not noticed, however, is that the parallel strengthens, rather than weakens, the nexus between fervent supplicant prayer and determined human action toward the goal of bringing God's just reign on earth.[85] Lukan-style prayer is thoroughly in the trenches, not in the clouds. Thus, to use an old evangelical image, our widow, far from being toned-down and kid-gloved, emerges as a vibrant model of a *prayer warrior,* fighting with God — both in the sense of actively *arguing with* and *allying with* God and God's just cause — with all her might.

Outside of Luke, the prayer warrior image associated with widows finds its sharpest expression in the prayer of Judith, set during the formidable Assyrian crisis threatening the Jewish nation. Recalling the "burning zeal" of her ancestor Simeon, who avenged by sword the Shechemites' defilement of sister Dinah, Judith boldly petitions:

> O God, my God, hear me also, a widow. . . . Give to me, a widow, the strong hand to do what I plan. By the deceit of my lips strike down the [Assyrian] slave with the prince and the prince with his servant; crush their arrogance by the hand of a woman. . . . Please, please, God of my father, God of the heritage of Israel, Lord of heaven and earth, Creator of the waters, King of all creation, hear my prayer! Make my deceitful words bring wound and bruise on those who have planned cruel things against your covenant, and against your sacred house, and against Mount Zion, and against the house your children possess. (Jth 9:4, 9-10, 12-13)

Here is a widow woman (this identity is emphasized) using urgent, fervent prayer as a launch point for literal warfare against the Assyrian marauders, which she will spearhead by her smooth talk and sword-wielding hand in

---

85. Metzger's recent study ("God as F[r]iend?") is a notable exception. While I formulated my perspective independently of Metzger, I was happy to find his elaboration and confirmation. Note the concluding statement to his stimulating comparative analysis of the parables in Luke 11:5-13 and 18:1-8: "In this case, anger with God (or, more precisely, one's god-representation) would signal that something is systemically wrong in one's environment and may serve as a primary impetus for social change" (57).

God's name ("you are God, the God of all power and might, and . . . there is no other who protects the people of Israel but you alone!" [9:14]). Here, and in Judith's defeat of Holofernes that ensues, passionate prayer, savvy speech, and aggressive action perfectly coalesce in victory and deliverance.

Although the widow in Jesus' parable does not match Judith's martial-national heroism, she does mirror, on a judicial-personal level, Judith's effective speech and handiwork — as a widow — against an oppressive official. Likewise, though the Lukan widow does not herself pray, her framed association with prayer may be linked with Judith's praying in a way that bolsters, rather than undercuts, the widow's bold pursuit and attainment of justice. If the prayer warrior image doesn't quite work for Luke's widow, we may shift images from the militaristic theater to the athletic arena, which has proved amenable to feminist interests. The parable's widow typifies *wrestling* (a cousin of boxing) with God in prayer, wrestling in persistent petition and candid lament and not letting go until God blesses and equips the prayer-wrestler to face and fight one's unjust foe.[86]

Faithful Fighter: The Eschatology Factor

In this section, we further explore Luke's eschatological context in 17:20–18:8 surrounding the parable of the widow and unjust judge, with particular focus on the climactic verse: "I tell you, God will grant them justice suddenly *(en tachei)*. And yet, when the Son of Man comes, will he find faith/faithfulness *(tēn pistin)* on earth?" (18:8, my translation). We will extend our discussion of God's "sudden" manifestation of justice (18:8a), introduced above, and attempt to tie this in with the coming Son of Man's quest for "faith/faithfulness" (18:8b), which the widow marvelously embodies. Once again, as with the spirituality dimension, I see the related eschatological factor enhancing, rather than enervating, the widow's feisty fight for justice *on earth*.

1. Bringing Justice   Biblical-prophetic notions of justice are ineluctably entwined with eschatological judgment, often focalized on a final Day of Reckoning, the "Day of the Lord," when all will be held accountable and all will be put to rights. In the language of the Lukan Paul before the Athenian court: "[God] has fixed a day on which he will have the world judged

---

86. See the feminist-hermeneutical appropriation of Jacob's famous wrestling match in Phyllis Trible, *Texts of Terror: Literary-Feminist Readings of Biblical Narratives* (Philadelphia: Fortress, 1984), 4-5; I quote this passage with commentary in chapter 2.

(krinein) in righteousness *(dikaiosynē)* by a man whom he has appointed, and of this he has given assurance to all by raising him from the dead" (Acts 17:31). Of course, though Paul does not name him here before this Greek audience, the God-appointed "man" he has in mind is clearly the risen Jesus (cf. 17:18); in Jewish terms, he is more specifically identified with the apocalyptic "Son of Man," destined to vindicate God's suffering people, judge the world, and complete God's just reign on earth (cf. Dan 7:13-27). So do we just wait around helplessly until the Lord's Day arrives, whenever that will be, in our clueless state of not knowing "the times or periods that the Father has set by his own authority" (Acts 1:6)? By no means! In the interim, "[God] commands all people everywhere to repent" in advance of the Day of Judgment (17:30), thus prealigning ourselves with God's ultimate rule of justice. Further, we must "be alert at all times, praying [to] have the strength . . . to stand before the Son of Man" (Luke 21:36).[87] No passive sitting in the waiting room twiddling our thumbs. We must actively get on board with God's just cause, precisely as the parable's widow does. To be sure, she has nothing to repent of in terms of personal culpability, since she is the victim, not the perpetrator, of injustice. But she does set her mind and body to pursuing justice, to judging an unjust judge and setting him straight, to pumping and strengthening herself for full participation in God's just kingdom. In effect, then, she prepares the way for the Son of Man as his right-making agent.

But why then would the widow need God's or the Son of Man's help, when she's already done all the heavy lifting? She's taken care of herself, thank you very much. The new heavenly sheriff promising to ride into town and clean things up has been indefinitely delayed. So the widow deputizes herself and takes matters of justice into her own capable hands. Case closed. Does not any continued talk about eschatological salvation reduce her achievement and reinforce her helpless state requiring male (*Son* of Man) rescue of the damsel in distress?

Such assumptions, I would argue, while bubbling on the surface, ultimately rest on a shallow and truncated view of biblical eschatology and psychology. Biblical *eschatology* is process- and goal-oriented, tracking an inexorable *movement,* more than an isolated moment, of God in human history on planet earth, toward a full, climactic realization of God's restored righteous rule over all creation. It does not say: "To hell with this rotten world now until God one day zaps it into shape." Rather, it drops

---

87. Note again how prayer in Luke is associated with strong action.

regular hints — signs, foretastes — of final justice in the here and now, *both* through periodic divine interventions *and* through human cooperations with God's cause. It realistically admits and allows for a *struggle* toward justice that only the divine Creator-Redeemer can completely resolve, without, however, discounting the *formative* contributions that God's people make in that struggle along the way.

In terms of biblical *psychology*, God's people need to know that their efforts in forging justice matter and are not in vain, that their deep sense of vulnerability in an unjust world is met with divine sympathy and empowerment. Our widow's fight for justice is far from over. She's won this bout, but more struggle no doubt lies ahead; and it would not be surprising if this unscrupulous judge is already scheming for a rematch. For all the widow's laudable self-reliant success in the present case, she cannot permanently conquer the forces of injustice all by herself. Nor can any other person, male or female.[88] The hope of God's climactic just reign spurs and steels her — and all God's people — to keep fighting.

2. Coming Quickly   As for the problematic timing of the consummation of God's just purposes for the cosmos, we suggested above that the Lukan Jesus' promise of a "quick" resolution has to do more with the *sudden* (unexpected) and *sweeping* (unstinted) nature of God's climactic kingdom when it bursts into view than with its speedy, imminent arrival on history's timetable. We may now elaborate this perspective — based on two illuminating uses of the same *en tachei* phrase in Acts in contexts of prayer — to include occasional sudden signs or previews of God's deliverance, conjoined with rapid human response. First, at the eleventh hour on "the very night" he was about to be executed, the imprisoned Peter is suddenly awakened by an angel of the Lord and told to get up and out *"quickly" (en tachei)* (Acts 12:7). The whole time he was bound in jail, "the church *prayed fervently* to God for him" (12:5), but their pleas do not receive instantaneous response *until* God decides to act suddenly, which then prompts Peter to move swiftly. This virtual "exodus" and "resurrection" of Peter[89]

---

88. On "human beings' strange combination of competence with helplessness; our problematic relationship to helplessness, mortality, and finitude," see Martha Nussbaum, *Not for Profit: Why Democracy Needs the Humanities* (Princeton: Princeton University Press, 2010), 30-31.

89. See Robert C. Tannehill, *The Narrative Unity of Luke-Acts: A Literary Interpretation*, vol. 2: *The Acts of the Apostles* (Minneapolis: Fortress, 1990), 152-58; Robert W. Wall, "Successors to 'the Twelve' according to Acts 12:1-17," *Catholic Biblical Quarterly* 53 (1991): 370-93;

buoy a persecuted church to keep plugging along in the hope of "universal restoration" expected at Jesus' final appearing (cf. 3:19-21). But their struggle as God's messianic community in this present evil age is just beginning; Peter's great escape from Herod's prison does not encourage a frenzy of escapist, "rapture" fantasy.

Second and similarly, Paul describes a visionary encounter with the risen Jesus "while [Paul] was *praying* in the temple," during the tense period of his early Christian ministry in Jerusalem. In this "trance," Jesus exhorts Paul to "get out of Jerusalem *quickly (en tachei)*" to flee those who would violently resist his testimony. But far from going into a covert witness protection program, Paul is suddenly sent to proclaim the gospel "to the Gentiles" (Acts 22:17-21), where he has enormous success but hardly a smooth ride. Indeed, he presently recounts this past visionary experience to an angry Jewish mob falsely accusing him of bringing a Gentile into the sacred precincts of the Jerusalem temple (Acts 21:27–22:29). From this point to the end of Acts, Paul will be held in Roman custody and will have to endure a battery of legal trials and hearings for disturbing the peace. So we see that, from the early days of his Christian call and commission, Paul's perilous mission combines (1) prayer, (2) intervention from the risen Christ, (3) his own decisive rapid response, *and* (4) continued trials and hardships. As with Peter and the early church overall, dramatic signs of eschatological salvation suddenly break through now and then, spurring Paul and the expanding church to swift action that propels them into new arenas of opportunity and hostility.

"I tell you: God will suddenly *(en tachei)* grant justice to his chosen ones who cry to him day and night" (Luke 18:8, my translation). Yes, God will one day, suddenly — when many are preoccupied with unjust business as usual — usher in the final age of righteous judgment. *But* in the meantime, God also suddenly breaks in now and then to post confirming signs of this glorious hope. *And also* in the meantime, God's promise of a sudden future explosion of justice is stoked by swift, responsive movement and witness on the part of God's human agents. Though Jesus' immediate commentary after the parable of the widow stresses *God's* acting *en tachei* to bring final justice, the wider Lukan narrative also allows us to appreciate the *widow's* working *en tachei* — rapidly, resolutely, decisively, as well as persistently — to obtain a measure of interim justice in a callous world.

---

and F. Scott Spencer, *Journeying through Acts: A Literary-Cultural Reading* (Peabody, Mass.: Hendrickson, 2004), 135-38.

3. Finding Faith　This continued focus on the widow's example is sharpened by Jesus' final concern about whether the Son of Man "will find faith on earth" when he appears. More fully, the "faith" *(pistis)* issue, as recent studies of this key concept have stressed, involves responses of both deep attitudinal *reliance/dependence* on God's redemptive love, mercy, and power and determined active *loyalty/commitment* to God's ways, or alternatively: *trusting* and *obeying, believing* and *being faithful.* It is a very real concern in Jesus' mind whether the Son of Man will find such faith/ fullness; it is not a given that such a disposition will abound, even among Jesus' followers. Even though they should be inspired by the hope of God's sudden manifestations of justice, both intermittently in this evil epoch and consummately in the coming age of God's rule, *yet (plēn* [18:8b]) Jesus seriously worries whether his disciples will come through; even with his closest apostle, Peter, Jesus must pray that "[his] own faith may not fail" (22:32). Apart from the constant onslaughts of Satan and his minions (cf. 22:31), there is that subtler, but no less diabolical, lulling into the usual business of consuming and commercializing, without due alertness to the impending visitation of God's judgment through the Son of Man. These are the casual and callous days of Noah and Lot, which Jesus so clearly associates with "this generation" and the "days of the Son of Man" in the passage immediately preceding the parable of the widow (17:20-32).

　　Will the Son of Man in fact find *(eurēsei)* any faith/fullness in these days? Jesus' wistful plea eerily evokes Abraham's desperate bargaining with God over Sodom's judgment in the days of Lot: "Suppose fifty, forty-five . . . ten righteous/just *(dikaioi)* persons *are found (eurethōsin)* there — will you still judge and destroy the city?" (cf. Gen 18:23-33). But of course, not even a small quota of righteous ones *is* found; it's even pushing it to suggest that Lot's spared family qualifies as righteous. The "days of Lot" — paradigmatic of the present days preceding the Son of Man's coming — are days conspicuous by their dearth of faith/fullness on earth. Will any faithful one be found? Will anyone stand out from an unjust crowd? Will anyone stand up in an unjust world for the cause of justice? Will anyone — here's the critical tie-in — *follow the righteous lead of the justice-seeking widow in the parable?* She emerges at the climax of Jesus' commentary as *the* model of faith/fullness in advance of the Son of Man's appearing, punctuated by the unusual definite article before the accusative (objective) case ("Will the Son of Man find *the* faith/faithful one [*tēn pistin*] on earth?"),[90] with the happy coinci-

---

90. Cf. Green, *The Gospel of Luke,* 637: "[A]ccording to the Greek text of v. 8, Jesus'

dence that "faith/fullness" also happens to be a feminine term in Greek. The parable's widow then supremely typifies that rare and special faith God seeks, which, driven by the hope of God's ultimate reign of justice, moves with brisk dispatch and bold determination to bring God's justice on earth. This is no clueless, helpless woman mired in the daily grind and overwhelmed by the grit and grime of business as usual. This woman tackles injustice head-on as an agent of God's kingdom. And she's no secret agent: she marches on city hall, as it were, publicly challenging the unjust local regime. Luke's narrative — parable plus commentary — only cements her sterling performance on center stage.

4. Glancing Back Again at Lot's Wife   Finally, the connection with Lot's days invites a concluding comparison with Lot's wife. Earlier we noted the similar plights of Lot's wife and the parable's widow in terms of financial and familial loss, amid a stark contrast in the justifiability of their misfortunes: the former denizen of Sodom receiving a fair sentence, given the unrighteous character of her city; the latter inhabitant of "a certain city" receiving unjust treatment from familial and judicial authorities. We may now also stress the incongruence of these distressed women's responses. Mercifully dragged away from her unjust environment against her will (and that of husband Lot's, too — he doesn't want to leave any more than she does), she looks back longingly and becomes petrified in her tracks, permanently encased in the bitter, corrosive salt of judgment. While we may sympathize with her family and community solidarity, which does not necessarily entail active engagement in evil deeds, we nonetheless are warned by Jesus to "remember" her passive complicity in Sodom's fate and failure to "get out quickly" and forge ahead on God's path of justice. Conversely, the parable's widow decisively presses with all her might against

---

question is not concerned with 'faith' (in general) but with '*the* faith' — that is, that manner of faith demonstrated by the widow in the antecedent parable" (emphasis in original); Metzger, "God as F(r)iend?" 50 n. 60. David R. Catchpole ("The Son of Man's Search for Faith [Luke XVIII 8b]," *Novum Testamentum* 19 [1973]: 81-104) discusses various semantic options for "faith" *(pistis)* in Luke 18:8 and argues for a meaning that coheres with the parable of the widow (he regards 18:2-8 as a literary unity in both Luke's source and redaction). Unfortunately, however, Catchpole's use of male generic language obscures the widow's example: "Hence, it [*pistis*] must stand for the fundamental and continuing attitude required of *man* within the relationship with God in question" (103). "It [God's judgment] insistently recalls *men* to that faith for which the Son of man will above all be concerned when he comes" (104 [emphasis added]).

the city's unjust forces arrayed against her, refusing simply to roll with the punches, opting instead to deliver what blows she can to the dominant system. And in the process she forges her own future in alliance with God's eschatological aims and shakes out a mighty measure of God's savory, preservative salt of justice. This is the true "salty" woman, grittily and savvily exhibiting a fervent faith/fullness the Son of Man will rejoice to find advancing God's righteous reign on earth.

8. A Capable Woman, Who Can Find?
We Have Found Some in Luke!

"A capable wife who can find?" So begins the famous alphabetic-acrostic epilogue to the book of Proverbs in 31:10-31, describing the ideal woman who dazzles with the range of her manufacturing, mercantile, domestic, and didactic capabilities. The poet has obviously "found" such a woman in his imagination, but we may well question the grounding of this portrait in social reality. The husband's dependence on her for his welfare and honor in the community (31:11-12, 23) is hard to fathom in ancient Israelite society.[1] As a feminine image for divine Wisdom, however, mirroring earlier projections in Proverbs 1–9, the "capable wife/woman" makes more sense: the socioeconomic success of young men depends on embracing and emulating Woman Wisdom (and eschewing Femme Folly), whose value "is far more precious than jewels" (31:10; cf. 3:13-16; 8:11). Still, for all this metaphorical appropriation and political idealization of capable womanhood, "it is difficult," as Claudia Camp comments, "to read Proverbs' paean to the power of wisdom personified as woman (chs. 1–9) and of woman as the ideal representative of wisdom (ch. 31) without imagining some related social reality at their base."[2]

Do we expect to find in real life the Superwoman dynamo of Proverbs 31, who does everything but leap tall buildings in a single bound? Not typically, if ever, and it scarcely helps women's flourishing by holding them up

---

1. See Kathleen M. O'Connor, *The Wisdom Literature* (Collegeville, Minn.: Liturgical Press, 1990), 77-78.

2. Claudia V. Camp, "Woman Wisdom," in *Women in Scripture: A Dictionary of Named and Unnamed Women in the Hebrew Bible, the Apocryphal/Deuterocanonical Books, and the New Testament* (gen. ed. Carol Meyers; Grand Rapids: Eerdmans, 2001), 550; cf. Carol Fontaine, "Wife," in *Women in Scripture* (ed. Meyers), 303-4.

to impossible, do-it-all standards. But within Israel's wisdom tradition, Proverbs does at least mitigate the misogynistic cynicism of Qoheleth.[3] Frustrated and dubious about the prospects of ever discovering the "deep, very deep" insights of wisdom ("Who can find it out?"), Qoheleth is quite certain that women provide no help at all. What he has "found" is that "the woman who is a trap, whose heart is snares and nets, whose hands are fetters," is "more bitter than death." Moreover, "one man [of wisdom] among a thousand I found, but a woman among all these I have not found" (Eccl 7:23-28). While agreeing with the rarity of finding pure woman-wisdom gold, the poem in Proverbs 31 still values the quest and suggests better odds of fulfillment.

If we are fortunate enough to find that priceless pearl of a "capable woman," what will she be like? The Hebrew profile of a "capable *(hayil)* woman" suggests a "strong, valiant, heroic" woman, matching qualities usually associated with *men* of valor in military and monarchic settings.[4] The Greek OT renders the phrase as *gynē andreia* — "a manly/virile woman" (Prov 12:4; 31:10). Wolters thinks that the "Song of the Valiant Woman" adapted a hymnic tradition originally dedicated to heroic warriors.[5] In its present setting in Proverbs, it immediately follows a maternal exhortation to King Lemuel, advising him not to succumb to women who would sap his capability or "strength" *(hayil)!* (31:3). So *hayil/andreia* seems to be a quintessential characteristic of male power that exceptional women might share when they are acting like honorable mighty men (think Deborah) and not like devious emasculating women (think Delilah)!

Be that as it may, the particular qualities of the capable woman delineated in Proverbs 31 are manifestly *not* militaristic or antagonistic to men, but rather beneficent, nurturing, and altogether humane: she "does [her husband] good, and not harm" (31:12), works hard and smart to provide

---

3. See Raymond C. van Leeuwen, "The Book of Proverbs: Introduction, Commentary, and Reflections," in *The New Interpreter's Bible*, vol. 5 (ed. Leander E. Keck et al.; Nashville: Abingdon, 1997), 260.

4. E.g., Josh 1:14; 6:2; 8:3; Judg 3:29; 6:12; 11:1 (Jephthah); 1 Sam 9:2 (Saul); 10:26; 16:18 (David); 1 Kings 11:28 (Jeroboam); 2 Kings 5:1 (Naaman). The term is also applied to a royal woman in the case of the queen of Sheba, though not to her character as much as the great wealth and "very large retinue" *(hayil kabēd)* at her disposal (1 Kings 10:2).

5. Al Wolters, "Proverbs XXXI 10-31 as Heroic Hymn: A Form-Critical Analysis," *Vetus Testamentum* 38 (1988): 446-57; cf. Richard J. Clifford, *Proverbs: A Commentary* (Louisville: Westminster John Knox, 1999), 273.

food for her family, manages the affairs of a large household, "opens her hand to the poor, / and reaches out her hands to the needy" (31:20), teaches the ways of wisdom, promotes the happiness of others, and embraces solid God-fearing values over superficial preoccupations with "charm" and "beauty" (31:30).[6] Such an ideal model focused on capabilities of character and virtue in everyday communal life finds a "real" exemplar, surprisingly enough, in Ruth the Moabite, whose story *immediately follows* Proverbs 31 in the Hebrew Bible.[7] Though groggy, a bit hung over, and more than a little startled by Ruth's sudden appearance at the threshing floor, Boaz pulls it together to sum up aptly Ruth's reputation: "All the assembly of my people know that you are a *worthy woman ('ēšet hayil)*" (Ruth 3:11 [NRSV]; "virtuous woman" [KJV]; "woman of excellence" [NASB]; "woman of noble character" [NIV]).[8]

This brief assessment of the OT's image of a capable woman, concerned with matters of character (who she is) and function (what she does), leads us back to the much broader contemporary Capabilities Approach advanced by Martha Nussbaum, with a strong humanistic orientation applied equally to all women and men — and by no means limiting women to the "good wife" role of Proverbs 31 (but also affirming women's full exercise of their capabilities as wives and mothers, if they so choose). She would like to see us finding capable women as the rule rather than exception in all societies. Her list of ten universal, central capabilities — under the rubrics of (1) life, (2) bodily health, (3) bodily integrity, (4) senses, imagination, and thought, (5) emotions, (6) practical reason, (7) affiliation, (8) other species, (9) play, and (10) control over one's environment — provides a useful template for summarizing and evaluating the depictions of women in Luke explored in this book. I included Nussbaum's descriptions of the first seven capabilities in my discussion of Jesus' mother Mary

6. Cf. Wolters, "Proverbs XXXI 10-31," 456-57: "On an overt and explicit level, the Song of the Valiant Woman constitutes a critique of the literature in praise of women which was prevalent in the Ancient Near East. As a distinct tradition, this literature was overwhelmingly preoccupied with the physical charms of women from an erotic point of view — in a word, their sex appeal. Against the ideal of feminine perfection reflected in this widespread erotic poetry, which was cultivated in the context of royal courts and harems, the acrostic poem glorified the active good works of a woman in the ordinary affairs of community, family — good works which for all their earthliness are rooted in the fear of the Lord."

7. Van Leeuwen, "The Book of Proverbs," 260.

8. Prov 12:4, 31:10, and Ruth 3:11 are the only places in the Hebrew Bible where *'ēšet hayil* appears. While Ruth exemplifies the character of a "worthy woman," she also uses her charm and beauty to good effect on the threshing floor.

in chapter 3 and will not repeat them fully here. Here I attempt to relate various characteristics of the women we've examined to all ten of Nussbaum's categories, though I acknowledge that some will prove more pertinent than others. I will also draw at various points on Pinar Uyan-Semerci's illuminating application of Nussbaum's capabilities list to the situation of poor, migrant Muslim women in the squatter settlements *(gecekondus)* of contemporary Istanbul, Turkey.[9] The social codes and values of these women in a traditional, Middle Eastern community resonate with those of many (though not all) women in ancient biblical eastern Mediterranean culture.

As for the women of Luke, while they are not fully "liberated" in the way modern feminists would advocate (Luke retains many kyriarchal attitudes of his milieu), they still prove themselves to be remarkably "capable women of purpose and persistence" (the subtitle of this book). As the diligent woman in one of Jesus' parables finds her lost coin, and as the determined widow in another parable models an affirmative answer to Jesus' question, "Will the Son of Man find faithful ones [like this widow] on earth?" (cf. Luke 18:8), I suggest an optimistic reply to the sage's question, "A capable [woman] who can find?" (Prov 31:10): to an encouraging degree, we have searched and found several — alongside the sweeper woman and savvy widow — in the narrative of Luke's Gospel!

1. Life

Nussbaum envisions this capability in terms of one's opportunity to complete a full life span, unimpeded by premature death or catastrophic debili-

---

9. Pinar Uyan-Semerci, "A Relational Account of Nussbaum's List of Capabilities," *Journal of Human Development* 8 (2007): 203-21. The study is based on interviews with twenty-two women from one *gecekondu* community, known as Ihlamurkuyu-Umraniye, and on two diaries by Nalan Turkeli. As the title of her article indicates, Uyan-Semerci's approach focuses on the "relational" dimensions of human capabilities, appropriate to these Middle Eastern women's communal-cultural identities and self-understandings (also common attitudes in the biblical world): "Particularly for women who live in poverty, one discovers that they do not see themselves as separate individuals from their families. They try to develop their own capabilities and their families' capabilities to get adequate nutrition, safe and clean water, better medical services, and education" (217). This perspective balances Nussbaum's primary attention to individual rights, autonomous agency, and "each person as an end." However, Nussbaum also remains keenly attuned to human beings' integral involvement in familial, social, and political networks.

ties that would render life "not worth living."[10] Among the women in Luke we discussed, only the life of Lot's wife was tragically cut short. Of course, from Luke's perspective her death would have been prevented if she had heeded the Lord's warning not to look back on her smoldering city. Ironically, as Jesus avers, only by "losing" her material-political basis of security in Sodom could Lot's wife "save" her life (Luke 17:33). Jesus' paradoxical-theological perspective anchored in the coming of God's kingdom clearly pushes beyond Nussbaum's nonreligious — though not antireligious — approach.[11] Moreover, as we mustered some sympathy for Lot's wife in her deep attachments to lost family and friends left behind, Nussbaum would no doubt raise questions about all the denizens of Sodom excepting Lot's nuclear family, including myriad innocent women and children, prematurely incapacitated — indeed, incinerated — by the holocaust. The plea of Abraham to God — "Will you indeed sweep away the righteous with the wicked?" (Gen 18:23) — still haunts us, though Luke does not wrestle with it in his brief appeal to "remember Lot's wife."

However, while Lot's wife does not score high on the "life" capability scale, other women in Luke fare much better. In fact, the only female character who dies in the narrative — Jairus's twelve-year-old daughter — is resuscitated by Jesus and restored to full capability at this crucial, (re)productive period in her life (Luke 8:40-42, 49-56).[12] The widow at Zarephath comes right to the brink of death, only to be saved, nourished, and made capable by the prophet Elijah of living a full and fulfilling life (though neither 1 Kings nor Luke completes her story). Elizabeth and Anna both live to ripe old ages, though not without complications: the former's barrenness and the latter's widowhood. But in each case, life still blossoms: Elizabeth's capability to bear life is miraculously provided in her golden years, and she also discovers a dynamic prophetic capacity; after Anna's husband's death, she flourishes in an eighty-year prophetic "career" in the temple precincts.

---

10. Nussbaum, *Creating Capabilities: The Human Development Approach* (Cambridge: Harvard University Press, Belknap Press, 2011), 33.

11. On Nussbaum's staunch support for freedom of religion and its connection with women's rights in a global context, see *Sex and Social Justice* (Oxford: Oxford University Press, 1999), 81-117; *Women and Human Development: The Capabilities Approach* (Cambridge: Cambridge University Press, 2000), 167-239; *Liberty of Conscience: In Defense of America's Tradition of Religious Equality* (New York: Basic Books, 2008).

12. However, in apocalyptic contexts, Jesus does warn of the impending suffering and death that will befall some women (as well as men). See Luke 17:35 (a woman grinding at the mill "taken/left"); 23:28-30 ("daughters of Jerusalem" facing destruction of the city).

Simeon's ominous forecast of Mary's sword-piercing destiny does not on the surface bode well for a long, satisfying life. But as we contended in chapter 3, this prophecy does not signal the physical cutting off of Mary's life, but rather her psychical (involving bodily, mental, and emotional capacities) cutting *through* the thicket of God's mysterious ways in a darkened, divisive world. In any case, whatever her pain and suffering, linked with the consummate pain and suffering of her son Jesus, Mary by no means concludes that life is "not worth living." Quite the contrary, Mary's Magnificat resounds from the start of Luke's Gospel as the glorious exclamation of God's uplifting, liberating, life-affirming purposes for humanity, especially those whose capabilities have been tamped down by oppressive forces.

2. Bodily Health

Closely linked with the potential for full human life, this capability focuses on basic dimensions of bodily well-being, including adequate nourishment, protective shelter, and reproductive health. Uyan-Semerci's fieldwork among the *gecekondu* women in Istanbul uncovered unrelenting struggles with malnutrition, unhealthy housing conditions, miscarriages, and a variety of incapacitating diseases compounded by inadequate medical care as "facts of daily life."[13]

While Luke is deeply concerned about hunger and other poverty-related problems in Roman Palestinian society, the women in his Gospel fare reasonably well. When deficiencies are exposed, Luke's God and Christ often intervene to restore bodily capabilities. Jesus' mother Mary may occupy a poor, "lowly" position in her world, but we have no indication that she herself was on the edge of starvation or homelessness; and rather than lamenting the condition of the destitute, she rejoices that God "has filled the hungry with good things" (Luke 1:53). She can't afford the Bethlehem Ritz, but a modest, crowded lodging near the household animals (kept indoors at night), with feed trough ready-to-hand as a makeshift crib, serves as a cozy, decent-enough place for giving birth to Jesus.[14] And the concep-

---

13. Uyan-Semerci, "A Relational Account," 206-7.

14. Popular legends of Jesus' birth in a cold, lonely outside stable or cave go beyond Luke's account. See Kenneth E. Bailey, *Jesus through Middle Eastern Eyes: Cultural Studies in the Gospels* (Downers Grove, Ill.: IVP Academic, 2008), 25-47. Whatever the comfort level of the lodgings, there may still be a thematic connection between Jesus' improvised birthplace in

tions, pregnancies, and deliveries of John and Jesus to Elizabeth and Mary, respectively, are attended throughout by joy and blessing. No miscarriages, excessive hardships (beyond Mary's trek to Bethlehem), or complications that we know of, and both sons "grow and become strong" under their parents' care and God's favor (cf. 1:80; 2:40, 52). Of course, Elizabeth's maternity reverses a lifetime of "disgraceful" incapability to bear children (1:25).[15] Both cases are also atypical in their miraculous elements, but as we have seen, these do not completely overshadow the natural, bodily means of reproduction. Elizabeth and Mary both conceive in their wombs, carry their fetuses to full terms, and deliver through normal processes. Divine power works in, with, and through human female capabilities. Almighty God becomes incarnate in a woman's capable body.

Though homes *(oikoi)* are often places of family conflict in Luke, most women at least have homes to live in or stay in, as we see with Mary, Elizabeth, Martha and Mary, and the searching woman in the parable sweeping *her* house. Joanna and Mary Magdalene might venture out on the road with Jesus, but they leave their homes voluntarily (they're not evicted) for a period of time, and as women of means, probably return to fairly cushy residences when they wish (Joanna may have a nice suite in Herod's palace, assuming she remains congenial with husband Chuza). They did suffer from some bodily maladies (quite serious, it seems, in Mary Magdalene's case), but Jesus' ministry of *restoring their physical capabilities* serves as a major motivation for their following Jesus (8:2).

The state of vulnerable widows' bodily health capabilities remains precarious in Luke, but by no means hopeless. Unscrupulous officials prowl about scheming to "devour widows' houses" and extort their last pennies. But God, God's prophets, and God's house (sometimes) nurture widows and enable their surviving and functioning, as evidenced in the temple's supporting the widow-prophet Anna, Elijah's feeding the widow at Zarephath, and Jesus' honoring the charitable widow at the temple treasury (though he doesn't help her or clarify how she's going to survive now with no money). Finally, we mustn't forget the indomitable widow in Jesus' parable who, in the face of economic exploitation and judicial corrup-

---

limited space and his itinerant ministry where he "has nowhere to lay his head" (9:58); see Raymond E. Brown, *The Birth of the Messiah: A Commentary on the Infancy Narratives in the Gospels of Matthew and Luke* (2nd ed.; New Haven: Yale University Press, 1993), 418-20, 669-71.

15. The related stories of healing the woman with the chronic (vaginal?) bleeding disorder and raising Jairus's pubescent twelve-year-old daughter from death (8:40-56) may also imply restored reproductive capabilities.

tion, proves quite capable of securing justice for herself, with or without God's aid.

3. Bodily Integrity

Bodily facility stresses freedom of secure movement from place to place. Applied to women, it particularly advocates protection from physical violence, both public and domestic, and free exercise of choice in reproductive matters. Uyan-Semerci's study reveals the severe limits of this capability among the Turkish *gecekondu* women. Apart from their discomfort with moving about the city of Istanbul because of financial restraints (transportation can be expensive) and communication limits (they lack basic literacy), their movements are closely monitored within their own households. Some reported: "'Getting permission from the husband' or 'to move in such a way that you do not make a noise so that the mother-in-law does not oppose' were considered as 'freedom.'" Overall, these women did not regard their bodies as their own, but rather as extensions of their husbands' bodies and exhibits of his and his male relatives' reputations: "The woman's body . . . represented the honour of her family. Fathers, brothers, husbands and the families of the husbands, even the people from the same or close villages, were all responsible for safeguarding the goodies of their daughter, brides, wives."[16]

Honor-shame codes certainly permeated Luke's first-century world and could serve to define and confine "a woman's place" in relation to the dominant men in her life, though not as narrowly or universally as some studies suggest, as if ancient women were literally shackled to certain quarters (think ankle monitors in modern terms for those under house arrest).[17] Then as now, women had to be careful about where they roamed and conscientious of social and safety implications, but they still had things to do and places to go in the normal course of life. In any case, without necessarily judging this as particularly radical for Luke's day, the women in his Gospel display considerable mobility (movement across space) and motility (gestural freedom within space). Mary of Nazareth

16. Uyan-Semerci, "A Relational Account," 207-8.

17. For a balanced and nuanced discussion of the varied applications of honor-shame codes to women in the ancient Mediterranean world, see Carolyn Osiek, Margaret Y. Mac-Donald, and Janet H. Tulloch, *A Woman's Place: House Churches in Earliest Christianity* (Minneapolis: Fortress, 2006), 7-9.

spends a good part of her pregnancy away from home, traveling both on her own to cousin Elizabeth's hill-country house and with husband Joseph to Bethlehem for the census registration. After Jesus' birth, she goes to Jerusalem for purification/dedication rites and Passover festivals. Her story in Luke 1–2 largely plays out in a journey setting, which will characterize much of Luke's two-volume narrative. The Lukan drama, for women as well as men, is plotted on the road. Unlike the other Gospels, Luke introduces many journeywomen — Mary Magdalene, Joanna, Susanna and company — with Jesus and the twelve male disciples early in the story (Luke 8:1-3), though these women are quickly shouldered off the main highway until the end of the journey. Among the three OT women Luke features, the queen of the South enjoys maximum mobility, traveling in style from the "ends of the earth" to Solomon's court. Lot's wife provides a notable counterportrait, frozen in her salty tracks on the way out of town. But the whole point of the story is that she *should have kept moving ahead*, with no stopping or looking back.

As for women's motility within space, the sweeper woman in the lost coin parable and the hostess Martha both move about freely and busily in their homes, without restraints from any paterfamilias. And upon finding the missing coin, the woman calls her women "friends and neighbors" over, perhaps to a shared courtyard, for a big celebration (Luke 15:9). Of course, both the sweeper woman and Martha employ their bodies in conventional domestic tasks, and Jesus approves of Mary's quiescent, sedentary posture in the face of Martha's protest. But as we have seen, Jesus also affirms, and in other situations emulates, Martha's hospitality and "much service," though he cautions her — out of care for her — against worry over and wearing herself out with her demanding work. He doesn't pick up a towel, basin, or apron to help her this time, but neither does he insist on being served. Jesus also features another strong, motile female protagonist in another parable, this time set in public judicial space. In addition to getting herself to the courtroom, once she's there, a savvy widow makes the most of her chance to secure justice against an oppressor, even before a notoriously callous judge. She punctuates her forceful plea with persuasive physicality. She might "punch like a girl," but literally or figuratively, it packs enough wallop to win the case against daunting odds.

Finally, the issue of reproductive choice came to the fore in our study of the Virgin Mary in chapter 3. While consistent with the biblical view of the primacy of God's sovereign choice and the privilege (and responsibility) of being fruitful and multiplying offspring, Mary's acceptance of her womb's "overshadowing" by God's "wild child" Spirit to conceive Jesus' human life is not portrayed as a passive, dispassionate resignation to the inevitable. Quite the contrary, Mary actively and repeatedly probes and ponders this reproductive use of her body, even by — or perhaps especially by — divine force and fiat. She proves herself to be a dynamically engaged creative partner with God. She chooses to embrace God's choice with all her heart, mind — and body.

4. Senses, Imagination, and Thought

This capability involves the full development and use of various cognitive talents and skills to produce creative works "of one's own choice, religious, literary, musical, and so forth." Critical to such intellectual and artistic pursuits are broad-based education in the humanities and sciences, protection of rights to free expression and religious exercise, and the ability "to have pleasurable experiences and to avoid nonbeneficial pain."[18] And we should recall that Nussbaum's scheme entitles *all persons* to such opportunities. Such a universal vision remains hard enough to achieve in modern democratic societies, much less ancient and contemporary traditional societies.

Most of the poor Muslim women in the Istanbul ghetto interviewed by Uyan-Semerci lacked basic literacy, and only one had graduated from high school. To their credit, some had availed themselves of adult classes in the community, but given their marginal social and economic conditions, it was virtually impossible for them to acquire an "adequate education." Their dream was to enable their children to go to school and eventually secure decent employment. To this end, *gecekondu* women primarily exercise their creative capabilities in domestic care of their children: feeding, clothing, cleaning, and other "housework." Their artistic (artisan) productions wind up on their children's plates and backs, though some handiwork (knitting, lacework) might serve more decorative functions. Though recognizing their limitations for what we might call their own personal growth, these women by no means resent their maternal duties. Quite the contrary, childbearing and child raising constitute their primary reasons for being, and "children continued to be their 'joy of life.'"[19]

As for the opportunity to think through religious issues and follow the

18. Nussbaum, *Creating Capabilities*, 33.
19. Uyan-Semerci, "A Relational Account," 209-10.

dictates of one's conscience, wherever they may lead, such freedom is in fact *unthinkable* for these Turkish women. They were born into their Muslim faith; it was simply part of the air they breathed and they never questioned it. (Of course, this religious determinism, based on familial-national heritage and environment, shapes the vast majority of the world's population.) Likewise, lamenting their harsh life situations as a religious problem was out of the question, lest they "offend Allah," whose will remains paramount and permanent.[20] We thus confront that common paradox of religion as both comfort and constraint: in this case, Islam contributes both to sustaining the impoverished Muslim women and to keeping them in their places (Judaism and Christianity have no right to smugness at this point). Nussbaum maintains *both* a passionate advocacy "for the intrinsic value of religious capabilities and of religious women and men as choosers of a way of life (a basic commitment of political liberalism)" *and* a critical concern for "the full range of the human capabilities that are sometimes at risk for women in traditional-religious cultures."[21] Religion as both boon (value) and bane (risk) — particularly for those in traditional societies with limited religious choice — is a precarious tightrope to walk, too tight in Uyan-Semerci's opinion, and in need of further reflection in assessing and promoting the political capabilities of women like those in the squatter settlements of Istanbul.[22]

Luke says nothing about the educational pedigrees of women. The illiteracy of most people in the ancient Greco-Roman world suggests this would be the case for most women in Luke's narrative. The young Jesus, as we have seen, is touted for his growth in wisdom (Luke 2:40, 52), especially on display in his discussion with the temple scholars. But this features more his God-given wisdom than his formal education (of which Luke says nothing), and Mary is more peeved about than proud of his precocity on this occasion. Luke's second volume commends Paul's advanced training in Judaism and knowledge of Greek language and rhetoric (Acts 21:37-40; 22:3; 26:4-5), but also admits the "uneducated and ordinary" backgrounds of Peter and John (4:13). In any case, as with Peter and John, so with certain women, their apparent lack of institutional schooling and even literacy does not entail a lack of thoughtfulness or imagination.

---

20. Uyan-Semerci, "A Relational Account," 210-11.
21. Nussbaum, *Women and Human Development: The Capabilities Approach* (Cambridge: Cambridge University Press, 2000), 188; cf. 167-240.
22. Uyan-Semerci, "A Relational Account," 219 n. 13.

Jesus' mother Mary provides the banner example, especially with her majestic blend of sense, thought, and imagination in the Magnificat. We can debate on literary and historical grounds how much of this hymn can be attributed to Luke (it does fit his style) or to a source tracing back to Mary/Elizabeth, but either way, Luke's Gospel places the hymn on Mary's inspired lips and thus presents her as a remarkably capable young woman in what we might call the creative religious arts. As for her exercise of religious freedom, Mary is thoroughly embedded in her native Jewish faith and practice, and we have no reason to think she ever considered any other option. Yet her religion is far from a rigid program she follows robotically. Her repeated pondering and probing, from Gabriel's annunciation throughout Luke 1–2, demonstrate considerable freedom and deliberation *within* her religious heritage. Her Magnificat again crystallizes this creative potential, as she rejoices in God's past mercies to "his servant Israel," affirms God's present choice of her for "blessed" purposes (and not only for her, but for all lowly people like her), and envisions a future cascade of God's redemptive actions "from generation to generation" (1:50; cf. 1:46-55). Here we find a woman reveling in the expansive liberty of God's grace. Like the *gecekondu* women, Mary's experience is rooted in her maternal identity and function. But her vision stretches far beyond their immediate preoccupations with the survival and hoped-for success of their own children. Mary lives in no fantasyland; she quickly learns how tough life will be for her special son (2:34). But her keen sense of God's life-generating purposes for her son Jesus — and through him for all who "fear [God] from generation to generation" (1:50) — drives her thoughts and imagination through the pain and suffering to a resilient hope of fulfillment of God's gracious promises of salvation (1:55).

Mary's freedom to think and question within her faithful Jewish religious framework — without getting zapped for it, like Zechariah does[23] — sets the stage for a couple of feisty women who vocally lament their situations. Martha complains to Lord Jesus about her excessive domestic workload, unassisted by sister Mary. While Jesus resists her demands and rebukes her frustration, he does not lambast her impudence (How dare you question me!) or dismiss her concern (What are you moaning about?

23. Though I also see the possibility of Zechariah's (temporary) muting not primarily as an act of punishment, but more as a move to compel his deeper reflection (throughout Elizabeth's pregnancy) on the significance of his son's special God-ordained birth and ministry. By contrast, Mary needs no silencing spur to intelligent inquiry: she thoughtfully and faithfully seeks to understand her maternal vocation from the start.

Where's dinner?). He addresses her sympathetically ("Martha, Martha") and takes her angst seriously. As we argued, he affirms her "good" service along with Mary's attentiveness, attempts to ease her anxiety, and implicitly invites her to the seminar. Later, the widow in Jesus' parable pushes even harder and smarter with her savvy insistence, "Grant me justice against my opponent" (18:3), which eventually proves successful. In its most immediate context, she argues in a secular court before an unjust, godless judge. But, as we developed at some length, she also serves within the wider frame of Luke 18:1-8 as a complex model for intelligent, passionate, and protestant pleading with God in prayer.

While most of the women in Luke share the Jewish heritage of Mary and Jesus, the three "foreign" OT women Jesus references encounter Israel's faith as outsiders and represent interesting cases of religious choice. Jesus notes that Elijah "was sent" to a destitute widow in the Phoenician city of Zarephath (she did not send for him). But the case Jesus reports is that of Elijah's feeding, not his evangelizing, the foreign widow during a season of famine. There is no hint of the prophet's attempt to convert the woman to the Jewish faith. As we discussed in chapter 6, the larger OT narrative in 1 Kings 17 depicts the widow's probing Elijah's relationship with his God and her eventual free acknowledgment of the veracity of YHWH's word (1 Kings 17:24). But such "conversion" or repentance is not Jesus' concern at this point. Rather he aims to convert his kinfolk to a more welcoming, inclusive attitude toward foreigners. Similarly, Jesus cites the queen of the South, not as a Jewish proselyte per se, but as a faithful seeker of God's wisdom embodied in God's authorized ruler of Israel and as an ultimate judge of the faithless "people of this generation" (Luke 11:31). Finally, however, lest we too enthusiastically and anachronistically trumpet Luke's and Jesus' espousal of the democratic ideal of religious liberty, we must "remember Lot's wife" (17:32). After being yanked out of her hometown, she remains free not to follow the dictum of her husband's fiery deity, but such freedom (to look back on incinerated Sodom) paralyzes her in a salt block, which proves it was no freedom at all. And on one reading we sympathetically explored, her back-glancing choice was not so much out of religious defiance of Lot's God or out of moral affinity with Sodom's wicked element as out of social and emotional solidarity with longtime family and friends left behind in the ashes and rubble. The *gecekondu* women, and many others traditional and otherwise, would have been right there with Lot's wife, frozen in their tracks, facing their beloved community with mouths agape and eyes awash with

tears. But isn't that what silly women get for their hyperemotional natures? Consider the next capability on the list.

5. Emotions

A profound distrust of emotions as distortive of sound reason and deleterious to human flourishing runs long and deep in Western thought.
Hence, emphasis has often fallen more on stifling or extirpating, as the
Stoics would advise, emotional capabilities than on developing and enhancing them.[24] For example, in praising the stoical martyrs of one remarkable family — Eleazar and his seven brothers and mother — during
the Antiochene persecution, the Hellenistic-Jewish author, steeped in
Greek philosophy, puts emotions (or passions) firmly in their subordinate
place: "It is evident that reason rules over those emotions that hinder self-
control, namely, gluttony and lust, it is also clear that it masters the emotions that hinder one from justice, such as malice, and those that stand in
the way of courage, namely anger, fear, and pain. . . . It is not for the purpose of destroying them [the emotions], but so that one may not give way
to them" (4 Macc 1:3-6). The martyrs succeeded in dying nobly for their
faith because they did not give way to weak emotions. Of course, being the
"weaker sex" (15:5), women were regarded as more emotional and thus less
rational, and inferior to men, particularly by dint of their maternal natures
dominated by love for children. It is all the more extraordinary, then, an
anomaly of epic proportions, when the widowed mother of Eleazar and
seven other sons coolly watches them being tortured to death, one by one,
approves of their brave loyalty to God, and then valiantly throws herself
into the executioners' flames. In short, she sheds her sappy womanhood
and acts like a rational-stoical man: "How great and how many torments
the mother then suffered as her sons were tortured on the wheel and with
the hot irons! But devout reason, *giving her heart a man's courage in the
very midst of her emotions,* strengthened her to disregard, for the time, her
parental love" (15:22-23).[25]

---

24. See Nussbaum, *Upheavals of Thought: The Intelligence of Emotions* (Cambridge:
Cambridge University Press, 2001); Genevieve Lloyd, *The Man of Reason: "Male" and "Female" in Western Philosophy* (2nd ed.; Minneapolis: University of Minnesota Press, 1993).

25. See S. Moore and J. Anderson, "'Taking It Like a Man': Masculinity in 4 Maccabees,"
Journal of Biblical Literature 117 (1998): 249-73; Robin Darling Young, "The 'Woman with the
Soul of Abraham': Traditions about the Mother of the Maccabean Martyrs," in *"Women Like*

In recent decades, however, we have witnessed a developing revolution in understanding the integral role emotions play in human experience inextricably connected with, rather than opposed to, rational thought and action. The interface of cognitive and affective processes in embodied life has captivated a range of fields in the sciences and humanities, especially neuroscience, biology, psychology, political science, literary studies, and philosophy. In the latter discipline, Nussbaum has been a leading figure in appreciating and analyzing afresh the emotional nature of *all* human beings, men as much as women.[26] It is not surprising, then, that her Capabilities Approach promotes emotional flourishing for all persons, focusing on "being able to have attachments to things and people outside ourselves," and in these relationships being able "to love, to grieve, to experience longing, gratitude, and justified anger" and, on the flip side, "not having one's emotional development blighted by fear and anxiety."[27]

Uyan-Semerci reports that while the Istanbul "women interviewed were at ease when expressing openly their emotions," the scope of their emotions concentrated narrowly on love and grief directed toward parents and children. Love for husbands appeared more formal and functional than romantic and passionate, and Uyan-Semerci, not surprisingly, says nothing about the *gecekondu* women's freedom to express anger or frustration.[28] By contrast, the women in Luke display somewhat fuller emotional lives, sometimes in tandem with intellectual pursuits. To be sure, we know nothing about how the three married women — Elizabeth, Mary of Nazareth, and Joanna — feel about their husbands one way or another, and Joanna's brief profile gives us little insight into her emotional state. We can only guess at the emotional condition of Lot's wife, but she seems more inclined to grieve over lost kinship and friendship ties back in Sodom than to cherish attachment to her husband and two daughters who have fled the

This": *New Perspectives on Jewish Women in the Greco-Roman World* (ed. Amy-Jill Levine; Atlanta: Scholars, 1991), 67-81; and from my chapter "Passions and Passion: The 'Loose' Lady, Woman Wisdom, and the Lukan Jesus" [on Luke 7:33-50], in Spencer, *Dancing Girls, "Loose" Ladies, and Women of "the Cloth": The Women in Jesus' Life* (New York: Continuum, 2004), 120-23.

26. Nussbaum, *Upheavals of Thought*; Nussbaum, "Emotions and Women's Capabilities," in *Women, Culture, and Development: A Study of Human Capabilities* (ed. Martha Nussbaum and Jonathan Glover; Oxford: Oxford University Press, 1993), 360-95.

27. Nussbaum, *Creating Capabilities*, 33-34.

28. Uyan-Semerci, "A Relational Account," 211-12.

city. In this case it might be fair to say, from Luke's perspective, that she let her emotions get the best of her and cloud a rational response to the angel's warning to evacuate and not look back (though from a modern viewpoint, would we view an apocalyptic doomsday message from an angel as *reasonable?*).

More positively, though, Elizabeth and Mary stand out as women capable of great joy and sorrow, mostly related to their sons, but also, as we have seen, in solidarity with the covenantal history of God's people, especially the lowly and hungry clients of God's powerful and merciful care. In its soaring strains "rejoicing in God my Savior," the Magnificat runs emotionally high and thoughtfully deep — an affective-cognitive tour de force. Elizabeth and Mary also experience negative feelings, but find ways to move through and past them. Elizabeth knows full well the "disgrace" of barrenness, but she perseveres in godly faith and hope finally to see her shame "taken away" and supplanted by joyous fertility (Luke 1:25). For her part, Mary's fear at the sudden angelophany (implied in Gabriel's "Do not be afraid" exhortation [1:30]) does not drive her to hysteria or shock: though "perplexed," she methodically ponders the situation, probes Gabriel with relevant questions, and presents herself as a cooperative servant-partner ("Here I am, the servant of the Lord" [1:38]). Later, Mary gives full vent to her and Joseph's "great anxiety" over young Jesus' AWOL activity (2:48) — an anxiety tinged with a confusing swirl of anger and love that parents across the ages have typically felt upon finding a missing child. Despite Mary's knowledge of Jesus' special gifts and vocation, confirmed all the more by his amazing performance in the temple, she does not hesitate to express her frustration and to question Jesus' conduct. In response, Jesus chides her and Joseph for "not knowing" his true Paternal assignment (2:49), another hint that familial emotions can distort good spiritual judgment. But nonetheless, as we have repeatedly stressed, Jesus still returns home in submission to his earthly parents, and Luke promptly underscores Mary's continuing deep internal reflection about "all these things" (2:51). Luke makes no attempt to suppress either Mary's emotionality or her rationality. These dimensions of her personality coalesce in forming her rich spirituality.

Eruptions of anxiety and anger also characterize, in different ways, the householder Martha who hosts Jesus and the plaintiff widow in Jesus' parable. Martha, like mother Mary, does not hold back on telling Jesus how she feels about him, even when it's not all love and adoration. She feels he doesn't care enough about her and her demanding work; further, she seems to feel he cares more about her sister by allowing Mary to sit at his feet rather than ordering her to help the beleaguered Martha. Note again, Martha *feels free* to tell Jesus just how she feels, without hesitation or apology. This honest communication with *her Lord* — she knows just whom she's talking to — speaks volumes about the frankness Jesus allows, perhaps even encourages, from his followers, signifying a solid, healthy relationship between master and disciple. Yes, Jesus rebuffs Martha — he speaks openly and candidly, too — but he doesn't demean her or her emotions. He is genuinely worried that her worry is making her miserable and souring her admirable "much ministry" (10:40). She needs to sort through her many thoughts and emotions, not squelch them in dehumanizing fashion, in order to discern what is most "good" *(agathon)* and "necessary" *(chreia)* on any given occasion (10:42).

The widow in Jesus' parable represents a banner case of expressing "justified anger" or "righteous indignation," matched only by Jesus himself in his denunciations of religious hypocrisy and protest demonstration in the temple courts. The widow's pressing demand for justice in the face of an unjust judge and exploitative adversary, punctuated by fist-jab gestures, if not actual punches, models a bodily engaged, emotionally charged action that proves as strategic as it is dramatic. Far from being a liability, her passionate, persistent display ultimately results in judicial victory against unfavorable odds. We are not told how she feels after this, but we might assume another apt emotional response similar to that of a successful woman in another parable. I can well imagine the widow who won her case, like the woman who found her coin, gathering her women friends and neighbors for a joyous celebratory party (cf. 15:6).

6. Practical Reason

The capability of senses, thought, and imagination already stressed the development of cognitive skills, including reason. Now the accent falls on the use of reason toward *practical* life goals, on the facility "to engage in critical reflection about the planning of one's life." Nussbaum regards this and the next capability (affiliation) as "architectonic" or integral to the entire list in their pervasive promotion of human dignity and liberty. Practical reason in particular "is just another way of alluding to the centrality of choice in the whole notion of capability as freedom"; "the opportunity to plan one's life is an opportunity to choose and order the functionings corresponding to the various other capabilities."[29] Moreover, practical reason entails the overarching capacity, enhancing all dimensions of human life, of "being able to behave as a thinking being, not just a cog in a machine," an opportunity Nussbaum flags as more often denied to women than men.[30]

Traditional societies, such as those in the biblical world and in the Muslim Turkish settlement investigated by Uyan-Semerci, in which patriarchal families commonly arrange marriages for young women (often in their teens), afford limited opportunities for women freely to chart their own lives outside the patriarchal "machine" in which they function as sexual-maternal "cogs." Any life-planning energy they might exercise is typically directed toward their children, helping arrange their marriages and promoting their sons' wider success in the world (recall Mrs. Zebedee's attempt to advance her sons' standing in Jesus' kingdom [Matt 20:20-21]).[31] For the most part, the women in Luke we have studied display all their other considerable capabilities *within* an established patriarchal-kyriarchal structure. They in fact operate as cogs in traditional domestic (Elizabeth, Mary, Martha/Mary, widow at Zarephath, Lot's wife) and forensic (widow who pleads her case before an unjust judge) systems, though with amazing effectiveness therein. But to argue that Lukan women are freely planning out their lives and careers would be egregious special pleading. Luke mostly provides brief snapshots, momentary glimpses of women's experiences, nothing approaching full life stories.

The fullest portrait is that of Jesus' mother Mary, stretching from her adolescent conception of Jesus to a predicted (though not narrated) life course of "piercing" conflict and sorrow. While, as we argued at length, Mary exhibits remarkable agency, imagination, and reflection *within* this plot, she does not chart her course. She chooses how to respond *within* the story but does not get to compose it. We must not ignore, however, at this point the core *theological* element in Luke's narrative. More than simply playing out her role within the dominant social structures of her day, Mary becomes a key figure in God's drama of salvation. She doesn't audition for her part; she is drafted and given no choice about *whether* she will perform her part. She is indeed a cog in God's scheme. But again she is allowed dramatic freedom in how she will interpret her role in creative partnership

29. Nussbaum, *Creating Capabilities*, 34, 39.
30. Nussbaum, *Women and Human Development*, 82.
31. Uyan-Semerci, "A Relational Account," 212-13.

with God. And most importantly, *she finds and facilitates redemptive free-dom for her and her people by fulfilling God's redemptive plan.* Here we con-front Luke's theological paradox (outside Nussbaum's humanistic frame-work), which we may express in modifying the principle Jesus states immediately after evoking memory of Lot's wife: "Those who try to con-trol and plan their lives on their own will lose them, but those who surren-der to and cooperate with God's liberating plan will find them" (adapting Luke 17:33).

Finally, back to a more sociological perspective, Joanna stands out in Luke as a married woman with some freedom to plan her own life. No doubt her elevated social class makes a difference here: aristocratic Greco-Roman and Herodian wives[32] enjoyed greater means, wider choice, and freer range of movement than their lower-class counterparts. At any rate, Joanna exercises considerable practical reason, with or without husband Chuza's endorsement, in opting to leave Tiberius to meet and follow Jesus, at least for a time, and to support his movement financially. To some ex-tent, she controls her own datebook and pocketbook. To a fuller extent, of course, the queen of the South controlled her schedule and considerable resources as sovereign of her realm. Although clearly a special case among women as a monarch of unknown marital status, her inclusion by Luke as a model of wisdom and discernment — in other words, *practical reason* — should not be discounted.

7. Affiliation

This capability, which along with practical reason ranks high in impor-tance and "suffuses all the other capabilities,"[33] runs in two directions: (1) *toward others* — being able to appreciate empathetically and support actively others' needs and interests; and (2) *toward self* — being treated with due respect and dignity by others, thus experiencing "nondiscrimina-tion on the basis of race, sex, sexual orientation, ethnicity, caste, religion,

32. Perhaps the most influential Herodian woman of her time was Bernice, sister and wife (for a time) of Herod Agrippa II. Luke briefly refers to her accompaniment of Agrippa in Acts 25:13; 26:30. For a fuller assessment of her political career, see Ross Shepard Kraemer, "Typical and Atypical Jewish Family Dynamics: The Cases of Babatha and Berenice," in *Early Christian Families in Context: An Interdisciplinary Dialogue* (ed. David L. Balch and Carolyn Osiek; Grand Rapids: Eerdmans, 2003), 130-56.

33. Nussbaum, *Women and Human Development,* 244.

national origin."[34] In short, affiliation facilitates "complex forms of discourse, concern, and reciprocity with other human beings."[35] "Reciprocity" particularly captures the two-lane flow of this capability. Not surprisingly, Uyan-Semerci again underscores the primary significance of *family* affiliations for her informants, the household being the main arena in which they "show concern for others." Indeed, this kinship-based ethic of care conjoined with religion constitutes "the ultimate meaning of life" for these Muslim women.[36] Though she would also encourage a wider circle of social and political engagement, Nussbaum strongly affirms familial attachments, "argu[ing] that the capabilities approach, which treats each individual as an end, is in no sense incompatible with the appropriate valuation of family love and care; indeed it actually provides the best framework within which both to value care and to give it the necessary critical scrutiny."[37] This need for critique would especially apply to the *gecekondu* women's poor sense of personal respect and dignity: their altruistic concern for other family members is rarely reciprocated. As Uyan-Semerci reports, "sexual discrimination was definitely stark," as her interviewees bluntly admitted: "They do not consider us [women] as human species."[38]

As women across time and cultures have typically led the way in (and borne the burden of) empathic care for others, especially other family members, mothers in Luke such as Mary of Nazareth and Lot's wife of Sodom follow the pattern, however different they otherwise may be. However, as we have seen, Luke features loving maternal figures sparingly and not always positively (as with Lot's wife). Also, female empathy for kinfolk does not shine through Martha's demeanor. She does not try to see the situation from sister Mary's point of view; that's precisely what Jesus encourages Martha to do, even as *he* shows concern for Martha's frustration. Turning the tables, however, from a capabilities perspective, Martha admirably advocates for her own affiliation needs, demanding to be treated with due respect and care ("Don't you care!" [cf. Luke 10:40]), not taken advantage of in the household by her "Lord" or her sibling. Further, on a more critical survival level, the widow in Jesus' parable showcases a woman's rightful — and successful — plea for respectful consideration in a disrespectful familial and legal environment.

34. Nussbaum, *Creating Capabilities*, 34.
35. Nussbaum, *Women and Human Development*, 82.
36. Uyan-Semerci, "A Relational Account," 213.
37. Nussbaum, *Women and Human Development*, 244.
38. Uyan-Semerci, "A Relational Account," 213-14.

Luke's presentation of three "foreign" OT women evinces a nondiscriminatory stance on the basis of nationality, class, gender, and, to some extent, religion. Jesus cites with approval God's sending Elijah to feed the poor widow at Zarephath; the wider OT story clarifies the dignity Elijah accords this woman, respectfully conversing with her and ensuring her physical survival with no strings attached: his ministry is not contingent upon her denouncing her Phoenician gods and people, though she ultimately confesses the truth of Israel's deity. On the opposite end of the social spectrum, Jesus commends the elite queen of the South for seeking out and certifying Solomon's God-given wisdom and even goes so far as to forecast her righteous prosecutorial role at the final judgment; but neither Jesus nor his OT source compels the queen to deny her "Southern" culture or religion and become an Israelite citizen or Jewish proselyte. Now, to be sure, the culture and religion of ancient Sodom are cut no slack by Genesis or Luke. But at least Lot's wife is still accorded the right of free choice: she might be yanked out of the city, but she's strapped with no heavy harness to keep her from looking back. It's hard to find much dignity in her salt-pillaring (or pillorying), but she still remains worthy of being "remembered." This trio of anonymous OT Gentile women, granted a whopping total of *four verses* in Luke's Gospel, hardly deliver an overwhelming egalitarian mandate. Luke's social-narrative world remains sexist, classist, and xenophobic, befitting its time and place. But the just reign of God inaugurated by Jesus in word and deed begins to shake, if not shatter, that world in many respects and forward the hope of a renewed household of God, a Spirit-charged community of reciprocal affiliation.

8. Other Species

Being able to live with concern for and in relation to animals, plants, and the world of nature.[39]

This capability, which Nussbaum elaborates at some length in a book stemming from her Tanner Lectures on Human Values,[40] reflects recent

---

39. Nussbaum, *Creating Capabilities*, 34. I quote the full descriptions of these last three capabilities, which I did not present in chapter 3.

40. Nussbaum, *Frontiers of Justice: Disability, Nationality, Species Membership* (Cambridge: Harvard University Press, Belknap Press, 2006), 325-407.

ecological sensibilities critical of self-preoccupied, human-centered values — a perspective of remote interest perhaps to poor, traditional folk struggling to eke out an existence (saving baby seals ranks low on the list when one's own babies are starving). Indeed, the women in Uyan-Semerci's study did not give this capability much thought. Unlike most modern Westerners, their relationship with animals and the natural world was more immediate and pragmatic: most of these women had labored in the fields tending crops and sheep in their native villages before migrating to Istanbul, and they continued to regard plant and animal life in utilitarian terms "as a more essential resource for human life than a spiritual value." Animals were not so much objects of "concern" as sources of food (milk, meat) for human survival.[41]

This is not the place to unpack Luke's philosophy of nature or theology of creation (both of which merit more attention in Lukan studies). But on a basic level, the environment of Jesus' upbringing and ministry reflects the agrarian/pastoral society of first-century Palestine. He is laid in a manger at birth, attended by shepherds from the fields, and later tells stories about mustard seeds, lost sheep, and workers who have "just come in from plowing or tending sheep in the field" (Luke 17:7), while also, however, teaching a lesson about a gardener instructed to cut down a barren fruit tree if it doesn't shape up (13:6-9) and sending a herd of swine plummeting to their deaths with the demons he expelled from a tormented man (8:32-33). Jesus shows a clear respect for the world as God's creation and object of God's sustaining care, but within an unapologetic hierarchy favoring human life ("Of how much more value are you than the birds! . . . How much more will [God] clothe you . . . ?" [12:24, 28; cf. 12:22-28]).

As for the women we've considered, what little we have to go on comports with Jesus' disposition toward the natural world. Mary matter-of-factly offers for sacrifice her two turtledoves or pigeons at Jesus' baby dedication as required by Jewish law (no need to ponder this), and the widow at Zarephath knew all too well how unyielding nature could be if God decided to shut off the rain spouts for three and a half years and how fortunate, by contrast, was God's last-minute creative provision of food through his prophet. Perhaps most interesting regarding female capability related to "other species" is Jesus' comparison, which we briefly discussed, of his protective care for Israel to that of a mother hen enveloping her

41. Uyan-Semerci, "A Relational Account," 214.

brood under her wings. Of course, this is ultimately a tragic allusion, as Jesus' maternal-natural capability for care is frustrated by the obstinacy and waywardness of the children of Israel (13:34-35).

9. Play

> Being able to laugh, to play, to enjoy recreational activities.[42]

Now it may seem that we've really moved into some privileged Westernized arena far removed from the real-world concerns of most of the world, particularly those myriad people mired in poverty and oppression. Playful "recreational activities" too easily evoke thoughts of ski junkets, camping excursions, island cruises, and all sorts of other leisure pursuits most people, especially women, simply can't afford in terms of time or money. But this is precisely Nussbaum's point — not promoting extravagant holidays for the rich and famous, but advocating that all persons need some time, resources, and opportunities to enjoy life, to not work themselves to death, to pursue creative and re-creative activities. And for no group is this more essential than for women worldwide who carry the heaviest labor burden, often involving relentless "double shifts" with outside employment to make ends meet followed by full domestic responsibilities for feeding, clothing, child care, and nursing (elderly relatives as well as children): "In general, protecting leisure time for workers, especially female workers, is an important issue in creating a decent society."[43]

Again, the *gecekondu* women in Istanbul prove woefully deficient in this capability. They recalled some occasions for play as children, but these were typically cut short by their need to help with household duties at a young age, not to mention their marrying young and soon having their own children to tend. Moreover, as wives and mothers, opportunities for play, even with their own children on public streets, were culturally stigmatized as shameful and "'acting beyond reason.' To be able to laugh was also something that could endanger the purity of woman's honour and therefore, expression of amusement was mostly limited to a smile rather than a laugh."[44]

42. Nussbaum, *Creating Capabilities*, 34.
43. Nussbaum, *Creating Capabilities*, 11 (cf. 10-11).
44. Uyan-Semerci, "A Relational Account," 214.

Fortunately, though again we have little information to draw on, the situation with women in Luke is not quite so dire. The joyous house parties of female family and friends celebrating Elizabeth's delivery of baby John (1:57-58) and the sweeper woman's discovery of her lost coin (15:8-9) evince a capacity for fun and festivity on special occasions. The latter example, we might even say, features a "recreational" break from the strain of domestic work. But again, it's a special case (this is not a labor parable promoting two coffee breaks and a lunch hour during the workday); there's no reason to think that the overworked *gecekondu* Muslim women would not also take time to celebrate a new birth in the community or someone's retrieving a lost precious possession.

Generally speaking, Luke's Jesus is not big on leisure pursuits. To be sure, he loves attending dinner parties, but he usually winds up spoiling the party with some critical word to the host about shoddy hospitality (7:44-46) or an elitist guest list and seating chart (14:7-24). Jesus embarks on God's urgent kingdom mission with no time to waste. He is much more likely to minister round the clock, through the night (4:40-42), than to take a break. He even works on the Sabbath, albeit to heal, not to profit, but still to the consternation of the religious authorities (6:6-11; 13:10-17; 14:1-6).[45] He does refer to playing once in a parable, but the reference is to child's play, which he applies negatively to the foolish and fickle "people of this generation" (7:31-35). So there's not a lot of playtime in Luke's narrative for men or women, but we take what we can get and rejoice with Elizabeth and the sweeper woman for at least a few verses.

10. Control over One's Environment

(A) *Political.* Being able to participate effectively in political choices that govern one's life; having the right of political participation, protections of free speech and association.

(B) *Material.* Being able to hold property (both land and movable goods), and having property rights on an equal basis with others; having the right to seek employment on an equal basis with others; having the freedom from unwarranted search and seizure. In work, being able to work as a human being, exercising practical

45. See F. Scott Spencer, *What Did Jesus Do? Gospel Profiles of Jesus' Personal Conduct* (Harrisburg, Pa.: Trinity, 2003), 178-89.

reason and entering into meaningful relationships of mutual recognition with other workers.[46]

This final capability extends Nussbaum's advocacy for human freedom, autonomy, and dignity into the political and material realms, though under the somewhat misleading heading "Control over One's Environment." "Control" carries unfortunate connotations of domination and manipulation, and "environment" is perhaps too broad in scope, suggesting the whole natural world (including "Other Species"). Maybe a label such as "Participation in Political and Economic Life" would be more apropos. In any case, the dual "political" and "material" capabilities Nussbaum outlines in her description are quite clear and specific. More than the other components of her "decalogue," this one has a resounding American constitutional, democratic ring to it, especially with its advocacy of voting and property rights and safeguards for "free speech and association" and "freedom from unwarranted search and seizure."

In modern democratic Turkey, the marginal settlement women interviewed by Uyan-Semerci have the right to vote, and they exercise it as good citizens. But they also report that "politics [is] something alien to their lives." That is, they regard the overall political process dealing with — or in the women's view, largely *not* dealing with — crippling social problems of poverty, unemployment, poor education, and urban blight as beyond their control (maybe that's the proper term after all), dominated by wealthy elites with little concern for the plight of the underclass. "Except for two women," Uyan-Semerci comments, "they all thought there was no chance of improving their situation, but also more generally improving Turkey's situation."[47] In other words, they had become stuck in a state of learned helplessness. On the economic front, these women might seem to have some security in the legal provision of joint ownership of household property by husband and wife. But the actual practice of property law in Turkish society seldom plays out to wives' or widows' advantage. As for employment opportunities, immigrant women in Istanbul typically secure domestic service work in others' homes or piecework in their own homes to make ends meet, even as they continue to bear the brunt of maintaining their own households. The "double shift" phenomenon is routine and certainly not compensated with "overtime" pay. In large measure, these

46. Nussbaum, *Creating Capabilities,* 34.
47. Uyan-Semerci, "A Relational Account," 214-15.

women's notion of material capability would involve the option to live comfortably *without* working for external wages and thus to have some opportunity for rest and "play" in line with the previous item on Nussbaum's list.[48]

All the women (and men) in Luke's Gospel live under Augustan or Tiberian monarchy (Luke 2:1; 3:1) — not American or Turkish democracy. Freeborn women in ancient Rome could be citizens but did not have the right to vote or hold public office. This is not to say that women could not have considerable political influence, but such power, as noted above, would be limited to upper-class women of substantial means. Joanna might well have enjoyed some political clout with the Herodian court at Tiberius, and of course, in her different context, the queen of the South reigned over her realm. But the other women in Luke we've studied live, in varying degrees, on the lower underside of Roman power and prosperity. But that doesn't mean they simply wallow there in abject helplessness, especially in the two dynamic cases of Jesus' mother Mary and the litigant widow in his parable.

The particular circumstances under which Mary gives birth to Jesus are inconveniently determined by the census edict of Augustus, requiring Mary and Joseph's trek to Bethlehem. Mary's full pregnancy at this time is of no concern to the emperor: he dictates the movements of his subjects according to his sovereign will. Such is the secular political state of affairs. But that is far from the whole story in Luke: nowhere does the beacon of Luke's dynamic *theological politics* shine through the oppressive world-system more brilliantly, illuminating what Mary has already heralded in the Magnificat. The proud and powerful ruler on his throne, who *seems* to be in control, is being subverted by the lowly and little child in a manger whom the true Savior-God of the world has authorized as the true Savior-Lord-Christ to lift and liberate the downtrodden and enslaved in the world (Luke 1:51-52; 2:10-12). And the Bethlehem venue will work just fine, not as Augustus's registration post, but as "the city of David" (2:11) bearing the messianic hopes for the redemption of God's people through God's royal son. In all this revolutionary divine plotting, Mary emerges as more than a mere functionary, but rather as a cocreative, consummately capable agent of God's kingdom.

The widow in Jesus' parable represents the only woman in Luke who directly challenges the dominant political and economic system in court,

---

48. Uyan-Semerci, "A Relational Account," 215.

and she does so with remarkable flair and force. She operates as a bold antitype of the helpless widow. The most plausible background to the widow's case, we argued, involved a legal right to family property, like that granted to Babatha and other Jewish women in ancient Roman society (and to Muslim women in modern Turkey), but which was not respected or protected by certain relatives (as in Babatha's case) and magistrates (as with the *gecekondu* wives and widows). But none of this deters the protagonist in Jesus' story, who presses her case against all odds, using all the strength and shrewdness she can muster until she receives the justice she deserves.

It would be better, of course, if the system supported this woman's material capability from the start; that is Jesus' (and Nussbaum's) ultimate point. But in the meantime, in the face of seemingly intractable injustice, this widow uses the capabilities she has developed — her senses-thought-imagination, her emotions, her practical reason, and let's not forget her bodily health/integrity, as she freely moves with flailing fists in a public forum — to acquire the capabilities she's being denied, namely, affiliation in terms of being treated with due dignity and respect and control of one's environment in political and material spheres. In her case, "control" in the nonideal sense of domination and manipulation applies: she has no choice; she does what she has to do and beats the system at its own game.

It is apt that we end this study with this multicapable woman of purpose and persistence we have "found" in Luke, but not only to celebrate her achievements. We must also lament with her the situation in Luke's world (both his narrative and social worlds) and continuing to today (both in our religious and secular worlds) that oppresses women, restricts their capabilities, and forces them to use exhausting, extraordinary measures to secure justice. "Good for the widow. Way to go, Lady!" we cheer. But we should also cry out in prayer, no less than in public discourse, "What a damn shame! Why put her through this legal maze to realize justice?" Or in the more polite, but no less pointed, words of Jesus: "And yet, when the Son of Man comes, will he find faith/fullness on earth?"

Index

Abishag, 157-59
Akhmatova, Anna, 257-58
Alter, Robert, 147, 149n.8, 150n.10, 151n.13, 152n.14, 152n.16, 153n.17, 153n.18, 255n.123
Ananias and Sapphira, 3, 130
Anna: heritage, 94, 190; as prophet, 16, 224-25, 297, 305-6, 321; as widow, 104, 283, 297, 303, 305-6, 319, 321
Aquila and Priscilla, 111, 130-31, 140
Asceticism. See Women ascetics
Aseneth, 197-201, 206, 208; marriage to Joseph, 198-201, 209; repentance and conversion of, 200-201, 208, 226, 242; as woman of wisdom, 242

Babatha, 123, 271-75, 277, 278n.24, 341
Bakhtin, Mikhail, 94n.98
Barren women, 56-57, 159, 162; Elizabeth, 57, 163-65, 168, 319, 330; Hannah, 79, 154-57, 168; Rachel, 151-54, 162, 168, 179; Sarah (Sarai), 31, 148-51, 162, 168
Bathsheba: and Abishag, 157-59; nominally related to the queen of Sheba, 236
Bauckham, Richard: on feminist biblical criticism, 29-30; on Joanna as apostle, 136-41
Baumgardner, Jennifer, 253

Beauvoir, Simone de, 52-54
Beavis, Mary Ann: on parable of the lost coin, 44-46; on parable of the widow and unjust judge, 264
Bent-over woman (Luke 13:10-17), 7, 11, 12n.30, 17, 101n.2, 191
Berlin, Adele, 158

Calvin, John: on divine providence, 65-66; on Martha and Mary, 175, 176
Camp, Claudia, 228n.72, 241n.95, 242n.97, 315
Capable women, 60-61, 74, 184-86, 280; hemorrhaging woman, 13; in Luke, 4, 14, 15, 19, 20, 317-41; Martha and Mary, 186; Mary of Nazareth, 21, 74, 316; in parable of widow and unjust judge, 23, 266, 301, 309; in Proverbs 31, 315-17; Ruth, 317. See also Nussbaum, Martha
Chrysostom, John, 174, 175, 176
Clement of Alexandria, 173
Collins, Patricia Hill, 193
Constable, Giles, 173-79
Cotter, Wendy, 267n.6, 288, 304

Danker, Frederick, 84n.70, 84n.71, 285n.38, 287n.43
Daughter of Jairus, 4, 13, 167, 213, 319, 321n.15

Daughters of Jerusalem (Luke 23:28-29), 168-69, 191, 213, 319n.12

Daughters of Lot, 206, 250-53, 255, 271, 278, 329-30

Daughters of Philip the evangelist, 131, 191

Daughters of Zelophehad, 271

Davis, Ellen, 38, 39-40

Deborah (judge and prophet), 56, 203, 290, 316

Delilah, 204-5, 284, 316

Derrett, J. Duncan, 266-67n.6, 287

diakoneō,-ia,-os, 13-14, 78, 105, 114-18, 120, 171, 172. *See also* Women's service

dialogizomai, diatarassomai, 68-69, 71, 93-94

diatereō, 99-100

Dinah, 86-87, 197, 201, 307

Divine providence: John Calvin's view, 65-66; and women's agency, 59-66

Dowling, Elizabeth, 292

Durber, Susan, 40-41

Eckhart, Meister, 179-80

Elizabeth: as barren woman, 56, 57, 163-65, 168, 319, 330; filled with the Spirit, 76, 164, 167; heritage, 94, 190; and Mary of Nazareth, 30, 35-36, 66, 75-78, 94, 100, 163-65, 167, 171; as mother of John the Baptist, 7, 321, 338; as prophet, 16, 100, 167, 319

Emotions of women, 328-31; Lot's wife's anguish, 253, 256-60, 263, 278-79, 329; Martha's frustration, 15, 22, 145, 168-71, 188-89, 326-27, 330-31, 334; Mary of Nazareth's anxiety and anger, 49n.75, 92n.94, 95-100, 165-66, 330; widow's righteous anger in parable of widow and unjust judge, 331

eperchomai, episkiazō, 71

epiblepō, 78-79

Esther (character and book of), 196, 197, 205

Eve, 25, 254

FBI (Feminist Biblical Interpretation), 1, 22, 33, 265

Feminist biblical criticism: focused on "others" and "foreigners," 194-95; of Luke's writings, 1-19, 40-54, 264-66, 290-93, 303-8; methodology, 27-40. *See also* Hermeneutics of suspicion

Feminist theology, 62-66, 77, 194

Feminist theory: applied to housework, 51-54; applied to Martha and Mary story, 184-89; concern for "others" and "foreigners," 192-95; and feminist theology, 62-64; womanist, 192-94; and women's agency, 59-64

Fendt, Gene, 257-58

Fewell, Danna, 157n.27, 160n.32, 162, 202-3n.29, 203n.31, 208n.40, 254n.120

"Foreign" women. *See* Queen of the South; "Strange" ("foreign") women; Widow at Zarephath; Wife of Lot

Fortune-telling slave-girl (Acts 16:16-18), 286

Francis of Assisi, 174-75

Gaventa, Beverly Roberts, 72n.42, 74n.47, 85n.75, 92n.94, 94

Gilligan, Carol, 161-62

Goldingay, John, 44

Greek women of high standing (Acts 17:12, 34), 211-12

Green, Joel, 24n.1, 28n.11, 118n.41, 246, 279n.28, 280n.29, 285n.39, 312-13n.90

Gregory the Great, 177

Gunn, David, 157n.27, 160n.32, 162, 202-3n.29, 203n.31, 208n.40, 254n.120

Hagar, 55, 56n.1, 76, 252; relationship with Sarah (Sarai), 148-51, 162, 165

Hannah, 16, 56, 168, 190, 191; relationship with Peninnah, 154-57, 165, 171; song of, 79, 157

Havea, Jione, 202

hayil, 316-17

Hays, Richard, 30-31, 34

Heffner, Blake, 174, 179n.75, 179n.76

Index

Hellenist widows (Acts 6:1-6), 10, 23, 90n.23, 117-18

Hemorrhaging woman (Luke 8:43-48), 12n.30, 13, 17, 101n.2, 104, 167, 214

Hermeneutics of conspiracy, 97

Hermeneutics of suspicion (doubt), 1-10, 15, 20-22, 24-54, 62-63, 77, 193, 206, 210, 291; and anti-Jewish biblical interpretation, 27; and the biblical lament tradition, 26; and ecological hermeneutics, 27; and the element of struggle, 38-40, 46-51; and feminist biblical criticism, 27-54, 206, 210, 264, 286, 290-93, 303; and feminist theology, 62-63; and feminist theory, 193; methodology, 32-33, 40-41; and personal experience, 36-38, 44-46; and warning labels on the Bible, 27-28, 30-31

Hermeneutics of trust (faith), 24-25, 30-31, 34-36, 46-51

Herzog, William, II, 278n.24, 289-90, 292n.55

Holy Spirit, 64; filling Elizabeth, 76, 164; in Martha and Mary, 179; overshadowing the Virgin Mary, 66, 71-73, 74, 75, 88, 324; as "wild child" of the Trinity, 66, 71, 324

Honor-shame codes, 12, 89-90n.89, 96, 163, 263, 266-67n.6, 287-90, 291, 301, 321, 322, 330, 337

hooks, bell, 193

Hospitality: of God, 82n.66; of Martha toward Jesus and others, 104, 116, 166, 169-72, 180-82, 186-89, 323; toward God and the Holy Spirit, 65-66; toward God's messengers, 101, 250-51, 255-56; of women, 101, 104, 115-16, 120, 144, 146, 203, 219, 238n.88

Household rivals type-scene: applied to Elizabeth and Mary of Nazareth, 163-65; applied to Martha and Mary, 165-89; applied to OT women, 148-62; basic elements of, 146-47

hyparchonta, 121, 139

hypōpiazō, 266-67, 279n.28

Ilan, Tal, 123-24, 138

Innocent III, 178-79, 183

Jael (wife of Heber), 202-4, 205, 208, 290, 316

Jezebel, 204-5, 208, 209, 221, 223, 224, 225, 226, 227, 245-46, 252

Joanna, 21, 30, 44, 323, 333, 340; as apostle, 136-41; benefactor (patron) and beneficiary (client) of Jesus, 103, 113, 121-24, 125-28, 135, 139-40, 143-44, 235; champion of the poor, 124-26, 137-38; chaste devotee, 128-31; double agent, 131-36; independent lady, 126-28; Mary Magdalene's friend, 103, 106, 112-13, 118-19, 120, 131-37, 321; widowhood, 126; wife of Herod's official (Chuza), 103-4, 106-7, 110-11, 123, 124-25, 132, 136-41, 167, 238, 321

Johnson, Luke Timothy, 277n.23, 292

Jones, Serene, 20, 60n.5, 62-64, 68

Joseph and Aseneth, 197-201. *See also* Aseneth

Judith (character and book of), 196, 197, 205, 208, 283, 290, 307-8

Junia, 140-41

Kahl, Brigitte, 35-36, 97, 99, 164-65

Klutz, Todd, 243-44

Kraemer, Ross Shepard, 200n.23, 272

LaHurd, Carol Schersten, 41-42, 49n.77, 53

Lapsley, Jacqueline, 24n.1, 47-48

Leah: relationship with Rachel, 151-54, 162, 165, 166, 176; type of Martha, 176, 178-79

Levine, Amy-Jill, 22n.53, 32, 101, 122-23n.51, 141n.120, 195-96, 207

Life of Saint Mary Magdalene and of Her Sister Martha, The (VBMM), 180-84

Livy, 285-86

Lopata, Helena, 270

Lorde, Audre, 192-93

Lot's wife. *See* Wife of Lot

344

Luther, Martin, 174
Lydia, 121-22, 212, 304

Magnificat, 6, 73, 77-80, 83, 119, 164, 212-13, 304-5, 320, 326, 330, 340
Makrothymia,-eō, 297-98, 300-302
Maloney, Linda, 47
Marbod of Rennes, 177-78, 183
Martha, 44, 116, 321, 332; as dragon-slayer and miracle-worker in medieval tradition, 182-84; frustration of, 145, 168-71, 188-89, 326, 330-31, 334; model of good works in history of interpretation, 173-84, 305; relationship with sister Mary, 165-89, 305, 323; service to Jesus, 116, 166, 169-72, 181, 182, 186, 188-89, 323, 326-27. *See also* Martha and Mary story (Luke 10:38-42)
Martha and Mary story (Luke 10:38-42), 15-16, 22, 44, 104, 145-47, 165-72, 190, 305; in light of feminist theory, 184-89; reception history of, 173-84. *See also* Martha; Mary (sister of Martha)
Mary, mother of John Mark, 121-22, 213, 304
Mary Magdalene, 167; businesswoman from Magdala, 122, 132-33; conflation with Mary, sister of Martha, 177, 180-84; disciple and benefactor of Jesus, 13, 18, 30, 35-36, 44, 104, 106, 110, 112-13, 120, 235, 321, 323; Joanna's friend, 21, 103, 104, 112-13, 118-19, 120, 131-36
Mary of Nazareth, 7, 16, 21, 30, 31, 34-36, 190, 334; birthing Jesus in Bethlehem, 80-88, 340; as choosing agent, 57-58, 66-100, 323-24, 332-33; destiny forecast by Simeon, 90-95, 165-66, 320; as disciple, 74, 78, 99; Gabriel's encounter with, 57, 66-75, 326, 330; in *Infancy Gospel of James,* 70; in *Infancy Gospel of Thomas,* 100; pregnancy of, 75-80; as prophet, 77-80; purification and presentation of baby Jesus, 88-90, 336; relationship to Hannah, 79, 164; relationship to Miriam

(Mariam), 67, 78; relationship with Elizabeth, 57, 66, 71, 75-78, 100, 163-65, 167, 171; responding to God's word, 72-73, 86-88; as sage, 85-87; seeking/finding young Jesus in temple, 49n.75, 95-100, 165-66, 330; as slave/servant, 74, 78-79, 90, 164; as virgin, 66-67, 70-72, 163-64. *See also* Magnificat
Mary (sister of Martha), 321, 332; conflation with Mary Magdalene, 177, 180-84; good/better choice of, 15-16, 171, 172, 178, 186, 305, 323, 327; model of contemplative faith in history of interpretation, 173-84, 305; relationship with Martha, 165-89, 305, 323. *See also* Martha and Mary story (Luke 10:38-42)
McLean, Kalbryn, 64-66, 71, 74
Merz, Annette, 303
Metzger, James, 299n.69
Mill, John Stuart, 74
Miriam, 16, 67, 78, 190, 191
Moberly, Walter, 37-38
Moltmann-Wendel, Elisabeth, 126-28, 141, 184n.85
Mother hen: image of Jesus as (Luke 13:34), 50-51, 200, 336-37
Mother-in-law of Simon Peter, 17, 113, 115, 116, 135, 142, 167
Mother of Eleazar and seven brothers (4 Maccabees), 11, 328
Mother of James (Luke 24:10), 213
Mother of James and John (Matt 20:20-23), 101n.2, 104, 332
Mother of King Lemuel, 316
Muslim women in Istanbul, Turkey, 318, 320, 322, 324-25, 327, 329-30, 332, 334, 336, 337, 339-40, 341
Mycoff, David, 180n.79

Naomi, 159-62, 165, 171
Nussbaum, Martha: Capabilities Approach of, 20, 21, 22, 60-62, 75, 89-90, 184-86, 281-82, 317-41; on shame and disgust, 89-90n.89; on the struggle

for justice, 310n.88; on women's
agency and dignity, 281-82

O'Day, Gail, 295-96
odynomai, 98
Okin, Susan Moller, 20, 50n.79
Origen, 173-74

Parable of the baker woman (Luke
13:20-21), 8, 17-18, 44, 283
Parable of the lost (prodigal) son, 7, 42,
48-49, 143, 213-14
Parable of the lost sheep, 42-43, 48-49
Parable of the sweeper woman (or lost
coin) (Luke 15:8-10), 8, 17-18, 40-54,
283, 321, 323, 331, 338
Parable of the widow and the unjust
judge (Luke 18:1-8), 8, 17-18, 23, 44,
214, 264-314; and biblical lament tradition, 295-302; boxing/fighting motif in, 266-68, 278-80, 283, 287-90,
308, 323, 331, 341; characterization of
the adversary *(antidikos),* 267-68,
276-77; characterization of the unjust
judge, 267-68, 277-78, 284-90, 294-
302; compared with Sirach 35:14-25,
299-302; compared with story of
Lot's wife, 259-60, 278-79, 313-14;
honor-shame elements in, 287-90,
291, 301; role of God in, 294-302; as a
sexually suggestive tale, 286-87; the
widow as model of faithful fighting
to the end, 308-14, 318; the widow as
model of persistent praying, 293-308,
327; the widow's aggressive agency,
280-83, 323, 340-41; the widow's financial and familial status, 275-79;
the widow's shrewd strategy, 284-90,
330-31, 340-41
Penninah, 154-57, 164, 165, 171
Philo of Alexandria, 108
Price, Robert, 128-31, 133, 141
Prophetic women: in Luke's writings,
16-17, 77-80, 94-95, 118-19, 190-91, 211,
292, 304-6; in the OT, 16-17, 56, 67,
77-79, 190-91. *See also* Deborah; Elizabeth; Hannah; Magnificat; Mary of
Nazareth; Miriam
Purity issues, 12, 88-90

Queen of the South (Sheba), 22, 191-92,
198, 204, 230-45, 260-63, 323, 333, 340;
compared with Jonah and Ninevites,
231-32, 238; in Josephus, 239-41, 245;
in Luke's literary setting, 230-32;
moral and religious character of,
236-45, 327, 335; sexuality of, 236-38;
significance of South/Sheba location,
233-35; socioeconomic status of, 235-
36, 252; Solomon's encounter with,
232-33, 236-45; in *Testament of Solomon,* 243-45; as woman of wisdom
and judgment, 231, 234, 236, 238-45,
335

Rachel, 168, 198, 205; relationship with
Leah, 151-54, 162, 165, 166, 176; type of
Mary (sister of Martha), 176, 178-79
Rahab, 22, 39-40, 203, 206-7, 226
Reid, Barbara, 5, 15-19, 42n.57, 67n.28,
109n.20, 110-11n.23, 225n.67, 265-66,
280n.29, 289n.49, 303
Resurrection narratives in Luke: of
Jairus's daughter (8:49-56), 4, 13, 167,
319, 321n.15; of Jesus (24:1-49), 4, 8-9,
13-15, 18-19; of widow's son (7:11-17),
4, 17
Richards, Amy, 253
Robert of La Chaise-Dieu, 177-78, 183
Ruth (character and book of), 30, 165;
as Moabite, 206-7, 208, 226, 227; rela-
tionship with Naomi, 159-62, 171

Samaritan woman at the well, 101n.2,
109, 119
Sarah (Sarai), 16, 31, 34-35, 55, 56-57, 168,
190, 198; relationship with Hagar,
148-51, 162, 165, 171. *See also* Barren
women
Sawicki, Marianne, 131-37, 138, 139, 140,
141

Schaberg, Jane, 5-9, 10, 11, 14, 15, 19, 108-9n.18, 111n.24, 128
Scheele, Barbara, 264-65, 304
Schottroff, Luise, 46, 279n.28, 293
Schüssler Fiorenza, Elisabeth, 5, 27n.9, 31, 33, 37, 58, 77, 102n.3, 102n.4, 210-11
Seim, Turid Karlsen, 5, 9-15, 19, 97n.106, 167n.45
Sen, Amartya, 280-81
Shame. *See* Honor-shame codes
Shiphrah and Puah (Hebrew midwives), 191, 203, 208
Shunammite woman, 224, 225
Song of Songs, 237
Stendahl, Krister, 28
"Strange" ("foreign") women, 194; in Deuteronomic history, 201-9, 236-37, 238-39; in *Joseph and Aseneth*, 199, 209; Solomon's wives as, 236-37; in Wisdom literature, 207-8, 241-42, 284
Streete, Gail, 202, 203n.31, 206
Susanna (character and book of), 186-97
syntereō, symballō, 83-88
Syrophoenician/Canaanite woman, 6, 39-40, 101n.2, 104, 209-15, 295-96

Tamar the Canaanite, 22, 171n.34, 206, 270, 282-83
Theissen, Gerd, 124-26, 131, 135, 139, 141
Theological interpretation of the Bible, 24-26, 28-31, 34-36; by Latina Christian feminists, 258n.131; related to Luke's portrait of Mary of Nazareth, 31, 34-36, 58, 79, 93, 332-33, 340; related to Martha's use of "Lord," 146-47n.1, 168-70; related to the parable of the sweeper woman (lost coin), 42-44, 47-48, 51-52; related to the parable of the widow and the unjust judge, 264, 266, 270, 293-96; related to the story of Lot's wife, 319
Trible, Phyllis, 2, 39, 148, 204, 205

Uyan-Semerci, Pinar, 318, 320, 322, 324-25, 329-30, 332, 334, 336, 337, 339-40

VBMM. See Life of Saint Mary Magdalene and of Her Sister Martha, The
Vocal women, 3, 15-17, 118-19, 291-92, 304-6, 330-31. *See also* Prophetic women

Widow at Nain (Luke 7:11-17), 4, 17, 101n.2, 104, 143, 167, 213, 225
Widow at Zarephath, 10, 22, 191-92, 198, 204, 213, 215-29, 232, 238, 245, 260-63, 271, 283, 319, 332, 336; Elijah's feeding by and of, 218-20, 228, 321, 335; in Luke's literary setting, 215-18; moral and religious character of, 226-29, 327, 335; pairing with Naaman, 224, 226-29; significance of Zarephath/Sidon location, 220-23; socioeconomic status of, 224-26, 252-53
Widows: in the Cave of Letters papyri, 271-72, 277; in Luke, 10-11, 104, 224-25, 283, 285, 321; Naomi and Ruth as, 159-62, 282-83; in the OT, 268-71, 275, 285, 289; in Sirach, 299-302. *See also* Anna; Babatha; Hellenist widows; Judith; Parable of the widow and the unjust judge; Tamar the Canaanite; Widow at Nain; Widow at Zarephath; Widow who gave her last coins
Widow who gave her last coins (Luke 21:1-4), 10, 18, 44, 104-5, 121n.47, 271, 283
Wife of Lot, 22, 167, 191-92, 198, 206, 213, 245-63, 319, 323, 332, 333, 334; days of, compared with days of Noah, 248-49, 312; in *Genesis Rabbah*, 255n.125; in Irenaeus, 256, 259, 260; in Josephus, 254-55; in Luke's literary setting, 246-47, 250-51, 258-59; in modern poetry, 257-58; moral and religious character of, 246, 250-51, 253-60, 334, 335; in relation to the parable of the widow and the unjust judge, 259-60, 278-79, 313-14; to be "remembered," 22, 167, 246, 258, 262, 263, 278, 319, 327, 335; significance of Sodom

location, 249-51, 335; socioeconomic status of, 251-53; in the Targums, 251, 255; in Wisdom of Solomon, 254
Wife of Pheroras, 123, 138
Wife of Potiphar, 199, 201
Wolters, Al, 316
Woman Wisdom: Jesus as prophetic emissary of, 235-36; in OT wisdom literature, 176, 234, 241-42, 286, 315
Women ascetics (single and celibate), 1-12, 103-4, 109-10, 128-31, 148, 166, 180, 192, 238
Women benefactors (patrons) and beneficiaries (clients), 102-3, 119-24, 126-28, 143-44, 218-20, 235. *See also* Joanna; Mary Magdalene; Women disciples
Women disciples, 6, 15, 16-17, 34, 35, 36, 43-44, 102, 122-23n.51, 127-28, 141-43, 293; Galilean followers of Jesus, 8-9, 13-14, 18-19, 21, 30, 44, 102-3, 105-6, 109-13, 118, 121-22, 167; Joanna as, 12, 13-14, 21, 125, 127-28, 138, 141-44; Martha and Mary as, 168, 172, 174, 176, 189, 331; Mary of Nazareth as, 74, 78, 99; widow who gave her last coins as, 121n.47; witnesses to Jesus' resurrection, 4, 8-9, 13-15, 18-19, 118-22, 133-36
Women in apocryphal acts, 129
Women in Matthew's genealogy, 22, 190, 206, 209-10
Women in OT wisdom literature: contentious wives, 284-85; "loose" women, 284-85; in Proverbs 31, 315-17; "strange" ("foreign") women, 207-8; Woman Wisdom, 176, 234
Women's agency and choice, 15-16, 56-66, 280-83, 331-33; and divine providence, 59-66; essentialist-constructivist debate regarding, 59-64; exercised by Martha and Mary, 184-86; exercised by Mary of Nazareth, 57-58, 66-100, 323-24, 332-33; in parable of the widow and the unjust judge, 280-83

Women's bodies (embodiment), 11, 18, 63, 64, 66, 74n.48, 89-90n.89, 186-88, 208, 215, 261, 283, 320-24, 329; Elizabeth's, 76, 321; of Hellenistic-Jewish women, 195-96, 197, 323; Jezebel's, 298n.40; Joanna's, 127, 321; of Lot's daughters, 251; of Lot's wife, 257, 258, 261; Mary of Nazareth's, 67, 70-72, 75, 81, 97, 100, 320-21, 323-24; of the queen of the South, 245, 261; the sweeper woman's in the parable of the lost coin, 52, 54, 323; the widow's in the parable of the widow and the unjust judge, 266-68, 278-80, 283, 293, 304, 308, 309, 331, 341. *See also* Women's movements
Women's movements (motility), 22, 102, 105, 107-8, 111, 141-42, 186-89; Joanna's travels, 111, 126, 128-30, 133-34, 141-42, 321; Martha and Mary's bodily movements in Luke, 186-89; Martha and Mary's travels in medieval tradition, 179-81; Mary of Nazareth's travels, 75-77, 80-81, 88, 320-21, 322-23, 340; queen of the South's travels, 236, 261; wife of Lot's movements, 253-61. *See also* Women's bodies
Women's service, 13-14, 74, 78, 103, 105, 114-20, 116, 169-89, 228, 323, 339-40. *See also diakoneō,-ia,-os;* Hospitality
Women's silence: Abishag's, 159; Bathsheba's, 158; Hannah's, 156; in Luke's writings, 3-4, 6-7, 15, 16-18, 22, 77-78, 93, 118-19, 165, 188, 190-91, 210, 211, 291-92, 304, 323; Miriam's, 77-78; Naomi's, 162, 165
Women's vocality. *See* Vocal women

Young, Iris Marion, 20, 22; on women's housework, 53-54; on women's motility, 186-88

Zipporah (wife of Moses), 191, 203